Edgartown PUBLIC LIBRARY

HITLER'S FIRST HUNDRED

TITLE

DAYS

Comments

Please share your thoughts about this book with
the next borrower. Thank you!

_____

_____

_____

_____

_____

_____

_____

_____

How do you rate this book?

EXCELLENT	GOOD	FAIR	POOR

HITLER'S FIRST HUNDRED DAYS

ALSO BY PETER FRITZSCHE

An Iron Wind: Europe Under Hitler

The Turbulent World of Franz Göll

Life and Death in the Third Reich

HITLER'S FIRST HUNDRED DAYS

WHEN GERMANS EMBRACED THE THIRD REICH

PETER FRITZSCHE

BASIC BOOKS
NEW YORK

Basic Books
Hachette Book Group
1290 Avenue of the Americas, New York, NY 10104
www.basicbooks.com

Printed in the United States of America

First Edition: March 2020

Published by Basic Books, an imprint of Perseus Books, LLC, a subsidiary of Hachette Book Group, Inc. The Basic Books name and logo is a trademark of the Hachette Book Group.

The Hachette Speakers Bureau provides a wide range of authors for speaking events. To find out more, go to www.hachettespeakersbureau.com or call (866) 376-6591.

The publisher is not responsible for websites (or their content) that are not owned by the publisher.

Print book interior design by Six Red Marbles.

Library of Congress Cataloging-in-Publication Data

Names: Fritzsche, Peter, 1959– author.
Title: Hitler's first hundred days : when Germans embraced the Third Reich / Peter Fritzsche.
Other titles: Hitler's first 100 days
Description: First edition. | New York : Basic Books, 2020. | Includes bibliographical references and index.
Identifiers: LCCN 2019041776 | ISBN 9781541697430 (hardcover) | ISBN 9781541697447 (ebook)
Subjects: LCSH: Nationalsozialistische Deutsche Arbeiter-Partei. | National socialism. | Germany—Politics and government—1933–1945. | Elections—Germany—History—20th century. | Germany. Reichstag—Elections, 1933. | Hitler, Adolf, 1889–1945—Influence. | Nationalism—Germany. | Social classes—Political activity—Germany—History—20th century.
Classification: LCC DD253.25 .F75 2020 | DDC 943.086/2—dc23
LC record available at https://lccn.loc.gov/2019041776

ISBNs: 978-1-5416-9743-0 (hardcover), 978-1-5416-9744-7 (ebook)

LSC-C

10 9 8 7 6 5 4 3 2 1

Contents

Quarter Past Eleven, One Hundred Days, a Thousand Years

T HE POCKET WATCH told the time: It was shortly before eleven o'clock in the morning on Monday, January 30, 1933. The most powerful men in German politics had gathered in the first-floor office of Otto Meissner, chief of staff to the president of the republic, Paul von Hindenburg, who occupied the second-floor suite. They met in the Chancellery Building in Berlin, where Hindenburg and Meissner had temporary offices while the Presidential Palace underwent repairs. The men in the room were determined: they would destroy the republic and establish a dictatorship powerful enough to bend back the influence of political parties and break the socialists.

The men were powerful for different reasons. Chief negotiator Franz Joseph Hermann Michael Maria von Papen, the nation's unpopular chancellor from June to December 1932, had standing among conservative, antirepublican elites and clout because of his friendship with President Hindenburg. A contemporary described the fifty-four-year-old Westphalian Catholic as an antiquated caricature: "a figure from *Alice in Wonderland*" perfectly cast with "long-legged stiffness, haughtiness, and bleating arrogance."[1] Press tycoon Alfred Hugenberg was powerful because he led the right-wing German National People's Party, which had lost most of its voters over the years but remained crucial to any plan for a nationalist unity government. His enemies considered him a "hamster"; even his friends remarked on the sixty-seven-year-old's lack of "political sex appeal."[2] And forty-three-year-old Adolf Hitler, a veteran of World War I and the postwar political struggles but otherwise without experience in government, was powerful because he was the indisputable leader of the nation's largest party, the National Socialist German Workers' Party, a violent, populist movement with an energized following that had swept with terrific force onto the political scene. To many observers, the man was a cipher. The satirist Karl Kraus remarked, "Hitler brings nothing to my mind." Hitler "doesn't exist," said another funny man; "he is only the noise he makes." True, Hitler was very loud, but people listened to him.[3] Other men were present in the room, including current cabinet ministers who had agreed to join the new government that Hitler would lead, but these three were in charge.

Not at the meeting were the leaders of the Catholic Center Party, which was as it sounded—Catholic and centrist—though it leaned more to the right than the left. Also missing were representatives of the Social Democratic Party, Germany's oldest (and, until 1932, largest) party and the most reliable pillar of German democracy, and the Communists, who, like the National Socialists, had gained votes by furiously attacking the "system" in the embittered years of the Great Depression. Together, the absent politicians represented more Germans than the conspiratorial men in the room, but they shared little if any common ground. There was no such thing as majority opinion in the country: not enough Germans supported Hitler, not enough supported the republic, and not enough supported the old-fashioned conservatives. Almost no one supported the old kaiser in exile. After all the electioneering of the previous year, the political system had checkmated itself.

Since July 1932, the two radical parties—the National Socialists, or Nazis (German acronyms usually incorporate syllables rather than letters), and the Communists, or the "Commune"—had composed a slim negative majority in the Reichstag. Given this, the other parties might have been expected to form a coalition to protect the constitution and preserve law and order. But German politics didn't work that way. To understand how they did work, one must first understand the political divide that made even moderate Social Democrats unacceptable partners to the right-of-center groups. The inability of Right and Left to communicate—divided as they were on the issue of the November Revolution of 1918, which established the democratic Weimar Republic, and the "stab-in-the-back" legend, which blamed the revolutionaries for Germany's defeat in World War I—disabled every level of government. The Right derided the new national flag, which replaced the imperial colors of black, red, and white, as a despicable mix of black, red, and "mustard." It dismissed volunteers in the republican civil guard, the Reichsbanner, as "Reich bananas" or "Reich bandits." The German Right's hatred and dread of the Left drove the plot against the republic and pushed these plotters into the arms of the Nazis.

Yet those gathered in the Chancellery Building had reached no agreement on the best political plan. It was now past eleven o'clock, when Hitler and Papen were scheduled to present the new cabinet to President Hindenburg. Hitler, hoping to attain a Nazi-dominated supermajority in the Reichstag in order to revise or suspend the constitution, pressed Hugenberg to endorse the proposal for one last round of elections. As the leader of a relatively small party without modern campaign machinery, Hugenberg refused, at the last minute jeopardizing the plan. Hindenburg was expecting them upstairs.

The assembled men felt a real sense of urgency. In the past week, three big demonstrations had crowded downtown streets in the capital: Nazi storm troopers (Sturmabteilung, or SA) on January 22 (shouting, "Germany, Wake Up!"), Communists on January 25 ("Red Front!"), and Social Democrats on January 29 ("Freedom!"). The negotiations to put Hitler in the number one spot, as chancellor, had been difficult. And most of the men in the room had heard rumors that the army command was unhappy, although no one was sure whether the Reichswehr opposed the return of Papen to that post—which journalists thought the likely but highly unfortunate solution to the present crisis—or intended to block the last-chance gamble on the people's demagogue, Hitler, whose brown-shirted storm troopers vastly outnumbered the government's regular soldiers. Maybe the army wouldn't move at all. In consultations, Hitler quickly promised not to use future election results to rearrange the composition of the new cabinet, in which Hugenberg and his allies occupied powerful positions. From the perspective of Hugenberg, who suspected that any plan calling for the dissolution of the Reichstag and new elections would strengthen the National Socialists and ultimately result in legislation overriding the constitution and giving the Nazi leader emergency powers, Hitler's pledge was beside the point.

The issue of elections was important. The decision would determine the division of power in the room that morning and the hardness of the envisioned dictatorship. Without new elections, the leaders of the nationalist unity government would rule by emergency decree, which required the consent of the president. The new autocrats would bypass the Reichstag, ignore its negative majorities, and push aside the democratic opposition. Such a solution would be frankly authoritarian, but it would leave power divided between the chancellor and the president and preserve the political influence of the various right-wing partners represented in the cabinet. Government structures would remain in place. This was the "illegal" path to a "partial" authoritarian state supported by Hugenberg and his German Nationalists as well as Germany's military, business, and civil service elites. As establishment figures, Hugenberg and Papen would serve as guarantors. With new elections, on the other hand, Hitler would pursue a "legal" though much more adventurous path. By cementing a coalition with Hugenberg, Hitler planned to lead the national unity government to an electoral victory, making the new Nazi majority powerful enough to revise the constitution and put emergency powers in his own hands. The "legal" path would lead to a "total" authoritarian solution that would allow the Nazis to dismantle the power of the presidency and consolidate the party's power, all without any constraint on arbitrary rule or revolutionary ambition. Hugenberg was the lone holdout against Hitler's proposal.

The men still had reached no agreement when Meissner entered the room, watch in hand. He pointed out that it was quarter past eleven. The eighty-four-year-old Hindenburg, whose face, "cut out of rock," was without "a flicker of imagination or light or humor," could be kept waiting no longer.[4] The odd man out, Hugenberg, at the last moment, agreed to new elections. The conspirators walked up the stairs to Hindenburg's office, and at eleven thirty the president administered the oath of office to Adolf Hitler, who became Germany's new chancellor.

This was the moment the Nazis had been waiting for. They intended to use the forthcoming election campaign to win the battle on the streets, eradicate the socialist opposition, and install their "Führer" as dictator of a one-party state. That the men in the room got to the second floor in basic agreement led to the greatest man-made disaster in twentieth-century history: the rise of Hitler, the establishment of the Third Reich, and the Nazis' war on the world.

Yet, at a quarter past eleven, on one of the last days of the first month of 1933, events still could have transpired very differently. Hugenberg could have stuck to his position. Hindenburg could have remained faithful to his long-standing refusal to appoint Hitler chancellor without a Reichstag majority. This path, which most republicans and big-city newspapers editors expected the president to follow, would have left German politics in January 1933 muddled but kept Hitler outside the gates of power.

There was nothing inevitable about Hitler's appointment on January 30, 1933, or self-evident about Germany's Nazi future. There was no crowd at the Brandenburg Gate or march on Berlin to push the National Socialists into power. The National Socialists were not riding a wave of newfound popularity; indeed, in the last big elections, in November 1932, they had lost votes. If the public desired anything, it was a political truce, which many saw as the prerequisite for economic recovery. When the transfer happened that morning, those present in the second-floor suite had detected no decisive shift in the national mood that suddenly worked in Hitler's favor. Although the Nazis were the largest party, Germany remained extremely fractured: cleavages divided those loyal to the republic and those who hated the "system," divided Protestants and Catholics, divided Germans who had a job or a business and those who had neither. All these conflicts cut across the almost unbridgeable political divide that separated neighbors who stood with the socialist Left from those who aligned with the nationalist Right.

There could only even be a "quarter past eleven" because the divisions in the country had created political paralysis, a stranglehold that concentrated power in the hands of a very few men around President Hindenburg. Hitler could seize power only by working with them. In the last half of 1932, everything hinged on the actions of the president. Hindenburg had the power to sign emergency decrees and bypass parliament, and this empowered his aides and counselors: his son, Oskar; Chief of Staff Meissner; former chancellor Papen; and current chancellor Kurt von Schleicher, an unpredictable, not entirely unsympathetic figure whose power base was the army. History only remembers the clock ticking in Meissner's hand on Monday morning because the National Socialists had been unable to win an absolute majority in any of the four big elections held in 1932. Nonetheless, as the largest party, Hitler's National Socialists were indispensable to the plot. Papen succeeded in bringing everyone together on January 30. In order to smash the Weimar Republic, the men in the room needed the Nazis, and to lever themselves into power, the Nazis needed the men in the room.

The last round of elections had shown that the National Socialists were no longer able to win over large numbers of new voters; they believed violence was the only available avenue if they were to attain and remain in power. Hitler and Hugenberg talked about purges, bans, and arrests to smash the socialist and republican opposition. The idea that they would punch hard was understood. Violence was built into the "legal" path since the Enabling Act to suspend the constitution in March 1933 raised the stakes to total power—Hitler's alone. The route from the drama in the Reich Chancellery Building to the horror of concentration camps such as Dachau in one hundred days was short and direct.

Quarter past eleven also tells the time of decision. Hitler's appointment released enormous energy; it pivoted many people down a path they were willing to travel to escape endless political conflict and economic hardship. Better "an end with horror" than "horror without end," asserted one Nazi leader, although he could not imagine that later Germans would repeat the same phrase to signal their acceptance of a harsh defeat at the hands of the Allies at the end of the war.[5] Hindenburg, the old field marshal, had long opposed the appointment of Hitler, a demobilized corporal, to the chancellorship. Yet, once he had agreed, the *Reichspräsident* put the tortuous parliamentary conflicts of the past behind him; he had "jumped over the last hurdle and now has his peace."[6] Millions of Germans felt they had done the same. The trouble of the present gave way to a future in springtime—and the Nazis described their new regime in, literally, sunny terms to both create and exploit this optimism. The national mood did change and swung in Hitler's favor—at first only perceptibly, in February, then decisively, after the elections of March 5, 1933.

More Germans were for Hitler than for any other thing in January 1933. And holdouts largely came around to him once he had become chancellor. Cascades of cheers accompanied the new dictatorship, testifying to its genuine popularity. As the clock ticked on after a quarter past eleven in the following days and weeks, the National Socialists who stood behind Hitler swept into real power through unprecedented violence against their enemies and newfound enthusiasm among cheering friends. A split-second decision had consolidated one of the most popular and wicked dictatorships in modern history with startling speed. A quarter past eleven led, in only one hundred days, to the Thousand-Year Reich.

The "crowding events of the hundred days," as Franklin Roosevelt said around the same time to describe the early accomplishments of his presidency in 1933, completely redirected Germany's national destiny by "crowding" out opponents and closing off alternatives. In just one hundred days, political actors rediscovered the power of collective action; the marching in 1933 would lead to war in 1939. The new regime was borne of coercion—but also of consent, even though the line between these two was as difficult to discern then as it is today. The story of Hitler's first hundred days is also about deferral and irresolution; no one knew for certain the depth of conversion, or the extent of mere appearance, or the effect of terror. The legitimacy of the Third Reich rested on a potent combination of genuine enthusiasm and doubt, the fact that no one quite knew who was a true Nazi believer and who was not.

C OUNTING one hundred days out from January 30 takes us to May 9. The Nazis had won the elections and passed the Enabling Act to suspend the constitution, appointed Reich commissars to take over the separate federal states—Prussia, Bavaria, Hamburg, and so on—and seized the operations of local government to assume complete political control. They had dismantled the trade unions, coordinated many of the institutions of civic life, and promulgated laws denying German Jews equal rights as citizens. They had mustered their "gangsters," as the British ambassador referred to Nazi paramilitaries, in the police force. Not only had the National Socialists destroyed their Communist and Social Democratic opponents, but many former Marxists had wandered into the Nazi ranks—even participating in ritualized burnings of their red flags on the market square and singing the "Horst Wessel Song," the Nazi anthem.[7] On the 101st day Nazi student organizations burned antipatriotic books in what *Time* magazine referred to as a "Bibliocaust" and *Newsweek* subheaded a "Holocaust."[8] Since supercharged university students lit the fires, the one hundred days revealed the calibration of the new era as much from below as from above. The fires in the immediate aftermath of the hundred days kindled the wildfires of persecution, war, and genocide.

In a few short weeks, once-firm ideological affiliations—Left versus Right, Catholic versus Protestant—no longer structured political thinking. It was Nazis versus non-Nazis. And the Nazis had seemingly established sturdy foundations for a fierce new national community, the Third, or Thousand-Year, Reich.

Everything changed, but how much?

Quarter past eleven tells us when—but little else. It does not tell us why the men were in the room or who the Nazis were or why they were so powerful. Nor does it explain the timing. Why the sense of urgency to make a decision on January 30, 1933? And why the apparent sudden shift in national mood in favor of the Nazis in the one hundred days that followed? To begin to answer these questions we must step back in time, first to the crisis of the Great Depression and then further back to the end of World War I and the November Revolution that established the Weimar Republic in 1918.

The enormous financial outlays by all the belligerents in World War I (1914–1918) upended the economic order. Extensive debt, inflationary pressures, overproduction, and unemployment after demobilization engendered a postwar decade hobbled by recession and currency devaluation. The late 1920s finally saw a measure of stability, but then came another crisis. The Great Depression, initiated at the end of 1929 with a sharp downturn in public stock valuation and thus private investment in the United States, the world's leading creditor, accelerated into a global crisis as international trade collapsed, factories closed, and a monetary liquidity crisis threatened banking operations. Government austerity measures aggravated rather than alleviated the situation.

The depression hit Germany, an industrial country heavily dependent on exports, particularly hard. Every winter pushed more workers into unemployment lines, and summer could not sweep enough back into temporary jobs in factories and construction sites. Between 1929 and 1932, one in three Germans lost their livelihoods. At the same time, young people had no prospect of entering the labor force. Given mechanization, international competition, and economies of scale, German farmers suffered terribly as commodity prices slumped.

What had been, first and foremost, a crisis of the "little man"—workers, artisans, and farmers—expanded to jeopardize the more prosperous middle classes in 1931, when unmet obligations and devalued investments caused banks to fail, which in turn prompted austerity measures limiting access to savings and cutting salaries and social entitlements. Germany's Depression-era leader, the Catholic politician Heinrich Brüning, a severe man and a veteran of the war, became reviled as the "Hunger Chancellor."

Compounding the economic crisis were political divisions familiar to other European countries but far deeper in Germany because of Weimar's revolutionary origins. Not only did fiscal conservatives square off against trade union representatives, but nationalists, who remained largely fixed to the ways and means of the prewar world, battled socialists, who were determined to engineer a new, postwar one. Even on the local level, Germans associated with their own social, religious, and economic sets. Neighbors rarely crossed the ideological divide that separated socialist workers from nationalist burghers. A visitor to towns across Germany found two football clubs (one red, one black), two nature societies, two sets of choral and singing societies, and, on occasion, two voluntary fire companies (one for uptown, the other for downtown). Although confounded by the severity of economic problems, politicians also followed their own partisan interests and failed to forge parliamentary alliances as the crisis deepened.

One critic expressed his dismay at the absence of a way out: "whether the question is reparations or disarmament, the planned economy or federal reform, the parliamentary system or French-German relations, everywhere the same picture appears—a field of rubble." The end of the war obviously had not halted the destruction on the ground. "We have undertaken all possible experiments," he explained in 1931; we "have consoled ourselves and let ourselves be consoled, we have tried all methods without believing in any particular one. Now general misery chokes us at the throat. The past years have left nothing behind but a single new word for the unprecedented hardship, an eerie one: contraction."[9] Miserable, choking contraction, with no solution or end in sight: a state of siege constituted the state of affairs. People felt imprisoned in times that could not continue but somehow did. Commentators wrote books on crisis and sought its origins in moral laxity, religious indifference, and political radicalization. Die Krise became a state of mind. Receiving a few marks as "crisis support," unemployed men and women fumbled the currency of despair in the pockets of their patched-up clothes.

Graphs mapped the crisis with a line that showed unemployment climbing from the bottom left corner to the top right, a line paralleled almost exactly by the growing numbers of Communist and Nazi voters. But the equation of hard times with radical votes is too simplistic. Circumstances in the wake of the 1929 crash did not create the economic and political pressure on their own; events in Germany in 1918 and 1914 had also shaped it.

Crisis talk about the Great Depression always incorporated debates about the "August Days" of 1914, which Germans remembered as a moment of great national unity at the outset of World War I, and about the 1918 November Revolution, which brought down the Kaiserreich and established the Weimar Republic. In some ways, the three dates compounded the sense of hopelessness because each illustrated what Germany had lost. Strung together, they plotted a trajectory of deterioration and decay and engendered a narrative of decline "concocted precisely by those who wanted to replace a democratic with an authoritarian system" under the sign of emergency.[10] Many Germans held fast to the olden days. Surprised when Hindenburg won the election for the presidency in 1925, observers surmised that voters really hankered for a substitute, or ersatz, kaiser. The most popular movie in the postwar years was not a Weimar classic like *Metropolis* or *M* but *Fridericus Rex* (1922–1923), a portrayal of the tumultuous life of the eighteenth-century Prussian king Frederick the Great. Film audiences flocked to features set in romantic, timeless settings: "the Rhine and Neckar rivers flow through Berlin's cinemas as if it could not be otherwise," complained the novelist Erich Kästner in 1927. "Couples hold their hands in the dark and borrow each other's handkerchiefs and shed a tear."[11]

Yet August 1914 and November 1918 also radically transformed the ways in which Germans imagined the nation. Both events had legitimized the people as the proper subject of political action, while delegitimizing the kaiser, class-based suffrage systems, and the pretensions of social elites. Between the experience of the August Days and the November Revolution, the future seemed to be Germany's. Indeed, a "dance craze"—new moves, not old routines—marked the end of the war. "Berlin has never experienced such a New Year's Eve," commented the *Berliner Tageblatt* after city officials lifted the wartime ban on public dancing at the end of 1918; "everywhere, here, there, and over there, on the northside, on the westside, on the southside, and in the suburbs, New Year's Eve balls." Weimar produced novelty nonstop: the international style of metropolitan architecture, fashionable bobbed haircuts, live radio broadcasts, and the weekend excitement of airplane rallies and zeppelin flyovers. Illustrated magazines and mass-circulation newspapers beamed back the images of *das neue Leben* (new life) and *die neue Zeit* (new times). "The new life forms are entirely independent of party affiliations," affirmed Eugen Diesel, son of the engineer, in 1931. "A lifestyle emerges from the spirit of technology to which we are all beholden, whether Communist or National Socialist."[12]

At first, the open spaces of the postwar years favored Germany's new democracy. In 1919, three-quarters of all Germans voted for the pro-republican Weimar Coalition made up of the Social Democratic Party, the Catholic Center Party, and the German Democratic Party. In an unacknowledged legacy of the revolution, political contenders of all types entered the public square. Their commemorations, assemblies, and marches attested to the energetic struggle to appropriate the future. Stepping out, the demonstrators, often in uniform, mirrored each formally; yet they deepened divisions between those who upheld the republic and those who rejected it and between radicals such as the Communists who dreamed of a "Soviet Germany" and the nationalists who looked to build a new German Reich.

For all these contenders, crisis represented jeopardy—but only in the first moment: It also presented opportunity, a break in the system that was also a break from Germany's painful past. Germans would no longer be at the mercy of history (although that is precisely where they found themselves twelve years later, in 1945). In this sense, crisis was synonymous with refusal, forecast, and future. Other European powers were divided between Left and Right—victorious France, for example, just across the Rhine. But France's citizens obsessed more about slow growth, old age, and feelings of constraint. Germany was a startling place in the years after the Great War in that political conflicts expressed themselves in the future tense and borrowed the rhetoric and choreography of rebellion and revolution.

In the end, antirepublican forces were the chief beneficiaries of action on the streets. The voices of refusal grew louder, and in little more than ten years, the republican majority had been cut in half. Nationalists instrumentalized the fear of Bolshevism—the Soviet Union loomed over Europe after the war—to smear both local Communists and moderate Social Democrats, claiming that members of these groups had stocked an insurrectionary home front, betrayed upstanding soldiers on the front lines, and manufactured

Germany's defeat. (In point of fact mutinous soldiers more often accosted bewildered civilians with ideas of revolution.) Opposition to the Treaty of Versailles, at first a rare point of unity among Germans, ended up completely defining enemies of the republic. And the Weimar Republic itself, modern in appearance and progressive in its social policy, was criminalized as an oppressive, untrustworthy "system" or, once hard times had cheapened its promises, dismissed as a transient phenomenon not suited to Germany's destiny.

Observers just had to watch how Weimar elections unfolded. Middle-class voters moved from liberal to nationalist parties, abandoning the German Democratic Party, which had offered leading "personalities" to accompany the mass of socialist working-class voters. This was "the yeast in the cake," so to speak, in 1919 for more extreme antirepublican alternatives. First came the German People's Party, a middle ground that appealed most to older, wealthy men, and then the more hardline German National People's Party, which esteemed the single person, the authoritarian leader modeled on Bismarck but delivered in the form of Hindenburg. More and more young people joined paramilitary groups and threw themselves into the throng of political activity on Sunday afternoons: the Wandervogel, the Bismarckbund, the Tannenbergbund, and the Stahlhelm decked out with black, red, and white imperial flags and even swastikas.

Although the Weimar Republic offered unprecedented opportunities to Germany's Jews by removing informal barriers to social advancement—in the 1920s, a Jew could find a position in a German university more easily than in an American one—anti-Semitism spiked. Students and educators, people often forget, were among the earliest and most eager supporters of Nazism. No group after the war suffered the opprobrium Jews did, and no institution was as contemptuous of Jews as the university campus. Watched over by sympathetic professors, fraternities not only banned Jews by introducing the "Aryan paragraph" but denied Jewish fraternities "satisfaction" by refusing to fight duels with their members or even to appear alongside their representatives in official university ceremonies. Shoes scuffed against the floor when Jews entered the lecture hall, and passersby shoved Jewish-looking students in hallways. The German university was not a bastion of free or critical thought before or after 1933.

The 1918 revolution authorized everyone to speak, and anti-Semites spoke loudly. Released from the restraints of the authoritarian but decorous *Kaiserreich*, radical anti-Semitic groups burst on the scene and passed their cheap currency. Posters pasted side by side and on top of each other on a wooden fence featured a series of appeals to the Spartakists and their Communist leader, Karl Liebknecht: a plea for the republic's "young freedom," a call on newly enfranchised women to vote for bourgeois parties, and an ominous warning against the Judeo-Bolshevik threat to home and hearth.[13] "In train compartments and streetcars," noted one reporter, "you hear people cursing the Jews," profiteers of the malodorous present who had extinguished the splendid past. Acquaintances casually distinguished Germans from Jews as from the French. "The Jew," complained one exasperated professor living in Munich in August 1919, "is blamed for everything: war and revolution, Bolshevism and capitalism." "It is a terrible tragedy" for Jews, of course, and somehow absurdly "comical at the same time."[14] During the crisis, graffiti lectured passersby, "The Jews Are at Fault."

Advocates pursued political and cultural life in the Weimar Republic by continuously sharpening the knife edges of existential confrontation and utopian aspiration. It was as if the belligerence of the war on the front came to incorporate all aspects of life at home after the defeat.

The Nazis stood out as exemplary warriors on this contested battleground; they were wilder and more audacious. They built on the antirepublican ruckus of the German National People's Party, which had emerged as Germany's second largest in 1924, and they recruited from the miscellany of nationalist youth groups. They furiously denounced the "system," glorified their leader, the "Führer," Adolf Hitler, and energetically took to the streets to display their martial valor and combative spirit. They sought out political fights.

What was true for the other parties in the republic was also true of the Nazis—the experiences of 1914 and 1918 and the war years in between shaped how politicians thought about the contemporary condition—but National Socialists mined the recent past in a different way. They idealized the people's community glimpsed in August 1914, assailed the alien republic established in 1918, and used the combative spirit of the war and the destructive energy of insurrection to remake the nation in a genuinely popular German form that looked forward to a new future rather than the restoration of a familiar past. In the spirit of war and revolution, the time had come to move *vorwärts*, forward.

The National Socialists thrived as no other group did on the idea of crisis as the ultimate tipping point when they would rally to destroy the republic and inaugurate new times and the Third Reich. But unlike other right-wing groups, they welcomed workers and the "little people" into their ranks. They were more effective at integrating diverse social groups into the movement. As the name indicated, the National Socialist German Workers' Party (NSDAP) reached out into the alphabet of society, eventually attracting more workers than any other nonsocialist party and more Catholics than any other non-Catholic grouping. In its view, the party provided the model for the national community it promised to construct once it seized power. The Nazis succeeded by building on right-wing mobilization without being a component part; they refused to join efforts to strengthen a nationalist unity block because they believed they had realized it on their own. They hated Hindenburg as much as Hugenberg and conservatives (reactionaries) and as much as Communists (the Red Front).

Like the party name, with its quirky combination of nationalism and socialism, the movement was full of paradoxes. It held out the prospect of national unity while being the most divisive, violent, and anti-Semitic political actor in the Weimar Republic. Germans responded with a mixture of great expectation, enormous apprehension, and utter contempt. They loved and reviled Hitler like no other twentieth-century politician. Given the prevalence of anti-Semitism in the 1920s, however, the party's vilification of Jews probably attracted more people than it repelled; it certainly did not make the majority of prospective voters uncomfortable. While anti-Semitism was not the hot-button issue in the big election year of 1932 that readers might assume when considering events from the perspective of the Holocaust, the public's acceptance of the persecution of the Jews in the early years of the Third Reich sheds light on how the Nazis resolved the paradox of promoting national unity by dividing the country.

They did so by promulgating a binary worldview. National Socialists gathered in friends and pushed out foes. They nurtured good Germans while clobbering bad ones. This two-way movement of inclusion and exclusion meant that the Nazis relied on both consent and coercion to fortify the Third Reich. National Socialists continuously strengthened and mobilized the virtuous against the enemies they themselves conjured, pitting patriotic Germans against subversive Communists, Aryans against Jews, the healthy against the sick, the Third Reich against the rest of the world. In the end, the Nazi view proved more compelling than not; the achievement of unity and prosperity, they claimed, rested on the destruction of corrosive elements threatening the German whole.

Whatever their philosophy, the Nazis were undeniably a highly mobile force, moving across Germany's patchwork geography, integrating diverse social groups, and taking up arms against enemies. After their electoral breakthrough in September 1930, they dominated political debate and strategy. Yet, by the end of 1932, they had clearly reached the limits of their ability to mobilize new allegiants; after four hotly contested elections in eight months, their electoral numbers hovered just below 40 percent. If some observers counted on the demise, at long last, of the Nazis, others, in a different political calculus, urgently resolved to collaborate with them while they were still at near-maximum strength in order to destroy the republic.

A quarter past eleven, on January 30, 1933, Hugenberg hesitated to agree to new elections because he well understood that Adolf Hitler was a ruthless political commander. The beginning of Hitler was the end of Hugenberg. At a deeper level, Hugenberg also realized that the National Socialists were far more suited to operating in the modern political landscape than were his own German Nationalists, old-fashioned political practitioners who had everything to lose in the tumult of mass politics. The Nazis constituted a huge political movement with a paramilitary force, party press, and extensive ground organization. But their superior capacity also explains Hugenberg's acquiescence. They could help with his party's larger goal: bringing down the republic and restoring Germany's national virtue. Hugenberg's long-standing aim to ravage the republic could not be achieved without the Nazis and, in a democratic age, after the mobilization on the streets in the years after the war, could only be realized on terms set by the well-populated ranks of angry, hopeful National Socialists.

Papen, the self-appointed ringleader of the antirepublican circus, which had more rings than he could imagine or control, fended off objections of more alert conservatives who warned against Hitler's appointment as chancellor. "We'll box Hitler in," he reassured. "In two months, we'll have pushed Hitler so far into a corner that he'll squeal." After all, said Papen, "we've hired him."[15] These extraordinary misjudgments about Hitler and the nature of democratic power in the twentieth century underpinned the risks that Papen was willing to take. In the end, both Hugenberg and Papen calculated, "Better Hitler than Weimar."

The risk taking on January 30 recalls the deep divisions in German society: conservatives' disdain for Hitler and the democratic currents where his movement thrived; Hitler and his co-conspirators' hatred of the republic; nationalists' fear and loathing of Social Democrats and the "system." It also indicates that the principals in the room believed that some combination of carrot and stick could establish a new authoritarian order to bury the Weimar Republic.

When things change, they tend to do so quickly and unexpectedly. The extraordinary drama of Hitler's first one hundred days reveals how a disparate, contradictory, and, in many ways, extremely angry democratic society—streaked in brown and red, very nearly cleaved down the middle—disappeared in a few short weeks to make way for a Third Reich, energetically organized around the center and divided only between the many who valued the collective norms of community, nation, and the German "people" and the few who dissented or were excluded altogether as non-German. Even Berlin, whose inhabitants had prided themselves on living in a "red," or socialist, metropolis, transformed into the shiny "capital city of the Reich." Though not representative of Germany— smaller towns, where most Germans lived, were more conservative and more receptive to the National Socialists—Berlin deserves special attention. Its proletarian profile, socialist voters, and animated, racy cultural life heightened the drama of economic crisis, the rise of the Nazis, and the convulsions of the first one hundred days.

It was an astonishing transformation, considering that the so-called Thousand Year Reich lasted barely twelve. People felt the republic die in winter 1933, after which they never thought about returning to Weimar—just as most exiled Jews never considered returning to Germany after the war. Did contemporaries completely embrace the fresh growth of the Third Reich? Germans realigned, but did they become fixed in place? How was it possible for the new to drive out the old so quickly?

To answer these questions, the Germans of the Third Reich had to read signs. Divining an answer was also a political statement—and so reading signs also invited misreadings and manipulations. People were careful, anxious, but also eager readers, and as interpreters they were writers who turned signs into arguments.

Both before and after 1933, Germans examined small signals to draw larger conclusions about genuine consent and forcible coercion. As a German Jew who had converted to Protestantism, Victor Klemperer, a second-rate professor of French literature but a first-rate diarist, was particularly mindful of where people stood in the Third Reich. "I'm constantly listening for 'symptoms,'" he noted as he walked around Dresden. The reckonings were themselves a topic of constant conversation: "The 'Good morning' or 'Good afternoon' is said to be increasing," he reported. Klemperer took his own poll. What was the result? "At Zscheischler's bakery five women said 'Good afternoon,' two said 'Heil Hitler,'" and at Ölsner's grocery store "they all said 'Heil Hitler.'"[16] "Whom do I see, to whom do I listen?" he wondered about identifying true believers. "Natscheff, Berger, the grocer, the cigar dealer in Chemnitzer Strasse, who is a freemason, the charwoman, whose forty-year old is stationed in the West and who is on leave just now, the coal heavers." "Vox populi disintegrates into voces populi," a frustrated Klemperer concluded.[17] The readings formed an ouroboros: signs both for and against chased each other in endless circles.

One interpretation, on closer examination, revealed itself to be its opposite, or neither, or both. "For professional reasons, I meet with a family that had earlier sympathized with the Communists," reported one informant who had slipped into Germany to figure out popular support after the regime had been in power for two years. "Immediately after we greet each other, the wife begins to loudly complain. Prices are rising faster, you can't buy eggs or butter anymore, potatoes have never been more expensive. We might as well just go hang ourselves." The traveler pressed a bit more: "Yes, but the people didn't want anything else; didn't they vote for the Nazis?" At once the housewife replied, "What do you think it would be like if the Nazis hadn't come along. Under the others we would have all perished a long time ago. At least all the parties have finally been cleared away and we have unity." The informant concluded, "People bitch like lunatics but are Nazis nonetheless."[18] In this case, the sounds of hostility were not reliable indicators.

Reading signs was always a matter of perspective. From the point of view of German Jews, who watched the singing and marching, the Germans had marched over to the Nazis in unison. But from the perspective of National Socialists, this tidal force of converts made it impossible to discern who was a true believer and who was without conviction but swept up in the wave. Klemperer himself set his vignettes carefully. As usual, the talk among the guests in March 1933 was about the signs of the spirit of the times:

Fräulein Weichmann visited us. She tells how in her school in Meissen all are bowing down to the swastika, are trembling for their jobs, watching and distrusting one another. A young man with the swastika comes into the school on some official errand or other. A class of fourteen-year-olds immediately begins singing the Horst Wessel Song. Singing in the corridor is not allowed. Fräulein Weichmann is on duty. "You must forbid this bawling," urge her colleagues. "*You* do it then. If I forbid *this* bawling, it'll be said that I've taken action against a national song and I'll be out on my ear!" The girls go on bawling.

At first glance, everyone seemed to be falling into line with the National Socialists. Klemperer should have been horrified. But

Klemperer's corroborators were fourteen-year-old adolescents who bawled and tenured teachers who trembled. Klemperer abstained from painting a compelling portrait of ideological conviction. He highlighted foolishness and fear. A careful reading of the diaries reveals that Klemperer constructed the entries in such a way that he could imagine himself living among Germans afterward, after the collapse of the Third Reich; he found his fellow citizens to be weak, feverish, poisoned, and bullied—but not basically criminal or fascist.[19] Klemperer did not let go of his love of Germany, which distorted his view. Was he foolish, or was he right?

The press mediated and manipulated signals. The radio looped nonstop acclamation of the new regime. "If I read the newspaper," reflected Klemperer, or "see and hear the film reports, then we're doing sooo well, we love the Führer soo much and sooo unanimously—what is real, what is happening?"[20] (In diaries from the Third Reich, the "sooo" appears all the time—a stretched-out syllable that indicates great enthusiasm but also alertness to hype.) National Socialists themselves worked hard to edit the representation of collective desire in the media. In rallies and marches, they stage-crafted events so that citizens could experience the awakening of the nation. These attempts often fell short of the promised nirvana, since people spent a great deal of time standing around waiting, and the dead time allowed participants to closely observe the disorganization or disinterest or drinking around them. But the Nazis also reframed disappointments so that blemishes did not disrupt ideals. As long as those ideals were accepted as valid, actual experience did not necessarily nullify pretty illusions. The end effect of this acceptance was that the values of national community were strengthened rather than weakened. Signs of the national mood were manipulated, but the self-deceit occurred at all levels.

The drama of the first hundred days centers on an apparent seismic shift in public sympathies as Germans became Nazis. Germans were puzzled by the solidity of the new world of the Third Reich in which they suddenly found themselves. Signs were not always easy to read. To this day, scholars argue about the degrees of deception and self-deception and the scales of desire, opportunism, and coercion that made up the phenomenon of National Socialism. The Nazi revolution shuddered through every household. It detonated abroad as well, completely disrupting the scenes of twentieth-century life. The enormous power of National Socialism is evident in its long afterlife—all the talk about the Third Reich as families gathered after the war, the thousands of books on Hitler and his confederates, the long debates about the relationship between Germany's history and the rise of the Nazis, the maximum effort to create a democratic civic culture of remembrance and repentance after 1945, the irresistible historical analogies to Hitler and his appeasement, and the rekindled anxiety about fascist desire in our times.

This story is littered with the "forest of upraised arms," "arms and hands over heads like leaves on the branches of a tree"; the voices in the unison of slogan and song; the marching columns unwinding the hours along cobblestoned provincial streets and the loud cheers booming out from newly purchased radios in response to aggressive, unyielding calls of speechmakers; the energetic public campaigns of charity drives and anti-Jewish boycotts; the cherished intimacy with "our Germany," the ravished maiden of world history; and the feelings of relief after a crisis seemed past, the call to duty to guard a nation's future, and the desire for private happiness at home; but also suspicions and misgivings about neighbors, their motives, and the tenacity of their beliefs.[21] Everything changed, but how much?

CHAPTER ONE

"Crisis, if You Please"

BERLINERS FAMOUSLY celebrated the dynamic energy of their home. "Go, go, go" and "tempo, tempo" were the refrains of the city. On the move, Berliners even turned the routine practice of people watching into entertainment, and the popular Berlin newspaper the *Morgenpost* sponsored a contest, "Augen Auf!" (Keep Your Eyes Peeled!), which invited readers to win 2,000 marks by spotting one of its reporters, his face featured on "wanted" posters, as he crisscrossed the city on a November Thursday in 1919. (Though he was not nabbed, several "false arrests" were made.) The newspaper had choreographed the casual, inquisitive, and sometimes suspicious or frightening ways that people surveilled each other.[1] The spectacle of looking became part of city life. But as the Weimar Republic gave way to the Third Reich, the amateur detectives who ran around Potsdamer Platz on a hunt to identify pedestrians and expose their disguises evolved into confident state administrators who made assignments according to unquestioned social and racial categories.

After World War I, German cities felt more perilous as social norms eroded. The popular crime movie *M*, a 1931 feature directed by Fritz Lang and starring Peter Lorre as a child murderer on the run, built on the pastime of watching passersby but screened this supposedly innocuous activity as terrifying operations of surveillance. In the citywide panic—"Who is the murderer?" screamed publicity posters—people scrutinized pedestrians. They kept watch over occupants of apartment buildings and worried about strangers lurking in stairwells. *M* anticipated the dangerous new formations that engulfed public spaces when the postwar state of flux deteriorated into a state of permanent crisis with the Great Depression. Berlin became much more belligerent after thousands of workers lost their jobs—nearly half the work-able population was eventually unemployed. It slowed down—no more "tempo, tempo"—as men and women pocketed streetcar fares and walked. More people loitered: the unemployed crowded welfare offices; itinerant peddlers and musicians worked the streets; beggars came up to the door. Policemen ordered idlers to "move on."

Berlin became louder as the Depression turned politics raucous and violent. Partisan rallies dominated landmarks like the Sportpalast, a cavernous venue that had opened on Potsdamer Strasse in 1910 with the ice capade "Fairie at the North Pole" and had always attracted thousands of spectators, who watched the frenzied action of the city's six-day bicycle races, ice hockey championships, and boxing matches in an atmosphere of "maddening hubbub, beer steins clashing, shouts, louder and louder, applause," patrons "hollered for grilled sausages."[2] It became the site of political demonstrations—crowds made up of strangers wore uniforms and badges, visible declarations of party loyalty to Nazis, Social Democrats, or Communists. Such mobs made ordinary interactions in the city fraught. People punched and shoved each other. The sounds of marchers and marching songs echoed through the streets. The economic crisis of the early 1930s demanded self-examination and self-surveillance.

After their 1933 seizure of power, the Nazis would make this metropolitan habit a matter of patriotic duty. They undertook an extensive campaign to permanently affix signs of illness, depravity, and jeopardy to Jews and Communists, identifying them as dangerous enemies, and to require citizens to comply with strictures of public order. If the premise of the 1919 newspaper contest had been the basic illegibility of the city, the signs the Nazis put up after 1933 assumed the fundamental legibility of a society that distinguished between "us" and "them," "Aryans" and "Jews," comrades and enemies. In this way, the Nazis resolved in violent fashion both the troubling signs of crisis and the crisis of reading signs. By fixing who belonged and who did not, they imposed a kind of literalness onto the city. The 1919 game could no longer be played after 1933.

E VEN BEFORE THE NAZIS, the economic crisis created two clear categories: those who belonged and those who did not. The degree to which the city had come apart struck observers in the early 1930s: "tempo" on one side, "tristesse" on the other. Berlin had always been a working-class and left-leaning city, with just over half of its electorate splitting votes between Communists and Social Democrats. "Berlin Stays Red," workers chanted. But unemployment reshaped the city, dividing it between those who had work and those who did not, between those who had something to do and those who had nothing but time, between those who could afford to go out for a beer and those who subsisted on potatoes.

Poverty itself was a business. One enterprising tour operator showed "sensation-hungry tourists" "the metropolis in crisis." The itinerary of his tour, called "Crisis, if You Please," included voyeuristic journeys to the "corridors where unemployed get stamped," "shuttered factories," and "empty new developments." In the evening, patrons could inspect asylums housing the homeless and attend political rallies sponsored by radicals. And if the sounds of anger and despair were insufficient to satisfy customers, street-corner adolescents were hired to supply the expected wails.[3]

Such profiteering on human misery aside, traveling to working-class districts did afford the best observation and understanding of the metropolis in crisis. One journalist found it remarkable: "You get on the subway and get out at the next station—it is another world. A huge chasm separates here and there." Regine, a character in the novel *Berlin 1932*, shuttled between two worlds. After visiting her parents in working-class Berlin North, she would take "Autobus #2 from Usedomer Street back home," traveling west. It was as if "she came out of the perpetual darkness of a mine shaft back into bright daylight" "when the bus left Elsässer Strasse and turned into Friedrichstrasse," putting behind it "the hideous city and arriving in a charming one." North and West composed "two fundamentally different cities, like hell and heaven in the film *Metropolis*." Residents, separated by "Autobus #2," "seemed to belong to totally different races." Since Regine herself had work and her husband did not, she experienced the shame, betrayal, and resentment that characterized each "race" in her own home.[4] Neighborhood nicknames often underscored that difference and its racialized nature; in other German cities, the proletarian underworld was known as "Little Moscow" (Stuttgart, Frankfurt) or "Algiers" (Lüneburg).

There were other crass differences as well. Regine described her parent's proletarian street as a "political street." "The Communists have always set the tone here, but recently the National Socialists have emerged as dangerous intruders," she observed. "The street is the scene of furious battles; gun shots," and "sirens of riot squads pierce the night." "There is never really peace or quiet," a contrast to her neighborhood. These sorts of differences were typical of Berlin. Thoroughly mobilized terrain bordered on peaceful precincts.[5] From the vantage point of the Great Depression, it was hard to say which of Regine's streets indicated the direction events would take.

To try to determine where things were headed, journalists arranged their own tour of the "metropolis in crisis." It usually began on Alexanderplatz, a large and busy intersection abutting the city's poorer districts. In his first days in Berlin, in November 1932, Abraham Plotkin, a forty-one-year-old American trade unionist associated with the International Ladies' Garment Workers' Union and charged with investigating Germany's social conditions, headed straight for Alexanderplatz. There he was "swallowed by the crowds," which "mill about you and suddenly disappear, reappear and vanish again." He found his way to Aschinger's, an inexpensive chain restaurant described by novelist Alfred Döblin in his classic 1929 novel *Berlin Alexanderplatz* as a place where "people who have no belly, can get one there" and "people who have one already, can make it big as they please." Outside, on the sidewalk, Plotkin noticed a young woman selling candy boxes for ten pfennigs each, the price of a daily newspaper. She was thin and blond and bitten by hunger. Suddenly she lurched, and Plotkin caught her before she fell. He picked up her boxes of candy and treated her to a bowl of soup at Aschinger's, but the frightened woman was clearly out of place in the milieu where she now found herself. One of the impoverished middle class whose future had vanished, she no longer belonged.

Moving on, Plotkin wandered to the nearby Grenadierstrasse, where he encountered a prostitute in a bar. She appeared more aware of her choices, referring to her respectable past while affirming, "I like this life" and the small extras that came with it. Nonetheless, she did not expect much from an existence that Döblin might have sketched. "Do you remember," she explained, surprised that Plotkin had read the novel, "that Döblin said that time is a butcher and that all of us are running away from the butcher's knife? Well that's me, and that's all of us. You too. I'll run until I fall. But until I fall, I want to live." Döblin would have been impressed that his book had become part of the world it depicted.[6] The pair of vignettes—at Aschinger's and on Grenadierstrasse—combined destitution, cynicism, and a little hope, but in a way that left the final resolution uncertain. Were Germans basically virtuous but unlucky, or had a wider moral decay set in?

Twenty-three streetcar and nine autobus lines traversed Alexanderplatz, enabling an easy commute from there to Berlin's poor working-class neighborhoods. The most notorious sight was "Meyer's Hof," a gigantic tenement at Ackerstrasse 132/33. From the outside, the building displayed "bourgeois dilapidation": "window upon window" with "little balconies tucked on the front," each with a flower box. The complex, five stories high, like most of Berlin's nineteenth-century tenements, stretched over interconnected interior courtyards that housed a jumble of workshops and businesses: "all sorts of professions are represented, judging by the placards," a "pumpernickel factory, ladies' and children's ready-to-wear clothing, metalworking, leather stamping, a bathing facility, clothing press, butcher." To get a better idea of the lives led by the 1,300 inhabitants of Meyer's Hof's 250 apartments, visitors had to wander into the back courtyards, "the sad first one, and the sadder second." Make sure, wrote a guide, to look at "the sallow children loitering around, squatting on the steps of the back building's three, four, or more lightless entryways, stirring and grotesque creatures," exactly as Heinrich Zille, Berlin's beloved illustrator, had once drawn them. In 1929 alone, at least five newspaper articles featured Meyer's Hof (or Zille-Burg, as it was known), and reporters kept coming back in the hard years that followed. Yet journalists were not sure whether they were looking at a proletarian fortress or a ruin of economic misery.[7]

From the busy store-fronted streets, visitors passed through the entryway into the first courtyard. Though darkened by shadows cast by surrounding buildings, the courtyards echoed the ever-tiresome noise of neighbors. Throughout the day, people came in and out: "rag-and-bone men hollered, and every morning an old man came by, who wanted to exchange firewood for potato peels." This was the bartering of people who were hopelessly poor, who needed wood bits to light the coal fires of their "cooking machines" or food scraps for a cow or an old horse kept in a shed in the back. In the afternoon, organ grinders appeared and played familiar, melancholy melodies. Radios blared sappy tunes—"what a racket!" There was even a hit song about the tenement courtyard: "Her name is Marie, Marie / I am so in love with her...at the window vis à vis." The popular repertoire acquired a greater sense of tristesse after years of poverty. "Somewhere in the world there's a little bit of happiness to be found," but it would have to fit the budget: "a penny for love, a penny for faith, a penny for a little tenderness—I don't want more than that." Shouts from residents mixed in with the music of tragedy. In the evening, workers returned home and barked from the open windows, "Pack those goddamn kids in bed! All this bawling, such a scene, never a quiet moment. What is this shit?"[8]

Passing through the door and up the stairwell, visitors noted that "the railing was loose, held together with wire. The plaster fell off the walls to reveal yellow-red bricks. In some spots, doodles and scrawls had been chalked: 'Lisbeth Schunkel is an old slut.'" On the way up, they smelled the exhaust of confinement, the odor of "cabbage and damp laundry and little kids."[9]

Abraham Plotkin's inquiry took him to Kösliner Strasse 2 in the Wedding district, where, the superintendent told him, only five out of eighty tenants had regular work. The hallway was so dark that his companion had to use a cigarette lighter to show the way. "A rat came scurrying down the hallway." Most Berlin apartments had electricity, which made radios popular, but in shabbier buildings such as this one, tenants still relied on gas hookups in their units. A third of apartments did not have running water, and anyone who needed to go to the toilet had to pass through badly lit, smelly common spaces.[10]

As he inspected streets, tenements, courtyards, stairwells, hallways, and apartments, Plotkin paved the way for the more sinister surveillance of the Nazis who set out to conquer (and convert) these proletarian tenants after coming to power. The first intruders, do-gooders like Plotkin, intended to produce sympathetic, investigative narratives; the second endeavored to enforce control over adversarial spaces. Plotkin merely wanted to examine family budgets, not search for subversive Marxist literature or arrest a veteran Communist. But cigarette lighters used to see the way in the unlit hall in 1932 would give way only a year later to battery-powered flashlights and pistols.

Plotkin's team knocked on the door at the Schoners'. "The darkness inside was something to get used to," even though it was only two o'clock in the afternoon. The apartment consisted of two rooms, standard for workers' accommodations. The Schoners were lucky because they only had one child, but three people shared the bed. There was a table, a chair, a cupboard, and a box on the floor.[11] For the two rooms, where "the walls were literally wet with dampness"—tenants joked about apartments that came with "running water"—the Schoners paid twenty-three marks a month in rent, more than one-third the monthly welfare payment the family received.

Abraham Plotkin took leave of the Schoners (the daughter "curtsied to me with the springy dip of the knees that is taught to all German children"). "We climb stairs" for a second interview, and "still higher" for yet another. ("Can you stand one more?") At each station, Plotkin counted iron beds and wooden chairs, added the amount of marks received as unemployment relief, and divided the sum by the number of children to calculate the miserable budgets that forced the families to scrimp on either potatoes or coal—to eat or to heat.

The household budgets Plotkin inquired about were closely examined throughout the Great Depression. One analysis detailed the situation of Herr Mielenz, a metalworker, and his wife, whose earnings as a cleaning woman covered the rent. After subtracting payments on debts incurred to buy furniture and clothes ("forgiveness is only for the better sorts") and the cost of bus fare, gas for heat, and electricity for light, the sum of 18.70 marks a week remained for food. Meat was reserved for the father because of the physical labor he performed; everyone else made do with vegetable soup and potatoes. Every day, the Mielenzes consumed five pounds of potatoes (2,250 calories), five pounds of vegetables (525 calories), and a loaf of dark bread (2,925 calories). With the addition of "butter," that is, margarine, and occasional bread rolls, the family of two adults and seven children consumed a daily total of 10,890 calories. Counting each of the younger children as half an adult and excluding the two toddlers altogether, the five "adults" in the family each consumed 2,179 calories. Yet, according to an expert cited in the report, "Prof. Heinr. von Hoesslin, chief physician at the hospital in Lichtenberg-Berlin," writing in "*Klinische Wochenschrift*, 1930, Number 20," a healthy person needed 2,540 calories. Each "adult" therefore came up 360 calories short. And to purchase the 10,890 calories, the Mielenzes spent 3.75 marks a day, or 26.25 marks a week. "What we have here is a deficit that has not become any smaller because of the rough calculations and the elimination of two members of the household." "Every week 7 marks 55 are short to guarantee a proper diet. . . . The result: malnutrition."[12] On the whole, Germans ate less than before the war and paid more for what they did eat.[13] As it was, the Mielenzes were more fortunate than many.

Whenever a worker received the *blauer Brief* (blue letter, the German equivalent of a pink slip), he queued up behind "the great grey mass of dead hands and superfluous brains."[14] The loss of employment not only capsized family finances but made everyone cranky because the male head of household "lounged about" the apartment. Newspapers dutifully chronicled how Germans made good use of all the extra time that suddenly became available during the "crisis," selecting stories with the "happy ending" readers preferred. Hilde, a twenty-four-year-old unemployed teacher simply continued to work without pay by searching out playgrounds and teaching children "finger games"; mothers sometimes gave her a sandwich as a thank-you. For his sons, Paul, a forty-five-year-old engineer, built a model railroad, including a "locomotive, a coal car, and a mail car," out of 550 empty matchboxes; "it took two months, but I finished it." Another unemployed man constructed a bird cage for his daughter: "day for day, morning and night, clean, precise, accurate work. Total cost 4 marks, 20—about 500–600 hours."[15] (In the crisis, people counted pennies but guessed hours.) It was a bourgeois interior that men kept in repair.

Unfortunately, the larger reality was duller, less accomplished. One chronicler reminded readers that between waking up, eating meals, and going back to bed, the unemployed were forced to sit "next to each other, or rather, opposite each other." "People get to know each other," "the little habits, breathing through the nose, clearing the throat, the footfall, sister hides her compact, brother his cigarettes." Children made for sharp observers. At school they were routinely asked about father's "line of work." Hans, Gertrude, and Johannes replied, "Papa doesn't have to work because he sleeps so long, 'til noon"; "my Papa sits around all day long and smokes"; "our Pap doesn't do nothing, just eats." Marie, Heinz, and Franziska saw it differently: "father at the stove, father wringing laundry, father sewing buttons, father beating mattresses." About half of unemployed husbands helped around the house. In the novel *Berlin 1932*, Regine's husband Martin "kicks the kitchen chair like a football. Goddamn chores! What kind of world is this." "My work, or what passes for work! Vacuuming and dusting and shopping and peeling potatoes and…" Regine tried to comfort her "boy," "it wasn't his fault," but when she called him "her big boy," he became that much smaller.[16]

Little Man, What Now?, the title of Hans Fallada's famous 1932 novel about an ordinary German man painted into a tight economic corner, asked the same question the unemployed posed each day as they sat around the apartment and finally made it out the door. Every week the unemployed had to go into town to visit the employment office to get a stamp certifying that they were available for work. Obtaining benefits was an arduous undertaking: applicants had to fill out long forms about where they had lived and worked, how much they had earned, whether other family members were still employed, or if anyone in the household raised rabbits for food.[17]

These visits were not just a matter of lining up with hundreds of others to show proper documents or get the right stamp; the employment office was also the transit station of downward mobility. After twenty-six weeks, unemployment insurance was exhausted, and then the unemployed signed up for more meager "crisis" support. When that ran out, they registered for penny-pinched welfare payments, which municipalities regarded as loans, sometimes paid out in food or in vouchers for discounted groceries, although this was often not of real support. "Let me ask you, what am I, a bachelor, supposed to do with onions?" one disappointed unemployed man lamented. (The Nazis canceled the debts in 1936.) A few temporary jobs were sometimes available but only underscored the general humiliation. "Two men to beat carpets," offered the man behind the desk, "but you have to know how. Eight pennies an hour." "Two men to hand out fliers. An eatery on Friedrichstrasse"—such an opportunity usually offered lunch rather than spare change in exchange for labor. In the lines at the employment office the "little man" drew up accounts of the dignity he had lost to what the Left called the "social order" and the Right the "system."[18]

With so much time on their hands, people without jobs lost interest in almost everything. Once they had gone "stamping," the unemployed had nothing to do, and so they walked. They were easily identifiable and picked out by the police as public nuisances. Around Berlin's Alexanderplatz, there was always new construction; men stared through slats in the wooden fences to watch activity at the building site—at least until the police hustled them away. Hans Schulze walked on, observing business routines from which he had been ejected and looking at the items in the store windows: "all the things displayed behind the shop windows, and with every step a new shop: butter, bread, cake, paper, books, flowers. At every corner, a bar, and then more butter, bread, cake, paper, sausage."[19] All over Germany, the unemployed wandered down the old grand avenues: Schlossstrasse, Kaiserstrasse, Wilhelmstrasse, and Hohenzollernstrasse. One half of the population, without work and outside the normal rhythms of society, watched the other half.

From inside the stores, shopkeepers kept a careful eye on the streets. They waited for customers who no longer came or bought margarine by the quarter pound or asked for two slices of bread; by 1932, 6,000 shops in Berlin—about one in six—had gone out of business. And small shops competed with larger ones that offered fantastic discounts: "Small Prices in Big Berlin" (Karstadt) or

"Never Before Such Low Prices" (Wertheim) or "Astonishingly Low Prices!" (Joseph and Co).[20] "Five and dimes" such as Woolworths advanced steadily; it increased the number of outlets in Germany more than tenfold to eighty-two stores between 1927 and 1934. Shopkeepers also worried about idlers who sometimes charged the premises and stole what they could before running away. After four such men robbed a market on Dunckerstrasse in the north of Berlin, the saleslady ran into the street and hailed a passing delivery van to pursue the perpetrators, who had fled on bicycles. Once the robbers realized they were being followed, they stopped the car and attacked the two occupants, an altercation that drew a crowd split evenly between supporters of the businesswoman and defenders of the shoplifters. Especially in winter, under cover of early darkness, four or five such incidents occurred in Berlin every day. And while the newspapers believed that the plundering was the work of organized gangs, not hungry young men, residents, at least on Dunckerstrasse, were not so sure.[21]

Frustrated by bureaucrats, threatened by police, and eyed suspiciously by passersby, Berlin's unemployed tramped lonely circuits through the city. "At first you take a lot of long walks, just to get out of the house," reported Hans, a nineteen-year-old. "You leave early and keep yourself out of view." The sense of being "expelled" was widespread. Men approached strangers to sell matches or knocked on doors to peddle shoelaces or simply asked for spare change. Once, the maid opened the door to find herself face-to-face with her own uncle, who stood silent and ashamed. Entire columns in the newspaper dealt with the question of how to deal with beggars. Was the strategy to simply give two pfennigs to anyone who asked or to offer food, which only every other beggar accepted, or to guard against the confidence game played by the "disabled man" who, when no one was looking, put his crutches under his arm to light a cigarette?[22]

The whole city slowed down as the number of commuters on streetcars, subways, and autobuses fell by 25 percent.[23] Walking, sitting around, playing cards—thousands of men idled in the streets. The unemployed were the most visible sign of social distress, political calamity, and individual failure, but no one was quite sure exactly what the nature of the problem was. "Keep Your Eyes Peeled!" People deciphered the combinations of virtue and vice in the "metropolis in crisis" without coming to any definitive answer about cause and effect. Were the unemployed an unfortunate part of "us" or an alien "them"? Were beggars frauds, the "hunger marches" Communist agitprop?

That many Germans were not destitute and had not received a "blue letter" compounded the dilemmas around such troubling questions. A depression cuts unevenly. If half the city was slowing down, the other half was speeding up. "We have become terribly demanding," commented *Tempo* in November 1931. "The nightclubs are filled. Every night, all the best places post signs: 'Closed Due to Overcrowding.'" American reporter Hubert Renfro Knickerbocker, from Yoakum, Texas, tried to inspect cabarets in Berlin West: "'Sorry but every seat's taken,' declared the doorman at the Rio Rita"; "'Impossible to crowd in,' explained the flunkey at the Julian Fuhs"; "'No room for the moment,' regretted the attendant at Koenigen Bar"; "'Try a little later,' recommended the porter at Jonny's Night Club"; "'You should have come earlier,' advised the liveried guard at Henry Bender's." When he did squeeze into a bar, Knickerbocker tumbled "over the legs of patrons crowded as closely as in a subway train." The "tempo of the times" was punctuated by the rise of those who were lucky and the fall of those who were not.[24]

Even in bad economic times, some 600,000 Berliners crowded train stations to leave for vacation in summer, and another 300,000 did so in winter. Special trains were pressed into service. All the big newspapers published travel sections. Since 1929, *Tempo* had sponsored an annual contest inviting readers to submit their best holiday snapshots. The Reichsbahn pitched the wildly popular "Fahrt ins Blaue," a one-day excursion to a secret destination. Victor Klemperer and his wife, Eva, took such a "mystery tour" in Dresden one Tuesday in August 1933. It was *the* fashionable thing—for the petit bourgeois, for the elderly, for those who have difficulty walking." Three buses took approximately thirty passengers each and set out with "a master of ceremonies, who made short humorous speeches...no anti-Semitism—the most harmless comedy," just "animal voices" and "dialects." The trip lasted about three hours. "We really drove in a zigzag into the blue to the accompaniment of a great deal of guessing."[25]

The "mystery tour" was an apt metaphor for Depression-era Germany, when the nation's destination and the stops in between had become so unclear. Anarchist poet Erich Mühsam made fun of Germany's political mystery tour in fall 1932: "A whistle and a jolt and steam. All aboard." "A bottle of wine, sausage, and bread in the rucksack," but "where does the journey go?" "Man, don't you notice that the train is going backward," exclaimed a tourist. "Is this still the Weimar line?" Suddenly Potsdam, the symbol of the old Kaiserreich, comes into view. Then the train switches course: "We are going to the right! Is our destination somewhere in the Third Reich?"[26] The Third Reich, Potsdam, or back to Weimar?

In the winter when 1932 became 1933, newspapers featured dozens of stories about skiing, a sport that had become wildly popular in Germany. Thousands of spectators lined the course to watch German athletes dominate the alpine event, which would be added for the first time in February 1936 to the program of the Winter Olympics held in Garmisch-Patenkirchen. Even Social Democrats admitted to suffering "ski fever" and showed as much interest in snow reports as in newspaper headlines, a sign of the times: "Voralberg 30 centimeters old, 20 centimeters new, powder." At the end of the Weimar Republic, there were the unemployment figures, and there was the ski report.[27]

Not a great deal is known about how skiers responded to the economic crisis. But the periodic letters written by Elisabeth Gebensleben, wife of the Lower Saxon city Braunschweig's conservative deputy mayor, to her daughter, Irmgard, or "Immo," who lived with her husband and children in Utrecht, Holland, provide a glimpse into how a middle-class family viewed the worsening conditions in Germany. When Chancellor Heinrich Brüning's government declared a long bank holiday on July 13, 1931, after a run on the banks following the collapse of the Darmstädter and Nationalbank, the economic crisis began to hit home. There was a "9% salary reduction" for civil servants such as Elisabeth's husband and higher value-added taxes for consumers, although these measures hardly amounted to attempts to "cold-heartedly destroy one existence after another," as Elisabeth claimed. Elisabeth retailed stories about the trouble acquaintances encountered when they could not withdraw sufficient funds: the Lawyer L. who was at "wit's end" because he was unable to distribute 80,000 marks of inheritance money to his clients; the "simple, ordinary girl who entered W.'s notions store sobbing. She had just arranged for her marriage license. For years she had saved for her wedding day, 1,000 M in the end"—that was close to an annual salary—"now she wants to marry, needs the money for a wedding dress and a small party. She too gets nothing." "I could just go on and on," Elisabeth added. For these middle-class neighbors, the problem was restriction, not destitution. Elisabeth thought of Immo and her husband in Holland as "lords of the manor" because they could travel wherever they wanted.[28]

Like other middle-class Germans, the Gebenslebens were unnerved that "so many people come to the door to beg," including "well-dressed individuals"—people who looked not so different from themselves. But the crowds of unemployed Communists who gathered in city streets—"poor misguided human beings"—frightened Elisabeth most. The sight of the men raised the prospect of "civil disorder," even "civil war."[29]

Back in 1929, Elisabeth had taken great care to find a proper live-in maid. That the "new 'Frieda'" came from an upstanding family was a relief. Her father was a member of the patriotic veterans' group the Stahlhelm, "and 'he,' whom she went 'out' with yesterday, is in the army. Religion luth." So, Elisabeth informed her daughter, "there is no fear that we have anything to do with 'dissidents' or 'Reds.'" During the crisis, however, Elisabeth noted Communists "creeping out of their nooks and crannies." It was "sinister" to "look at the groups standing everywhere around on the street." Even on Sundays, when Elisabeth strolled down the promenade Steinweg, she encountered "Communist bicyclists" shouting, "'Heil Red Front!' It sounded very scary."[30] She stayed on alert as she walked around town.

Middle-class Germans shared Elisabeth Gebensleben's fears. Though not usually threatened by economic destitution, they worried about the political effects. What might happen as more unemployed men came to the door to beg or traveled into town from the countryside to register at local employment offices or milled around streets shouting slogans? Germany looked different; Germans felt less at home in their own towns. At first, Elisabeth believed that "law and order" would prevail. She trusted in the "discipline and industriousness of the German people." But gradually she figured that, in the crisis, only Hitler's National Socialists could protect Germany from the Communists. "It is a wonderful sight," Elisabeth confided to Immo, "to see the brownshirts in whom I and thousands and millions of others have such faith."[31]

When he journeyed to Berlin in winter of 1932–1933, Abraham Plotkin also made the connection between the crisis and growing support for the Nazis, whose meetings he attended in the Sportpalast. He recognized Hitler's insurgent appeal but ultimately believed that "nationalism" founded on "prejudice and dictator-ship" and on "intensity of emotion" would crumble—unless, he added, the Nazis "win power quickly." He recalled "the history of our Ku Klux Klan," which had been powerful in the 1920s but "suddenly collapsed." The Social Democrats seemed to be made of sturdy stuff when he mingled with working-class crowds rallying on the Lustgarten, the square across from the old Hohenzollern palace. As they sang "The Internationale," Plotkin observed, "ev-ery voice was raised in song, song as deep and ritual as the rolling sound of an organ in a cathedral. Every head uncovered in the fog and every throat voicing its hope and faith in the promised sys-tem of a workers' control of human destiny." "Is this the real Ger-many?" he asked himself. "I know that within their hands today there is nothing resembling real power. I stood watching them and listening to them as they marched and sang—and wondered."[32] He had been assured by his German contacts that Hindenburg would never appoint Hitler, but, then again, "Herbert Kline of the Chi-cago Tribune told me that anything is possible." (If Plotkin felt that there was "something brewing," the next day, on January 28, he re-ported on a brew of a different flavor: "the season for masked balls is now in full swing. . . . The young boys and girls of Berlin shook as mean a leg of jazz as the best."[33])

If Plotkin had identified the Nazis as the looming threat, Elisa-beth Gebensleben had concluded exactly the opposite. It was the Communists who composed a mass of "misguided, hate-filled people." She worried about a sudden, violent coup. The Nazis, she wrote, rallied patriots "willing to lay down their lives and sac-rifice themselves for their cause: Germany's freedom!" For Elisa-beth, the brownshirts represented the real Germany. Newspapers reported at the end of November 1932 that Hjalmar Schacht, the former Reichsbank president who had thrown his support to Hit-ler as "the only man who can save us," predicted that "if Hitler does not become chancellor now, he will in four months; Hitler can wait." Elisabeth was not so sure. "Our politics are so muddled!" she worried, and in the four-month wait for Hitler's appointment, "the Bolsheviks will become ever stronger as desperation pushes people into their camp." Her letter went back and forth. "Although I am very *upset*, I am not in *despair* precisely because I *know* the *National Socialists exist*."[34]

Someone like Plotkin followed his nose, attending rallies and demonstrations, listening to speeches and songs and slogans. He climbed the stairs of dilapidated buildings in Kösliner Strasse to interview tenants. Gebensleben avoided the Communist street, Mauerstrasse; what she knew about Braunschweig's poorer people, she learned from her maid, Frieda, whose tall tales about friends on the "dole" eating "schnitzel with cream sauce at Frank's for 75 pf." hardly generated sympathy. But Elisabeth took walks up and down Steinweg. She picked up stories, watched the crowds, and took measure of the unrest. Reporting on conditions in letters to her daughter across the border in Holland, Gebensleben stepped into the role of investigator.

J OURNALISTS TENDED to blend the signs of crisis into the tempo of everyday newspaper reportage. At the end of 1932, with millions of Germans unemployed, newspapers reported on the latest fad: the yo-yo. Perhaps that Berlin took so energetically to the toy was not surprising. After all, it was "a specialty of Berliners to twist others around their finger while still pulling the strings." The crisis cradled almost every observation. "To go sledding!" exulted one enthusiast after a new layer of snow had blanketed Berlin, noting bitterly, "we are the ones usually being sledded."[35]

If newspapermen walked into the first apartment building courtyard to report on economic destitution, they did not walk into the second one to investigate political radicalism. For all the investigative reports on the crisis and the trips to the "Zille-Burg" on Ackerstrasse, there was little attempt to map political ideas onto economic anxiety. Perhaps big-city newspapermen could not imagine themselves as Nazis or Communists and so refrained from examining these political pockets when trying to make sense of the crisis, or perhaps they wrote under the demand to find a happy ending.

You could not ignore the "screams on the street," however. A sense of "terror that is without an object" permeated the prosperous "streets in the west" of Berlin, wrote an observer who also made out the far-off noise of a "National Socialist gang" and the "penetrating odor" of Communist riots in outlying proletarian districts.[36] The gigantic Karstadt department store stood out ten stories high on Berlin's Hermannsplatz like a "bone-white stump" against a dark and inky sky. Sounds of thunder rolled over the restaurant garden on the roof. What first sounded like "the trundle of the underground subway" came and came back, "in rhythm," "three times." "Probably voices chanting in chorus." "Hail Moscow? Or Germany, Wake Up? You could not really understand the words. They were too far away."[37] Sounds in the city broke into menacing slogans. Scraps of song in the distance constantly distracted Abraham Plotkin as he walked around Berlin. "Five o'clock, approaching Charlottenstrasse, I thought I heard some singing." Suddenly, it was plain to hear. A few afternoons later, leaving the Deutsches Museum, Plotkin and his friends wandered in the direction of "the noise of a military band" and "came across a parade of Nazis" who had "started to sing."[38] Slogans and songs had become part of the urban soundscape.

Witnesses located the noise at a remove as if to signal the approach of new dangers. Thunder and lightning, *sturm* and *drang*: political mobilization in the city was unmistakable. Along crowded streets, passersby heard lethal fighting words: "fascism," "terror," "Drop Dead." More uniforms marched along. Citizens talked constantly about politics, especially during the 1932 elections. They gathered around newspaper kiosks to discuss the latest political news. In front of the employment office, workers debated loyalties to one party and the treachery of another. "There were constant political arguments, fruitless and bitter," reported Sebastian Haffner, a young law student. They took place "in cafés and bars, in shops, schools, and in family homes." Even cigarettes on sale signaled political affiliation—New Front, Alarm, and Drummer were popular brands among Nazi storm troopers and markers of identity. As the numbers of extremists grew, life seemed to diminish. "What was no longer to be found," concluded Haffner, "was pleasure in life, amiability, fun, understanding, goodwill, generosity, and a sense of humor."[39]

Revolutionary parties seized locations around Berlin. At the Sportpalast, when the favorite Hein Müller was knocked out by Otto von Porat in the sixth round on October 21, 1932, many in the stands understood the boxer's fate: "life goes easy until it suddenly gets very hard and then not at all." Eventually, competitors were pushed aside by combatants who booked the Sportpalast so many times over that the place became indelibly associated with the Nazis. Communists such as Ernst Thälmann and Walter Ulbricht also held rallies in the Sportpalast, but it was Hitler and Berlin's Gauleiter, Joseph Goebbels, a master campaigner and future minister of propaganda, who learned the arena's acoustics and perfected their entrances to fill its 15,000 seats week after week. In 1937, a guidebook to "National Socialist Berlin" parked tourists in front of the building on Potsdamer Strasse. "The Sportpalast is the grandstand," it explained, from which "we spoke to this enormous city."[40]

National Socialists also shoved their way into Berlin's most beloved beerhall, the Neue Welt (New World) on the Hasenheide. Decorated in kitschy Alpine decor, with hills of fir trees climbing up the staircases, the Neue Welt was best known for the "Great Bock Beer Festival" to which Berliners eager to swill strong, dark Bavarian beer crowded in the winter weeks before Carnival. The parties lasted all night and featured a "Great Beef Roast," dancing to the musical fare of brass bands, and irresistibly popular contests for the "most beautiful brunette bob," or "the heaviest lady under thirty," or the "smallest rosy mouth." "Another beer and another and one more and another—these are the vital signs of life once the new year has begun" for those Berliners who stopped to curse in order to yodel; in January, they called out "Holdrioh" instead of "Hello" or "Heil" and sang "Schnadahuepfli." It was at the boozy Neue Welt that Hitler addressed an overflowing crowd of 5,000 students on December 4, 1930, to promise that "the best will come over to us and unify the people." In the audience that night was a local professor of architecture who had been urged to attend by his students. He remembered the evening as a kind of epiphany and joined the Nazi Party soon thereafter.[41] One of "the best," Albert Speer later became Hitler's close aide and personal architect.

The political programs at the Sportpalast and Neue Welt brought thousands of activists into the streets before and after events. Supporters and opponents angrily shouted slogans at one another, slugged it out in street fights, and laid siege to the surrounding neighborhood. The seizure of public space was no different in smaller towns such as Northeim in the very middle of the country where the 1910er Zelt, customarily used for carnivals and dances, was booked solid by the Nazis, who rallied large crowds of sympathizers as well as socialist adversaries, each side taunting the other along the cobblestoned streets. Late into the night slogans echoed: "Jews, Drop Dead!" or "Red Front!" When political rallies got too big, the police cordoned off the streets—in the old days, it had been the kaiser's parades that had blocked traffic—but when they got really big, it was vendors selling grilled sausages, beer, and party trinkets who set up cordons of kiosks on the sidelines.

There were not many Nazis at first; no more than 800 storm troopers in Berlin in 1928 and about 2,200 at the end of 1930, with about twice as many regular party members. The period of real growth only began at the end of 1931. But National Socialists deliberately blocked out their movements in public to grab attention and create friction, marching five abreast in close formation, picking up speed by driving trucks through the city, traversing working-class neighborhoods with slogans and songs, and storming the fancy "Westend" district of Berlin to shout vulgarities. "The synagogue is burning," they chanted. "Sarah, pack your bags!" (History books composed after 1933 to commemorate the Nazi's "period of struggle" noted all this detail.[42]) Taking to the streets in this way, Gauleiter Goebbels explained, the National Socialists "suddenly stood at the center of public interest. Like a hot summer gale, the party blew into the lethargic calm of Berlin, and people had to decide whether they were for us or against."[43]

CHAPTER TWO

Mystery Tour

N<small>O PARTY</small> in German history charged into a position of power as quickly as the National Socialist German Workers' Party did in the years between 1930 and 1932. From 2.8 percent of the vote in the 1928 Reichstag elections, the Nazis achieved an electoral "breakthrough" just two years later, on September 14, 1930, with 18 percent of the vote. In that single day, Adolf Hitler became a figure of intense public interest, interviewed by high-profile international papers, and the National Socialists emerged as the violent, outsized protagonists of the German drama. They doubled that share less than two years later, in the July 1932 elections. No party in the Weimar Republic had managed to gain a foothold in as many precincts as quickly as the Nazis did, and no party could match their diverse electorate, which mostly comprised middle-class Protestants, farmers, shopkeepers, and civil servants but also included the "bourgeoisie of education and property"—voters like Elisabeth Gebensleben—as well as workers and Catholics.

The Nazis campaigned tirelessly to court such support. The party promised a "landslide in which it would send out 1,500 certified speakers to hold 34,000 rallies in the month before the election. In cities, Hitler himself attracted audiences that numbered in the tens of thousands. On August 3, 1930, he traveled to Frankfurt, the "stronghold of Jewish capital," where he filled the 17,000 seats of the Festhalle at a ticket price of 1.20 marks; thousands of latecomers had to listen to the speech on loudspeakers outside. On September 10, 16,000 Berliners crammed into the Sportpalast to hear him. The Nazis never stopped campaigning. In a typical week, Hitler pulled his skin-tight leather driving cap around his ears like a gas mask, climbed into his Mercedes, and crisscrossed the country to give speech after speech. A memorandum prepared by the Prussian Ministry of the Interior in May noted that "even in small districts, not a single day passed without Nazi leaders holding several rallies." "One meeting followed and was chased by another," crowed one enthusiastic brownshirt at the end of 1930, a total of "150,000 in 365 days in every town and every village." One of the first historians of the party would compare the Nazis to a force of nature—not locusts, not fire, but the flood. "It is not waves of assemblies washing up over the shore. It is a ceaseless rolling ocean. There is not a single village, hamlet, or suburban development in which their agitators have not advanced."[1]

The Nazis maximized weekend bustle. "Night after night, Sunday after Sunday, in wind and rain," activists spread the Nazi gospel on bicycles and trucks across the countryside.[2] Dispirited Communists described these Sunday rallies as a "curse on the land," but Nazi supporters traveled around the country, joining up in numbers to occupy one town after another. Once the brown-shirted strangers arrived, they organized a busy medley of weekend events:

"reveille, roll call, honoring the dead at the war memorial, propaganda march through the small town, a review of SA troops," as well as sports competitions, band concerts, an evening speech, a night-time torchlight parade, and a final tattoo.[3] When Sturmabteilung (SA) soldiers came into town, they did not seek, like the socialists did, to assemble local sympathizers in a big show of protest. Instead, they marched through the streets in closed formation to impress distracted bystanders, to win the sympathy of "weak" burghers, and to intimidate "strong" enemies.

Who were these Nazis? Why did they give up their Sundays to go on the road? And what possessed neighbors in little towns across Germany to gather around with such excitement? Many observers thought there was nothing more to the movement than the noise it made. Out-of-town Nazis brought welcome entertainment to sleepy hamlets, just as a county fair or traveling circus did. At a time when circuses across Germany were folding up their tents forever—five in 1926, four in 1927, seven in 1928, and eight in 1930, stranding menageries of lions, tigers, and giraffes—this conclusion was not misplaced. In *Little Man, What Now?*, for example, Hans Fallada's character Lauterbach joined the Nazis out of boredom—a path that many readers could recognize in themselves and their neighbors. His "lust for life was finally satisfied," even in the "small town" where "almost every Sunday" he fought alongside Nazi toughs.[4] Nazis showed up as swashbucklers.

Or perhaps the loud variety show on Sunday simply drummed together everyone with a grievance. Given the party's multivalent name, people saw in the Nazis what they wanted to see. Half of the electorate voted for the "National Soc. German Wkrs. Party," the other half for the "Nat. Socialist Ger. Workers' Party."[5] One historian refers to the National Socialists as "a catch-all party of protest." "If the party's support was a mile wide, it was at crucial points an inch deep."[6] The Nazis attracted support from a broad spectrum of disaffected social groups. Apprentices trained for jobs that no longer existed; students lacked prospects; farmers held crushing debt; shopkeepers watched customers finger pockets for pennies. But voting trends in the early 1930s were not volatile. As millions of Germans abandoned their traditional political homes, be it the old middle-class parties or the Social Democratic Party or even the Catholic Center, they moved in only one of two directions: to the Nazis or the Communists. Terms like "protest" do not describe their political behavior well as the political realignment was deliberate rather than scattershot or reactive.

The National Socialist German Workers' Party was a startling new political entity, but it was not without political lineage. A broad grassroots coalition of patriotic clubs, paramilitary groups, and the two main conservative parties—the German People's Party and the German National People's Party—succeeded in electing seventy-seven-year-old former field marshal Paul von Hindenburg as president of the republic in 1925. He was not an "ersatz" kaiser but the figurehead of a newly energized nationalist movement that took to the streets and began to push the Social Democrats, Germany's most capable political force, onto the sidelines. After 1930, antirepublican forces like Hindenburg's supporters recognized the National Socialists as useful and then indispensable allies. In fact, the electoral bloc that Hitler pulled together in the depth of the crisis had assembled before, in 1925 in support of Hindenburg, whom Hitler opposed in the elections of 1932. Votes for Hindenburg in 1925 were the single best predictor of votes for Hitler in 1932.[7]

Nor was the Nazi Party a creature born of the Great Depression. It is tempting to compare the dramatic rise in the number of Nazi voters in the years after 1930 with the equally dramatic rise in the number of Germans without work. But the unemployed did not generally vote for the National Socialists, while well-to-do burghers did. Statistics indicate that the wealthier the precinct, the higher the Nazi vote. Moreover, voters began to abandon the old parties long before unemployment surged.

Another American—not Abraham Plotkin, but Theodore Abel, a professor of sociology at Columbia University—undertook the first detailed investigations into why Germans became Nazis. He was thirty-seven when he arrived in Berlin in June 1934, and after settling into his room, he went for a walk around Potsdamer Platz and had a drink in the Haus Vaterland entertainment emporium. Abel busied himself counting "Heil Hitlers," a greeting that he found was used "only in official places," while *Guten Morgen* and *Auf Wiedersehen* prevailed in "everyday contacts."[8] He had come to Germany to launch an ambitious research project on the Nazis, and his project had an interesting twist. Abel wanted to ask National Socialists directly why they supported the Nazis, using the case study method pioneered by the Chicago School of Sociology. He looked to the "Old Fighters," those who had joined the party before 1933, and had them write autobiographical statements. For this approach, he needed the help of the Nazi Party, which cooperated by sponsoring a writing contest. The contestants, who competed for cash prizes, penned essays describing how they had looked at the world after 1918.

The propaganda ministry, headed by Joseph Goebbels, feared that Abel "would not do justice to the imponderables and the declaration of faith and only use the factual material," but the professor reassured the party's top brass that he was not interested in reducing ideology to sociology. He intended to compose "life histories" rather than correlate statistics. When he published his 1938 book, *Why Hitler Came to Power*, which featured six long autobiographies, Abel acknowledged the importance of social and economic factors (that is, the role of the crisis), but he emphasized above all ideology, a kind of conversion experience in which the unsettlement of the war, the experience of revolution, and emotional attachment to the idea of the nation created a generation that incorporated the revolutionary message of the National Socialists.[9]

Abel discounted economic destitution and anti-Semitism as major factors in the rise of the Nazis. The Weimar "system," which had ostensibly promised freedom but in fact, in Abel's subjects' view, delivered the bondage of the Versailles Treaty and trapped "little people" in the economics of austerity, molded Germans into National Socialists. Nazis hated the November Revolution, but they were also radicals who embraced the idea of revolution and its potential to finally sweep reactionaries and "Marxists" alike from power. They repeatedly invoked the statement "The German people have triumphed all along the line," a mantra of the 1918 revolution, to demonstrate that the German people had not triumphed at all—and to vow that they would. The crisis created faith in the possible as easily as it did desperation.

The Nazis built on sturdy foundations of antirepublican activism first laid in the early days of the republic. About half of Abel's respondents reported that they had been members of the patriotic associations and youth groups that had sprouted up after the end of the war. The marching that began with the mobilization for war in August 1914 never really ended. Homecoming parades for soldiers returning from the front in November 1918 gave way to the patriotic demonstrations of the Stahlhelm veterans' group in the 1920s and of the SA storm troopers in the early 1930s. Politics followed everywhere. Even when Germans took vacations at the seaside, they built sand castles as if they were still digging trenches at the Somme, fighting for the kaiser and an earlier version of their country. They planted the old black-white-red colors of the Kaiserreich on turrets and destroyed the battlements of opponents. "In the summer of 1927, we were in Travemünde," remembered one German. Everyone "on the beach had a small 'castle' with a flag," and "most of them hoisted the black, white, and red colors.... We had two big black, red, and gold ones" in order to show loyalty to the republic, but "after a few days the flags disappeared and our covered wicker beach seat was floating in the water."[10] This all recalls the tenacious effort of millions of Germans to break the Weimar Republic.

The National Socialists seized on popular feeling and escalated the offensive against the republic while widening its scope by rejecting restorationist tendencies for the revolutionary aims most people preferred. They scorned the old class prejudices and limited social horizons of traditional nationalists. In many respects, Hitler deliberately adopted the Social Democratic playbook, copying the socialists' organizing methods and taking up their (former) revolutionary élan as well as their contempt for elites. As a young man, Hitler had been transfixed by the sight of "the endless columns of a mass demonstration of Viennese workers," marching four abreast, a "gigantic," frightening "human dragon slowly winding by." He resolved to assemble a "menacing army" of his own in order to rouse a dragon to stir up "physical terror."[11]

Such displays were highly effective. Reading through the auto-biographies National Socialists wrote for Abel—essays with titles like "Why I Found the Way to My Führer," "My Path to the NS-DAP," and "My Life Journey to Adolf Hitler," echoing Hitler's own *Mein Kampf*, "my struggle"—one is struck by how many Germans converted because they had either seen Adolf Hitler speak or witnessed the SA marching through the streets. Hitler's oration found "the right words to heal broken bodies."[12] Hitler spoke in the name of the people, whose judgment against the "November criminals" he expressed in ferocious terms. When the speaker railed against the Weimar "system," the audience cried out, "Hang them up! Bust their ass!" "If our movement succeeds," Hitler asserted, "we shall erect a people's tribunal before which the November criminals shall expiate their crime, and I frankly predict you shall then see their heads rolling in the sand."[13] The Nazi leader appealed to popular fears and resentments and transformed them into final judgments and the promise of direct remedial action.

Voters responded to Nazi promises to clean house, to clear the barn out with an "iron broom": "Get out!" "Make room!" "Enough already!" were electoral slogans in 1932. And Germans seemed to agree. "Every conversation I had in Germany with anyone under the age of thirty," recalled American journalist Dorothy Thompson, "ended with the phrase: '*Es kann so nicht weiter gehen. Es muss etwas geschehen.*' 'It can't go on. Something must happen.'"[14] The Nazis won over voters by responding to the crisis with a fight.

Not everyone was moved. Sometimes Hitler spoke in pouring rain, and the atmosphere of acclamation did not take hold—in other words, no "Hitler weather" at all. Plenty of people heard Hitler and considered him mad, a distillation of ordinary scum and diabolical fantasy. However, "those he had converted followed him." They "laughed with him, felt with him," wrote American journalist Hubert Renfro Knickerbocker. "Together they mocked the French. Together they hissed off the Republic. Eight-thousand people became one instrument on which Hitler played his symphony of national passion."[15]

SA marches also left a deep impression on spectators. "Old Fighters" felt swept up in the throng and aroused by the disciplined bearing of the brownshirts. Columns marched with a sense of purpose. They assembled in the center of the town, cheered the Führer, breached "red" working-class neighborhoods, and ultimately arrived in the Third Reich. One convert remembered when he fell in step on the sidelines with marchers on the streets:

Spring 1925. The early evening darkens the streets of the East Prussian capital and a spring shower whips rain into my face. Gas lamps flicker like big bright spots. Shivering, I pull up my collar and think of the Bergstrasse where the trees have long since bloomed and the tender green of the forests shines. I'm lost in thought as I make my way home. Suddenly I hear the footfalls of a marching column. Reichswehr, I think, or one of the dozens of patriotic troops? The next lantern releases the group from the darkness of the street: brownshirts appear, arm bands glimmer, the flag flutters blood red, the sharp contours of the swastika contrast with the pale ground. It is only a small troop, not even twenty men. I am completely taken. I can't do anything but turn around and march alongside.[16]

Elisabeth Gebensleben, the wife of Braunschweig's deputy mayor, could not join the all-male marchers, but she cheered on the 100,000 Nazis (including just about every SA man in the country that the party could muster) who occupied her left-leaning city of 150,000 for a few days in October 1931. "Germans once again breathed freely and proudly," she noted, meaning that Nazi soldiers, who appeared in "endless numbers," had succeeded in pushing aside Communists, who didn't "dare show their faces." She listed the patriotic sights: "exemplary discipline," "marching bands," "exuberant singing." "Germany is truly awakening," she concluded. From this moment on, she identified "the national cause" with "the Führer."[17]

S CHOLARS OFTEN consider the National Socialists a movement that sought to build a new Germany by pursuing "transcendent" aims.[18] If read only as synonymous with "otherworldly," "fantastic," and "supernatural," the word "transcendent" does not immediately convey its meaning in the Nazi context or indicate its radical impetus. The Nazis conceived of a national union that would *transcend* the existing sociology of the nation by breaking down the socioeconomic milieus that kept the nation divided. This meant eroding the all-important emphasis citizens placed on categorical identities like Protestant or Catholic, rich or poor, bourgeois or proletarian, nationalist or socialist. It also meant destroying the democratic system that represented divergent interests and the liberal order upholding cultural and ethnic diversity. In the Third Reich, the various parts of the German nation would express the greater transcendent, homogeneous whole. This overarching vision of the *Volksgemeinschaft* (people's community) made National Socialists especially appealing.

The whole Nazi project rested on the resolve to reverse the tide of history by vanquishing the revolutionary traitors of 1918 to establish a new Reich based on the patriotic union of 1914. It relied on two myths: the dark suspicion that socialists, Jews, and other enemies had stabbed Germany in the back at the end of the war for the purposes of erecting a false, divisive republic, and the overly optimistic, naive idea that the spirit of 1914 had fashioned Germany into a genuine national community in which a unified people had discovered their collective strength and ethnic sovereignty. Whenever Nazis "countered November 1918 with August 1914," reflected one observer, they "always had an easy victory." "Neither myth had much basis in reality," the historian reminds his readers, but we also know that history has been made when millions of people "deeply believed things that were verifiably untrue."[19]

The world war that German soldiers fought between 1914 and 1918 offered a military model to follow to move from the lingering present-day November back to the ideas of August 1914. Any new war with Germany's old enemies would be predicated on civil war against new enemies at home, and for the National Socialists, the front ran right down the middle of the country. The "November criminals" had to be destroyed and the Weimar "system" dismantled—only then could a newly invigorated Germany break the shackles of Versailles and austerity.

A barrage of militant slogans narrated the operations of the storm troopers. War was openly declared: "Red Front, Smash It to Pieces," Nazi soldiers chanted. "Attention, the SA Is Marching, Clear the Streets!" "Jews, Drop Dead!" they shouted in rhyme with

"Germany, Wake Up!" (Juda *verrecke*, Deutschland *erwache*). After the National Socialist seizure of power, "Old Fighters" recalled "battle experiences" from the "time of struggle," and the Nazis commemorated their casualties alongside the soldiers who had fallen in the Great War. About one-third of Nazis who mustered up were veterans of that conflict. Hitler had earned the Iron Cross as a corporal on the western front, and Hermann Göring, his close advisor and designated successor, was a decorated fighter pilot.

But many more belonged to "the generation of 1902," or the "nineteen-hundred-and-sad" generation, the so-called victory watchers who had been too young for combat. They had played pretend games like "Sink the American Steamer" or "German Zeppelins over London," yet experienced the humiliation of defeat without the tragedy of war. The National Socialists were an extraordinarily young movement. They still believed in romance and idealism but rejected the democratic and socialist successors who came to power in 1918, considering them old and rotten. These two generations of young people, stirred up and scarred, provided the Third Reich with its recruits.[20]

If you asked the brownshirts who they were, they answered by giving their "military rank in the civil war." They were soldiers through and through; "they had totally forgotten that they were salesmen or accountants or postal employees or unemployed." When the ban on uniforms was lifted in June 1932, SA men called it a "day of rejoicing." After months "in which we hung around everywhere as unemployed" lads, "now at least we are once again somebody, SA men."[21] The remark is telling: The men did not join the SA because they were unemployed and bitter; unemployed or not, they wanted to be SA men. It was no accident that, as chancellor, Adolf Hitler wore the brown uniform of the SA when he opened the election campaign in the Sportpalast on February 10, 1933, or appeared before the Reichstag to introduce the Enabling

Act establishing the dictatorship on March 23. The Führer was first and foremost the commander of a political army.

They spoke of street skirmishes in military terms: storm troopers set up "guard posts" as they prepared an "attack" on Communist "positions." "The field of battle is not the trenches in France but Hedemannstrasse" in Berlin. "Stomach shots, fractured skulls, stab wounds in the lung, in the neck, in the arm"—"This was no longer a hospital, but a field hospital," remarked another observer looking at the wounded lying about after the SA had clashed with Communists. (One nurse reported that she could immediately identify the injured patient's party since "those with head wounds inflicted by beer mugs and chair legs were Nazis, and those with knife wounds in the lung were Communists."[22])

You could hear the SA men before you saw them—the march step of the boots before the soldiers' singing. The scrape of leather on the pavement was sinister, almost threatening. "Suddenly I heard a noise I had never heard before," remembered one pedestrian. "Tack-tack-tack—an explosive, popping staccato." Uniformed men marched in lockstep, with "a serious, fierce, even ferocious look," and created a "draft in the air" that "took my breath away." The observer "sensed the violence emanating from this block of bodies" and felt "fear, rage, but also powerlessness."[23]

Then came the music. "Singing we will march into the new era," commented one SA enthusiast.[24] Songs fostered a feeling of community and discipline among the marchers and inspired and intimidated spectators; it was at once "energizing" and "inflammatory." Accompanied by a brass band, the SA sang standard military tunes that had become popular during the war but rewrote the lyrics to reflect present circumstances. The socialist enemy supplemented the old foreign ones, and a new hero featured. The pledge of allegiance in the song "Up, Up, Let's Fight," formerly "We have sworn to Kaiser Wilhelm, Kaiser Wilhelm we give a helping hand," became "We have sworn to

Adolf Hitler, Adolf Hitler we give a helping hand." The Communists also had their version, inserting the names of Karl Liebknecht and Rosa Luxemburg.[25] This shared culture of martial singing indicated how the culture of war infiltrated Weimar lives and how easy it was to relocate the front from the borderland to the homeland.

It was a Berlin SA man, Horst Wessel, who composed what became the most popular Nazi fighting song. The "Horst Wessel Song," which the Nazis designated as the national anthem alongside the "Deutschlandlied" or "The Song of the Germans" in 1933, had become especially beloved by the Nazis after Wessel was murdered in 1930. In the "war of songs" that spilled into German neighborhoods in the early 1930s, the Nazis sang the "Horst Wessel Song," and Communists and Social Democrats struck back by belting out "The Internationale." Thousands of people in the early 1930s sang one or the other at the huge rallies that each party organized in market squares and sports arenas. Like "The Internationale," the "Horst Wessel Song" celebrated an ongoing struggle for liberation. The four stanzas replayed the war in a domestic setting, but this time Germany emerged victorious. The first (and fourth) stanza paired soldierly resolve with soldierly martyrdom:

> *Raise the flag! The ranks closed tight!*
> *SA marches with firm steady tread.*
> *Comrades shot dead by Red Front and Reaction.*
> *March in spirit within our ranks.*

In the second stanza, soldiers moved aggressively into the public spaces and into the arms of an adoring public:

> *Clear the streets for the brown battalions!*
> *Clear the streets for the storm trooper!*
> *Millions, full of hope, look upon the swastika.*
> *The day of freedom and bread is dawning.*

Victory was close at hand by the third stanza:

For the last time the attack alarm is sounded!
All of us are ready to fight.
Hitler flags soon wave on every street,
our servitude is nearly over!

Both the Nazis and their socialist opponents projected loudly to display the acoustic power of their ranks and shout over, and thus symbolically destroy, the enemy.

"Who Betrayed and Spat?" came the call, followed by the soldiers' scornful response: "Why It Was the Social Democrat!" "Who Has Dirtied Up the Nest? The Communist!" "Who Will Make Us Free and Hearty?" brought the final fiery answer, "The Hitler Party!" This call-and-response, embedded in the salute "Sieg, Heil," anticipated the signal to attack the enemy. It did not take long for working-class militants to gather in the streets to shout out the counteroffensive: "Red Front! Red Front! Red Front!" they chanted. "Down with Goebbels's Bandits. Out, Out, Out!" The verbal assault continued, "Fascist Dogs, Beat Them Dead." The SA returned fire, screaming, "Germany, Wake Up! Germany, Wake Up! Germany, Wake Up!" And then the Communists: "Nazis, Drop Dead! Nazis, Drop Dead! Nazis, Drop Dead!"[26]

Just who prevailed in these engagements was unclear. The Communists transformed neighborhoods into formidable fortresses. Activists defaced sandstone facades with graffiti, painted gigantic slogans on firewalls, and draped streets with flags and banners that read, "On Every Corner, the Flag Is Red" or "Nazis, Drop Dead!" Any visitor could walk around and read this open book of left-wing militancy. "Overnight, Nostizstrasse had been turned into a Thälmannstrasse."[27] Yet the "Thälmann streets" of "red" Berlin (so-called for Ernst Thälmann, the tough Communist Party chief whom the Nazis arrested in March 1933 and murdered in August

1944) were disconnected from the rest of the city, stretching for a few blocks—Nostizstrasse, Kösliner Strasse, Wallstrasse. This was a weakened position for the Reds. Nazi supporters, by contrast, were spread more evenly across the city. Compact working-class "barricades" were surrounded by numerous Nazi assault teams, which were more mobile and aggressive. The Left had no hope of "conquering" middle-class neighborhoods; the Nazis had better luck infiltrating "red" ones.

Sometimes the Nazis turned the corner and found themselves attacked by residents as stones and bottles, flowerpots and chamber pots sailed through the air. "Boiling water spilled out of the windows onto the street," wrote one novelist who reconstructed the scene in the Nostizstrasse. "The girls and the women boiled it by the pailful. And down on the street, a few men hollered: ouch, damn!"[28] The weapons were mostly improvised. There were bricks and boiling water in the Nostizstrasse, chair legs, beer steins, and ash trays in the battles that broke out in the Saalbau Friedrichshain, where Goebbels and the Communist Walter Ulbricht took part in a January 1931 "Battle of Words." The fighting escalated when both sides began to arm themselves with more fatal weapons, like knives and pistols. "Strike the Fascists Wherever You Meet Them" was the popular Communist slogan, a directive that militants followed even after party leaders disavowed it in favor of propaganda intended to win over rather than punch out SA proletarians. "Where Are the Nazis Hiding?" was the victorious call, followed by the response "In the Basement!" The crowds gleefully booed. And sometimes the SA succeeded in passing through "red" streets, entitling the Nazi press to belittle the "poor KPD" and call out, "Where Is the Kommune? In the Basement. Boo-hooooo!"[29] (In small towns, SA marchers were more often greeted as guardians of order, showered with "apples, pears, and grapes," and served hot coffee.[30])

The fight was over whenever police reinforcements arrived to clear the streets, arrest troublemakers, and transport the wounded to hospitals. If shots had been fired, police searched tenement buildings for weapons and snipers, which led to further arrests. Residents in working-class districts became used to the sound of sirens and glare of floodlights. In Berlin, during these crisis years, thirty to eighty people a day were taken for questioning to the political section of the police, Department I, on Alexanderstrasse; on election weekends in 1932, the numbers increased to three or four hundred.

Local taverns transformed into SA *Sturmlokalen*, with local Nazis guaranteeing owners steady receipts in return for exclusive use of these new "homes," giving Goebbels important bases from which to launch his "struggle for Berlin." By the early 1930s, the SA had succeeded in establishing outposts first along the edges of working-class districts, then right down the street from Communists and Social Democrats. In the Klein Wedding district of Charlottenburg in Berlin, for example, the three hundred SA men of the notorious Mordsturm 33 (Murder Squad 33) set up base in the tavern Zur Altstadt on Hebbelstrasse, just around the corner from Werner and Zum Hirsch, Communist bars on Wallstrasse. These all-male outposts worked to the advantage of the Nazis because the encroachment gave courage to local sympathizers. They worked to the disadvantage of socialists whose basic pledge, "Berlin Stays Red," had been compromised.

Sturmlokalen made Nazis out of neighbors. An SA leader wrote about political combat in close quarters, observing, "Our SA lives in the same buildings, in the same streets as the Reds; they work together in the same factories." Brownshirts boasted that they were aware of "every step, every movement, every word" of the enemy.[31] This was an exaggeration, but such reconnaissance was indispensable when police began arresting Communists and Social Democrats in March 1933. From their taverns, the Communists watched too, chalking warnings on the wooden floorboards of tenement buildings. "Careful, mate! / Beware / The young Red

Front is watching." A swastika in a hangman's noose added lurid detail.[32] Communist threats—"The Streets Belong to Us!"—and Nazi challenges—"Clear the Streets for the Brown Battalions!"—placed neighborhoods on a war footing.

The scope of violence appalled those Germans who realized that Nazis sowed the very violence from which they promised to protect peaceful citizens. Yet precisely the fighting spirit of the Nazis, the fact that they were "consequential," willing not so much to restore old peace as impose new order, made them attractive. The Nazis won support because of their militance. By launching furious, uncompromising attacks on the "system" and physically engaging their enemies, they dramatized the combustibility of the present. Through action, they overcame the paralysis of the crisis and opened the way into the future.

Hitler knew that he was not repelling potential supporters when he defended violence. "I want no softies in my movement," he affirmed to a reporter for the *Daily Mail*. "I want fanatics." The black-white-red colors of the Nazi flag might have recalled the "good, old days" of the Kaiserreich, but, as one activist explained, "The red predominates because we want to make a genuine revolution, our revolution." "And the swastika," he continued, "the ancient pinwheel, strikes fear in every sorry fellow." The Nazis were ideal protagonists for those Germans who thought themselves living in an embattled environment that brought out panic in the face of total collapse, brutal hatred of political enemies, and hope for the future.[33] The fighting songs—"Wake Up!" "Drop Dead!"—revealed a desperate struggle for the fate of German bodies.

Few countries have witnessed political mobilization on the scale of Germany in 1932. Even in towns as small as Northeim, with some 10,000 inhabitants, as many as 1,000 people crowded the 1910er Zelt or the Cattle Auction Hall to attend Nazi or Social Democratic rallies. The elections that year—a presidential election on March 13, a runoff on April 10, Prussian elections on April 24, and Reichstag elections on July 31 and November 6—intensified the drama of political life in which choice seemed reduced to stark binaries. The Nazis or the Communists, the "Third Reich" or the "system," the republic or extremism, Hitler or Hindenburg.

With the slogan "Hitler over Germany," which cast the Nazi leader as a messiah, Hitler campaigned by airplane, speaking in as many as five cities in one day. Over the course of six months, in three separate tours, Hitler flew to a total of 150 events attended by perhaps as many as 4 million people. "That was more Germans than any other German politician could have mobilized in such a short period of time," notes one historian. Over 200,000 Berliners crowded the Lustgarten on April 4, 1932 (a huge number but proportionally only half as many as had turned up for events in little Northeim, reflecting the party's entrenchment in small towns). The Nazi campaign in the presidential runoff in April 1932 was the "most modern and technically perfect" Germany had ever seen.[34]

"All of Berlin has been stirred up," the *Berliner Tageblatt* lamented at the end of March 1932. Public space was almost completely covered with political script. Huge white banners stretched across streets, declaring, "Vote for Hindenburg." Slogans painted on walls promised, "Hitler is coming!" or "Class against class, for Thälmann."[35] Walking the streets or riding the omnibus, Berliners everywhere confronted the outsized posters of the stern patriarchal Hindenburg or Hitler's white face against a pitch-black background. In what became known as the "poster war," *Klebekolonnen* (pasting parties) put up new posters on Berlin's 3,000 advertising pillars. Every day, people gathered around the columns to see what new arguments the parties had advanced and to argue with one another. A contemporary novelist set the scene: "These were tough words that were printed here, words of fire, of hate, of anger, of outrage."[36] The people "who stood in front of these posters were nervous, antagonized, convulsed, but few were indifferent." The day before the April 10 runoff, Berliners were "snowed under" with leaflets. "Falling out of the sky, tossed out of cars, and passed out on street corners," four-squared fliers dumped Germany's sharp-edged political divisions at the feet of passersby.[37]

The 1932 presidential election offered the Nazis the chance to assume power legally since, as president of the republic, Hitler would be able to govern by emergency decree. Hitler and his advisors genuinely thought that they were going to win. "Everyone is confident of victory." A "blissful" Hitler thought so too, noted Goebbels in his diary. But by ten o'clock on the evening of March 13, "it becomes clear: We're beaten." "The dream is over." Hitler was "terrifically surprised by the result."[38] Hindenburg received 49.6 percent of the vote, Hitler only 30 percent—although Hitler did force Hindenburg into a humiliating runoff, which the president won on April 10 with 53 percent. The Nazis had miscalculated, mistaking the enormous enthusiasm that Hitler generated in city after city for nationwide acclamation. Hitler could see the teeming crowds, and a book published shortly after the election to commemorate "Hitler over Germany" invited readers to do the same by offering foldouts of wide-angle photographs. The sheer scale of Hitler's rallies was astonishing: "more than 100,000" supporters in Chemnitz, "over 100,000" in Görlitz, 120,000 in Altona.[39] But Hitler and his rally-goers did not see the deep pockets of Catholics and Social Democrats who did not attend the rallies. With each election, the Nazis would find it more difficult to reconcile their ability to mobilize the German people as no other political movement had before with the simple refusal of large numbers of voters to be swayed at all. The Nazis would always come up short. At the end, only behind-the-scenes intrigue in January 1933 and ensuing street violence in February and March would put Germany's largest party over the finish line.

If a "poster war" waged by campaign activists on the advertising columns had characterized the spring presidential elections, the Reichstag election scheduled for July 31, 1932, gave rise to a "flag war" carried out by ordinary voters who hung the political flag of choice out of apartment windows. Most of the flags were red, the color of distress. There was the red flag of the Nazis with the black swastika against a white circle, the red flag of the Social Democrats with three black arrows (poised to smash the swastika), the red flag of the Communists with a golden hammer and sickle. "From the ground floor up to the skylights, these flags wave in the wind," noted one observer. They came in all sizes. "There are huge and powerful symbols of the courage of the family's loyalties that stretch over the entire story, and there are little kiddie flags that decorate the flowerpots on the balconies." The medley of political allegiances on display in a single building never failed to catch the eyes of observers. The *Vossische Zeitung* introduced readers to one on Berlin's Müllerstrasse: on the second floor, tenants had hung a banner to accompany the Nazi flag that read, "A people without arms—a people without honor—a people without bread." Neighbors on the next floor responded with a Communist banner: "We are settling accounts—we want bread!" "What is the mood of the inhabitants in this building?!" the newspaper wondered. "It serves as an emblem of all the deplorable divisions breaking apart the German people." One was left to wonder about the residents: "Maybe neighbors used to greet each other without suspicion"; now "they take care to avoid bumping into each other."[40]

Waves of violence accompanied the Reichstag election campaign in summer 1932. Living in Berlin at the time, British novelist Christopher Isherwood depicted the ugly mood, writing that the city was "in a state of civil war. Hate exploded without warning, out of nowhere; at street corners, in restaurants, cinemas, dance halls, swimming-baths; at midnight, after breakfast, in the middle of the afternoon.... Bullets slashed the advertisements on the poster columns, rebounded from the iron roofs" of latrines stashed in the back of courtyards.[41] In June and July, police reported 332 acts of street terror that left 72 people dead and 497 seriously injured. Even Hitler's entourage ran into trouble. "A campaign in the Ruhr is a life-threatening venture," Goebbels admitted on July 14, 1932. "A raging mob" had assembled in Elberfeld after "Communist riffraff" recognized the car's Berlin license plate. "Murderer of workers," "Outlaw," and "Bloodhound," opponents screamed. It was not uncommon for rocks or bullets to hit the windshield of Hitler's Mercedes. Hitler and Goebbels sped through the crowded streets with revolvers drawn—"the Führer" had proven himself to be "an absolutely sure marksman" in practice. Hitler with his pistol ready is an unfamiliar picture, but then it falls into place.[42]

The summer's worst incident occurred in the old section of Altona, a truly poor city near Hamburg, where a march of several thousand SA men through the narrow streets on Sunday, July 17, called forth a furious Communist response. Miming cutting throats, the Nazis shouted, "We'll hang Karl Liebknecht from a tree." From the sidewalks the crowds hooted back, "Red Front!" "Heil Moscow!" "Fascist horde!" At the corner of Grosse Johannisstrasse and Schauenburgerstrasse, where the numbers of angry onlookers had grown larger and the chants of the SA more vicious—"when Jewish blood splashes from the knife / then things go twice as nice!"—two brownshirts were shot and killed. Panicked crowds scattered as police, suspecting Communists snipers on rooftops, shot back indiscriminately, killing sixteen unarmed men and women and wounding scores more. No snipers were found—they rarely were—but the police had already shifted gears from "neutral" to "right." The tragedy quickly came to be known as "Bloody

Sunday," bloody enough to serve as a welcome pretext for Chancellor Papen to remove the democratic state government of Prussia on July 20. "Day for day, Sunday for Sunday," Harry Kessler observed, "we are getting closer and closer to civil war."[43] "Bloody Sunday" was a dress rehearsal for the Reichstag fire seven months later, which was also automatically blamed on German Communists and provided justification for the emergency legislation that closed up the republic. The pattern was established: right-wing disorder justified assaults on democracy.

Terror came closer and closer. One day around this time, Hans, a first grader, walked out of his building in Berlin-Steglitz on his way to school and saw a man lying in his own blood on the sidewalk. The stabbing victim wore a swastika armband on one arm, and his other hand clutched a fistful of pamphlets. A few moments later, a rickety ambulance picked him up and took him away. By 1932, it was not unusual for ordinary people going about their business to hear pistol shots or witness street fights.[44]

Closer and closer—that is how the novelist Oskar Maria Graf imagined the Nazi seizure of daily life. Sitting at home, Graf's protagonist, the old Social Democrat Hochegger, suddenly "flinched." "Somewhere down in the distant city there were shots, three or four of them." A while later, he could make out the echoing tat-tat-tat of boots marching somewhere down the street. The bootsteps rounded the corner, and Hochegger could clearly hear the singing. "Raise the flag! The ranks closed tight! / The SA marches with firm steady tread." Maybe this was all just "the last hurrah" of the Nazis, a friend told him; they were a faddish "party of the moment," bursting onto the scene before fading away. But then maybe not. A while later, in the streetcar, Hochegger bumped into his youngest son, who laughed when he realized that his father had caught sight of his Nazi badge. Albert's companion in arms, Mantler, extended his own personal greeting to Hochegger, saying,

"By the way, we both live in the same street" and "I often see you." "They are lurking everywhere": the Social Democrat felt short of breath as the circle tightened around him. It got worse. Mantler was dating Hochegger's daughter, Lotte, and had moved into the same building. "They are quite open about it," reflected Hochegger. "All the neighbors are talking.... It is like living in a mousetrap." His oldest son, Joseph, the only child to remain true to the socialists, described the "National Socialists' attempts to infiltrate at the building level," enabling them "to keep exact books on every single resident." Once Hochegger opened the door to Lotte's room to find "two little swastika flags attached to the wall over the bed" and a Hitler portrait, as well as photographs of Albert and Mantler in SA uniforms, he knew that the snake next door had slithered into his own apartment. He kicked Lotte out, but the security of home had been destroyed.[45]

"Poster wars" in the streets and "flag wars" in tenements split apart families. In novels transcribing the end of the Weimar Republic, sons rejected the authority of fathers, professing loyalty to Communists rather than Social Democrats. In Hans Fallada's *Little Man, What Now?*, family members exchanged insults, calling each other "social fascist" and "Soviet slave." Or siblings surprised each other when a brother joined the SA or brought home a Communist newspaper ("bombs exploded at home"). Many "Old Fighters" remembered domineering Social Democratic fathers who cursed their sons, prohibited them from putting on the brown uniform, and felt ready to deal them a slap in the face, but they also recalled sympathetic older sisters.[46] Sometimes family members did not fully understand where they had come to stand politically until Hitler came to power. Albert Speer and his mother kept their Nazi sympathies secret from his liberal father and also from each other until after Hitler was made chancellor.[47] The coming of the Third Reich staged a violent, revolutionary drama among friends and family, one that was nightmarish, transgressive, and liberating.

On July 31, 1932, 84 percent of eligible voters cast their ballots for the Reichstag. Never before had so many citizens participated in an election. The National Socialists won over significant numbers of Social Democratic and Catholic voters, although most supporters came from the old anti-Weimar parties on the right. Even with its "middle-class belly," the Nazi Party could claim to be what Germans call a *Volkspartei*, a "people's party," straddling the country's social, economic, and religious divides,[48] although the Nazis were not the foreordained people's party they imagined themselves to be. Despite defections, the Catholic and "Marxist" base held, so that Germany remained an extremely fractured country. Infiltration was not usurpation, at least not yet. Depending on the local precinct, observers could plainly feel the mistrust separating Catholic parishioners from SA men in Bavaria or socialist from Nazi neighbors in Berlin. Facing an opposition that would not go away, Nazis realized they wouldn't get "an absolute majority" through demagogic election campaigns or thunderous Sportpalast rallies. One has only to read Goebbels's diary to understand the train of thought: "we have won a tiny bit. . . . Result: now we must come to power and exterminate Marxism."[49] The Nazis would have to run the final lap another way.

Still, the election results on July 31 gave the Nazis a great victory. With over 37 percent of the vote, they emerged as Germany's largest party, overtaking in one giant leap the Social Democrats, Germany's largest party since 1890, who slipped to 21 percent. Although National Socialists were not as popular as either of the two "Marxist" parties in Berlin's working-class districts—Neukölln, Wedding, Prenzlauer Berg—they did come in a close third. In fact, "red" Berlin supplied the Nazis with one-half of their total citywide vote. Together, the National Socialists and the Communists gained more than half of all the votes in the country, a negative majority that, along with the Papen coup against Prussia days earlier, crippled the prospect of democratic government.

And yet, as scary as it was, the Nazi victory could not hide the fact that no one had really won. The Nazis had failed to get a majority; the republican defenders of the constitutional state, the Social Democrats and the Catholic Center, appealed to fewer than a third of voters; and Chancellor Franz von Papen's authoritarian government itself could hardly count on the support of one in ten Germans. The result was a political stalemate in which each side could only plausibly argue that the other lacked a mandate and peddled a swindle. Only Hitler's appointment as chancellor on January 30, 1933, broke this impasse.

In the days after the election, the Nazis punched back and punched again. Did they do so out of triumph or frustration? Jewish diarist Victor Klemperer had breathed a sigh of relief after the election, writing, "The republic saved," only to be dismayed when the specter of more Nazi violence and even a putsch loomed. "Hitler ante portas—or who else?" Germans could feel pressure building, the seams in the ship of state bursting. "Terror increasing," the Nazis said. "Deliverance."[50]

In separate attacks on election night, July 31, unknown culprits in Königsberg forced their way into the homes of well-known local Communists, leaving one dead and the daughter of Reichstag deputy Walter Schütz seriously injured. The same night, the offices of the local Social Democratic newspaper, *Volkszeitung*, were attacked with firebombs, and the editor was shot and wounded in his home. Shouting "Hello, Hello, Clear the Streets," local Nazis also shot up and set fire to gas pumps at a Königsberg garage. In Braunschweig, police counted a total of eight bomb attacks against businesses and homes, including the apartment of the mayor, Ernst Böhme, a Social Democrat. A Nazi father-and-son team shot one Social Democrat and knifed another in Schierstein, near Darmstadt. As many as sixty Nazis assaulted three Social Democrats with steel rods and blackjacks in Eberswalde, outside Berlin, and later a firefight between Nazis and Reichsbanner men left a sixteen-year-old girl dead in the street.[51] In retrospect, this offensive was a harbinger of attacks on Social Democratic and Communist functionaries in the weeks following the Nazi victory in the March 5, 1933, Reichstag elections, when Böhme was in fact thrown out of office and badly beaten and Schütz arrested and tortured to death.

NEGOTIATIONS BETWEEN PARTIES after the July 1932 elections were difficult. As the leader of the largest party, Hitler demanded the post of "presidential" chancellor, in which he could govern without Reichstag support but through the president's emergency powers. He calculated that the "bonus" of holding power would allow him to enact emergency "enabling" legislation, deploy "vigilante" methods against his enemies, and dismantle parliamentary institutions. His claim to exercise the same "presidential" powers that previous, less popular chancellors had was strong. Moreover, he knew that Germany's power brokers could only build the authoritarian state they desired by working with the Nazis. "We bring into the business of government 75 percent of the capital investment," Hitler correctly noted; other partners contributed "only 25 percent." In this regard, Hitler was in a good position when he entered negotiations with President Hindenburg. In early August, initial discussions with Kurt von Schleicher, the Reichswehr minister and a Hindenburg confidante, suggested that Hitler might get his way. Nazi leaders exulted that "the great hour" to build the Third Reich had come. August 11 was Constitution Day in Weimar Germany, Goebbels noted; he was convinced it would be the last.[52]

The rub was that Hindenburg's willingness to work with Hitler did not mean he supported Hitler's "all-or-nothing" strategy in which he held out for full power, unencumbered by coalition partners, by threatening to remain in the opposition. Millions of voters who saw Hitler as Germany's savior desperately wanted to see him in office, but they were divided on precisely the issue of power sharing. This weakened his negotiating position, and Hindenburg did not feel compelled to give extraordinary power to the leader of a single party, particularly one so intolerant of other views. Hindenburg was concerned not so much about Nazi hostility toward Social Democrats as about Hitler's ability to work with other right-wing elements in the proposed government of national unity. The issue was not protecting the constitution because Hindenburg was willing to give wide emergency powers to Papen. The issue was the Führer himself, and Hindenburg expressed "his 'irrevocable' will" not to allow the "Bohemian corporal" to govern without a Reichstag majority.[53]

A humiliating interview on August 13 and an official press release suggesting that Hindenburg had acted in the national interest by rebuffing Hitler's demand for total power left the Nazis with few options. Goebbels admitted that the party had "only this one iron in the fire."[54] There were, on one side, disagreements about whether a demand of "all or nothing" made sense and, on the other, conflicts about whether the Nazis could afford to continue to pursue a strictly constitutional as opposed to insurrectionary path to power. SA units pounded the pavement in Königsberg and Braunschweig for the order to violently seize power in Berlin. "Among party members there is an enormous sense of hopelessness," Goebbels reported, "and the SA is at wit's end."[55] In the following weeks, the party launched a furious offensive against Germany's "old guard" and Papen's newly assembled "cabinet of barons."

Locked out of the halls of power, the Nazis attacked the establishment. Shooting from the left, they attacked Papen and German Nationalist leader Alfred Hugenberg, whom many Nazi voters imagined would join up in a cabinet of national unity. Among sympathizers, this fed growing doubts about Hitler's ability to put country over party. "I want everything or nothing," Hitler admitted to the left-leaning French newspaper *L'Oeuvre* on September 7, 1932.[56] Hamburg schoolteacher Luise Solmitz, who rapturously recorded her enthusiasm for Hitler in the spring, reported on people who walked away in the fall. "E. M. says," she noted in her diary, "that he is ashamed to ever have voted for those lads." As new elections approached, discussions grew heated and a dinner party was canceled. "Lieutenant Colonel Simon declined on behalf of his wife—because we are against Hitler!!!! She is so short-tempered when it comes to politics." Solmitz herself felt deep regret because "for us, the National Socialist Party was a love match" and the "German Nationalist marriage we want to enter is a marriage of convenience," without the old "pep." "Hitler meant everything to us!" she lamented at the end of the year. "Doesn't he realize that?" Even die-hard supporters struggled to convince themselves that Hitler's "all-or-nothing" strategy was the way to go. In Braunschweig, Elisabeth Gebensleben affirmed that Hitler must be "true to himself; he *cannot* accept conditions that clash with his convictions"; yet she thought the divisions in the nationalist camp a genuine "tragedy." What before had been so clear now seemed muddled.[57] The invincible forward march of the Nazis stalled at the moment of the party's greatest electoral triumph.

Worse was to come. On November 6, 1932, another round of Reichstag elections registered the first Nazi losses since 1928. The campaign had been "languid." After so many elections, voters were exhausted and the parties broke. Nazi flags were still flown, but there were fewer of them, and the wet fall weather caused the white field to bleed into the red background. "The red in their flag is as fake as their socialism," remarked one worker at the sight of the besmirched banners.[58] Turnout declined by about 5 percent, but Nazi losses added up to 10 percent (from 37.3

to 33.1 percent). At this rate, the party would be finished in fifteen months. Local elections in Lübeck and Saxony a week later indicated that the Nazis had lost another 25 percent of their voters. In some precincts the Nazis were down 40 percent from their July highs. "The aura of unstoppable victories has vanished," cheered the *Vossische Zeitung* about the election's "judgment of God." "The mass propaganda has lost its appeal; no one listens to superlative promises anymore. Now the recovery can begin." On a lecture tour to promote his recent book on the Nazis, journalist Konrad Heiden concluded that Hitler was "just another misguided fanatic," one "who overreaches and achieves nothing. A falling comet in the November fog."[59]

The election did not change the political calculus. Hitler's November negotiations with Hindenburg ended with the same result as those in August. Hindenburg agreed to appoint Hitler chancellor if he could find a Reichstag majority to back him but would not hand over emergency powers to the party leader. In the event, Hindenburg, persuaded at the last minute that sticking with Papen increased the dangers of civil war, appointed General Kurt von Schleicher chancellor instead. Germany's "mystery tour" set off in a new direction.

Schleicher, known as "the Spider" for his extensive behind-the-scenes contacts, was a slippery character—his last name can be translated as creeper, sneak, or prowler, which is exactly how many politicians on the left and then on the right came to see him. During the war and its aftermath, his reputation rested on his mastery of logistics and interdepartmental affairs; "his battlefield was the desk top, his weapon, the telephone, and his tactic, negotiations."[60] Fifty years old in 1932, "Spiderman" had emerged as a key figure pushing Germany onto a decisively authoritarian political course. He turned against Chancellor Heinrich Brüning in May, engineered Hindenburg's subsequent appointment of the deeply unpopular Papen (a "hat" on Schleicher's head, the general admitted), and facilitated the coup against the democratic Prussian government in July. (The Nazis would murder Schleicher and his wife on June 30, 1934.)

Yet, in fall 1932, Schleicher maneuvered himself into the public eye as a champion of a "softer" authoritarian approach. In a lead article, Theodor Wolff, editor of the liberal *Berliner Tageblatt*, was taken in. Schleicher considered inopportune "experiments" to revise the constitution or restrict the franchise. "With the mellow voice of a soldier," he appealed to fundamentals over doctrine. "First of all, the people need to finally get something to fill their bellies, that appears to me to be the most important task at hand." With the appointment of a special commissar for job creation, Schleicher signaled that employment would take priority over austerity.[61]

In a radio address in mid-December, Schleicher took an unusual stance, declaring that he was an adherent of neither capitalism nor socialism. He fondly recalled his childhood, commending his father for teaching him that servants were to be treated with respect. Yet this old-fashioned paternalism also set limits on what Schleicher could achieve among suspicious Social Democrats. In place of the "Hunger Chancellor," Schleicher stepped forward as the "Social General," though the moniker signaled both approval of his empathy and disapproval of his flirtation with any kind of social justice. It was precisely Schleicher's intention to find a more popular base of support for his government that aroused mistrust among the nationalists who had long been his partners in crime. "Unquestionably," the chancellor represented "a step back to parliamentary business as usual," warned the conservative *Berliner Lokal-Anzeiger*.[62] (Right-wing suspicions about the "Social General" ultimately brought down "Spiderman" after fifty-six days.) His fortunes boosted by the Nazis' malaise, Schleicher enjoyed something of a political honeymoon in December 1932. It was not exactly clear what policies the new chancellor would propose, but he wasn't Hitler. Or Papen for that matter. Perhaps he would lead the country— away from the bitter, fractious politicking that had dominated the year.

In the hundred days before Hitler was appointed chancellor, many Germans believed the worst was over. At the end of the year, the Nazis suffered one reversal after another, and newspaper headlines in mid-December exposed rifts among party leaders on questions of strategy. One thing was clear: The Nazis could not afford a new round of battering elections. The Sportpalast emptied out—Goebbels admitted "poor attendance" at one event, although the band had been "very good." Membership also fluctuated dramatically in turnstile fashion that saw more members exiting than entering.[63] "We are all very depressed," Goebbels wrote, describing the mood in his apartment after Hitler had come to visit on December 8, "especially when faced with the prospect of the entire party falling apart and all our work ending up being for nothing."[64] At the same time, Germany showed modest signs of economic improvement in production, trade, and stock valuation. "Land in sight!" proclaimed the influential business page of the *Frankfurter Zeitung* on New Year's Day 1933.

Hitler's losses were probably more decisive in brightening the public mood than anything Schleicher did or said. Either way, the liberal press desperately wanted to read the signs of the times in a positive light. Reporters dug to find special elections to confirm the Nazis' falling fortunes. In local elections in Ostritz, near Dresden, on December 18, the National Socialists tumbled from being the town's largest party to its second smallest; "the surge subsides," the *Vossische Zeitung* crowed on its front page. A little more than a month later, 276 voters in the tiny Pomeranian village of Binow had cut the Nazis' support in half.[65] The socialist newspaper *Vorwärts* even featured an editorial titled "Hitler's Rise and Fall." On

New Year's Day, the *Berliner Tageblatt* imagined future readers asking, "What was his first name again, Adalbert Hitler?"[66] The whole world used to talk about him. Whatever happened to him, they would wonder. It was the inevitable destiny of a "beer hall agitator" who could not be taken seriously.

The press rediscovered the virtuous qualities of the German people who stood firm against fanaticism. The November elections showed that the electorate was not so "politically immature" after all. "This great, patient, courageous, undaunted people of engineers, craftsmen, workers, and farmers," the *Vossische Zeitung* extolled, had "held its ground" in the "crisis of nerves." What had seemed an all consuming "fire" turned out to be a temporary "fever."[67] Reporters walked along city streets, finding relaxed consumers rather than impassioned partisans. Retailers were cheered that "browsing folks" had finally become "buying folks" and angled for purchases without becoming "all elbows," "tight-fisted and go-getting." "People are kinder to their fellow human beings," observers agreed, "more pleasant, amiable, calm, and considerate." After the "sacrifices and struggles" of the last years, the German people deserved to be "spared political blows" and to enjoy the small gains of improved circumstances.[68]

The sense of relief around Christmas was widespread, and the liberal press pushed the theme. A popular toy like the yo-yo at the end of the year seemed to confirm the faddish nature of all things foolish, including political fantasies like National Socialism. The yo-yo, twenty centimeters of fresh snow, Adalbert Hitler—the apocalypse had not spilled over the banks of everyday life.

There was nothing inherently wrong with this analysis, and even at quarter past eleven, on January 30, 1933, Hitler's chancellorship was not foreordained. In the absence of poll data, the mood of the nation was hard to discern. But all the commentary about Germany's "recovery" overlooked persisting signs of distress. "Hunger demonstrations" crisscrossed lines of Christmas shoppers on Berlin's Kurfürstendamm. Holiday crowds had been dispersed by tear gas bombs thrown by the Nazis into department stores in Darmstadt, Giessen, and Mainz.[69] Run-ins between Communists and Nazis picked up in the new year as well. Even with Schleicher as chancellor, guests at a dinner party took up the debate almost as soon as they sat down: When would the National Socialists "seize the government." "I can scarcely think of anything else on earth," admitted journalist Aurel Kolnai.[70]

However, there was something misguided about analyses that repeatedly invoked the healthy *Volk*, the German people, who wished for nothing more than "peace and quiet," separating out a few fanatics and troublemakers. Schleicher's strategy of cobbling together a "diagonal front" by going around the parties to deal directly with trade unions and patriotic associations was based on the like-minded conviction that people should be approached in a less partisan way. Yet the Nazis looked at the German problem very similarly, presenting themselves as the guardians of a basically sound moral order threatened by "Marxists" and Jews. The liberal sigh of relief at the end of 1932 buttressed the idea of "normalcy," which is exactly what the National Socialists enforced with great vigilance against perverted "anti-German" elements after 1933. Did the desire for political peace in Weimar's last hundred days prepare the populace to accept the political resolution the Nazis imposed in Hitler's first hundred days?

The Nazis had appeared weaker that winter because most commentators evaluated their dilemma in parliamentary terms. The thinking was that Hitler risked the future of his movement if he failed to compromise with the other nationalist parties and to abandon his demand for emergency powers. The assumption was that he would have to work within the system and adjust to the sobering reality that his movement had exhausted its electoral potential.[71] Observers stressed what the Nazis did not yet have rather than what they still had. Yet the National Socialists remained Germany's largest political movement, with half again as many members and party branches as the Social Democrats. The Nazis had established a presence in every place of note in Germany. Moreover, the paramilitary SA had twice as many uniformed soldiers as the combined forces of the Reichswehr and the Prussian police, even if the numbers had declined. According to one historian, SA membership "stagnated" at 427,000 at the end of 1932, down from 455,000 in August, but 427,000 was comparable to the size of the SA in early July. Morale problems notwithstanding, the SA was not "nearing collapse."[72]

In a democratic age, power is reckoned in voters, party members, activists, and the press, a basic calculation that disqualified unpopular "presidential" chancellors such as Papen. That calculus also ensured that the Nazis remained the major player in German politics. Hitler was on the mark when he weighed the political variables after listening to Schleicher's first radio address to the nation. "Is that all?" he asked. "We have the youth," Hitler added. "We have greater courage, a stronger will, and more tenacity."[73]

Maybe we should count the fact that there was no decision in the "decision year" 1932 as a plus for German democracy, and democrats certainly counted on Hindenburg to keep Hitler out of power. But this was hardly a political strategy. The Social Democrats themselves were paralyzed, torn between supporting the republic against the Nazis and, yielding to Communist pressure, opposing reactionaries such as Schleicher who might have saved it. Party leader Otto Wels opened a meeting in Berlin after the November 1932 elections by comparing the political future to the morning fog: "As I was driving this morning to Berlin, I had to drive very slowly because of the heavy fog.... For all of us, the political situation is as foggy as the weather outside." The Social Democrats did not know where they were going. Along the way, however, they passed by the taverns that had once been party strongholds. "Many of the familiar faces have disappeared from among the wooden tables," observed one visitor to the countryside. Remaining were "the village youth in brown shirts, suddenly mobilized into military storm troops and divisions."[74]

At the inconclusive end of 1932, the real decision-making moved from the streets and parliaments to the corridors of statecraft around President Hindenburg, who retained the power to issue emergency decrees. Schleicher had emerged as the key figure over the course of 1932, but Hindenburg remained close to Papen, the stricken chancellor, whom he had presented with a portrait inscribed with the traditional lament to honor a fallen soldier, "Ich hatt' einen Kameraden." The corpulent, bespectacled Otto Meissner, who served as state secretary in the Office of the President, and the president's son, Oskar von Hindenburg, also gained influence. Lobbyists for the powerful business and agricultural interest groups appealed to these men. This meant that the drama of 1932 became more compressed: only a few people, whose choices had immediate and far-reaching consequences, wielded political power.

It is relatively easy to get into the heads of these men. One hundred Communist deputies and thirty-four fewer National Socialist deputies in November 1932 made the prize of winning over the Nazi Party more valuable and reservations about Hitler's leadership less relevant. Indeed, Hitler himself hammered that "economic misery has not lessened, unemployment is rising, Bolshevism is spreading."[75] Consternation about Schleicher's socialist whisperings and recognition that Papen was not an alternative—his return to power would likely ignite civil unrest—also worked in favor of accepting Hitler, the people's tribune, as chancellor. Basically, the desire to establish authoritarian rule was so strong that even though Germany's nationalists believed they would be able to "tame" Hitler, they accepted the risk of not being able to do so. In any case, the Nazis already occupied the third-highest office in the country after the bourgeois parties themselves had voted in favor of the Nazis' nomination of Hermann Göring as president of the Reichstag in August 1932. Göring, one of the Nazis whom nationalists sought out for negotiations, replaced the long-serving Social Democrat Paul Löbe, which was exactly the kind of radical scenario right-wing forces sought.

Throughout January 1933, the few men who counted on the stage around Hindenburg concluded, one by one, with Papen in the lead, that the appointment of Hitler as chancellor was the only way to establish an authoritarian state. "The Iron Hindenburg," whom Germans had clad in metal when they hammered nails into oversized statues that dotted the landscape during the war, proved a "wooden titan" after he finally, to the shock of Weimar's democrats, followed Papen and acquiesced at quarter past eleven.[76] The conspirators were not trying to solve a serious problem, the crisis in governance or finances; they were working hard to reach an ambitious ideological goal—to destroy the republic by any means necessary. It took a long, long time, when Germany was already in ruins, for conservatives to understand that they had made a pact with the devil in 1933.

Liberal public opinion, such as it was, abetted the position of antirepublican string pullers. Leading newspapers such as the *Vossische Zeitung* supported Schleicher and regretted his resignation on January 28, 1933, "one hundred meters before the goal," but vociferously opposed Papen's return, which they believed to be the most likely and highly dangerous next step.[77] The army also warned against Papen.

Hitler had more cards to play than one might expect after his election losses. During the party's crisis in December and January, Hitler demonstrated what he could do, which strengthened his hand. He rallied his dispirited party, led it to victory in a crucial state election, and ordered his SA soldiers back onto the streets after the Christmas truce.

After the disappointing November election results, Hitler managed to hold the party together and consolidate support for his "all-or-nothing" strategy. "A striking aspect of Hitler's response to his precarious position," writes one historian, "was the composure he maintained in the face of daunting circumstances." There was "no loss of nerve." During the weeks that followed, the "Divine Hitler," the superman who knew that "Providence had decreed that he should always be right," was born. The end of 1932 was formative because it determined how Hitler would later respond to other crises in the Third Reich: the invasion of the Soviet Union in June 1941 or the defeat at Stalingrad in February 1943. "I hold the firm conviction that this battle will end not a whit differently from the battle I once waged at home!" Hitler exclaimed in November 1940. Goebbels struck a similar note in the Berlin party newspaper, *Der Angriff* (The attack). He extolled the power of sheer will: "The Reich will not collapse as long as we believe and continue to fight and work!" he wrote in a Christmas 1932 article titled "The Great Miracle," which came to pass six weeks later ("the great miracle has occurred!" he exulted on February 2) and, in the words of Zarah Leander's popular 1942 song "I Know There Will Be a Miracle One Day," was supposed to come to pass one more time after Germany had begun to lose the war.[78] The common vocabulary is remarkable.

Hitler also benefited from good timing. State elections were scheduled in the Lilliputian state of Lippe for January 15, 1933. They gave the Nazis an opportunity to reverse their political fortunes. The party poured resources into the 1,215-square-kilometer area inhabited by 163,000 "Lippe men and Lippe women," about one-quarter the population of the Berlin district of Steglitz. The press thoroughly enjoyed mocking the grand moment of the "little land." "Lippe men and Lippe women went to the polls and passed judgment on the life and death of parliament, on the power or impotence of the rulers and of those who hope to become rulers." And what did the "oracle of Lippe" say? The Nazis improved on their

November 1932 results without beating their July totals, and while they constituted the largest party, Communists and Social Democrats combined received more votes. "It was not a big victory. But even so," after "unprecedented efforts, a small success," concluded *Tempo* tartly. The elections in Lippe strengthened Hitler's hand at a crucial moment in his negotiations with Papen, Hugenberg, and Hindenburg's advisors.[79]

Hitler stood at the very center of everybody's thinking in January 1933 because the Nazis ably worked the streets as well as the ballot box. When the Nazis planned a memorial service for Horst Wessel, the SA leader murdered three years earlier, they provided a reminder of the kind of power that counted in the democratic age. Liberal newspapers expressed outrage that the SA had been given permission to hold a march past the Karl Liebknecht House, Communist Party headquarters on the Bülowplatz, on the way to the Nicolai Cemetery; the city center had to be completely locked down. On Sunday afternoon, January 22, some 16,000 SA soldiers, surrounded by just as many policemen armed with machine guns, "conquered" deserted streets. It was not a "heroic feat," remarked the *Berliner Tageblatt*; it was a "disgrace."[80]

The march allowed the Nazis to present themselves as "masters of the street, fearless and superior." "For the first and last time in party history, the Nazis staged a demonstration before huge photographs of Marx, Lenin, and Thälmann," while shouting, "Heil Hitler!" "Germany, Wake Up!" and "We shit on freedom, and we shit on the Jew republic!"[81] The Nazis boasted that the Communists had suffered an "immense blow to their prestige." Social Democrats acknowledged that "the fact that on January 22, 1933, in Berlin Hitler's brown hordes were allowed to march outside the windows of the KPD headquarters" was a "very bitter pill for the *entire* labor movement" to swallow.

The next day, Nazi papers declared victory: "Berlin, belongs to us," sticking it to the socialists who had always declared, "Berlin

Stays Red." Not quite consummated, but nearly so, the act of taking possession ("belongs to us") anticipated events in the coming weeks and indicated how confident the brown revolutionaries remained. Goebbels regretted that "we haven't yet won over police"; otherwise the Communists and their Karl Liebknecht House would be "finished." *Der Angriff* looked forward to "exterminating" the "poisoned spawn" of Communists "as one would exterminate rats or bugs."[82]

The SA did not march simply to win a battle against the Communists; they did so to deliver a message to nationalists. Look to the Nazis, and no one else, to protect you, they said. And they sent a message to Hindenburg's circles about their ability to assemble the people's power. The Nazi march created what Goebbels called *dicke Luft*, the sense that "trouble is brewing," anything can happen. "Over night," on the Friday before the Sunday march, Abraham Plotkin, the American in Berlin, reported, "There has come into the air a tenseness that is new and startling"; "the cafes tonight were jammed with men and women who could talk of nothing but what tomorrow may bring."[83] The Nazis were ready to move.

The Nazis displayed the power of the crowd across the whole city for an entire day. The SA men were in front of the Karl Liebknecht House while Hitler spoke at the Nicolai Cemetery before appearing at half past six o'clock at the Sportpalast, which followers in "drunken enthusiasm" had filled to the rafters. Hitler anticipated the coming Reich that would guarantee "the life of our people for many centuries to come."[84] Once the point had been made, Hitler left the Sportpalast to pursue closed-door negotiations with Hindenburg's people late into the night.

Historian Henry Ashby Turner provides a dramatic account: Oskar von Hindenburg and Otto Meissner slipped out of the opera after the house lights dimmed and took a taxi to the Dahlem villa of Joachim von Ribbentrop, a former journalist and wealthy wine dealer who would become Hitler's foreign minister in 1938. There, they found waiting for them former chancellor Papen, Hitler, and Hermann Göring, who had just arrived from Dresden. In time, Hitler took Hindenburg fils aside, and Göring conferred with Meissner. At the end of the evening, Papen signaled his willingness to accept a Hitler chancellorship and settle for what he himself had once offered Hitler, the vice-chancellorship.[85] It was a dramatic reversal.

The meeting was a turning point, but the choreography—a dance of the principals' sudden departures and arrivals, the dinner they enjoyed, the private conferences in side rooms—is only one way to think about power in January 1933. Another is to consider Hitler's activities on January 22. He arrived in Berlin in the afternoon after participating in party events in Frankfurt an der Oder, spoke to thousands of SA marchers at the Nicolai Cemetery, and then delivered a speech at the Sportpalast in the evening; only once these public events had been concluded did Hitler go to Dahlem. To understand how a handful of negotiators engaged each other in the villa at night, consider how thousands of Nazis staged themselves in the streets during the day.

"Germany, Wake Up!" "Nazis, Drop Dead!" Call and response. On January 25, the Communists answered the Nazi rally with their own. Tens of thousands of comrades marched to the Bülowplatz to reclaim the place. Social Democratic newspaperman Friedrich Stampfer published a strikingly sympathetic account of the masses with whom he mingled on the icy Wednesday night. "Bülowplatz once again," he began.

> They marched for hours in shabby coats, in thin jackets, in torn shoes in the sharp frost and piercing wind. Tens of thousands of pale faces reflected the distress but also the courage to stand for a cause they believe to be right. Their voices rang out hate, a thousand times justified, for a social order that has condemned them

to misery and poverty, rang out protest, a thousand times justified, against the grotesque madness of the glaring inequality of
our social conditions. The tens of thousands marching yesterday
across the Bülowplatz were not "subhumans" or "red murderous
beasts"—they were workers exactly like the workers organized in
the Social Democratic Party.[86]

Once Stampfer was able to see Communists as comrades, he could
represent socialist fellowship as the basis for an enduring German
community. Maybe Berlin would stay red.

Social Democrats organized an even bigger demonstration of
their own on Sunday, January 29, the day after Schleicher's resignation. It was a huge march that newspapers neglected to report on
fully in the rush of events on Monday, the day of Hitler's appointment, but on Sunday afternoon, Berliners must have felt the long
brush of men, women, and children making their way to Lustgarten, where as many as 100,000 socialists rallied the battered city.
Wasn't this Berlin? Abraham Plotkin thought so. Youth groups,
uniformed Reichsbanner men, trade unionists, and party members
"marched with a zip as effective as that of the Nazis." "Red banners flying high" made "a stirring sight." Endless chants of "Freedom, freedom, freedom" drowned out the speeches. People on the
sidewalk and neighbors at the window answered back. "Berlin,"
marchers called out, again and again. "Berlin Stays Red," people
shouted in loud response.[87]

At midnight on January 29, the stakes were high. How strong
were the Nazis? For how many Germans did they speak? What
would the Communists do? Had Social Democrats finally mustered freedom-loving citizens? From the SA march on the Bülowplatz to the socialist rally in the Lustgarten, the last week in January
composed a street drama in which the people of Berlin took part as
actors on stage, as members of the chorus, as spectators in the audience. It certainly held the attention of the negotiators in Dahlem.

The ending, the one that comes in the fifth act of a Shakespearean drama, was a mystery—not determined until almost the last minute. At noon, on Monday, January 30, the press agency announced that President Hindenburg had appointed Adolf Hitler chancellor of the German republic in a cabinet that included Franz von Papen and the German Nationalist leader Alfred Hugenberg.

There were many questions in the hundred days before January 30, 1933: "A turning point to the crisis?" asked the *Berliner Tageblatt*. "Will it get better?" wondered the *Kölnische Zeitung*. Some could hear "quiet chimes of hope," but others paid more attention to the stock market: "volatile," "later falling."[88]

At the end of January 1933, looking back on the last twenty years, Germans knew they lived in a "new world," but what sort of new world was it? The kaiser was gone; a war had been fought and lost, scarring every family tree; bright neon signs lit up the night on the Kurfürstendamm, while gas lamps still dimmed early evening at village crossroads. Into which "new world" had Germans stepped? The Neue Welt on the Hasenheide in which Albert Speer heard Hitler speak in November 1930 or the Neue Welt in which Neukölln's workers celebrated May Day with singing and dancing? The Neue Welt in which trick mirrors allowed customers to see up the skirts of women who crossed the "devil's bridge"? The Neue Welt was a place of delightful "simultaneity," commented French philosopher Jean-Paul Sartre after he watched the show on his own visit to Berlin in 1933.[89] It was always the same place, or was it?

Alfred Döblin made sure to take his leading man, Franz Biberkopf, to the Neue Welt in the novel *Berlin Alexanderplatz*. "Life's one damned thing after another; we shouldn't make life harder than it is." The bock beer festivals "got into their bones, with every measure and between beer mugs they tittered and smirked, hummed with the music, moved arms in rhythm; booze, booze, guzzle and booze. Leave all your trouble at home. Booze, booze, guzzle and booze. Leave all your trouble at home.... Then life's a happy refrain." "It is a guaranteed cure that does your whole body good," added a local newspaperman. "The patients enter gloomy, lonely, and bored and leave (mostly in pairs) happily singing and dance stepping on their way out." Cigarette and cigar smoke choked the air—Döblin pushed Biberkopf past the cloakroom into various back rooms, where he fell into conversations about the horizons of the "new world." "Arm in arm the crippled man and Franz sat at the bar: 'Say, lemme tell you they reduced my pension, they did, I'm gonna join the Reds.'" They drank. "Where did you serve in the army?" "The veteran whispered, his hand before his mouth, he belched," and drank some more and this time leaned right. "Are you a German, honest and true? If you run with the Reds, you're a traitor." And a traitor could not be a friend. He embraced Biberkopf, though, asking urgently again, "Are you a German, are you German to the bone?"[90]

CHAPTER THREE

Assault

M ONDAY, JANUARY 30: Everything tumbled out at once. It was a terribly cold, wet winter day, the first business day after Kurt von Schleicher's resignation two days earlier. In "Siberian Berlin," the revolutionary banners draped across the Karl Liebknecht House declared war on "War Mongering, Fascism, Hunger" and "Frost." In the small town of Waldshut, in southwestern Germany, the Bausch family gathered to eat lunch just after noon. "Hans," the father, an old Catholic politician, told his eleven-year-old son, "tune in Beromünster. Let's see if we already have a new government!" There was no news from the reliable Swiss station, but when young Hans switched on the Süddeutschen Rundfunk at 1:15 p.m., the family learned that President Paul von Hindenburg had appointed Adolf Hitler chancellor.[1]

The news spread quickly through Germany's neighborhoods. Hitler was the twenty-third chancellor in the history of the republic, but this appointment was different. At forty-three, Hitler was the youngest. He commanded a formidable political army and promised not to improve government but to build a new empire, the "Third Reich." When "Vati" came home for lunch in Braunschweig, he brought an extra edition, and "his face had broken into a huge grin." "At last, at last," his wife, Elisabeth Gebensleben, rejoiced, recalling the moment a few days later. In Berlin, a doorbell rang, neighbor greeting neighbor with a broad smile and palpable elation, exclaiming, "Our Hitler has become Reich chancellor! All the hard times are over!...A great new era will begin!" Ursula Sobottka's mother was worried: "I don't know, I am not as sure as the Hitlerite next door." Living in Paris, German writer Thea Sternheim "threw up" when she learned the news. (Later that night, watching the Nazis parade through the Brandenburg Gate, painter Max Liebermann remarked that he "couldn't possibly eat as much as he wanted to puke."[2])

Everywhere, people clustered together to talk: outside on streets, against the door in tenement hallways, around dining room tables. In Leipzig, writer Erich Ebermayer had invited Klaus Mann, with whom he was planning to draft a play based on Antoine de Saint-Exupéry's adventure novel *Night Flight*, to dine with him and his parents before Klaus continued on to Munich to visit his father, the German novelist Thomas Mann. Conversation turned to the day's unavoidable subject, Hitler. All at once, "it seemed to me as if a dark shadow had been cast over the world, as if something terrible, irrevocable, fateful had occurred." "Six weeks," interjected Ebermayer's agitated mother, "it won't last longer than that." Many people viewed Hitler with the same skepticism; they could not take the "uninvited house painter" seriously and regarded the conservative cabinet members around Hitler as the key players. It seemed clear that the cabinet's reactionary agenda would neither solve Germany's economic problems nor attract sufficient political support to gain a parliamentary majority. Ebermayer's father, a prominent jurist, was more pessimistic. With hardcore antirepublicans like Hitler, Franz von Papen, and Alfred Hugenberg, he said the cabinet did not look like one that would simply resign in the event of a no-confidence vote; it seemed ready to embark on dangerous constitutional experiments. At seventy-four years old, he doubted whether he would live to see the day when the new government would fall. Six weeks, or a lifetime—what was the staying power of Hitler's government, and how ruthlessly would the chancellor apply that power? Erich Ebermayer joked that the government "would last until after the next lost war." Everyone laughed.

This was the last time the two friends ever saw each other. Klaus Mann left for Munich that night and fled Germany six weeks later. Ebermayer stayed. When Mann returned after the war in June 1945 in an American uniform as a reporter for *Stars and Stripes*, he turned down Ebermayer's invitation to meet.[3]

Ebermayer's joke about the lost war attested to the lingering effects of World War I. Hundreds of thousands of Germans associated the unrepentantly patriotic Nazis with bellicosity, and they were terrified. "Hitler means war!" they shouted. But war or no war, a new start was exactly what millions of Germans hoped for after years of crisis, and Nazis profited from this feeling.

More Germans were for Hitler than for any other thing in January 1933. On the afternoon of January 30, Nazi newspapers announced rendezvous points for rallies across Germany. In Berlin, *Der Angriff* proclaimed, "Torchlight Parade, 7 o'clock Grosser Stern (Tiergarten). The parade will pass through the Brandenburg Gate to the Wilhelmstrasse." SA men assembled in a crowd of thousands of curious Berliners. No one was quite sure what to expect, but one thing was certain: Adolf Hitler, whose only experience was his own hyperenergetic campaign for power, was a totally new kind of politician.[4]

I N MELITA MASCHMANN'S FAMILY, politics was always part of breakfast. Morning papers prompted conversation about foreign policy, elections, and emergency decrees. Melita knew that, as German Nationalists, her parents were farther to the right than most. In their view, Germany's "special path" since the war had been a rocky, miserable trail. The country had lost the war, even though no other "nation had mustered such brave soldiers"; a shameful peace had "torn apart" its territories and caused the economy to "waste away." "The word 'Germany'" was something "I loved," remembered Melita. It evoked something "mysteriously overshadowed with grief, something infinitely dear and threatened by danger." This much she shared with her Protestant parents, but the fifteen-year-old also rebelled against the "unquestioning obedience" that the children were expected to show. She silently took the side of their maid in household quarrels. Drawn to the "little people," the "uneducated folks" whom her mother disparaged for allowing themselves to have political opinions at all, she was ready to hear what the Nazis had to say. The dressmaker who had come by to refit mother's dress for Melita spoke glowingly of Hitler; her "dark eyes sparkled."[5] Despite their prejudices, Melita's parents escorted her and her twin brother into Berlin to see the torchlight parade pass under the Brandenburg Gate. Although loyal to the old kaiser, the parents stepped up toward Hitler. It was a revealing moment: the Maschmanns were motivated by a sense of national duty that even the Nazis were able to call upon. People who had plenty to say about the inadequacy of Hitler celebrated the moment when nationalists and Nazis took over. Their no morphed into a yes.

"Fathers holding children up in their arms" to catch a glimpse of Hindenburg prompted the nationalist newspaper, *Deutsche Allgemeine Zeitung*, to hail the "spontaneous" patriotic union. The march gradually turned into a "people's festival"; vendors arrived on Wilhelmstrasse to sell sweets.[6] It was everyone's carnival, not somebody's rally. "The crashing tread of the feet, the somber pomp of the black, white, and red flags, the flickering light from the torches on the faces and the songs with melodies that were at once aggressive and sentimental" made a lasting impression on Melita. "For hours the columns marched by," though she continued to feel the "icy blast" of her parents' reserve in the winter night. At one point, someone broke out of the marching columns and started beating up a man on the sidelines. Melita wondered if the man had said something out of turn. "I saw him," she remembered, "his face bloodied, fall to the ground," screaming. Her parents immediately pulled her and her brother out of the way, but Melita had seen the blood. The adults' persisting aloofness, their willingness to cover for the new regime's violence—this was also a "no, yes" moment.

If the sights and sounds of the new era—blood and screams—alarmed her parents, they exerted a powerful attraction on Melita herself. Although Melita could not get the image of the bloodied man out of her head for days, she wanted to follow the tracks of the soldiers on the street, "for whom it was a matter of life and death." In her thinking, violence marked the idealism, fueling the country forward and christening the "people's community," or *Volksgemein-schaft*. Melita had first heard the word "from the lips" of the dressmaker, and "on the evening of January 30, it acquired a magical glow." It meant a declaration of "war on the class prejudices of the social stratum from which I came," and it offered "protection and justice to the weak." Melita narrated the evening as a personal liberation from the world of her parents and as a collective, even bloody conquest of space that enabled the liberation of the German people. The parents reluctantly accepted the National Socialists and overlooked the violence, while the children embraced the promise of the Third Reich and the blood sacrifice it demanded. "Hitler means war"—in this case Melita wanted to sign up.

The torchlight parade became a defining moment for the Nazis. It was much more than a victory celebration. The tens of thousands of Berliners who gathered from across the city formed an "honor guard" through which the SA squadrons marched, in what was heralded as the "rebirth of the nation." "At every turn, more flags, more marches, more forests of raised saluting arms," exulted *Der Angriff*. "What came to pass yesterday evening," when thousands of jubilant Nazis marched to the presidential palace and the Reich chancellery on the Wilhelmstrasse, where Hindenburg and Hitler stood at open windows, "can be compared to no other event other than the first days of August 1914 when an entire people stood up to the last man against a world of enemies and joyously expressed its will and resolve to fight." The frequent references to 1914 were intended to nationalize a partisan celebration, to let National Socialists stand in for the entire beleaguered nation.[7]

The Nazis promised to restore national greatness, but 1914's August Days did not in reality mark a conclusive victory. They were the start of general mobilization for a long war. As Thomas Mann pointed out, comparisons to "the mood of 1914–15" meant that "logically '16, '17, and '18 had to follow," the years when the unity of jubilation disintegrated and the country slid into moral and spiritual degradation. People in 1933 did not want war—so many Germans were against it, in fact, that later in the 1930s, Hitler's popularity rested on keeping the peace rather than waging war. But the bloodied face in the parade indicated that renewal of the "spirit of 1914" would be achieved precisely by vanquishing the victors of November 1918. The people who cheered the Nazis integrated these dueling pasts, accepting the violence of November 1918 in order to restore the ideal of August 1914.[8]

Nationally minded Germans like the Maschmanns accepted the National Socialists as the guardians of a national revolution that had finally unified patriots, which included veterans of the Stahlhelm and storm troopers of the SA. Enchanted with the parade, the influential conservative daily *Deutsche Allgemeine Zeitung* portrayed it as a genuine demonstration of various castes gathered together without distinction and "united in the cause of the fatherland," despite the late hour and winter cold. The reconciliation of Hindenburg and Hitler symbolized the "great national concentration."

That night Joseph Goebbels watched Hindenburg closely. "A towering heroic figure" from the Great War, he seemed completely in his element: "with his walking cane he time and again beat out the time to the rhythm of the military marches." (Berliners also had other ideas about Hindenburg, passing on the irresistible joke the very next day. The aging president, at the sight of the brown columns marching past, was said to have turned to his state secretary, Otto Meissner, with the remark, "I can't imagine, Ludendorff, where all these Russian prisoners of war come from."[9])

The Nazis portrayed themselves as heirs of Germany and its struggles, going so far as to equate murdered SA men with the fallen soldiers of the war. Nationalists saw the events of January 30 a little differently. They honored the brownshirts as fellow patriots but persistently enrolled the Nazis in a wider coalition ("Hindenburg, Hitler, and Seldte" or the "Hitler-Papen Union") subordinate to the idea of a reawakened German spirit, "everyone singing 'The Song of the Germans.'" This welding of Nazis and nationalists into a greater, better Germany was dubious, since the Nazis quickly exerted almost complete control and all but swamped their coalition partners in a sea of brown. The cabinet was not a government of "national concentration" because Hitler hardly worked with his coalition partners. But the idea of "national government" and the "national awakening" it oversaw proved useful, as it allowed the Nazis to label "Marxist" opponents as un-German traitors and terrorists. If the nationalist pedigree of "us" remained contested, the identities of "them" were always crystal clear.

The conservatives did not just want to tag along; they desperately wanted to be part of a great "national awakening." But since they did not have the numbers and people flocked to see Hitler and not Hugenberg, conservatives allowed the National Socialists to represent themselves as sentinels of the national interest. In the *Deutsche Allgemeine Zeitung* article, the Nazis entered the parade as SA storm troopers and came out the other end as German patriots.

Numbers, or perception of numbers, mattered in those first hundred days. The Nazis, who were always much better at multiplication than addition, claimed that the crowds beneath the Brandenburg Gate numbered 1 million, a total that practically constituted a plebiscite.

But it is very hard to believe that one out of every four Berliners journeyed to the city center that evening. Social Democrats claimed that only "several tens of thousands" of marchers had appeared, which more or less squared with the number of SA men organized in Berlin in January 1933 (between 30,000 and 35,000 men, or 1 percent of the city's population) but left out Stahlhelmers in the rear and those who joined in to troop behind the uniformed marchers. It left out the curious and sympathetic citizens, such as the Maschmanns, lining the streets. (The next day, socialists led a flag-spotting walk through the city to prove that there was only "lackluster enthusiasm" for the Nazis: "over there a little flag, and another one, but then...nothing at all." To them, a Nazi flag was not a flag but a *Fähnchen*, a flimsy banner in variable winds.) Since the Nazis' march down Wilhelmstrasse lasted nearly four hours, and about 100,000 well-disciplined troops could pass a viewing platform in one hour, an estimate of 30,000 or even 50,000 participants is surely very low, perhaps even by a factor of ten, while the police estimate, which put the number at 700,000, should probably be cut in half. More likely it was a quarter million, on par with the biggest demonstrations held in the capital during the Weimar Republic. The disagreement was about the Nazis' power of attraction and about the evidence to ascertain this power. The Nazis had not captured all of Berlin by January 30, but they had captured more of the city (and the country) than socialists believed.[10]

The Social Democrats were right to dispute the Nazis' claims that brown had a national mandate. The Nazis always looked too closely at the unprecedented size of their rallies and overlooked the absent socialists and Catholics. The parade was a means to represent the Nazi seizure of power, but it was not accurate as a measure of public opinion. As Hitler had discovered after he lost the two presidential elections to Hindenburg in 1932 and would learn again in the March 5 elections of 1933, loyalties to the opposition parties remained strong. But the Social Democrats missed the acceleration of people moving into the Nazi fold. The next weeks would reveal the Nazi advance in what, on January 30, was still a very divided Germany.

Hitler's Nazis were not the only thing spreading through town; a flu epidemic shuttered schools across Germany. Half of all grade school children and more than one-third of all teachers were absent before the city of Göttingen canceled classes altogether. In Berlin, two hundred grades had been sent home. Goebbels became so sick that he collapsed and had to go to bed: "Tuesday, had visions the whole day...fever climbed to 104°." Heinrich Brüning, the old chancellor, was sick too. Years later, novelist Heinrich Böll, who had been in bed himself with the flu as a fifteen-year-old, half-jokingly wondered whether historians had not neglected the epidemic as a key factor to explain the popular delirium accompanying Hitler's seizure of power.[11]

The rhythms of Germany's streets in January 1933 included shopping at a discount. Despite the fevers, Berliners hunted for bargains at the annual department store "white sales," and newspapers happily reported on the dreamworlds carefully arranged out of piles of cotton and satin. "The great atrium" in the Kaufhaus des Westens "presents itself in green and white," wrote the *Berliner Morgenpost*, "a bright, airy, theatrical patch of forest with snow-white trees, white branches, blossoms, and fruits." At the next crossroad, "the grave visage of the penguin oversees the white sales at Karstadt"— the funny-looking birds in black and white making sure that customers "diligently purchased" linens, sheets, and blouses. The "winter paradise" on the fourth floor at Hertie lured shoppers with a ski theme: "Ober-Engadin on the Hermannplatz."[12] The letter Q was woven into the decorations at Israel's big store to drive home the axiom that it is "cheaper to buy quality" (though soon enough, Israel disappeared from the advertising pages of newspapers).

Crowds milled; life moved. On one Sunday toward the end of February, streetcars and subways transported 1.86 million Berliners to merry destinations: 60,000 headed to the International Automobile and Motorcycle Convention on the Kaiserdamm under the banner "Full Gas Ahead," a one-day record; sledders had to stand in long lines on Berlin's "mountain tops" before taking their turns— so much snow had fallen in the city that 1,300 unemployed men were recruited to shovel it away. In the Rhineland, carnival celebrations pushed politics to the side; special trains pressed into service brought as many as 400,000 revelers to Cologne on Rose Monday, when the city came to a complete standstill to celebrate "carnival as it once was."[13]

On February 1, the virtuoso Jewish American violinist Jascha Heifetz performed at the Berlin Philharmonic; it would be his last visit to Germany. Berlin's Jewish museum on Oranienburger Strasse opened on January 24. A sharp-eyed reporter noticed one artifact on display, an ancient clay oil lamp from Palestine decorated with a swastika and a Star of David. "Isn't it charming?" Max Osborn concluded; a sign of "mutual compatibility." The museum would be shuttered and its holdings confiscated on November 10, 1938; Osborn, a Jewish art critic, would emigrate soon thereafter, going into exile in France and then New York City.[14] But in the first weeks, the signals were not easy to read.

At the end of the first week of Hitler's chancellorship, activist Kurt Schumacher, at thirty-eight one of the Social Democrats' youngest Reichstag deputies and a wounded veteran of the war, wondered in what basement the National Socialist revolutionaries were hiding. In a speech in Augsburg on Saturday, February 4, he mocked the Nazis, who had repeatedly announced that within twenty-four hours of seizing power, "everything would be different": "The honorable gentlemen have been in power five times twenty-four hours, but the long knives are still sheathed." Schumacher had no illusions about the National Socialists. He had spoken plainly to the Reichstag in February 1932, depicting them as thugs who appealed to "the inner swine in human beings." He did not take them seriously a year later, in 1933, because he believed Hitler's reactionary cabinet held him in check. "He used to be an interior decorator and now he himself is a decorative piece," chortled Schumacher. "The cabinet is called Adolf Hitler's, but the cabinet is Alfred Hugenberg's. Adolf Hitler is permitted to speak, Alfred Hugenberg, however, will be the one to act." "National capitalism" and not National Socialism "is the genuine article," he concluded, "the last bastion of a bankrupt capitalist system."[15]

This analysis mistook the number of German Nationalists in the cabinet for real power, ignoring the numbers Nazis wielded in the Reichstag and on the streets. It was a common miscalculation. "The general opinion," remembered Sebastian Haffner, a young law student at home in the tony West End of Berlin, was that "it was not the Nazis who had won, but the bourgeois parties of the right, who had 'captured' the Nazis and held all the key positions in the government." "Hardly the Third Reich, barely a 2½" Reich, calculated one diplomat.[16]

Schumacher and others were missing small but perceptible changes in the public mood. It was as if the frame holding things together began to slip just a bit, day after day. "When I came home" the day after Hitler's appointment, recalled one neighbor, "I saw how an SA man in full uniform stood at the window directly opposite." He had "never before seen a member of the SS or SA" in his working-class Altona neighborhood. If you walked down the street "on the day of, or the day following, the 'takeover,'" you saw "quite a number of people suddenly running around in SA uniforms." On January 31, foreign observers saw new uniforms, flags, and badges—so many, in fact, that they could not fathom who had the foresight to manufacture all the accessories in advance. Just three days after January 30, a doctor noted patients showing up wearing Nazi pins. People were startled at how many neighbors spoke quite openly about political intimacies they had never before confided: "our Hitler." National Socialists all over Germany organized victory celebrations that continued where the torchlight parade in Berlin had ended; these drew in more people, while the protests organized by Social Democrats and Communists were more occasional and marginal. With each victory march, the Nazis moved closer to center stage.[17]

In Northeim, with its 10,000 inhabitants, eight hundred Nazis and two hundred Stahlhelm men marched on Saturday, February 4, to the market square, which was filled with crowds "bigger than any heretofore seen." Townspeople flocked to the 1910er Zelt for an "evening of entertainment." The speeches, in favor of national unity and against the Communists, continued the next day. "The Nazis gave the impression that the town was completely theirs." In Hamburg, the same weekend, patriots organized a huge victory celebration to which, despite the late hour, Luise Solmitz and her husband, "Fredy," took their daughter, Gisela. "Afterall, she has to + must finally feel what the fatherland is," Luise said. It was late— ten o'clock—before the first torches appeared, and "then they came in like waves in the sea, 20,000 brownshirts, their enthusiastic faces reflected in the torch light." "Three times a hail to our Führer, our Reich chancellor," they cheered, and the Solmitzes hailed back, "Heil! Heil! Heil!" The whole event was charged, imbued with an emotional sense of "us" and "them," the German people versus the enemies of the state. The smell of civil war was in the air, the approach of a final reckoning and, just out of sight, a new beginning. "Heil! Heil! Heil!"[18]

Three days after coming to power, following perfunctory and failed negotiations to find a parliamentary majority, Hitler persuaded Hindenburg to dissolve the Reichstag and call for new elections on Sunday, March 5. The liberal press worried about "new feverish convulsions" of another election campaign that threatened "the body of the people" with grievous harm. The point of new elections was to provide the new government a Reichstag majority that would serve as the basis for suspending the constitution. Without elections, the constitution would determine the execution of emergency rule, applied at the discretion of Hindenburg, not Hitler. A further goal of elections, the *Vossische Zeitung* soberly explained, was "the stabilization of one-sided party rule that under the national flag excludes and eliminates those who believe in and want something different."[19] The "exclusion" aimed to destroy the power of the "Marxists" and the "stabilization" to marginalize the influence of the German Nationalists like Hugenberg, whom mobilized Nazi divisions would completely outnumber on the streets (and later in the Reichstag).

Hugenberg well understood the quandary he was in; in his campaign speeches, he conceded that he opposed the elections because they would inalterably secure the overwhelming power of the National Socialists. Both Hugenberg and Hitler were hard-core antidemocrats. They were grave diggers for the republic and wanted to eliminate German elections, to put an end to all the "electioneering" and impose a "state of emergency."[20] But they differed on the date of the "last election"; for Hugenberg, it had already taken place in November 1932, which had secured for his party a measure of power. Hitler's was to take place in March 1933, when Nazis were no longer insurgents outside the gates of power but revolutionaries on the inside gripping critical levers of executive authority.

THE MARCH 1933 election campaign allowed the Nazis to occupy the public space necessary to simulate a plebiscite. In an age of mass communication, radio was key. The Nazis mobilized the resources of the state to completely dominate the campaign

and intimidate opponents. More important, the National Socialists built on the January 30 torchlight parade to choreograph party
events as national festivals. They introduced themselves as spokes-
men for the nation. The campaign for "List Number One" culminated in the "Day of the Awakening Nation" on March 4, 1933. The
lessons on how to exploit radio and configure the audience as national representatives had been well learned.

The Nazis spoke for the nation when they made "the state the
domain of the party" on the occasion of an unprecedented and
grandiose state funeral for "Hanno" Maikowski, the squadron
leader of the SA "Mordsturm 33," and Josef Zauritz, a policeman
accompanying the brownshirts. The two men had been killed on
the night of January 30 after Nazi marchers returning home took
a detour through one of Red Berlin's "Ernst-Thälmann" streets,
Wallstrasse in Charlottenburg's Klein Wedding district, and came
under fire. Exactly who shot Maikowski has never been established, and an SA renegade may have been the culprit—but the
new regime immediately blamed the Communists, naming them
dangerous "terrorists" who imperiled the state. That Zauritz had
been killed alongside Maikowski was a stroke of luck since it allowed the Nazis to argue that Germany's policeman had died for
the same nationalist cause as had the party's SA man and that the
streetfighter Maikowski lost his life in the same line of law-abiding
duty as the policeman.

The February 5 funeral service was given all the dignity of a
state ceremony and held in the magisterial Berliner Dom cathedral. It was Hitler's first public appearance since becoming chancellor, and he stepped into the cathedral wearing an SA uniform. The
British ambassador could not believe "the amazing conditions now
obtaining in this country." The policeman, he explained, "who was
a Catholic, and the gangster, who was an agnostic, lay in state in
the Lutheran Cathedral in Berlin, and, to crown this travesty of a
solemn ceremony, the ex–Crown Prince laid wreaths on the coffins

of the gangster and the policeman, who turned out to be a staunch supporter of the Left."[21] It was Day 7 of the Third Reich.

As the ambassador noted, the funeral revealed friction between the fading Weimar Republic and the incoming Third Reich. When the government proposed that Maikowski and Zauritz lie in state in the Neo-Renaissance cathedral, Protestant authorities refused and permitted only a funeral service. A local church council also rejected the proposal to bury Maikowski in the Luisenstadt cemetery on the grounds that the funeral was a political affair and improperly planned for Sunday. The policeman's family tried to sidestep Nazi choreography, informing the press that Zauritz was a trade unionist and republican and demanding that his body be consecrated by a Catholic priest in St. Eduard Church in Neukölln after the service in the cathedral and buried in his Silesian hometown. There, the priest in Ottmachau publicly admonished Germany's new leaders for following the principle "If you won't be my brother, I'll smash your head in!" ("La fraternité ou la mort!" French revolutionaries used to say.) When local SA men attending Zauritz's funeral objected to the admonition with loud coughing, the priest replied with a plain-spoken rebuke: "Yes, indeed, and even if you cough, I stand here to tell the truth!" In the first days after January 30, it was still possible for local authorities to speak up in the name of law and principle. More could have done so.[22]

Zauritz's people talked as if they were still living in the Weimar Republic, but the boom of the Third Reich was unmistakable. According to Nazi arithmetic, over 600,000 Berliners assembled around the cathedral on a blustery, rainy day to witness the state funeral—twice the number of revelers at the Brandenburg Gate the previous Monday. The crowds included middle-class Nazis from the city's southern and western districts as well as workers, who filled out the ranks of the SA squadrons, from the north and east. Abraham Plotkin, the American in Berlin, looked over the "solid mass of brown, while the slow music of the Nazi funeral march joined in with the chimes of the Cathedral." The Nazi pastor, Joachim Hossenfelder, hallowed martyrdom and assured the mourners that the two men had sacrificed themselves for the "Führer," whom God had delivered to the German people to provide bread and work. Zauritz had done his duty, he added, by protecting the "brown lads" as they marched alone through the "red inferno."[23] The funeral cortege followed the route to the Invaliden Cemetery, where Hans Eberhard Maikowski was buried alongside Germany's great heroes.

The radio carried the state ceremony live in a nationwide broadcast, and listeners heard how the funeral memorialized the fallen SA street fighters as the heirs of the soldiers who had fallen in the Great War. As an SA honor guard carried the caskets out of the cathedral, a radio reporter "remarked that he witnessed Frederick the Great dismount from his famous perch [on a statue] high over Unter den Linden, walk slowly to the caskets, and personally thank Hans Maikowski for his loyalty to the death."[24] The broadcast of the funeral enrolled the entire nation as an honor guard.

The whole affair emboldened the SA to escalate attacks on the Communists. Storm troopers practically occupied the Wallstrasse after the shooting incident. With the state funeral they also advanced on the entire country. As one appalled journalist explained, the Nazis had "dared to equate a narrow instinct for violence with the spirit of the nation." They had allowed the "sport of party agitation" to trample "church customs." "On this rainy afternoon," there was no other conclusion: a "genuine conservative" piece of Germany had also been laid to rest.[25] The National Socialist election campaign would bury many more pieces.

Hitler kicked off the 1933 campaign with a mammoth rally in Berlin's Sportpalast on Friday, February 10. Although Berliners had grown up with the "sport" of the Sportpalast, especially the boxing matches and six-day bicycle races, and after the war would return to the fixed-up hall for rock concerts to hear Pink Floyd, Jimi

Hendrix, and Franz Zappa until it closed in 1973, the Sportpalast came to be linked to the Nazis. It was in the Sportpalast that Hitler addressed Berlin's public for the first time in 1928 and Goebbels held his notorious speech calling on the German people to accept the dictates of total war on February 18, 1943, two weeks after the defeat at Stalingrad.

Hitler's February speech was broadcast over the radio and over hundreds of loudspeakers installed in market squares and at busy intersections across Germany. The scheduled program immediately broke away to the event, to broadcast "live," however scripted. Mid-note in the music program, an announcer's voice came over the radio: "We interrupt this concert and switch to the German Broadcasting Station." Then the sounds of the rally suddenly filled the airwaves.[26] The switch-over simulated the eruption of the nation.

The Nazis' chief propagandist, Joseph Goebbels, adapted the format of Hitler's speech for the radio by broadcasting it like a live sporting event. He himself reported over the airwaves on the sights and sounds of the thousands of animated fans crammed into the Sportpalast. By ten o'clock in the morning, the first loyalists had arrived with picnic lunches to get good seats, and by six o'clock in the afternoon, the police had closed the hall so that late arrivals had to listen outside. The anticipation mounted as people waited for Hitler to speak. Goebbels reported on the "fervent, feverish excitement." He also spoke directly to the Germans gathered around loudspeakers: "You can already hear the noise getting louder as the frenetic suspense begins to build." Radio could transmit the background noise, the shouting and singing, and later the call-and-response when crowds erupted in "Sieg!" then "Heil!" after Hitler's declarations. "The entire Sportpalast resembles a gigantic anthill." Goebbels asked his radio audience to imagine the colossal building and its first and second balconies. "You can't even make out individual people anymore; all you can see," and here he paused to amplify the cries and chanting before continuing, "are streams and streams of people—a great mass," the scene of acclamation. He structured the broadcast to allow the people themselves to speak: "You can hear how the cry 'Germany, Wake Up!' erupts from the crowd." The honor guard bearing the flags appeared and marched toward the podium. "The entire mass enthusiastically sings along to 'The Song of the Germans.'" Goebbels paused his voice-over report so that the loudspeakers across Germany filled with "swelling, enthusiastic cries of 'Heil.'" "You can hear that the Führer has just arrived! The entire audience is standing up and saluting him."[27]

Radio dramatically reproduced the emotional relationship between Hitler and his followers. The broadcast of the crescendo in the Sportpalast recapitulated the national awakening that made the National Socialists stand for the future of the country as a whole. Although radio transmitted Hitler's speech, the acoustics in the hall were more critical than what Hitler was actually saying. When Hitler had first addressed the nation, on February 1, he spoke too fast and too aggressively; a second recording was then broadcast three times the next day.[28] For the Sportpalast speech nine days later, Hitler carefully modulated his voice, but in a way that elevated the excitement in the arena to a higher and higher pitch. He stepped up to the microphones, hands clasped behind his back, and was silent for a half minute before quietly addressing his "German comrades." He deliberately punctuated his opening delivery with emphatic pauses and controlled gestures to legitimate the harsher, louder judgments to come.

Listening to the early recordings of Hitler's speeches, one biographer was struck by their "peculiarly obscene" and "copulatory character": "the silence at the beginning," then "the short, shrill yappings," followed by "minor climaxes and first sounds of liberation," and then "the ecstasies released by the finally unblocked oratorial orgasms." Writer René Schickele once spoke of Hitler's speeches as being "like sex murders."[29]

On February 10, many Germans were hearing Hitler for the first time. He hammered a few themes: the ruination of the country by "Marxists" since the November Revolution in 1918, the miracle of Germany's national uprising fourteen years later, and the resolve of the Nazis to join the fight to save the country. Bloodied heads and healed bodies were intimately connected in this view. "There can be only one victor: either Marxism or the German *Volk!*" Hitler never spoke so much about God as he did in the first weeks after assuming power, and he ended his speech at the Sportpalast on a note of ecumenism and reconciliation. In rousing verses reminiscent of the choir in Handel's "Messiah," Hitler promised, "The hour is at hand in which the millions who today hate us will stand behind us." They will "welcome the new German Reich that we have jointly created," "a Reich of greatness and honor and power and glory and righteousness. Amen." With that amen, a note of "great pathos" at the very end, Goebbels commented, "all of Germany will just go wild"; "the nation will fall into our hands without a fight."[30] He estimated that 20 to 30 million Germans—500,000 in Berlin alone—had listened to the live broadcast. The numbers were proof that radio was "the most modern and most important instrument to influence the masses" and "unite the German people in a common vision."[31] It was Day 12 of the Third Reich.

After the Sportpalast speech, Hitler took to the skies to campaign by airplane. Journalists expressed astonishment at how Hitler, who did not particularly like flying, transformed himself from "a detached passenger munching on butter sandwiches and flipping through illustrated magazines" into a fanatic "Messiah of militant nationalism."[32] Wherever he spoke, Hitler addressed record-breaking crowds. In the last week of the campaign, he spoke in Leipzig, Breslau, Berlin, Hamburg, and finally, on election eve, Köngisberg. For the first time, newspapers provided thorough coverage of the National Socialist campaign. But it was the radio that allowed the Nazis to establish the most direct and intimate connection with the electorate.

Although Weimar-era guidelines prohibited radio from broadcasting advertisements and political speeches, they permitted government ministers to address the nation. So Hitler, Hermann Göring, and Interior Minister Wilhelm Frick, as well as Papen and Hugenberg, completely dominated the airwaves. Nazi politicians had never had access to the radio, and now they resolved to take full advantage. As Goebbels explained, "The radio belongs to us, to no one else!"[33] In the period leading up to the March 5 elections, cabinet members interrupted regular programming to deliver campaign speeches over the radio forty-five times. On February 23, for example, Hitler could be heard over stations in Frankfurt, Stuttgart, and Breslau, while another minister spoke over those in Königsberg and Hamburg. The next day, Munich broadcast Hitler, while Cologne broadcast Papen, and in the evening all German stations transmitted a recording of Hitler's February 19 campaign event in Cologne.[34] And whenever Hitler addressed the nation, Goebbels provided his "atmospheric reportage" to energize the national audience gathered at home and in taverns. Radio listeners mingled in this broadcast world as newspaper readers never could, discussing the oratory among themselves, saluting "our Hitler," and singing along with the national anthem.

Radio had always advertised itself as bringing the "world into the living room"; now it brought the Nazis.[35] As many as one in five Germans owned a radio, and they purchased more to hear Hitler's speeches. The pacing of the broadcast and the shouts, chants, and songs of the crowds drew listeners into the political spectacle. The whole range of acoustics gave the broadcasts a stirring, immutable, even sacred quality. They were noises not from another world but from *the* world and the elemental percussions that so evidently constituted it. Later, when the May 10 book burnings were broadcast live from Berlin, listeners could take in how "the flames lap at the wood, like rags in the wind, then the wood cracks and the branches snap."[36] "We listen to the speeches on the radio every evening," wrote Elisabeth Gebensleben. Even those Germans who could not stand Hitler's voice, which, one horrified listener remarked, sounded as if a knife had lodged itself in the Führer's throat, switched on the broadcasts of his speeches.[37] Both friends and foes harkened, anxious to monitor the roar of the crowds and direction of the country. Broadcast radio reported on political weather.

In Hamburg, Luise Solmitz felt herself a "second-class contemporary." Without a radio she could not participate fully in the "national awakening." Luckily, the "old Mich.'s" down the street had one and invited Luise and Fredy over. Although Gisela, their thirteen-year-old daughter, was sick with the flu, her father took her to hear the rebroadcast of Hitler's speech on February 2. At the Mich.'s, Luise heard Hitler's Sportpalast speech little more than a week later, impressed by the sights and sounds ("What a march! What enthusiasm!"). The next day she was back with a bottle of wine to listen to Papen and Hugenberg speak in the Sportpalast. When the "Song of the Germans" played, she and her neighbors stood up and sang along "deeply moved." On February 25, she heard Göring's "enthusiastic" speech, but by the time she had finished listening to Papen the next day, she felt that her "need for political speeches had been covered."[38]

When the weather got warmer, Goebbels urged radio listeners to open their windows so that passersby could hear Hitler's speeches. The radio broadcasts were designed to create a collective Nazi voice and a collective national experience. A few years later, Victor Klemperer recalled the day he "ran into the middle of Hitler's Reichstag speech" on the Bismarckplatz in Dresden; "I could not get away from it for an hour. First from an open shop, then in the bank, then from a shop again." In Hildesheim, residents distinctly remembered the Führer's voice in the business district, on

Hohen Weg and Almstrasse, and blasting from the hotels across from the train station.[39] Since most people listened to the radio together, the only way to escape was to leave the room, difficult to do discreetly. Radio listening made family gatherings more strenuous affairs for skeptics. Neighbors quickly became aware of listening habits, and later, failure to turn on the radio to hear Nazi broadcasts could engender suspicion. There was pressure to purchase a radio, social pressure, yes, but also pressure applied by the Nazis themselves. Goebbels warned, ominously, "Whoever excludes themselves from participating in national broadcasts runs the risk of missing out on the life of the nation."[40] As radio was part of national life, people listened to it—and after 1933 they also listened to other people listening to the radio.

Hitler debuted on the radio right around the time that it became an easy-to-use appliance. Technological improvements meant listeners no longer had to constantly fiddle with the knobs to stay tuned to a station. Instead of the finnicky plaything of the male connoisseur, the radio became an everyday amenity for men and women. Municipal electrification, largely completed by the early 1930s, meant every house in a city could have one. The entire family could simply relax and listen to the radio, undisturbed by other noises in the room. Powerful amplifiers replaced the crackerjacks' headsets. Radio achieved its sovereignty in the household as the "fifth wall."

Everyone suddenly wanted a radio set. Sales went up, even as other popular entertainments, such as cabaret and the circus, declined. With its variety programs, radio provided company to the housewife, a happy distraction while "ironing, washing, or sewing." Live reportage allowed listeners to follow spectacular events such as the voyages of the zeppelin or boxing matches and football games. With dozens of new stations across the continent, listeners turned the dial and embarked on what they cherished as a "small tour of Europe"—fully two-thirds of German radio audiences listened to foreign broadcasts. Recalling his nightly "travel circuit" in his memoirs, one fan counted off the cities he visited by ascending wavelength: "Budapest to Hanover, followed by Fribourg, Ljubljana, Lausanne, Geneva, and Basel via Moscow and Leningrad; then Hilversum," and "finally the Eiffel Tower" with Radio-Paris. "Hello! Radio Planet Earth Speaking!" imagined one enthusiast. There were so many international tourists that nationalists worried about the "ether storm offensive of the enemies."[41]

As National Socialists quickly discovered for themselves, the wireless offered the chance to create an undisrupted program of national uplift in which everyone heard the "same words" and participated in a unified national culture. Both Hitler and President Franklin D. Roosevelt took great advantage of the national intimacy of radio, the one in cheer-splattered declamations against "enemies," the other in "fireside chats" among "friends," so in the United States, radio created community in a different register. "When walking home in the hot summer evenings after window shopping on Madison Street," a Chicago man recalled, "one could follow the entire progress of *Amos 'n' Andy* from the open windows," a wildly popular radio sitcom rather than live broadcasts of political rallies serving as the shared experience.[42] Social scientists confirmed that the radio had the extraordinary ability to create national collectives by broadcasting "a calendar of 'sacred' national events, from folk festivals to sporting events" and, in Britain's case, "great royal ceremonies." This effect was strengthened by the fact that radio listeners believed that broadcasts were truer to fact than broadsheets.

"Foolproof" radio became reliably loud. It broadcast out of open windows and across tenement courtyards. Radio "blares, shrieks, screams, proclaims, yells, crackles, and wails," wrote novelist Annette Kolb. It was the "death of silence," according to another listener. The "musical medley" grew louder and pressed itself into the background as permanent noise. As a result, the public sounds of the radio fundamentally changed the constitution of private spaces. "We exchange the losses in our personal life for the gains of taking part in collective, public being," concluded one commentator.[43]

The neighborhood radio evenings and patriotic marches culminated in a nationwide extravaganza that the Nazis put on the evening before election day. It was Saturday, March 4, 1933, the Day of the Awakening Nation. Hitler was scheduled to speak in Königsberg, where he would stoke "a never-before achieved concentration of all propagandistic and agitational possibilities." "From the bleeding eastern frontier," Goebbels proclaimed, the gospel of awakening Germany would speak to the entire nation. Columns of singing, uniformed Nazi marchers led Hitler's supporters to market squares, parks, and meeting halls or restaurants to listen. In Berlin, twenty-four separate torchlight assemblies gathered around loudspeakers, filling the streets with music and casting over the city a glowing "red reflection against the night sky." An estimated (but unlikely, given Nazi tendencies to inflate numbers) 40 million Germans tuned into the live broadcast. Erich Ebermayer marveled at this use of the mass media: "What, wasn't there any radio before January 30? Just unbelievable!"[44]

Reporters mingled with the crowds. *Paris-soir*'s Jules Sauerwein stationed himself on Winterfeldplatz in Berlin where mostly young and middle-aged men had rallied. Holding torches above their heads and chanting, "Jews, Drop Dead," they composed a street-corner church in which the loudspeaker broadcast the echoes of Königsberg like a "new Sinai." And the congregation knew that similar flocks had assembled on market squares and in front of ancient cathedrals and old city halls across Germany. On the Reperbahn, the infamous strip in Hamburg, brown soldiers mixed with young ladies on the warm, humid evening, and in the distance the anti-Semitic chants added perilous harmony to the sweet atmosphere.[45]

With "passion and devotion," Hitler described how he and Hindenburg had extended their hands to each other. Imagine—the field marshal, who in the world war had liberated East Prussia from the Russian enemy, and the ordinary infantryman, who had fulfilled his duty for four years on the French front. Hitler ended his speech by declaring, "We are all proud that by God's gracious help we have again become true Germans." The hymn "The Dutch Prayer of Thanksgiving" followed, and the broadcast ended with the sound of the bells pealing for five minutes. (No one listening over the airwaves could know that local church authorities refused to ring the cathedral's bells because Hitler's speech was a political event; radio Nazis simply put on a record instead.) That night, as Germans walked back home, they could see bonfires ("freedom fires") burning on the tops of surrounding hills, reminiscent of the Wars of Liberation against Napoleon. Participants found themselves inserted into the long arc of German history, more powerful than the event itself.

Goebbels was sure that the festivities would pull "the last procrastinators" into the Nazi camp. He reflected on the evening with great satisfaction—"The whole of Germany resembles a single, huge, bright-burning beacon"—anticipating that the people would march behind Hitler and vote for "List Number One" the next day.[46] To detractors, the Nazi occupation of the public sphere—"everyday parades, torchlight marches, radio speeches, applause at the cinema newsreels"—was one big "circus," and a circus "without bread" at that. Yet the "racket every night" generated genuine enthusiasm and drew real tears.[47] It was Day 34 of the Third Reich.

The Day of the Awakening Nation became the model for the Nazis' attempts to choreograph the unanimity of the nation in the first hundred days. The live broadcast of the opening of the Reichstag in Potsdam on March 21, designed to demonstrate the reconciliation of the old and the new Germany, and the "Day of National Labor" on May 1, when the Nazis showed themselves to be the complete masters of German history, did not simply transmit events taking place at the center but put the radio at the very center of hundreds of local ceremonies. The torchlight parade on January 30, the Maikowski funeral, the Sportpalast speech on February 10, and the Day of the Awakening Nation—never before had a political party so effectively occupied national space.

I F JOSEPH GOEBBELS was the brilliant strategist, waging Germany's election campaign to win a majority of the vote, Hermann Göring, the last commander of Manfred von Richthofen's fabled "flying circus" in World War I, was the brutal enforcer. Göring's big role in the Third Reich was the one he played in the first months when, as Reich commissar for the Prussian Ministry of the Interior, he exercised police powers—extraordinary powers granted by the federal government after Papen's coup there in 1932—over two-thirds of Germany's territory. Göring used his position against the Nazis' enemies with increasing ruthlessness. Hitler had laid out the program in his Sportpalast speech on February 10. "There can be only one victor: either Marxism or the German *Volk*!"

The blows of SA fists rained down on socialists immediately after Hitler assumed power. Mostly instigated by the brownshirts, the violence recalled the wave of shootings and fire bombings that had followed the July 1932 elections. Shouting, "So, let's finally settle the score!" a Nazi trainman in Harburg took out his gun as soon as he returned to work on the morning of January 31 and shot two of his colleagues, killing a Stahlhelm man and injuring a Social Democrat. The next day, the Nazi Pallack murdered the Communist Schäfer with hammer blows to the head in the small Rhenish town of Verlmert. On February 4, a National Socialist high school student shot and killed the Social Democratic mayor of Strassfurt, a town near Magdeburg. Fifteen SA brownshirts fired into the Communist tavern Slop Box in Berlin's Rubensstrasse, killing the landlady with a bullet through the stomach.[48] Every day, the liberal press reported on more "clashes throughout the Reich," and every day the nationalist press reported on the "left-radical wave of terror throughout the Reich."[49]

Göring's model, established early on, served the Nazis well as they steadily consolidated power. SA violence was written up as Communist provocation necessitating "measures against Communist terror." In the spectacular case of "Bloody Sunday" in Eisleben, a small industrial town in Saxony, conservative newspapers insisted that the SA men who had stormed the "Class Struggle Building" on Breite Strasse with shovels on February 12 were actually the victims of an ambush. They put guns in the hands of Communists when it was brownshirts who had hacked off fingers and poked out eyes, and they claimed that Communists had hidden behind children in the playroom, forcing them to serve as human shields so that snipers could continue to shoot at the police.[50] All this "mainstream" commentary constituted a total disregard of fact to achieve one end: the destruction of the republic, which meant the destruction of fact, morality, and law. Insist on the crime, switch out the perpetrators, plant the evidence—it did not take much effort to convince Hindenburg that Communists were taking up arms. On February 2, the president issued the emergency decree "For the Protection of the German People." Subsequent decrees were all cast in the same watchful, solicitous way: the "Law for the Protection of ...," the "Law for the Restoration of ...," "The Law for the Prevention of ..." The February 2 decree banned the Communists from holding open-air meetings and authorized officials to censor newspapers that had shown "contempt" for the government. This was Day 4 of the Third Reich.

The National Socialists gave the German newspaper kiosk a real face-lift. The punitive measures crippled the ability of political opponents to campaign effectively or publicize the violence to which they were subject. The Social Democratic newspaper, *Vorwärts*, was already temporarily banned on February 4 for publishing an appeal to "citizens" to "rise up against your oppressors"; the article's phrasing was softer, employing words like *Bedränger* (persecutors), not *Unterdrücker* (oppressors), and "citizens," not "workers." It called on citizens to mobilize against "the leisured classes, against the wafer-thin upper crust of big capital." Here was an enemies' list that showed how mixed up smart socialists were about their real adversaries in the Third Reich. The entire Social Democratic press in Mecklenburg-Schwerin was banned a day later. Over the next weeks, Göring's team suspended papers left and Left for slander: *Vorwärts* and Berlin's *8 Uhr-Abendblatt* for eight days, Cologne's Social Democratic paper, *Rheinische Zeitung*, for six days, and Kassel's *Volksblatt*, Görlitz's *Volkszeitung*, Magdeburg's *Volksstimme*, and Heidelberg's *Volkszeitung* for five days. The popular boulevard newspaper *Tempo* was forced to suspend publication on February 17.[51]

Sebastian Haffner, a law student, raised his hand to object. " 'I take it as a personal affront," he said, "that one prevents *me* from reading the newspaper I want." "Don't you?" he pointedly asked his friends. One of them replied "cheerfully," "Not at all ... Why? Were you reading *Vorwärts* or *Rote Fahne* up to now?"[52] Early February would have been the moment for citizens to protest the arbitrary exercise of police power, which gravely threatened the freedom of the press and the constitution. Yet citizens did not speak up because they had always divided themselves up between those (others) who read *Vorwärts* and those (of us) who did not. You can only preserve the civic order if you step in for your opponent and speak out against your ally.

Conservative newspapers covered up the violence of the National Socialists, only to concede its existence when they threw it back into the faces of Social Democrats. The *Deutsche Allgemeine Zeitung*, a reasonable newspaper, not wicked as other rightist publications could be, noted that the socialist press kept on complaining that "Everyone has to fear for their life!" But it raised an objection, wanting to know what Social Democratic "dignitaries" had done when a few years earlier the Communists attacked the Nazis with the murderous slogan "Strike the Fascists Wherever You Meet Them!" The newspaper was prepared neither to speak up nor to listen. "When those who sow the wind harvest the storm, then they should beat their own breasts out of contrition."[53] This was Day 17 of the Third Reich.

A week later, as SA violence targeted politicians in the Catholic Center Party—Heinrich Brüning used back doors to leave meetings; Adam Stegerwald was assaulted—the editors remained unconcerned. In an article on "election fever," they maintained, "To wail about victims doesn't get us anywhere." "A new chapter in German history began on January 30, a counterrevolution, if you will," the *Deutsche Allgemeine Zeitung* explained, "and this struggle must be fought through to the end." It was important to keep the number of victims small, the paper conceded, but the "war of brother against brother" would only end with the decisive victory of the nationalist parties on March 5. In other words, only the destruction of the republic could protect republicans. For conservatives, there was nothing about Weimar or the parliamentary system or the constitution to defend. Germany stood before a binary decision: "either Right or Left, either the Republic of November 9, 1918, or the new Reich of January 30, 1933."[54] This historic struggle required "robust soldiers"; it could not be fought "with caution or a sense of delicacy, or with tact or guess work."[55]

In the middle of March 1933, the *Deutsche Allgemeine Zeitung* was more uncertain about the violence of the SA. Although "rogue operations" and "arbitrary actions" had occurred, editors assured readers that Hitler, the new standard, had issued "sharp and unmistakable orders" to restore that state of law. Editors recognized that "a frightened panic has spread across some quarters of the big cities" but advised readers to relax since the police had been alerted to "locations in which incarcerated 'political prisoners' are said to have been held by individuals acting on their own." The editors knew this: "personal blood vendettas are no longer taking place."[56]

In other words, the newspaper came out against Nazi terror once it had been consigned to the past or to a corner. It was an odd position; although terror was bad, the newspaper had no principled equipment to combat it. The conservatives first denied violence, blaming Communists and not the SA. Then they made excuses by indicating that the victims had once been perpetrators—not personally, but somehow collectively—or they justified the violence as one of the onerous burdens of counterrevolutionary struggle. Then they ignored it. Law and order and accountability were not allowed to muddy what had to be clear: "the Republic of November 9, 1918, or the new Reich of January 30, 1933." Conservatives, nationalists, and even Sebastian Haffner's friends did not speak up for the basic freedoms of civil society because they were too busy dancing alongside the Nazis.

When the *Deutsche Allgemeine Zeitung* regretted that "differences of opinion," at least among nationalists, could not be expressed in "a more amicable way"—the issue in this case was the boycott against Jewish businesses on April 1—it was too late to express regret or expect the broad-mindedness of amity.[57] In two months, editor Fritz Klein was fired and the paper coordinated.

Did the justifications of civic institutions such as newspapers embolden the Nazis, or did the Nazis' rapid progress toward dismantling the republic cause newspapers to provide more excuses? In either case, the lack of civic courage in defense of an open society was striking. "Hello, Hello, Clear the Streets"—you could hear the successive explosions the squadrons detonated, but you heard no one shouting stop, only the chorus "no, Yes": no whimpered against unnecessary excess, then the boisterous Yes in the name of the national revolution. No to November 1918, yes to August 1914.

On February 17, Göring instructed his Prussian policemen to avoid "even the appearance of a hostile attitude" toward the patriotic parties. He issued a "shoot-to-kill" order against terrorists "without regard to the consequences." The "failure to act" against

Communists was a more serious dereliction of duty than use of excessive force. It was Day 19 of the Third Reich.

On February 22, Göring mobilized tens of thousands of SA soldiers to serve as auxiliaries, or *Hilfspolizei*, to Prussia's law enforcement officials. With that decree, from one day to the next, law and order became Nazi rule; gangsters stood up as guarantors of the state's law enforcement. As Goebbels put it, "The watchword is as follows: 'Against November 1918.' It will be followed resolutely."[58] Henceforth, recalled one senior police official, the Nazis' "revolutionary energies" were "liberated in a drunken rampage in which Hitler's speeches provided background music."[59] The political parties campaigning to uphold the Weimar constitution, the Catholics, the Social Democrats, and even the conservative Bavarian People's Party could hardly find room to move or campaign. It was Day 24 of the Third Reich.

Executive power passed almost completely into the hands of the Nazis after the Reichstag fire on February 27, 1933. The fire broke out around nine o'clock at night. The sight of smoke and flames in the center of Berlin and the sound of live reports over the radio transfixed Germans. It symbolized the death of representative government and the rule of law. Almost immediately, a lone Dutch Communist was arrested at the scene and charged with arson. For the National Socialists, the fire provided the opportunity to declare a state of emergency and consolidate one-party rule. The Communists were the first targets, but all independent political organizations were eliminated or coordinated in the months to come.

In what émigré political scientist Ernst Fraenkel later described as the "constitutional charter of the Third Reich," a raft of federal decrees suspended civil liberties, expanded protective custody, and sanctioned the removal of state governments without any of the division of powers that Weimar-era emergency decrees had contained to ensure against their arbitrary application. The emergency legislation on February 28 established the foundations for the Enabling Act of March 23 and for the Nazi dictatorship, transforming the "constitutional and temporary dictatorship" into an "unconstitutional and permanent dictatorship." (The pro-Nazi journalist Friedrich Hussong agreed, referring to the legislation as the "Magna Carta of the Third Reich.") According to Fraenkel, the "constitution" of the Third Reich was simply a permanent "state of siege." The fire allowed the Nazis to create a society where it was always wartime, the single act of terror a justification for emergency rule.[60]

Hitler rushed to the Reichstag even before the fire had been contained. "His face glowed red with excitement," recalled an eyewitness. He looked as if he was about to "burst," screaming in an uncontrolled rage, "We will show no mercy anymore; whoever gets in our way will be slaughtered." The steps delayed when Hitler first came to power could now be taken. "Every Communist functionary will be shot as soon as we nab him. We can't wait until tomorrow to string up the Communist deputies." Reaching deep into civil society, Hitler ran down the list of enemies. "We also have to move against the Social Democrats" and their paramilitaries, the Reichsbanner. "We are not sparing anyone."[61] "This fire is just the beginning," he promised, "the beginning of a great new epoch in German history."[62] That night, Göring dictated a press release and immediately ordered the police to arrest those whose names already appeared on typed-up lists. "It is wonderful to be alive," remarked Goebbels, Berlin's Gauleiter.[63] It was Day 30 of the Third Reich.

The link between the fire and the decrees was a matter of sequence and opportunity, not causation. Since January 30, Göring had made wide use of emergency police powers in Prussia, and he did so without fires or Communist firearms. More important, Hitler, Hugenberg, and Papen all aspired to establish a new authoritarian state, the difference among them being audacity not principle; they did not need the fire to publish the decree. Papen himself had invoked emergency legislation to remove Prussia's democratic government on July 20, 1932, establishing the police powers Göring took full advantage of. And Hitler stated his plan to move forward on an Enabling Act as chancellor in his communication with Hindenburg's advisors on November 23, 1932. In campaign speeches in February 1933, Wilhelm Frick, the National Socialist minister of the interior, repeatedly threatened voters with a state of emergency in the event they denied the national government an absolute majority in the Reichstag.[64]

Responsibility for the Reichstag fire has never been established. It remains today what it was for contemporaries in 1933: "the Third Reich's enduring mystery." While most historians have concluded that a lone wolf set the fire, new evidence points to Göring and a small number of SA conspirators. (Göring professed his innocence in custody in 1945, contending that he did not need a pretext and plans to arrest Communists had already been drawn up.[65]) There is no doubt that only the National Socialists stood to benefit from the crime. Hitler himself may have genuinely believed in a Communist plot; even during World War II, in his monologic "table talk," he continued to blame the Communists. Whoever was responsible, almost immediately, an astonishing number of people asked, "Cui bono?" When Erich Ebermayer told his father about the fire, the supreme court judge responded in Bavarian dialect, "Den ham's doch natürlich selber ang'steckt!" (Well, obviously, they set the fire themselves.) On the very next day, diarists wrote about questions raised. "People gossiped," reported Matthais Mehs in Wittlich. "You can't say it aloud," but lots of people "take it for granted that the whole thing was organized by the right-wing parties."[66]

The whispers of Ebermayer, Mehs, and other Germans about Nazi conspiracy were drowned out by the loud, uncritical headlines denouncing the Communist terrorists whom the Nazis lined up behind the lone arsonist. Arrests began the same night. Police headquarters on Alexanderplatz was a "beehive" of activity as patrol cars began to arrive and police officials reached for the lists of state enemies. The next day, a reporter for London's *Daily Express* watched the police and SA auxiliaries at work, "swooping on the pubs and the flats where the Communist rank and file had their hideouts, and carrying away whomever they found there."[67] The lucky ones went to jail, the unlucky ones to "wild" concentration camps hastily set up in the back room of an SA tavern on Charlottenburg's Goethestrasse, in the machine room of an old water tower in Prenzlauer Berg, in the bowling club on Petersburger Strasse in Friedrichshain.

The following day, "restless, nervous" crowds pushed along to the Brandenburg Gate and the Reichstag building. The breeze carried the "sweet smell of fire." After a few days, the authorities took anyone who was interested on guided tours of the wreckage between noon and five o'clock. From the entrance at Portal 2, the way led past the cloakroom, through the Reichstag restaurant, along the corridors lined with scorched club chairs and sofas to the wrecked plenary chamber: "nothing, nothing, nothing has been spared here."[68] Thousands of people lined up to inspect the building, which gave the Nazis the opportunity to explain their version of what had happened and who was responsible. The tours confirmed that the Weimar Republic was now history. What was the ordinary person to make of these extraordinary events? The most compelling answer was to be "thankful that the authority of the state is prepared to step in with an iron hand against such nefarious plots."[69] As a curious traveler on a train from Frankfurt to Cologne bought one newspaper after the other, he realized that the press reported basically the same thing. "I could have spared myself the 15 pfennigs," he grumbled. "How nice," though, he concluded, that "finally there is just one truth: the official version." He overheard the half-murmured remarks other passengers made to themselves as they paged through the same papers: "'Göring will take care of it,' said one; 'arson, carrying a weapon—death sentence,' judged another; 'these scoundrels should be stood up against the wall and shot,' remarked a third."[70] With the Reichstag fire, Hitler seemed to have been proven right about the Communists, his course of action since January 30 justified. The specter of terrorism served the Nazis by creating consent.

In a 1933 film about the SA "struggle for Berlin," storm troopers torch an advertising pillar plastered with the election appeals of a half dozen parties—the Catholics, the Social Democrats, the Communists—the signpost of the discordance of civil society. Nazis had burned down the tall, disputatious "Reichstag" on the street many times over. Did they set fire to the Reichstag itself? Germans were not sure, but they expressed more cynicism about the arsonists than regard for the burned-out husk of democracy. "You might as well tear down the baker's oven in which you can no longer bake bread."[71] Whoever torched the Reichstag, the fire marked the advent of the authoritarian age; for some, it was the last day of the Weimar Republic, for the rest, the first day of the Third Reich.

T HE NAZIS DOMINATED what Germans saw and heard in February 1933, as well as what historians many decades later have recounted—parades, torchlights, bonfires, the Reichstag fire. Yet the nationalist tide did not wash away Social Democrats and Communists, who together had received more votes in the November 1932 elections than the National Socialists. You could add up the anti-Nazi votes, but left-wing voters remained deeply divided among themselves, and the old Weimar coalition of Social Democrats, the German Democrats, and the Catholic Center no longer represented three out of every four Germans, as they had in 1919. Now, it was only one in three. The republic lost more than half of its supporters over the course of fourteen years and the Social Democrats one in three in just four. The party slipped into resignation: It waited for the collapse of capitalism or improved business conditions to sweep the unemployed back into trade unions. In the short term, it relied on Hindenburg to block Hitler. Once that faith in Hindenburg proved misplaced, the Social Democrats had to face their own weakness. The sharp anti-Marxism of Hitler's cabinet and the Nazis' ability to rally the nationalist base left socialists more isolated. The bitter divisions between socialists and nationalists in every neighborhood in Germany nullified any concerted resistance to National Socialism.

Wherever socialists looked, they saw a National Socialist. The Nazis had made impressive gains among workers. It was not at all unusual for Social Democrats to live with family members who had gone over to the brownshirts—"Old Hochegger" had his Nazi children, Albert and Lotte. After January 30, party leaders debated the wisdom of extra-parliamentary action such as a general strike, which had put a quick end to a right-wing putsch in March 1920. But Social Democrats feared being outmaneuvered by a military response, especially if the army joined forces with the SA. And how many people would rally to protect the constitution in hard times when so many people blamed the "system"? The party felt the drag of 6 million unemployed like a "ball and chain." Given the anti-democratic "will of the people," the Social Democrats convinced themselves that a policy of strict legality offered the best chance; they would allow the conflicts in Hitler's cabinet to play themselves out. Along with the Communists, they never imagined how ruthless their Nazi opponents in fact were. If they contemplated persecution, they did so with Bismarck's antisocialist laws from the 1880s in mind. In the end, the united anti-Marxist front that had brought Hitler, Papen, Hugenberg, and Hindenburg into the same room on January 30 overwhelmed the divided antifascist opposition in almost every other place in the country.[72]

The Social Democrats could do one thing: demonstrate the existence of the other, democratic Germany in the hope of checking the audacity of the National Socialists. It was almost as if they rallied for the sake of the history books, to be awarded credit for their unbending antifascism. From points around Berlin, thousands of Social Democratic workers marched to the Lustgarten on Tuesday, February 7. As far as *Vorwärts* was concerned, this was the true face of the city. Red Berlin. "A million-headed working-class city." "Thunderous singing," louds calls for "freedom," and fists "flung into the air" clearly impressed Abraham Plotkin. But Plotkin also saw that the demonstrators were fenced in, like animals in a zoo. Long lines of police stretched along the perimeter, in front of the cathedral, behind the old museum, and along the bridges that led to Unter den Linden. In the small town of Northeim, the Social Democrats also found themselves corralled. February 19 was the last socialist rally. The police diverted the working-class demonstrators into a walled-in beer garden, while the SA gathered freely in the streets.[73]

The calls for "freedom" were exhilarating, but the Social Democrats coughed and hacked, enveloped as they were by the spread of German nationalism. In the midst of the boisterous flag waving on the streets, the Social Democrats began to back down. They tended to step out in public speeches as veterans. Emphasizing their service in the war, they burnished the ideas of August 1914. Social Democrats rushed to acknowledge that workers had a fatherland. They talked about hills and fields and home. Versailles, the German guilt clause—big talking points on the nationalist agenda—socialists had always stood opposed. And the "system"? Well, only fifteen of Weimar's eighty-eight cabinet ministers had been Social Democrats. They had only been in power for five years and could not be responsible for the last fourteen, as the Nazis charged.[74] Implicitly, these arguments disputed the details of responsibility but conceded the principle of corruption. Social Democrats ensnared themselves by using nationalist words to counter Nazi arguments. They could not compete with the martial rhetoric and patriotic marching, clutching at flimsy reeds, "the pieces" that the socialists said they would have to pick up after the Nazis had bankrupted themselves. Socialists would act in the future, but they could not in the present. "After Hitler, it will be us." But the popularity of the Nazis was such that the future kept slipping away, and the pieces the socialists finally did pick up in the late 1940s were destroyed cities and millions murdered.[75]

The Communists held their last big rally in Berlin in the Sportpalast on February 23, 1933, but the police shut it down almost immediately, claiming that Wilhelm Pieck had defamed religion. As they filed out of the hall, the outraged demonstrators sang "The Internationale" and chanted "Red Front."[76]

Although Social Democrats continued to organize campaign events in the suburbs, the last mass demonstration in Berlin's city center was held in the Sportpalast on Sunday, February 27. The program opened with a "chorus of five-hundred voices." "It was a raising of voices in the songs of revolt," recorded Plotkin, the American in "Hitler's Berlin," "not the songs of revolt that one hears every day, but the songs of revolt that stir one with the age-old desire to challenge and to dare." The audience listened "in the depth of the silence that can come only when a huge crowd is deeply moved." He rightly added, "It may be that this particular chorus will never again be permitted to sing." When the speeches began, the crowds jumped to their feet and lifted their fists in the air three times, shouting, "Freedom, freedom, freedom!" The police shut down their meeting too, and as the people filed out of the Sportpalast, they sang "The Internationale," as their Communist comrades had a few days earlier. They chanted the call "Berlin" with the louder response "Stays Red." The chant grew along the streets. Outside, on Potsdamer Strasse, "the first sight that greeted us was the several hundred steel-helmeted Polizei standing in front of the gates of the building. We were not to cross the street. We must move on our side of the street only." Once again, police had fenced in the socialists. "Suddenly the 'Berlin' cry rang against the building, and 'bleibt rot' the response, rang back again. Everyone was either shouting Berlin or shouting back the answer. Fifteen thousand people strung along for blocks," and "the shouting continued for a good half hour." "The people in distress," the socialist daily commented the next day, "but a people that has sworn to uphold freedom." "Despite everything!" it signed off.[77] That night crowds said good-bye to the republic and to freedom.

After the rally, Plotkin made his way to an inexpensive restaurant on Friedrichstrasse in the city center, where he heard the news about the burning of the Reichstag. *Vorwärts*'s morning edition of February 28, 1933, reported proudly on the Sportpalast socialist rally and ominously on the "gigantic fire"; it was the last edition of the paper to appear in Germany until 1948.

THE REICHSTAG ELECTIONS on March 5, 1933, were not free, if "free" assumes freedom of the press and freedom of assembly. Almost all opposition parties including the Catholic Center Party had been harassed. Communists campaigned in very difficult circumstances. And with the arrests of Communist functionaries after the Reichstag fire, few Germans dared to fly the hammer and sickle or the three arrows of the Social Democratic flag, gestures that would identify them as virtual enemies of the state. To show the colors was to risk being marked on some Nazi list or to court the violent retaliation of a Nazi neighbor. In the previous year's elections, tenement houses had been a "who's who" of political loyalties.

What did working-class residents think about as they looked out on the streets without the blaze of red? Neighbors kept their flags rolled up and unclasped party badges from their coats. Perhaps they quietly sang to themselves Claire Waldoff's well-known "Die Ballade vom Linken Been" (The ballad of the left leg), about a poor girl from Wedding who wanted to make herself look pretty for a fine gentleman. She wore dressy clothes and a "Florentiner" hat topped with a "crocodile" feather. But no one wanted to go with her because she walked with a limp. To fix herself up, the girl from Wedding had her left leg amputated and threw it in the Panke River, but the left leg continued to run after her anyway. Whether it was "rainy, hailing, snowing, or sunny," wherever she was in Berlin, she could not get away from it.

> Det linke Been, det musste et bezeujen (the left leg, it had to tell
>   the truth)
> Det linke Been, detse vom Wedding stammt (the left leg, it came
>   from Wedding)
> Det linke Been, det konnte man nich leujnen (the left leg, it could
>   not tell a lie)
> Det war noch nich so recht kurfürstendammt (it wasn't ever
>   Kurfüstendamm ready)

Wedding could not be dressed up and covered up like the Kurfürstendamm, and "red" could not be so easily painted over in black-white-red. Claire sang, as she had for decades in locales like Berlin's Neue Welt, but after the Nazis came to power, she was silenced, since she was a "left leg" herself.

Most workers in Wedding walked with a limp on the left. Would they continue to limp or amputate their political sympathies so they could stroll along the Kurfürstendamm of the Third Reich? And if they did, would the past run after them?

On election day, only the black-white-red colors of the Nazi swastika and the old imperial flag decked the city streets. Some richer districts were more conservative and showed black-white-red; others, more radical, flew the Nazi flag, and many residents like Luise Solmitz in Hamburg attached a swastika streamer to the imperial banner. Workers were right to worry about their left-wing legs since people like sharp-eyed Solmitz took note of who flew what where. Her own Kippingstrasse was "festive, as never before" with "blck. w. r + swastika wherever one looks." She wrote in her diary as if taking notes. On nearby Heimhuderstrasse, she counted only a "½ dozen blck.w.r flags"; "otherwise all the way down, absolutely nothing, neither nor. What kind of people live there nowadays?" she asked.[78] This was the beginning of the regime of surveillance that characterized the Third Reich and emboldened its citizens to denounce each another.

"On the afternoon of the election," the British ambassador, Horace Rumbold, "drove through miles of streets in the outlying districts in Berlin" (it is interesting that he took modest suburban neighborhoods as national bellwethers). "I did not see a single Republican flag, but there were many Nazi and Nationalist flags flying," and "there was a total absence of flags in the districts inhabited by the working classes." One reporter journeyed through Berlin by subway, by streetcar, and on foot for a full hour without seeing a single Communist or Social Democratic flag. Big banners across the streets showed who was now in charge of the neighborhood: they wrote out the plea "Give Hitler All the Power" or mocked with satisfaction, "Where Is the Kommune? In the Basement. Huhu!" Policemen and SA auxiliaries patrolled busy thoroughfares, confiscating the placards of the few Social Democratic "sandwich" men who dared walk around. In Munich and Frankfurt, there were not so many swastika flags, but almost no other flags were flying in working-class districts. In Cologne, the number of Nazi flags in traditionally left-wing districts surprised observers. Hamburg proved the exception, with working-class neighbors sometimes showing the hammer and sickle and the three arrows, but also displaying the swastika.[79] This was Day 35 of the Third Reich.

"If flags and pennants, banners and signs, posters and leaflets are taken to be visible expressions of the actual attitude of a city," commented the *Kölnische Zeitung*, "then the Reich capital belonged solely to the loyalists of the government parties."[80] With a high turnout, which primarily helped the Nazis, on March 5, 1933, 44 percent of all voters cast their ballots for the National Socialists and 8 percent for the German Nationalists. Though not a great showing, it sufficed to give Hitler's government a majority. Strikingly, though, the vote share of the German Nationalists had declined compared to November 1932. "Decent conservatives" had done little strategic voting to temper Nazi radicalism, as the right-wing press had recommended. Nationalists simply went for Hitler.

"Germany has awakened!" wrote Goebbels on the morning of the election. "We are all rolling around in ecstasy." But 52 percent also meant the nation remained bitterly divided, and the Nazis would repeatedly refer to the 48 percent they needed to "conquer" through propaganda and other forms of pressure. And startlingly, despite massive intimidation and radio news, the Social Democrats had held up well, losing only 70,000 voters (about 1 percent) since November. While the Communists lost 1 million voters, the proscribed party still received more than 12 percent of the vote. (The Communist vote results were annulled on March 8, which meant the Communist Reichstag deputies who had been elected were not counted when it came time to calculate the two-thirds majority in the Reichstag necessary to suspend the constitution.) In electoral districts throughout Germany and, significantly, in precincts throughout Catholic Bavaria, the Nazis emerged as the largest party—but often fell short of a majority. The Nazis got more votes than any other party in Berlin, yet were outpolled by the combined strength of rival Social Democrats and Communists. National Socialist advances were so large that most Berliners no longer voted for "red" parties, as they had since before the turn of the century. Goebbels may have been wrong to suggest the total "absurdity" of the argument that "Berlin Stays Red," but he was right that it no longer applied in 1933.[81] Observers parsed the results, but the tallies were psychologically disabling to the opposition.

With more than 17 million voters, the Nazis had picked up 5.5 million supporters around the country since November 1932 and substantially added to the 13 million who had cast ballots for the party in the July Reichstag elections. Nonetheless, in the illiberal circumstances of March 1933, Hitler won fewer votes than Hindenburg had in the raucous joust between the two men in the April 1932 presidential runoff. The Nazis also won a smaller percentage of the vote than did the two socialist parties in 1919 (but a larger percentage—the largest in German history—if one includes the German Nationalists, as one should since black-white-red voters knew that they were voting for Hitler as chancellor). Berlin's biggest newspaper summarized the result as "a conspicuous shift of the pendulum to the right-hand side."[82] The drama of the coming months would revolve around how the Nazis proposed to erode the other 48 percent and how the (mostly socialist but also Catholic) 48 percent would come to terms with the 52 percent who dominated the public square.

CHAPTER FOUR

The "Communist Beast"

T o what degree did Hitler's dictatorship rest on coercion, and to what degree was it built on consent? In just one hundred days of power, the Nazis not only wiped out their adversaries in calculated acts of counterterrorism but made the opponents who survived doubt their own ability to appeal to the electorate. Highly suggestive images of national acclamation completely disarmed critics. A complicated combination of coercion and consent was at work. The magic of stage management made it difficult to demarcate where the National Socialists were required to use force to get Germans to go along and where they could rely on Germans to willingly join in. Such pageantry—most notably, a string of commemorative events celebrating the nation's awakening—was both intimidating and appealing. To this day, historians disagree about the power of what one scholar calls the "Ministry of Illusion," the regime's ability to create a seductive reality of national renewal that

Germans more or less willingly consumed without experiencing a genuine revival.[1] It is not clear what part of the story, the coercion or the consent, we must tell first in order to explain the success of the Nazis.

The picture of a young man, Karl Dürkefälden, a thirty-one-year-old draftsman, standing with his wife at the window of their house in the little village of Hämelerwald watching townspeople celebrate the Day of the Awakening Nation on March 4, 1933, indicates the priority of consent. The ceremony was in the forest outside the village, and Karl could hear the speaker, who made clear that "we offer the open hand and not the closed fist." A big bonfire beneath the trees flickered to "purge souls of the sins" of the years 1918 to 1933. Taken together, all the "mass parades, fireworks, drums, bands, and flags," the "oaths and vows" in the forests, and Hitler's voice over the loudspeakers in town squares created an unmistakable impression of general acclamation. The Nazis' "worldview" gradually became the "world in view" in which most Germans crossed the threshold, joined up, and became insiders, and only a few stood by as lonely outsiders.[2] But consider another scene, the next day, when Germans voted in the Reichstag elections. The British ambassador had himself driven through the working-class districts of Berlin. Without "red" flags, the buildings were mute; yet most residents there voted for the "red" parties on March 5, 1933. In Hämelerwald, the many eclipsed the very few—yet in Berlin, a large, silent "48 percent" stood against the loud "52 percent."

During World War II, émigré sociologist Hans Speier said if seductive propagandists such as Joseph Goebbels were "entirely successful," then harsh disciplinarians such as Hermann Göring and, later, police and Schutzstaffel (SS) chief Heinrich Himmler "would be unemployed."[3] Thus coercion was part and parcel of consent. What was more important? A new beginning with great fanfare or the bludgeon of the SA man's fist? The appeal of the Third Reich changed over time. State terror forced compliance just as the

improvement of economic conditions encouraged former opponents to rethink their positions.

In the end, violence preceded acclamation and proved to be one
of its key ingredients. It became a regenerative force in the making of the national community. As the torchlight parade on January 30 indicated, the promise of the Third Reich demanded blood
sacrifices. The absence of red flags flying on apartment buildings
filled with red voters on March 5, 1933, confirmed how intimidated
people were by Nazi thugs. In chants, *verrecke* (perish) came first,
before *erwache* (awaken).

The week that followed the elections was the single most consequential in German history. It featured attacks on Jews as well
as Communists and Social Democrats and set the stage for the
takeover of Germany's political and administrative structures. A
twenty-year-old Hitler Youth understood the order of priorities.
"Can we really," he asked, "forge the two spiritual fronts, on the
one hand, Marxism, pacifism, liberalism, and, on the other, idealism, a martial spirit, and the will to sacrifice, into a single community?" His answer was no—"the first has to be stamped out, and
only then can we pursue the struggle for the hearts and minds of
workers." The destination was August 1914, but the first stop was
November 1918: the "clenched fist," not "the open hand."[4]

Everything was still in place in February 1933. Children sledded
down hills; shoppers purchased linens at white sales; doctors con-
sulted patients; secretaries opened mail at trade union offices. The
Neue Welt advertised its annual "Bock Beer Festival," and the unemployed got themselves "stamped." But the frame of events tilted
just a little bit every day after Hitler's appointment as chancellor,
and soon things started to slide out of place with greater speed.
Opposition newspapers were suspended and political opponents
attacked or silenced. Seemingly far-away events that people read
about in the papers one week, they suddenly saw happening down

the street the next. The Weimar Republic was finished off in a sequence of events over just a week or two in March 1933.

The Nazis claimed public spaces, tenement buildings, and private apartments and made life-and-death judgments on the people who inhabited them. The violent actions began with the occupation of space and ended with the seizure of bodies and the incarceration of thousands of Germans in concentration camps. In March and April 1933, government actions in the capital guided the upheavals, but countless grassroots initiatives also moved them forward. They took place simultaneously, in almost all spheres of life, creating an extraordinary turbulence that increased in both intensity and extent and overwhelmed conventional checks and balances regulating social interactions.

"1890: Wilhelm II dismisses Bismarck," reflected journalist Sebastian Haffner. "Certainly, a key event in German history, but scarcely an event at all in the biography of any German outside his small circle of protagonists. Life went on as before. No family was torn apart, no friendship broke up, and no one fled his country.... Those in love, whether happily or not, remained so; the poor remained poor, the rich remained rich.... Compare that with '1933: Hindenburg sends for Hitler.' An earthquake shatters 66 million lives."[5]

E VEN BEFORE the Reichstag fire, the specter of communism justified the harsh police measures of the regime in the name of public order. Assertions about terrorism produced a concrete policy of counterterrorism that installed the dictatorship. On February 23, police cordoned off the side streets around the Bülowplatz to launch a spectacular raid on the Karl Liebknecht House, headquarters of the Communist Party. No photo gallery of the Weimar Republic would be complete without an image of the five-story

Karl Liebknecht House, with its massive banners draping the facade, proclaiming the party's struggle against hunger and fascism. From the roof, an imposing red hammer-and-sickle flag flew. (The building represented "the hopes many people shared for a more socially equitable society and the horror others saw in an increasingly Stalinist and bureaucratic party of functionaries whose antagonism toward the Social Democrats was partially responsible for the division and defeat of the German workers' movement and the end of the Weimar Republic."[6]) Police had often raided the premises, but this was the first time they occupied the building. They also brought along Nazi auxiliaries. A few days later, the grand red banners were pulled down and the black-white-red swastika flag raised. Authorities promptly renamed the building and the adjacent square in honor SA martyr Horst Wessel.

Göring himself prepared the press release to announce the takeover, and newspapers quickly typeset the headlines and published what the police had discovered: a secret door hidden behind the tiles of a washroom leading to a chamber stockpiled with weapons, underground passages or "catacombs," and "tons of seditious material," which was actually bundled to provide physical cover in case of an attack. "It has become clear," the sober-minded *Vossische Zeitung* concluded, "that the Communist Party and its allied organizations pursued a second, illegal existence beneath the surface."[7] Outside observers felt that the whole case had been written up in "the style of Edgar Wallace," the screenwriter for *King Kong*, or belonged in a "Nick Carter mystery novel."[8]

After the Reichstag fire, on the evening of March 1, Göring addressed the nation by radio, providing details on the "Communist beast" and the terror attacks Germany had barely averted. Live broadcast heightened the sense of crisis with its unvarnished, confidential tone and the tight timeframe of events—the Reichstag fire forty-eight hours earlier, the breaking news of conspiracy, and the "close call" averting disaster by a matter of days or hours. The

Communists, Göring charged, planned an assault on Berlin on the night of the election, March 5, in an effort to divide the patriotic front by dispatching "terror groups" of one hundred to two hundred men camouflaged in SA uniforms to blow up department stores and public buildings and attack the police. Other Communists were known to be operating clandestinely, stockpiling weapons and communicating via secret codes from transmitters hidden in forests. Special terrorist teams had been trained to booby-trap bridges and train stations, poison the water supply, assassinate public figures, and kidnap the wives and children of senior officials to use as human shields. Göring claimed that "terror groups" planned attacks on as many as "8,000," and then he added up another "10,000" targets; it was not hard to imagine every single one of the 300,000 members of the Communist Party as a dangerous conspirator and every Communist Party or newspaper office and "red" sports club as an extension of the catacombs that spread out from beneath the Karl Liebknecht House.[9]

"Our hair stood on end," wrote Elisabeth Gebensleben after listening to the radio. "This matter-of-fact report probably had a more chilling effect than a passionate denunciation would have.... Thank God we have this resolute government," she reassured herself. It was time to "get rid of the Communists, and the Marxists too" (that is, the Social Democrats). The hidden world of forests and catacombs seemed entirely believable even to liberal newspapers. Although a few editors stated that they expected Göring to keep his promise and release documents to the public, for most observers the Reichstag fire was itself sufficient evidence. It created a sense of urgency that made rigorous and immediate counterterrorism measures necessary. Since the conspiracy was mostly a Nazi fantasy, the evidence was never made available.[10]

Much of 1933 was about coloring the world in a vivid, threatening way. When Göring looked out at the republican landscape, he conjured up the devastation of the western front. Images of the Great War made the fantasies of Communist attacks all the more lurid, utter ruin reflecting the trauma of loss and indicating how that trauma could be processed through the repetition of its violence in pursuit of absolute victory. Göring declared the need to fight the Communists and "Marxists" as Germans had fought the French and British in World War I. "Everything lies shattered on the ground," he said, surveying the no-man's-land of the Weimar Republic, to party members in a bombastic, battle-scarred speech in Frankfurt on March 3. "A killing field. It lies before us, desolate, eradicated. Nothing grows, nothing blooms. Everything is laced with the poison of the gases that for fourteen years have corroded and torn to pieces all living forms of life."[11]

In these apocalyptic visions, the Nazis always returned to one particular origin story when the "Red Army" shot seven hostages, including a noblewoman, on the grounds of Munich's Luitpold-Gymnasium during the April 1919 civil war. (Annals of the Third Reich scrupulously indexed the name Hella von Westarp.) This isolated example of "red terror" fit perfectly into Nazi conceptions of Communist conspiracy against good society. The Luitpold-Gymnasium was cited to justify unspeakable crimes, beginning in 1933 with the torture of trophy prisoners such as Hans Beimler and Erich Mühsam—both leading figures in the Munich Soviet Republic who had nothing to do with the executions—and culminating in 1941 in the mass shooting of Jewish civilians in the Soviet Union.[12] The compound of fact and fantasy, the faulty multiplication of "terror groups," the imaginary catacombs, and the nauseating memories of the devastation of war—all this served to sustain an extraordinary level of anti-Communist violence throughout Germany in March 1933.

Four days after the Reichstag fire, Göring gave a speech in Frankfurt that put his soldiers, the SA brownshirts recruited into the police, on alert. "When I give the signal, the attack will proceed along the entire front." The offensive would not be conducted, the war veteran explained, "in a bourgeois manner and with bourgeois timidity." "Legal considerations" had no place; "I am not here to think about justice, I am here to destroy and to exterminate, nothing less!" To Social Democrats who took offense at being thrown in the same pot as the Communists, Göring replied, "Poisonous Communist gases came out of your pot!" Addressing both "red and pink-red gentlemen," he declared a "fight to the death, in which I will grab your necks with my fists."[13] This was an extraordinary declaration of war against civil society, casting opponents as lethal villains to be annihilated. Hanging over everything was the smell of poison gas.

ONCE THE ELECTION RESULTS were announced over the radio on March 5, the National Socialists emerged as the largest party in thousands of cities and towns across Germany. "There was something in the air" that night, remembered a newspaper editor in Starnberg, a pleasant, touristy town twenty miles south of Munich. Rumors were passed on, "quickly contradicted, confirmed once more, again denied, and then repeated as fact." The editor was reminded of 1918, with its perilous lexicon: "arrest hostages," "against the wall," "surrender weapons." In Starnberg, all the threats made during the election campaign "took shape."[14] On Monday, March 6, a group of armed SA men marched into the public buildings to raise the swastika flag. By the time they reached the train station, a crowd of several hundred local citizens had gathered. The Nazis had a drink at the local tavern before marching to the homes of "red" functionaries, beating some up, and arresting others. Everywhere you looked you could see it for yourself—"a vast Nazi flood is now really inundating all of Germany."[15]

On Tuesday, March 7, 250 SA men stormed and occupied the Social Democratic trade union headquarters in Breslau, an action that left dead and wounded on both sides. Dozens of buildings around the country would be occupied before the end of the month.

On Wednesday, March 8, Nazi leaders in Koblenz spoke to large crowds in front of city hall, denouncing the mayor for refusing to allow brownshirts into the building to raise the swastika. "To hell with you," "Down with Rosendahl," and "String him up!" the crowds in the market square roared. When the mayor, Hugo Rosendahl, a Catholic Center man, backed down and agreed to raise the flag, the Nazis demanded he make an appearance at the window. When he refused, SA men forced their way into his office and escorted him to the window to hear speakers pronounce on his political fate. "Mister Lord Mayor! If you are not with us, you have to go," "Mister Lord Mayor! We will be settling accounts with you and the Catholic Center!" And "Mister Lord Mayor, you are fired!"

Carrying placards reading, "Germans, Patronize German Shops," groups of uniformed Nazis in Essen forced the Althoff and Woolworth department stores and all Jewish businesses to close their doors. Despite the rain, large crowds gathered to watch unauthorized people shut down retail establishments.[16]

On Thursday, March 9, "companies of snotty-nosed brats" in brown uniforms marched around Breslau with spades, rubber truncheons, and revolvers in their pockets, pushing and punching pedestrians. On the Kurfürstendamm in Berlin, SA bullies beat up passersby whom they took for Jews and stood guard at department stores to keep shoppers from entering. In Munich, they smashed the windows of Jewish stores, occupied newspapers and trade union buildings, and rallied in the city center to demand the resignation of the Bavarian government led by conservative Catholic politician Heinrich Held.

The barely concealed purpose was to create enough unrest to give the federal government in Berlin grounds, under the emergency Reichstag fire decree, to appoint an interim governor to supposedly ensure the "law and order" that the Nazis themselves were undermining. Held was replaced by Hitler's Reich commissar, General Franz Ritter von Epp. With Epp in control in Bavaria,

Hitler had successfully appointed Nazi Party Reich commissars in each of the German states.

That same night, a company of SS came to arrest Bavaria's deposed minister of the interior, Karl Stützel, who had consistently taken a hard line against the Nazis. They found him at home in bed. When he refused to get up, they packed him in a car and took him to Nazi headquarters. "You can just imagine the jamboree" in the "Brown House," snickered Lina Heydrich, the wife of the black-hearted SS leader, to her parents a few days later. "In his pajamas and socks, the interior minister stands in the hallway surrounded by a whole lot of SA and SS who are doubled over with laughter. Then they approach the weeping interior minister and with their heavy boots step on his big toes so that he hops from one leg to the other." The sixty-year-old Stützel was lucky to be arrested in early March instead of later in the month. He was released rather than transferred to a concentration camp for further humiliation.[17]

Early on Friday morning, March 10, five men in "SA uniforms" broke into the home of Paul Barnay, director of the Union Theater in Breslau. They grabbed him and drove to an outlying suburb, where they beat him with truncheons and dog whips, running away only after a policeman caught sight of them. The incident is revealing because German newspapers still reported it as a crime, although reports neither mentioned the fact that Barnay was Jewish nor directly blamed the SA. The men in question wore "SA uniforms"—the press played along with Göring, who had warned against "red" terrorists in brown camouflage.[18] Jochen Klepper, a Protestant writer married to a Jewish woman, described the "pogrom atmosphere" prevailing in Berlin and the "terrible pressure" and "terrible fear" that oppressed the couple even in their own apartment. Klepper anticipated the total isolation of Germany's Jews.

The same day in London, His Majesty's Government assured members of parliament that the Home Department "would protect this country from any undesirable influx of aliens" in response to a question about "steps to prevent any alien Jew from entering this country from Germany." "In view of the present situation," Edward Doran, a Conservative member of Parliament from Tottenham North, believed that "hundreds of thousands of Jews" were ready to "drive a carriage and pair through the Aliens Act."[19] It was cold recognition of the plight of Jews in Germany, and the word "alien" became further freighted with meaning in 1933, in Germany and in Britain.

Also on Friday, March 10, Göring delivered an unapologetic speech in Essen in which he expressly aligned government policy with the SA violence exploding on the streets. It summarized what had happened since the election on Sunday and what was still to come. The Nazis were always quite clear about their intentions. To the "old aunties" who complained about abuses of power, Göring said, "I reject the idea that the police are a defense force for Jewish department stores!" The record noted "boisterous acclamation" at the Nazi rally. Göring signaled to his brown revolutionaries. The police "are not there to protect rogues, vagabonds, usurers, and traitors! (loud applause)." Were there abuses? "If people say that here and there someone has been taken away and mistreated, I can only reply, You cannot make omelets without breaking eggs!" Göring promised, "I have just begun to clean up; we are nowhere near finished."[20]

After Vice-Chancellor Franz von Papen placed a telephone call to the chancellor to register concern about the violence in Berlin, where several foreigners had been mistaken for Jews and beaten up, Hitler erupted in rage. He responded by writing a scathing letter on Saturday, March 11, to "Herr von Papen," an address he repeated again and again as he put the vice-chancellor in his place. "I want to make the following observation: never in Germany's history was a greater crime committed than the villainous act of November 1918." He continued, "I myself returned, Herr von Papen, as a half-blind man to the homeland and found myself welcomed at Munich's central train station by having my ribbons and my Iron Cross first-class ripped off." In the years of struggle that followed, "thousands upon thousands of my followers had to take off their shirts, and here in Berlin, Herr von Papen, the police were so rude as to order men to take off their pants in public simply because they were colored brown. They were forced to take off their boots because the leather was brown." Hitler stood loyally with his SA soldiers, admitting that he "almost trembled at the judgment of history, Herr von Papen, because it will not spare itself the accusation that in this historic hour we, perhaps already contaminated by the weakness and cowardice of our bourgeois world, handled our enemies with kid gloves instead of an iron fist." "I must ask you most insistently, esteemed Herr Vice-Chancellor," he concluded, "not to allow yourself to bring these complaints to me in the future....I am fighting not the government of Frederick the Great but the November regime of mutiny and deceit."[21] Hitler destroyed both.

In the week of March 6, newspapers were still able to report on the assaults that occurred across the country and for the first time, since the seizure of power, to take note of the SA's anti-Jewish actions, although they did so in a tone of cautious exasperation. In his speech, Göring expressed his surprise that the papers were still around to say anything at all, and, sure enough, by the end of the week government officials issued warnings to compel the press to coordinate its editorial line with regime policies. The "fact" that the "Marxist" press had already been prohibited, explained a spokesman for the new federal commissar in Saxony a week after the Reichstag elections, "imposed upon the entire press the responsibility to exercise extraordinary restraint" when reporting on the steps the government was taking in the state of emergency.[22] Expectations became stipulations.

Newspapers reported on the abduction of the Social Democratic Reichstag deputy Wilhelm Sollmann in Cologne on March 9, but the SA's attack on the small working-class village of Ottendorf-Okrilla outside Dresden the next day left no trace in the public record. Truckloads of brownshirts descended on the community, searched homes, and lit a huge bonfire with the newspapers, books, and flags they confiscated. Men presumed to be "Marxists" were rounded up and taken to Zum Schwarzen Ross tavern, where they were badly mistreated. The public entertainment ended after the SA had the prisoners undo their belts, run a gauntlet of a double line of storm troopers, and jump over the fire. Since the men were forced to hold up their trousers, they could not protect themselves from the Nazi blows. One disabled man, a Communist, was thrown around so badly that he died of his injuries.[23] Incidents like this were talked about but then forgotten. By the beginning of April, readers acknowledged that the "German papers were useless."[24] As a result, news of the terror instigated by National Socialists dissipated into hearsay and rumor. No one can be sure how many acts of terror vanished from the collective memory.

Two days after the elections, the Nazi's Rhineland paper, *Westdeutscher Beobachter*, ran the headline "Next Sunday: The People's Assault on the City Halls." At first glance, it referred to local elections scheduled throughout Prussia on Sunday, March 12, and urged voters to give National Socialists the majorities they needed at the local level. But the article was really a signal for the SA to take over city halls with force. Raising the Nazi flag was the first step in the seizure of power, largely completed in March 1933. The elections returned large Nazi pluralities and even majorities, at which point the brown *Volkssturm* acted on the authority of the people, the "52 percent."

Typically, the occupation of a city began when a mob of Nazis challenged the authority of a mayor, county administrator, or newspaper editor. Once they stormed the office, the victim was at the mercy of crowds, who shoved, choked, and pulled hair to force him to resign. At this point, the SA or local police arrived, ostensibly to restore order but more often to take the person into protective custody, from which the offender would be released once he signed papers giving up his post. Although less bloody than street fights between more or less equally matched opponents, these encounters were more aggressive because the Nazis invoked the "will of the people" to crush their enemies and assume power. The term *Volkssturm*—designating a "home guard" to avenge the people's wrath—indicated how "the people" validated "the storm." As the Nazis stepped forward, so did sympathetic citizens, who quickly staffed the whole apparatus of the new order to muster into the SA; the more elite and powerful paramilitary guards, the SS; the Hitler Youth; the National Socialist women's organizations; and the party's charity groups and professional associations. A new public sphere emerged; in the name of "the people," the Nazis occupied the civic spaces of self-government to impose their will.

The events in Braunschweig indicated how Nazi invaders and republican defenders settled into their roles as undisputed victors and the unquestionably vanquished. With successive acts of escalating violence, the Nazis invaded, captured, and occupied civic space. Sometimes the events happened quickly; other times, more slowly. In Braunschweig, as elsewhere, the forces concluded their offensive with public demonstrations designed to display the people's will against the traitorous, almost comical usurpers they had toppled to indicate that all things had been put right.

Braunschweig was a brown state with a red capital, and the air was particularly tense around the time of the March 5 Reichstag elections. A few days earlier, hundreds of Nazi soldiers, whom the state had just deputized as auxiliary police, marched through the working-class districts of the city, a show of force they had not dared carry out in October 1931 when 100,000 SA men had rallied in the city. Street brawls between "Marxists" and Nazis spilled into the weekend of the election. On Tuesday, March 7, SA and SS musicians held an open-air concert in the Ackerhof, a small square in front of the Rotes Schloss, which housed the offices of the Social Democratic Party and the newspaper *Volksfreund*, to celebrate the absolute majority the Nazis had won in Braunschweig. The Nazis were within striking distance of the enemy.

The next day, Wednesday, March 8, SA and SS squadrons marched from one government building to another to raise the swastika. At city hall, the assault stalled. The Social Democratic mayor, Ernst Böhme, had not yet arrived, and so the Nazis waited. When they finally met the mayor to demand the keys to the building's steeple, they hesitated. The delegation of brownshirts in Böhme's office insisted that he take his hands out of his pockets when speaking to them. Böhme responded by asking the Nazis to take off their caps. "We won't take them off," they replied, "the uniform requires caps." Böhme simply responded, "Pshaw, uniforms? Not to me they aren't." In the end, the Nazis returned with a locksmith and raised the flag, but Böhme's free-speaking manner indicated that he still imagined that his political opponents would respect the office and show him deference. He badly misjudged the National Socialists.[25]

The Nazis were better prepared the next day. At around four o'clock in the afternoon on Thursday, March 9, several trucks unloaded SA and SS men in front of the Volksfreund House. Employees quickly locked the doors, but the brownshirts smashed the windows and opened fire, killing a salesman. They ran up the stairs and broke down locked doors, hauling out frightened trade union officials and secretaries, who, surrendering with their hands in the air, were detained for hours before being released with kicks and slaps. The SA ransacked the building and threw the debris onto a huge bonfire that burned for three days. Eyewitnesses remembered that the city resembled an "armed camp." "Hundreds of heavily armed Nazi guards patrolled the city, chasing and beating up pedestrians." On Thursday, the National Socialists acted much more violently than they had on Tuesday or Wednesday, but the bourgeois press kept pace with the Nazis. The nationalist *Landeszeitung* pointed out that the Volksfreund House had long been a "trouble spot." In these "new times," almost from one day to the next, the Social Democrats, including the mayor, had become enemies of the state, dangers to public order.

After the occupation of the Volksfreund House, the Nazis acted with greater impunity. On Saturday, March 11, the SA held its customary band concert in the city center, attracting large crowds. The tunes set in motion the macabre dances of the Nazis; suddenly, according to one (small-town) newspaper account, "large numbers of the crowd, including women, poured down Schuhstrasse" and with a "wild hello," the "hello" of the new masters, smashed in the show windows of the big department stores. Thereafter Nazi rowdies scattered across the city to beat up socialists and Jews.[26]

Greater violence did not keep members of the audience from standing to applaud the Nazis for restoring order in the city. On Sunday morning, March 12, Elisabeth Gebensleben and "Vati" strolled along "the Sack," one of Braunschweig's old medieval streets; "the huge show windows at Frank's, Karstadt, and Hamburger's" were all "completely destroyed and are nailed up with plywood." Later that day, National Socialists passed by the house on the way to a wreath-laying ceremony in the cemetery. "Vati stayed up on our balcony to get a good view," and Elisabeth excitedly followed along. Once back in the city, she stepped into the old cathedral "just as the formal prayer service began. Brownshirts packed the two aisles." "A very impressive picture," she concluded with satisfaction; "the city has really come to life." Inspecting the wreckage, hailing the Nazis, praying in church—it was exactly one week after the March 5 elections.

In Braunschweig, events escalated. On Monday, March 13, large crowds of Nazis rallied in front of city hall, and uniformed men pushed their way into the building itself so that the city council had to suspend proceedings. Order was only restored when the police arrived to take the mayor, who in the meantime had received notice from the Interior Ministry relieving him of his duties, into protective custody. Although Elisabeth regarded the incident as "insupportable," she was more focused on contradicting news reports that her husband, who served Böhme as deputy mayor, had shown the man sympathy. "It may be that at the last moment," she explained to her daughter, "Vati got a little misty-eyed as he heard the jeers of the crowd" and "helped the mayor, who started trembling, into his overcoat. But tears—out of the question." She also pointed out that Böhme left city hall unharmed and was released the same night, whereas the old mayor back in 1918 had been forced "by the Reds to march at the head of a parade holding the red flag." Yet the liberal mayor, Hugo Retemeyer, was not made to resign and served until 1925. The events of 1918 resonated in 1933, and although the Nazi revolution was more brutal and thoroughgoing, the existential threat posed by November 1918 justified the violence.[27]

The Nazis were now in total control. It had taken them six days to seize power in Braunschweig. In the same period, Mayor Böhme had finally backed down, trembling, whereas earlier he had scolded. A final act remained: the display of the Social Democrat not as a political opponent but as a transgressor, a criminal, a predator. On March 23, an SS squadron arrived at Böhme's residence to arrest him. He was able to call the police, but when they arrived, the SS Sturmführer ordered them to leave, saying, "You can see we are already here." The SS packed Böhme into a car and took him to the Volksfreund House, where the local SS leader, Fritz Alpers, a particularly brutal man, was waiting for him. They demanded that the forty-one-year-old Social Democrat resign his seat in Braunschweig's state parliament, preparing to physically harm him if he did not obey. In response, Böhme called attention to his war injury; Alpers directed the torturers, "Not the arm." The SS ripped off Böhme's clothes and, for over an hour, whipped him on his buttocks and back. Whenever he lost consciousness, his captors doused him with water. After the "negotiations" had compelled

Böhme to sign the letter of resignation, the SS soldiers ordered him to get dressed and put on his overcoat and hat. Then, draping a red sash around him, they marched him through the streets of Braunschweig to the local prison.

Böhme's mistreatment was only one of many frightful scenes in the Volksfreund House, and Nazis repeatedly "worked over" Social Democratic politicians to persuade them to resign their mandates. Böhme was in fact lucky; he was released from prison after one month. He moved to Berlin, where he survived the Third Reich as a tax advisor and bookkeeper; British occupation authorities returned him to the mayor's office in 1945. Yet, of the nineteen Social Democratic members in Braunschweig's state parliament, nine were sent to concentration camps; seven died there.[28] It was an extraordinary purge.

Although photographs of Böhme's public humiliation do not show crowds assembled in the streets to watch the spectacle, picture postcards sold to the public later achieved the same end. The procession through the city center to the Rennelberg prison revived the rituals of the pillory in which the Nazis publicly displayed "traitors" who had transgressed the norms of the newly constituted "people's community." National Socialists borrowed haphazardly from barely recollected customs dating back to the Middle Ages, intending with precisely the antique character of this "people's theater" to dramatize the popular will, the "people's anger," and the "people's wrath." The ritualized violence registered "the extreme, fateful seriousness" of events.[29] The spectacle did not celebrate a victory of one side over the other. It put self-evidently and incontestably wicked transgressors on public display in order to affirm the virtue and coherence of the community. In this way, violence served to produce acclamation.

Nazi violence was choreographed as "people's justice" to render enemies ridiculous and to bind spectators together as an injured but restored community. Postcards provided liner notes for the scene on March 9, 1933, when the SA arrested Social Democratic Reichstag deputy Bernhard Kuhnt, sat him down in a coal cart, and forced two Social Democratic city councilmen to pull him through the streets of Chemnitz to join a brigade of arrested "Marxists" busily cleaning campaign slogans off walls and fences. "Looking good! Naval mutineer Bernh. Kuhnt on the way to his new workplace (cleaning up dirt)." The juxtaposition of the references to mutiny and cleaning reflected the Nazis' ability to portray the incident both as the restitution of history and the restoration of order. That postcards circulated in the first place provided evidence that the Nazis had not committed a crime but served justice. Like a dunce cap in the classroom, the wagon ride through town subverted empathy for the victim, who was displayed as the clown, the idiot, the traitor. "Finally, the red spook" had been "cleared out," the local paper breathed with a sigh of relief.[30]

Watching these "scrubbing parties," which in the wake of the 1933 elections had taken the place of the "pasting parties" of the 1932 campaign, Madeleine Kent, an Englishwoman married to a Social Democratic functionary, commented on the peculiar horror of "this degradation of the human spirit." She stood at the windows of her apartment in Dresden watching storm troopers guarding "long lines of men...grovel[ing] on hands and knees" and "industriously scouring the asphalted road with bath brick and scrubbing brushes" to erase "the Communist and Social Democratic election slogans painted in white." She was astonished at how "the normal morning life of the street threw the nightmare scene into relief. The postman appeared on his round, and crossed and recrossed the road as unconcernedly as though the kneeling figures through which he had to thread his way did not exist." Kent noticed that "the milk cart had to be edged along close to the pavement but the milkman rang his bell as merrily as though he were accustomed to finding half his customers scouring the street under guard." Even without crowds or loud "Heil Hitlers!" the streets had become places where

insiders sorted themselves out from outsiders, the "wicked Marxists" who were wicked because they had been "brought low" and
displayed as obviously wicked.[31]

The most spectacular action against Weimar's politicians took
place in Karlsruhe on Tuesday, May 16, 1933. Larger and larger
crowds followed the script. After the appointment of a Reich commissar for the state of Baden on March 8, National Socialists arrested leading Social Democrats, including the Reichstag deputy
Ludwig Marum. After the "Marxists" had spent two months in jail,
where they were joined by Adam Remmele, Baden's former prime
minister, the Nazis organized the transfer of the prisoners to the
new concentration camp in nearby Kislau. Already on the day before, the Nazi daily, *Der Führer*, announced that "Baden's biggest
November criminals" would be brought from the prison to police
headquarters at eleven o'clock in the morning to be transported
to Kislau, and it invited Karlsruhe's inhabitants to "send them off
with a last farewell."[32]

The prisoners were seated on the open bed of a police truck
in such a way that they directly faced the thousands of people
who lined the streets. The procession brought traffic in the city
center to a standstill. As the Nazis led their captives through the
streets of Karlsruhe at a slow, walking pace, excited crowds whis-
tled and jeered and repeatedly sang the verses of the well-known
German folk song "Das Wandern ist des Müllers Lust" (Wandering
is the miller's joy). The Nazis chose the song because it described
the "journeyman's years," appropriate for the Social Democratic
"knaves without a fatherland," as the old kaiser had once derided
them. The verses were also directed at Remmele, who as a young
man had apprenticed as a miller, a figure often at odds with peasants,
and later, as minister, banned the song as an insult to his authority.
The leaflets the Nazis distributed bore the title "The Transfer" and
included the names of the prisoners as well as the score and all
four stanzas. Military bands along the way played "Das Wandern

ist des Müllers Lust" uninterruptedly to encourage spectators to join in the singing. Marum described the public humiliation as an "emotional trauma." (All the prisoners were eventually released except for Marum, a Jew, who was strangled in his sleep on March 29, 1934.)

Today the city of Karlsruhe rightly regards the "show ride" as a "shameful ride," but that was exactly how local Nazis conceived it.[33] The National Socialists designed the "show ride" to display the power they held over their seditious opponents, who had scandalized the community. The ritual worked on many levels. It served as a warning to others, to the hesitant 48 percent: The Nazis were lords over the body. The power to laugh and to mock had become the power to strike physical blows. Ritual also demonstrated the eagerness of the Nazis to transgress boundaries. They would stop at nothing. The brutality worked more deeply too, creating a border between the "people" and its "enemies," so that the acts of violence continually created both virtuous "friends" on one side and wicked "foes" on the other. Social Democrats were cast into infamy as "people's enemies," traitors and fat cats, representatives of the old "system," and illegitimate parasites with no right to voice or redress. The spectacle of humiliation instigated further violence, since the idea of protecting the people's body depended on the destruction of the alien forces continuously threatening to corrode its integrity. Thus, terror in 1933 expanded into the terror of Reichskristallnacht in 1938 and the terror of the deportations in 1941. Violence was *Volkssache*, a "matter of the people."

Once the National Socialists occupied city hall and commandeered the local police, storm troopers fanned out into the neighborhoods and broke into tenement buildings and private apartments to arrest the Communists whom they had fought in countless street battles before January 30, 1933. This was a much crasser operation. It did not imagine a few "parasites" corrupting the people but acknowledged, as Göring put it in his notorious speech in Essen on March 10, 1933, that "for us" there are "two parts of the *Volk*," "one part that commits itself to the German people and to which the German state also commits itself, and the other part, which wants to undermine and destroy and which the state will crush."[34]

The night after the Reichstag fire, two trucks with headlights dimmed drove into Charlottenburg's Wallstrasse, where "Hanno" Maikowski had been killed four weeks earlier. Police and uniformed SA men sat on benches in the open truck bed and awaited the whispered orders.

"Third floor on the right—Zander."

"House eighty-eight—Fischer. Eighty-five—Katorek!"

The SA provided the police with the names and addresses of local Communist activists, and the police provided the SA with firepower.[35]

The forces arrested Fischer and Katorek. In Jan Petersen's fictionalized but autobiographical chronicle of "our street," Franz Zander was able to escape out the back window just as policemen banged on the front door. His sister opened the door to face the bright light of flashlights and the gleam of gun barrels. The police searched the small apartment thoroughly, rummaging through the beds, throwing mattresses to the floor, and pushing the kitchen cabinet from the wall. A square-shouldered SA man "smashed the portrait of Lenin against the edge of the table." Entering the bedroom, he tossed clothes out of the wardrobe and reached into pockets and "even fingered" the seams. Finding nothing, the police decided to stay the night and wait for Franz to return.

Petersen's chronicle reveals the disruption of social life in working-class streets. On the night of the Reichstag fire, residents in the Wallstrasse stood around in the doorways debating, despite the late hour. After the police started to arrest residents, the mood on election night a few days later was very different: "knots of people stand around the branch office of a newspaper. I join them.

The night edition with the final results of the Reichstag elections has just been posted. Those who have finished reading step aside and leave. No remarks are made." Even the faces in the group were without expression. "How excited the discussions after earlier Reichstag elections used to be!" The raids in which the police hauled out Fischer and Katorek changed everything. "Our former tavern" on Wallstrasse was shut down, the election placards scratched off the walls, and the Communist slogans painted over.

In the week between the Reichstag fire and the Reichstag elections, police and their SA auxiliaries arrested some 5,000 people, mostly Communists. In Berlin alone, they shut down three hundred Communist taverns. What the National Socialists referred to as "intellectual instigators" were also picked up. Vanguard journalist Carl von Ozzietzky had received warnings but felt safe since he had taken the precaution of removing the name plate in his apartment hallway. Taken away in his pajamas early one morning, anarchist poet Erich Mühsam refused to leave town because he worried about his house pets. Police headquarters on Alexanderplatz became "a Who's Who of writers, artists, lawyers and politicians despised by the Nazis. 'Everyone knows everyone else,' one of them later recalled, 'and every time someone new is dragged in by the police, there are greetings all around.' Some were soon set free again." But others, including Mühsam, were in for a horrific fate. The term "intellectual instigators" became notorious and justified the arrest and execution of Jews across Europe during World War II. "Mass arrests everywhere," announced the front-page headline in the Nazi daily, the *Völkischer Beobachter*, on March 2; the "fist hits hard."[36]

After the March elections, the "big action" against the Communists began targeting Social Democrats. In the first two weeks of March, 1,500 people were arrested in Düsseldorf, 1,000 in Cologne, 400 in Breslau, and 300 in Aachen. By the end of the month, the Prussian police and SA had made 15,000 arrests, a figure that leapt to

30,000 by the end of April. In October, a total of 100,000 "Marxists" found themselves in protective custody in Germany. The arrests hit the Communist Party very hard. In the weeks after the Reichstag elections, 450 of Essen's 2,000 members had been arrested. In the small town of Hilden, near Düsseldorf, the proportion was even higher: 80 out of 250 members, about one in three. The blows were extremely dispiriting. Residents of working-class neighborhoods, who had prided themselves on defending "our street" against the Nazis, found themselves completely at the mercy of SA soldiers.[37]

On March 8, the SA "Mordsturm 33" took up quarters in the middle of the "Murder Commune" they intended to pacify, taking over the Social Democratic "People's House" on Rosinenstrasse, no more than one hundred meters from "our houses." The feeling was uncanny, recalled Petersen: "It seemed as if an invisible billboard has suddenly been hung over the street: 'Beware! Area Closed!' Pedestrians avoid Rosinenstrasse. At night the neighboring houses appear to empty. Hardly a light burns." In the renamed Maikowski House, the SA now conducted "a little conversation" there with locals they suspected of having contacts with Communists. Neighbors on Rosinenstrasse could hear the screams of prisoners. A few months later, Wallstrasse was renamed Maikowski-Strasse, the street sign lettered in old German type. A plaque attached to the wall at number 52 commemorated the Nazi martyr. As an afterthought, the authorities found a small lane nearby to rename Zauritzweg. (Maikowskistrasse was renamed Zillestrasse in 1947, and the plaque honoring Maikowski was replaced with one honoring residents found wrongly guilty of the SA man's murder; Zauritzweg remains.)

Residents no longer recognized "our street." Communist activists agreed not to greet each other in public and took detours to avoid busy intersections when they walked to work or back home. Comrades kept their apartments "clean," burning incriminating material in their coal ovens in case of a police raid. They also dressed in a way that would not attract attention: Rothacker went to secret meetings wearing a "grey fedora" and holding the *Deutsche Allgemeine Zeitung* in his left hand. Ede was also in *Zivil*—"he is in a blue suit and has a soft felt hat."

Despite the SA's occupation of the neighborhood, the Communist activists living in "our street," like Jan Petersen himself, were sure that on the inside "the heartbeat of the street was still the old one." "You have to learn how to read a face. From the outside, it shows the indifference behind which those who are at the moment weak conceal their vigilance. What the street really reveals is deep, iron-clad refusal." The street may have fallen silent, "but the people in the windows, the groups at the entryways, speak, for those who know how to hear, the mute speech of solidarity." The street was like "an animal in danger that rolls itself into a ball and plays dead," ready to attack when the time came.

But the confidence of the Marxists was misplaced. Petersen's characters admitted to the difficulties they had reading the street. After the first arrests, they suspected that neighbors had denounced local activists to the SA or that Communists who had been arrested had named names during torture. Mistrust settled over the street. Franz and other Communists saw old sympathizers make their peace with the new regime, although they were not sure why. "Here and there a street attracts my attention," observed one comrade: "the black-white-red flags and the swastika flags hang all around." "The race for showing 'loyalty' has begun." But "in other streets again, only a few" flags. In August, when Nazis dedicated the Maikowski plaque, residents were expected to show the swastika. SA men knocked on the doors of residents who lived in the front building facing the street, offering a flag for free but in a tone that made refusing difficult: "They are scared" or worried about their jobs. Few people wanted to attract attention to themselves. However, other residents purchased flags all on their own; "the Meyers" and "the Radlis," for example, who used to "sympathize with us." Ede was outraged that "our comrades are already making propaganda for the Nazis." The solidarity of the red flock dissolved. "Swastika flags are flying in the Wallstrasse!"

More people appeared on the street wearing the uniform of the SA, but all the brown was not clearly legible either. It didn't always mean fervent political affiliation. "There are always a thousand reasons why they cannot risk their jobs," Petersen explained. "They wouldn't be able to take their girls to the movies. They'd have to stop smoking. They don't want to have to eat meals cooked at home by their mothers." Around the city, Berliners slowly fell into step with the new times, whether in a crooked way or more resolutely.

Denunciations led to arrests and arrests to confessions so that the political police, or Gestapo, quickly destroyed underground Communist and Social Democratic networks—on Wallstrasse and elsewhere. Activists became more isolated. Anytime neighbors displayed the Nazi flag, activists grew more uncertain about who was "true" and who was not, who was a "real" Nazi and who was just going along. "In our section," Petersen's group conceded, "only seven loyal comrades are left"; otherwise "everything fell apart."

With the tread of boots in the stairwell and the knock on the door, "the sounds of the night," Nazis entered the private apartments of individuals. They got in other ways as well. Residents on Wallstrasse reported on what children wanted for birthday or Christmas: uniforms. Not wanting to miss the excitement, young people joined the Hitler Youth.

A feeling of enormous fear gripped working-class neighborhoods. "The punitive raids, the violations of house and home, the arbitrary arrests, and prolonged periods of incarceration," the French ambassador reported on March 16, created widespread "disquiet." In almost every street in the poorer districts of Berlin, wrote the *Manchester Guardian* on March 28, the inquisitive foreigner was informed "that the Nazis murdered So-and-so living at number so-and-so; they have beaten So-and-so living around the corner."[38]

In some places, people talked: It was impossible to "enter a café or an underground railway train, without hearing of these horrible brutalities."[39] But in the tenement buildings themselves, residents fell silent; when suspects were arrested they could see neighbors peeking cautiously out the window. Maybe people thought that only criminals were arrested, that they were safe on the right side of the law; maybe they were afraid for themselves.

National Socialism penetrated the body, which moved with more caution, and it entered the mind when people were sleeping. Immediately after the March 5 elections, people had nightmares because the dictatorship had "the power to make nightmares real."[40] They dreamed of Göring and Hitler; they dreamed of denunciations, house searches, and arrests. They had visions of friends and comrades dressed up in SA uniforms. In other words, these were dreams about unexpected coercion and unexpected consent. In one dream, a doctor felt completely exposed. He was "stretching out on the couch" after his consultations when "suddenly the walls of my room and then my apartment disappeared.... I looked around and discovered to my horror that as far as the eye could see no apartment had walls anymore," and at once he heard the boom of the loudspeaker announcing the "decree of the 17th of this month on the Abolition of Walls." The Third Reich created the effect of suddenness: From one moment to the next, individuals felt completely isolated. Without being able to live in four walls or rely on social norms, individuals were extremely vulnerable. "I awoke bathed in perspiration," recounted another dreamer. This had happened on "countless previous nights.... I had been shot at, tortured, and scalped." She was running for her life, "breathless flights across fields, hiding at the top of towers...cowering down below in graves, everywhere the Storm Troopers at my heels." Active dreamers sometimes barricaded their bedrooms before going to sleep.[41]

Given the spate of anti-Jewish attacks after the elections, Jews had especially vivid dreams in spring and summer 1933. They felt marked, hounded by both the authorities and members of the public. One diarist reported on intense dreams he never used to have: "I am walking with a group of people across a rising field of snow. While the others climb effortlessly through the banks, I sink to my hips with each step and, despite desperate efforts, cannot keep up." Then there were dreams of America: "I am crossing the street of an American city. A policeman approaches me on his bicycle. I can't shake him and he keeps following me. Finally, he dismounts the bicycle and informs me that I am going the wrong way. I apologize and say I am a newcomer." Or "I am crossing the street of an American city and find myself in the midst of a horde of black kids on bicycles who nearly run me over. A policeman rescues me, points to the light that I crossed against, and gives me a very stern lecture. Again I apologize, telling him that I am a foreigner." Kurt Rosenberg was dreaming about his own incapacity.[42]

The dreams show two things. There was the physical fear that the dictatorship enacted in the body, and there were the actions of people around the isolated individual that augmented this fear: the administrative zeal of the police, the racialized behavior of the crowd, the indifference of bystanders.

WITH THE ARRESTS on Wallstrasse, the Nazis made good on their 1932 promise to arrest and sentence "all Communist and Social Democratic Party functionaries," to "smoke-out the deadliest districts," and to throw "suspects and intellectual instigators in concentration camps."[43] The concentration camp would become one of the most recognizable symbols of the Third Reich. Yet, when the Nazis came to power in January 1933, they did not have concrete plans to build the infrastructure of an extralegal system of incarceration. They talked more about "heads rolling in the sand" than about protective custody or punitive detention. The unlawful detention of tens of thousands of Germans, most of them men and most of them Communists, in concentration camps was the logical consequence of the outsized role the SA played in the seizure of power. The SA sustained the extraordinary energy of the Nazi movement; "every day," Hitler explained, the men "have to climb into their trucks, protect meetings, stage marches," and "exert themselves night after night."[44] After January 30, the SA continued to engage Communists and the Reichsbanner in street battles but with the great advantage of having the government on its side, which aggravated the violence. Once the Prussian government deputized the SA as auxiliary police—and other German states followed suit—Hitler's soldiers possessed weapons and the power of arrest, allowing them to act as police and to interrogate and imprison enemies. The occupation of trade union buildings and party and newspaper offices also gave the SA valuable real estate to do as they wished without being overseen by regular police in precinct houses.

After the Reichstag fire and the Reichstag elections, the number of arrests ballooned, and the SA acquired more real estate. They established "wild" concentration camps in the immediate field of their operations, requisitioning abandoned factories, run-down hotels, sports' facilities, and even restaurants such as "the Schützenhaus in the town of Annaberg in Saxony; its landlord was the local SA Sturmbannerführer, who ran the new camp while his wife prepared the prisoners' food." SA taverns doubled as makeshift prisons so that instead of SA violence flowing from the pub to the street, as was the case before 1933, it flowed from the street back into the pub.[45] The Maikowski House, the Volksfreund House, and Gestapo headquarters at Prinz-Albrecht Strasse 8 in Berlin defined space in the Third Reich. This same topography would eventually be recognized in all the cities the Nazis occupied across Europe: Gestapo headquarters was located at 84 avenue Foch in Paris, at al Szucha 25 in Warsaw, at Euterpeststraat 99 in Amsterdam.

The SA bore the marks of the violence they sought out. One veteran street fighter scrutinized his body: "I have knife scars on the back of my head, on my left shoulder, on my lower lip, on my right cheek, on the left side of my upper lip, and on my right arm." From 1929 to 1932, the size of the Nazi Party increased eightfold, but SA insurance claims for injuries sustained in the line of duty jumped by sixteenfold to 14,006. Years of struggle had brutalized the SA, who shared a culture of violence and adopted a gangland slang so that "a truncheon was an 'eraser' (*Radiergummi*), a pistol, a 'lighter' (*Feuerzeug*)." They called one another "Pistol Packer" or "Potshot Müller" and referred to their squadrons as a "Robber Band" or "Murder Squad."[46]

In hundreds of "wild" concentration camps over the course of the spring and summer of 1933, SA soldiers tortured Communist and Social Democratic activists to give up the names of comrades who made up the underground networks of Nazi opponents. The small groups of brave resistors hardly posed a threat to the state, but graffiti on a wall and a leaflet stuck in a mailbox disrupted the Nazi narrative of total national acclamation. SA interrogators thought of themselves as instructors in a "choral society": "you will soon be amazed at how beautifully you will be able to sing for us," and by the end of the year, relying on "brutal" but "tried-and-true" methods, the Gestapo destroyed most of the fragile lines of communication in the underground. If suspects remained defiant in the first round of interrogations, most broke down after a "difficult night," revising testimony with statements that began, "Now I will tell the pure truth" or "I must correct myself."[47]

The real purpose of the violence was not to extract information but to break the spirit of Communists and Social Democrats, to display the unassailability of the new lords, and to force the enemy to accept the unconditional terms of defeat. Since the aim was psychological rather than instrumental, the physical assault on prisoners was highly ritualized. And prominent SA officers such as the Hohenzollern prince August Wilhelm, or "Auwi," pulled up a leather lounge chair to watch the show.[48]

A steady stream of abuse accompanied prisoners as they were taken to the SA command centers: "You asshole...bastard...murderer...dirty Jew." One of the first things that victims noticed was that the rooms and hallways were covered with the booty looted from the "Karl Liebknecht" and all the other "people's" houses the SA had occupied. Red flags, placards, uniformed shirts, and group photographs hung on the walls. The best items were later installed in the "Revolutionary Museum of the SA Division 6," which opened in Berlin in May 1933. ("Open daily from ten o'clock in the morning to ten o'clock at night, entrance fee 0.30 marks; in uniform, schoolchildren, and unemployed, 0.15 marks.") A tour guide described the attractions: "An unusually comprehensive and well-arranged collection of trophies of Berlin SA's struggle against Red Front and Reaction."[49]

The plunder played a central part in the torture and humiliation of prisoners. The SA often administered beatings over a table draped with the black-red-gold flag of the republic. Teams of handlers held the arms and legs of the prisoners, pulled down their pants or, in the case of female prisoners, pulled up their skirts and pulled down their slips, and beat the bared flesh with switches and rods twenty, thirty, or more times. The flag muffled the screams but also made it difficult to breathe. In the report of her interrogation on the night of March 20, Marie Jankowski, a Social Democratic councilor in Berlin, reported that she was forced to explain the meaning of the colors of the black-red-gold flag; when she got to "gold," the SA demanded that she use the word "shit." She refused and was beaten. Jankowski and her fellow prisoners were also forced to assume a military bearing and sing the German national anthem. Interrogators often asked spurious questions about big salaries or the embezzlement and misuse of municipal funds in order to link socialist opponents with the "system" or to impugn their personal integrity. Jankowski was accused of stealing shoes from unemployed workers. One trade union secretary was released only after promising in writing to provide his wife with an adequate housekeeping allowance. "I found the interference of these half-grown adolescents in my marital relations outrageous," he said.[50]

The principle guiding most of the violence was simply to cause suffering rather than death. In the Columbia House in Berlin, the beatings were administered according to scale: "wind force 1, 2, and 3," that is twenty-five, fifty, or one hundred blows. Jankowski was lucky: she was released after one night. Many other prisoners were beaten bloody until they lost consciousness and endured many more nights in the makeshift prisons, which echoed with screams of victims and the *Klatschklatsch* of leather whips. The rooms in the SA command center on the Hedemannstrasse in Berlin were known as the "blood cellar."[51]

Historians cite Rudolf Diels, the head of the "political department" of the Prussian police, who described what he saw when he took his own tour of the prison in the SA's headquarters in Berlin after he received reports about mistreatment. After having himself driven to Hedemannstrasse on March 29, 1933, he forced his way into the prison cells. "The victims that we found," he recounted in his postwar memoirs, "were half starved to death. For days they had been locked up standing in narrow closets in order to force 'confessions.' The 'interrogations' began and ended with a thrashing. A dozen lads worked in rotating shifts to flail the prisoners with iron rods, rubber truncheons, and whips. Smashed teeth and broken bones testified to the torture." When Diels arrived, the "living skeletons," bludgeoned and bloody, lay listless, one next to the other, on beds of rotten straw. There were no moans, just "silent stares as the men waited for the end." They were like "lumps of clay" or "strange dolls" with oddly bobbing heads. Writing after the war, long after the wickedness had cemented into genocide, Diels concluded, "Hieronymus Bosch and Peter Breughel had never glimpsed such horror."[52]

When the terrifying commotion quieted down, prisoners could sometimes hear "the rustle of wagons" or "the honking of automobiles" outside. As they waited for the next round of torture, captives felt shipwrecked in "the center of a modern city in the middle of the twentieth century." Even after their release, they remained out of touch with the civilized world, dizzy and lost.[53] There were exceptions, but most people who had been tortured did not resume conspiratorial activity against the Nazis.

The 48 percent of the population well understood the terror. After the March 5 elections, Social Democratic officials received a flurry of resignations from members across the country. Within a week or two, both the Communist and Social Democratic parties had ceased to exist at the local level. Most of the 52 percent of the population deflated the rumors because they considered harsh measures necessary to restore order.

Hitler's biographer, Joachim Fest, contended that "a nation cannot decide, like Richard III, to become a villain."[54] This assertion is certainly right in the sense that is it misguided to scrutinize Germany's national character for unusual evidence of deviancy or criminality. But it is off the mark in that the Nazis continuously displayed violence as spectacle, introducing their victims as "November criminals" and corrupt beneficiaries of the "system" in rituals of humiliation that created audiences who were invited to participate in the chastisement. There was nothing secret about the concentration camps, the abandoned factories and military barracks rebuilt as temporary stockades to relieve prisons, which had become overcrowded with political prisoners.

It was perhaps coincidence that the first news items announcing the establishment of concentration camps in Dachau and Oranienburg appeared on March 21, the day Germans celebrated the Day of Potsdam—the ceremony for the opening of the new Reichstag—on the very first day of spring. But the two events reinforced each other.[55] It was telling that both Hitler and Goebbels skipped the church services that preceded the ceremony to visit the graves of SA fighters who had lost their lives in street fights. By doing so, they signaled that national unity depended on martial combat. The National Socialists made it clear that there was always something permanently embattled about the ideal of the "people's community." The Day of Potsdam was a "day of national celebration" that "occurs very rarely in the history of a people." "The flags have now been lowered, the cries of the crowds have died down," Elisabeth Gebensleben wrote in a happy glow, but she added that the "boundless rejoicing" could not absolve the government of the responsibility to "apply an iron fist." She understood how the newspaper items fit together, explaining at the end of her report on these "great times" that Communists "have to undergo a three-year probation in a concentration camp," and the "same goes for the Social Democrats."[56] The coincidence of the date did in fact force a decision to accept the camps as the price of national unity.

The revival of the lurid debate about the best way to execute prisoners convicted of capital crimes—the hand axe or the guillotine—shows just how far Germans were willing to go to destroy the enemy. While some state prosecutors found the handheld axe, which had to be specially weighted to give it the necessary cutting force, "repellent," others felt that the intimate style of execution upheld the "superiority of the state" and thus the "dignity of the community." "Beheading by muscle power" had "something real, manly, natural about it." The hand axe was a symbol of "swift, direct action," while the guillotine was "dead, soulless, impersonal" or else represented a "sickly humanitarianism." Hitler eventually decided in favor of the guillotine, but that did not stop people from imagining how the first Communists, convicted in the Altona case, were executed on August 1, 1933: "presumably with a hand ax" instead of, as had been the case in Hamburg, the guillotine. (Most executioners had learned the trade of butcher.[57])

The concentration camps were a "matter of the people" too. Elisabeth's speedy arrival at the idea of camps in her chain of thought reveals how many Germans believed that Communists and representatives of the "system" needed to be incarcerated. The "national awakening" implied the assertion of national feeling that distinguished between friends and foes. Of course, counterterrorism was not the necessary means to fight terrorism; rather, it was the reverse: the incidence of terrorism was necessary to install a counterterrorist order, impose a state of emergency, and suspend the rule of law. A playful but staged photo essay, titled "The new game: 'the SA storms the Karl-Liebknecht-House,'" published in the Nazi illustrated in mid-April, indicated the routinization of Nazi violence. It depicted children playing a German variation of "Cowboys and Indians" as boys stormed the "Libknechthaus"—a deliberate misspelling that underscored the homespun nature of the (counter)assault—nursed their wounds, and afterward got tucked into bed, but not before imprisoning captured "Communists" in a "concentration camp."[58]

Once understood in terms of "Cowboys and Indians," the epic struggle for political space, the concentration camps made more sense. The National Socialists introduced the concentration camps as integral parts of the new Reich. One newspaper hailed the "long life" of the concentration camps. "Today Dachau is not just a temporary measure [*Episode*]"; "it is the program and watchword for all those who neither have proper faith nor goodwill." "Dachau" was "Auch da," an anagram spelling out "also there" or "always there."[59] The press covered the concentration camps extensively, even as newsreel shorts and radio reportages whitewashed their brutality.

Camp commanders went on record to defend harsh measures. "It would be foolish," admitted Oranienburg's Werner Schäfer, who published a unique account justifying the camps, "to conceal that some of the arrested have meanwhile received none too gentle treatment." This was hardly surprising in light of the fact that the SA had been for so "many years chased, beaten bloody, outlawed, [and] expelled from their jobs and their homeland." "Spiritually impoverished," most prisoners had been "misled" and "poisoned"; they would eventually be released. But a few were not reclaimable for the *Volk* on racial grounds. "There are some one would not like to meet in a dark alley," explained one newspaper; it was possible to "see how years of incitement can transform a person's features into something brutal . . . sly, false, and insidious." The "incorrigible Bolshevist" was easy to pick out. For bearers of such a "half-animal face," even "the most draconian education would be fruitless. These atavisms have always existed."[60] The figure of Communists as "subhuman" had emerged already in the Weimar Republic and anticipated Nazism's "Judeo-Bolshevism"; it was a grotesque but inalterable biopolitical entity to be eradicated, as Hitler had promised many times.

The institutionalization of concentration camps in national life was evident in jokes that began to circulate in summer 1933: "Dear God, make me mute / So that I don't end up in Dachau," with regional variations that substituted Dürrgoy (near Breslau) or Wittmoor (Hamburg) for Dachau (Munich).[61] Dachau was also widely cited to convey a threat on the part of the regime against recalcitrant elements. "There is still lots of room in the new camp, which will open its gates already on Wednesday," warned one small-town newspaper in Bavaria. "Ab nach Dachau," or "off to Dachau": newspapers reported on a new transport leaving the local train station for the concentration camp at "12:40." And Dachau served as a cudgel held up by ordinary citizens to keep unhelpful bureaucrats or disliked neighbors in line. "Ready for Dachau," people warned each other, or "Dachau—only eighteen kilometers!"[62] The sheer number of arrests—upward of 50,000 in April 1933—and the extensive press coverage quickly made places like Dachau and Oranienburg parts of everyday conversation.

Released or escaped prisoners who managed to publish retrospective accounts abroad furnished details about the concentration camps, but the horrific information they provided made it back to Germany only in fragmented underground accounts. Concentration camps were run like military camps, which would have been familiar to many inmates since almost every male over the age of thirty-three had served in the German army in World War I. Daily routines included roll calls, marches, drills, and forced athletic exercises that doubled as punishment: push-ups, knee bends, running, crawling, hopping. It was the "stone pit—parade ground—stone pit—parade ground," day in, day out.[63]

However, guards bore little resemblance to senior military officers in rigidly hierarchical institutions; they treated prisoners as they believed they would have been treated if the Communists had seized power. "If these pigs had come to power, they would have cut our throats," reminded a commander in Dachau; "but now we are in power." "We have not come here to treat these bastards in a humane way," he exhorted. "We see them not as human beings but as second-rate."[64] What followed was not simply routinized brutality but licensed sadism, which made particular guards, known by frightening nicknames—"Firebrand," "Ivan the Terrible," the "Long Shadow"—notorious. Inmates quickly learned about terrifying places: "Room 16," where interrogations in Oranienburg took place, or "Barracks 7," which housed the "Jew company" in Dachau.[65] Guards apprenticed in Dachau went on to staff senior positions in the wartime death camps.[66]

New arrivals in total institutions such as the military frequently endured initiation rituals, but the "welcome" prepared for prominent newcomers to the camps set the stage for horrific violence meted out to select prisoners for the "entertainment" of the rest of the inmate population.

The arrival in Oranienburg of "onetime greats" Friedrich Ebert, son of the former president of the republic, and Ernst Heilmann, a Social Democratic Reichstag deputy, made front-page news. The camp commander imagined the satisfaction of the inmates as they watched the two ready themselves for work with shovel and broom. "Now rut around as you like, you red agitators," gloated the *Völkischer Beobachter*. When Ebert and Heilmann were transferred from Oranienburg to Börgermoor a month later, they were forced to "introduce" themselves. "I am Friedrich Ebert, son of the traitor Ebert." And then came Heilmann's turn: "I am the super-scoundrel Heilmann.... I have deceived the German people and betrayed the workers." They were the "big racketeers" who had squandered the "workers' pennies." Of course, the confessions were not believable, but once articulated they served to separate out the representatives of the "system" from the rest. Ebert was eventually released, but Heilmann, as a Jew, remained in the camps to endure the worst humiliations. According to one account, he was "made to creep on his hands and knees" into a kennel and "bark like a dog, bow-wow, bow-wow!" The guards resolved to slowly finish him off. Alone, shunned by most comrades as "unmanly," which was the point of the treatment, Heilmann was murdered in Buchenwald in April 1940 just before his sixtieth birthday, seven years after being picked up at Café Josty on Berlin's Potsdamer Platz on a sunny Monday, June 26, 1933.[67]

To further humiliate Social Democratic big shots, the SA guards attempted to stir up long-standing hostilities between Social Democrats, cast in the rituals of the prison as corrupt big-time spenders, and Communists, who served as the chorus. Guards made prominent Social Democratic prisoners stand up and shout out, "I am the fat cat who betrayed the workers!" The confessions sometimes prompted laughter and applause among Communist inmates who viewed the former functionaries as "social fascists," no better or even worse than the National Socialists. Many reports confirmed that Communists belittled Social Democrats, but Communists had also been arrested earlier and in much larger numbers and were usually detained longer. Communists and Social Democrats were all degraded when forced to listen to Hitler's speeches or to play parts in radio and film broadcasts of *The Oranienburg Concentration Camp at Play*, singing Nazi anthems such as the "Horst Wessel Song" or their own, suddenly old-fashioned-sounding socialist hymns. A perverted mix of old Weimar and new Nazi rituals stranded inmates in the totally new time of the Third Reich.[68]

Raids against Communist and Social Democratic activists continued through summer and fall 1933. "Prisoners in protective custody arrive from Dachau," the newspaper reported on the timetables of Germany's underground railway in August 1933, and "a new transport departs."[69] A new class of more ordinary prisoners also filled the cells of jails and barracks of concentration camps. On March 21, 1933, the Day of Potsdam, a new law criminalized malicious, even mischievous talk against the regime. Special courts expedited the trials by curtailing the rights of defense and eliminating sentencing hearings and appeals. In most cases, defendants had passed on rumors and jokes that bore some resemblance to reality. These malcontents imperiled the whole idea of the national community.

Lengthy newspaper reports served as a warning but could not hide the gratuitous and cruel nature of the regime's special courts. Berliners read about fifty-two-year Theodor Fons, the "father of four children who barely supported his family by selling butter and margarine door-to-door after losing the support he had received for losing an eye in the war," sentenced to one month in prison for maintaining that "numerous" Jews had been beaten to death. The twenty-nine-year-old salesman Martin Hein received fifteen months for spreading the news that the SA had forced "Communists" to drink castor oil in the prison on Hedemannstrasse and had abducted and stabbed a young Jew. Workers sitting around talking about Dachau in a stonemason's hut in a Bavarian village each received a three-month sentence for sedition.[70]

Since so many defendants had been overheard talking on the streetcar or in the tavern or had let down their guard and gossiped while selling door-to-door, they had clearly been denounced by other civilians. In spring and summer, a wave of denunciations swept over Germany, providing the authorities with names and addresses of Communist suspects, but also overwhelming them with false or misleading information passed on by (mostly male) neighbors and acquaintances with a grudge. The police quickly figured out that at least half of the tips they received were not worth pursuing, but the new modes of spying on and interacting with neighbors added to the atmosphere of suspicion and fear that SA justice had first created. "Everyone can get everyone else locked up," even for something as minor as not returning the "Hitler greeting," wrote novelist Irmgard Keun. "There aren't many" that can "withstand the temptation to make use of that kind of power."[71] As it was, most Germans did not denounce their neighbors; yet denunciations became an entertaining part of public life. The circulation of the scurrilous weekly newspaper Der Stürmer, which baited readers with dozens of stories about Jews and other "enemies of the people," rose tenfold to 500,000 in the three years after 1933. The practice and threat of denunciation became part of the folkways of the Third Reich, demarcating how divisions between insiders and outsiders insinuated themselves into daily life.

Political prisoners were released during the traditional Christmas amnesty at the end of 1933—just nine years after Hitler himself had been allowed to walk out of Landsberg prison early on December 20, 1924. "Out of Custody, Back into the People's Community," read a Berliner Morgenpost headline. But inmates had to promise to remain silent about their experiences and refrain from further political activity if they wanted to remain free. This did not stop people from talking about the camps as the circulation of one joke makes clear.

Two men meet [on the street]. "Nice to see you're free again. How was it in the concentration camp?"

"Great! Breakfast in bed, a choice of coffee or chocolate. Then some sport. For lunch we got soup, meat, and dessert. And we played games in the afternoon before getting coffee and cakes. Then a little snooze and we watched movies after dinner."

The man was astonished: "That's great! I recently spoke to Meyer, who was also locked up there. He told me a different story."

The other man nods gravely and says, "Yes, well, that's why they've picked him up again."[72]

When former inmates did not speak up, "broken teeth, battered bodies, and terrified silences" testified about what had happened. Many were traumatized. Felix von Papen, nephew of the vice-chancellor, who had been arrested for pro-monarchist activity, reported on his broken self: "I am ashamed to be alive and to have accepted all this.... For the rest of my life, I will never get over this. I should have defended myself. Although I knew with absolute certainty that if I had resisted in the least I would have been shot like a dog."[73]

Even after just a short time in the camps, former prisoners could not recognize the country to which they returned. They felt out of place in the new routines of life in the Third Reich. Former politicians took up the trades they had learned in their youth or took employment as accountants or coal dealers or salesmen. That was hard enough, but it was shocking for them to see relatives and friends more or less fall in line with the National Socialist regime in a mixture of compliance and consent. When Communist activist Fritz Ausländer returned home in June 1935, he found that his wife had joined the Nazi women's organization and his children the Hitler Youth. Neighbors heard him screaming at his wife, "That is how you raised our kids—they're Nazis!"[74]

The big fight that Social Democrats and Communists lost to the National Socialists in February and March was one in which the nation was bitterly divided. The prisoners who returned home at the end of 1933 took the measure of how quickly Germany had changed from a country of highly articulate partisans who flew flags and pinned on badges of allegiance into a country of believers and conformists who, for reasons that were not always clear or verifiable, had made their peace with the new regime. This was the Nazis' achievement in the two short months between the Reichstag elections on March 5, 1933, and the day celebrating German labor on May 1. The "48 percent" who had not voted for Hitler almost entirely disappeared from view, its remnants treated as miscreants and "asocials," agents of national and social corrosion, drowned rats in the sea.

CHAPTER FIVE

The German Spring

INMATES RELEASED from concentration camps were dismayed by how comfortably the German public seemed to have settled into the Third Reich. On the train home, they saw passengers chatting banally about weekends and movies—a disconcerting experience for former prisoners who, for months and years behind barbed wire, continued to live in a perverted fun house version of the Weimar Republic with denunciations of "fat cats," SA guards bullying "Marxists," and conflicts between Social Democrats and Communists. One novelist imagined a released prisoner feeling like an escaped zoo animal, a "bear on the Kurfürstendamm, who doesn't know whereto" or a "wolf who has strayed onto Potsdamer Platz and gets run over by an omnibus."[1] In their eyes, Germans had become the contented citizens of the Third Reich. And in many ways, a children's army led the long march into it. But that march was uneven and the signals to which it stepped cacophonous—something that the former concentration camp inmates, bowled over as they were by the seeming unanimity of Germans in the Third Reich, could hardly see.

Dissidents put into relief the greater part of the consent that Germans had given the new regime. Matthias Joseph Mehs, a forty-year-old innkeeper and Catholic Center councilman in Wittlich, a town on the left bank of the Rhine between Koblenz and Trier, had cleverly tabled a resolution to make Adolf Hitler an honorary citizen of the town by suggesting that a committee be appointed to detail (that is, to ascertain) the precise contributions the new chancellor had made to it. This was a small act of defiance. Nonetheless, he registered the liveliness of his hometown after the March 5 elections. "Yesterday evening, 8 o'clock; marching steps, drummers, fife-players, flags.... Something is going to happen." He asked, "Are we climbing into the Third Reich?" He himself kept an ironic distance. "Germany is marching!" he wrote on the Day of Potsdam, "but it will only awake when the marching, drumming, fife-playing, tooting, and singing stops." What Mehs called "tam-tam" was even greater when Wittlich celebrated the Day of National Labor, on May 1. He was appalled by the sheer excess of celebration, which began at six o'clock in the morning along the streets beneath his window and played nonstop on the radio until early the next morning, and he disapproved of the exclusively Nazi stamp to the display of national unity. During the ceremonies, the only songs were "fighting songs, Hitler songs." It all smelled too much of Berlin and too little of Wittlich. He himself did not step into the parade because, as he snidely put it, somebody other than the town's Jews had to watch it.[2]

In his diary, Mehs noted that his daughter, Marialein, wanted a brown uniform of her own. "A little angel's dress or a Hitler one?" her father followed up. "A Hitler dress," she replied, adding that she expected her father to get himself a proper "Hitler suit" so that she could be seen "out on a walk" with him.[3] To walk the streets of the Third Reich was to don a new look, to revel in Germany's spring.

Spring 1933 was when a man went to the barber shop to get his hair cut. A startled Englishwoman living in Dresden noted that "anti-Nazis could now be recognized at a glance by the style of their haircut," even though everyone "might be indefatigable in giving the Hitler salute.... [I]t was remarkable how much more Western they looked than the Nazis, whose cropped hair revealed straight-backed heads and bulging necks."[4] Men and boys outfitted themselves in uniforms, which were not inexpensive. The gear required just to join the Jungvolk, the youngest section of the Hitler Youth, cost over 100 marks, more than one month's income for a working-class family, and included the purchase of "brown laced shoes" (13 marks), a knapsack (22 marks), a military waist belt (2.50 marks), shoulder straps (1.50 marks), and a field canteen (4.50 marks). Children too young to join a paramilitary formation sucked black-white-red "lollis" and collected armies of Elastolin soldiers. The favorite toy soldier was the most expensive: Hitler as field commander who came in his own extra box lined with crepe paper. At 2.50 marks, the collector's item featured a movable right arm that could be raised into a Hitler salute. Luise Solmitz herself received such a doll as a birthday present from her thirteen-year-old daughter, Gisela; a little embarrassed, she later gave it to her English friend, Erneste Hetherington. (The "Führer" figure can still be bought on the internet for about three hundred euros.) Out shopping one Saturday, Luise did buy a flip book, *The Führer Speaks*, a cinematic sequence she quickly flicked through. It was a great sensation when she showed it to her friends, although Solmitz considered other kitschy items, such as sofa pillows embroidered with "Heil" or hair braid clasps fastened with a swastika button, "revolting—just like 1914."[5]

If the sight of an "SA man in full uniform" standing at "the window directly opposite" surprised the old Social Democrat in Altona on January 30, brown uniforms turned up everywhere in the weeks that followed. One Sunday afternoon, Willy Cohn took a walk down Breslau's Rennbahnstrasse: "all in white, the beautiful splendor of chestnut trees, whereas an earlier stretch was totally red. Unfortunately, the scenery echoes with the song of the marching SA troops, which disrupts the peace and quiet." Law student Sebastian Haffner sat in the meadows of the Grunewald, the woods outside Berlin, with his girlfriend Charlie. "The world was full of the peace of springtime." Yet "every ten minutes or so a group of young people would go past," accompanied by teachers, and "every one of these classes, as they passed, shouted, 'Juda verrecke!' to us in their bright young voices, as though it was a sort of hiker's greeting." It was a "surreal" scene, he remembered. "We kissed and caressed each other," and the boys "cheerfully told us to perish." In Weimar over the summer, Erich Ebermayer found the city unbearable: "the nonstop smack of SA boots on the pavement, the cries of 'Heil Hitler' ringing through the quiet streets."[6] Military music played in the cafes.

All over Germany, young people brought the sights and sounds of the Third Reich home with them, singing the newly learned verses of the "Horst Wessel Song," which had been hastily pasted over other songs in the grade school songbook. One day in May, as Mehs was packing up documents to send to relatives who needed to attest to their "Aryan" identity, his other daughter, Margaret, broke into song. It was the "Horst Wessel Song," and it had "thoroughly acidified" even the youngest children, Mehs reflected, but he noticed Margaret stumbling over the lyrics. She pronounced "reactionaries" as "treactionaries" when she sang, "Comrades shot by the Red Front and reactionaries." "What can she know about 'Red Front' and 'reactionaries'?" Mehs asked himself. Later, when his daughters sang, "Clear the streets for the brown battalions, clear the streets for the storm trooper," while they were getting ready in the morning, Maria asked her father to help her get dressed, singing, "Clear the streets, put on my dress!" When Mehs asked her what she actually meant by all those "brown battalions," little

Marialein replied, "The uncles clearing the streets." "What uncles?" her father inquired. "The ones who always sweep the streets," she answered—the municipal street cleaners who wore brown overalls.[7] Margaretchen's garbled "treactionaries" and Marialein's ideas about "Uncle Streetsweeper" indicated how confused the Nazi message may have been. What the girls lost in translation stands for a larger problem when Germans observed neighbors becoming Nazis. The more Mehs paid attention to the Nazi phenomenon on the streets, the more puzzled he became. "Treactionaries" poses pressing questions about the depth of ideological identification and the roles that fear, opportunism, and even misunderstanding played in the process of conversion.

In Hämelerwald, Karl Dürkefälden kept careful notes on how friends and family responded to National Socialism. He had to contend with his parents and his sister, Emma, who were "fanatic adherents of Hitler," and he detailed how neighbors reconciled themselves in less obvious ways. He wrote that on a trip to Hanover with his wife, Gerda, to visit her parents over Easter, "we also talked about the political situation" and learned that they had "not yet changed their opinion." His brother-in-law, Walter Kassler, had not "adjusted himself" either. But Karl's turn of phrase indicated that other acquaintances had accommodated themselves. Hans Kinne, the husband of Gerda's friend Irma, for example, "is now a Nazi because of his job, but only for show." Although the local barber had joined the SA, Karl thought he did so for "economic reasons" only. Karl later added the words "not so" to the diary entry, which suggests that he initially had trouble believing that many people converted for any other reason than opportunism. Only later did it become clear to him that conviction had also played a role, calling into question his assumption that adjustments were "for show" only.[8] Dürkefälden struggled to read the mixed signals of conversion.

All the sardonic references to newly minted Nazis, to the *Märzgefallenen* (casualties, those who "fell" to the Nazis after the March elections) or the quick new growth of "March violets," followed by *Maiglöckchen* (lilies of the valley) or "May bugs" and "June roses," confirmed that National Socialists themselves were fully aware that the new Nazis of spring 1933 could hardly be ranked alongside loyal "Old Fighters" from the pre-1933 time of struggle.[9] The appeal of Nazism was real, but the extent and depth of this appeal remained uncertain. Not only who had become a Nazi but how was the subject of endless discussion and ongoing scrutiny as neighbors witnessed the marching and singing and counted flags, badges, and brown suits among their circle of relations.

When Germans referred to the *Märzgefallenen* to denote the 1.6 million men and women who joined the Nazi Party between January 30 and May 1, 1933, at which point a ban on new memberships went into effect, they snickered ironically at precisely those who had not pledged themselves with their hearts but taken advantage of opportunities or given in to threats. Since the vast majority (1.3 million) of the *Märzgefallenen* fell in the ten days after the announcement of the forthcoming ban on April 20, expediency seemed to trump conviction.[10]

The status of *Märzgefallenen* would seem undesirable, but it also offered a kind of exoneration. It allowed Germans to forgive themselves for their weakness and to refrain from thinking about their complicity in the Third Reich. In retrospect, with the accumulation of the Third Reich's crimes, most Germans thought of themselves quite unironically as *Märzgefallenen*—as conformists, not believers. "I didn't do it," said the *Märzgefallenen*. "Adolf Hitler, he was the one." The emphasis on conformity is hardly controversial: the violence of dictatorship forced most citizens to live "dissonant lives." The public presentation of the new conformist self often clashed in uneasy ways with the cultivation of the old self in private. But this explanation cannot account for the collective enthusiasm in spring 1933. Opportunism, conformity, fear—yes, but also ideology, patriotic excitement, racism. The quick-witted cabaretist Werner

Finck looked back in 1947 on the crowds he had entertained ten years earlier: "If only I had known then what we know now, that they were all just Mitläufer," hangers-on, the casualties of March. "Some were so good at camouflaging themselves they made it all the way to Gauleiter," he added.[11]

Even the aggressive gesture of the *Heil Hitler!* salute was not unequivocal. A few months after January 1933, most people in Germany raised the right arm and exclaimed, "Heil Hitler!" several times every day. One still heard Berlin's *Guten Tag* or Hamburg's *Moin* or Bavaria's *Grüss Gott*, but *Heil Hitler!* (or simply *Heitla!*) had wormed itself into the country's lexicon to such a degree that 1945 was remembered as the moment when "we never have to say *Heil Hitler* again!"[12] In July 1933, civil servants were required to use the greeting in official communication. Schoolteachers "Heil Hitlered" their students at the beginning of class, conductors on the Deutsche Reichsbahn "Heil Hitlered" passengers when checking tickets, and post office clerks "Heil Hitlered" customers buying postage stamps. Victor Klemperer was astonished to see "employees constantly raising their arms to one another" as he walked through the buildings of his university in the summer of 1933.[13]

With *Heil Hitler!* Nazi Party members attempted to recompose the body of Germans. It required practice, and students drilled in raising their arms, "hands outstretched, to eye level."[14] Raising and stretching drastically expanded National Socialists' physical claim on public space. A political declaration accompanied the assertive gesture. Unlike *Guten Tag*, which sought to reconcile neighbors, *Heil Hitler!*, with its exhortative exclamation mark, aimed to create and enforce political unity. Signs in stores and offices bore the command "Germans Greet Each Other with Heil Hitler!" As more Germans said, "Heil Hitler!" to each other, not responding in kind became harder. The standardization of the salute thus enhanced the sense of acclamation but also created room for just going along.

Foreigners found the salute contagious as well; on motorcar trips through Germany, Martha Dodd, daughter of the American ambassador, and novelist Virginia Woolf " 'heiled' back" at enthusiastic Germans lining the road. After a group of international journalists posted at the Nuremberg rally listened to the speeches broadcast in their hotel, the "audience to a man and woman rose to its feet with its arms raised in the Nazi salute and joined in the emotional singing of 'Deutschlandlied' followed by the 'Horst Wessel Lied.' " Singers included the previously suspicious *New York Times* correspondent Frederick T. Birchall, who reported on the incident.[15] But precisely because *Heil Hitler!* became ubiquitous, it blurred the boundary between genuine and half-hearted support for the regime.

In a final scrambling of signals, the perfunctory show of the palm could be instrumentalized in ways that served the collective. In the 1944 movie *Die Deggenhardts*, the "old man," played by the illustrious Heinrich George, is identified by his old-fashioned courtesies—the handshakes, the greeting *Moin, Moin*, the very mumbled *Heil Hitler!* His time is up, and the "old man" is retired after twenty-five years of service in 1939. Ashamed, he fools his family by pretending to go to work every day until the truth comes out; then the accumulating hardships of war result in his reinstatement and thus the reconciliation of old and new, the reluctant Nazi and the national community. Such reconciliation can, the movie implies, be achieved through the higher purpose of war.

How to evaluate going along with the *Märzgefallenen* and raising the right hand in the Hitler salute? Matthias Joseph Mehs himself counseled friends not to resist the pressure to join the Nazis if they feared personal disadvantage or loss of employment. He urged them to become "fake" Nazis. When he looked out at the crowds singing the "Horst Wessel Song" and shouting, "Heil Hitler!" he saw shame in the participants who remained loyal Catholics in their hearts. Yet Mehs also criticized acquaintances who allowed themselves to be "systematically misled and intoxicated." He himself failed to distinguish clearly between the bad choices his fellow townspeople had been given and the stupid choices they made.[16]

Like Mehs, scholars are positioned on the outside looking in at a strange phenomenon that occurred many decades ago. They carefully take a nuanced approach to understand popular support for Hitler. Rightly skeptical about making large claims for different kinds of people, historians have been uncomfortable with the proposition that many or most Germans desired the Nazis. A document such as Matthias Joseph Mehs's diary highlights the role of pressure, conformity, and opportunism. These pressures are easy to reconcile with conventional assumptions about social behavior. Historians unpack words and actions, examine context, and scrutinize social origins, so they often do not take desire seriously. They have been reluctant to recognize genuine belief or true love.

Most Germans preferred the Nazi future to the Weimar past. Millions of citizens were attracted to national renewal and the ideal of service to community, nation, and race. National Socialists repeatedly projected images of a reunited nation, and more and more Germans consumed and embroidered them. Outsiders such as Mehs depicted national celebrations as occasions when the regime enforced regimentation. Yet the scenes also revealed how many people participated in the collective activity, reinstating the nation and the *Volk* and thereby affirming the virtues of National Socialism. What Mehs sometimes regarded as coordination, most Germans experienced as spiritual renewal and uplift. This majority did not reassemble on every point of Nazi policy, certainly not on the deportation and murder of Germany's Jews. Nonetheless, Germans came to identify their own prospects for a better, richer life with the fortunes of the new order; private happiness became deeply entangled with the establishment of the Third Reich.

To explore consent instead of coercion means to engage with the social descriptions of collective life that the National Socialists themselves applied to modern politics: the importance of will and belief and the credibility of concepts such as national community, the people, and race. This is a vexed undertaking. Some might object that this method is "too colored by Goebbels' propaganda";[17] yet we can only understand the glue holding the Third Reich together by recognizing how Nazi ideas moved people, by taking Nazi words seriously.

The enduring popularity of the Nazis rested on the idea of the *Volksgemeinschaft*, the national or people's community. This was not a Nazi idea or perceived as imposed or strange. On the contrary, Germans credited the Nazis with finally putting into place the national solidarity they had yearned for after the lost war and years of revolution and counterrevolution. Appeals for unity resonated because they promised to resolve the crass divisions of 1932. This is important because constituents who did not necessarily identify with National Socialism cherished the collective energy and unity of the national revolution in 1933. The legitimacy that Hitler and his regime enjoyed rested on a foundation of goodwill larger than the Nazi Party or its base. The so-called national revolution came before the Nazis, even if the Nazis were the indispensable means of its realization.

While in principle antidemocratic, Nazis and their supporters genuinely believed they represented the German people. They shifted the terms of representation so that, in their conception, the people represented a unified and enduring community—one in which the sacrifices of past generations had laid the foundations for the achievements of the future. Free elections could not attain the will of the people; only the state's task in preserving and strengthening the collective existence could achieve that. National vigor mattered, not individual choice. Considering ancestry and progeny meant thinking about biological stock in the long term. This sort of National Socialism underwrote policies designed to safeguard the nation against parasites, interlopers, and outsiders.

The Nazis took the concept of the *demos* to a radical conclusion. There was always something dramatically embattled about their *Volksgemeinschaft* as they continuously seized on the evidence of German suffering. They assailed internal and external enemies— Jews, profiteers, "Marxists," the Allies—who allegedly obstructed national regeneration. They offered a comprehensive and appealing vision of renovation but married it with the alarming specter of national disintegration. In the Nazi view, 1914 stood for renewal and life, while 1918 threatened revolution, chaos, and ultimately death. Getting to the ideals of 1914 necessitated refighting and eradicating the ideas of 1918. One of the most prominent words in this period was *verrecken* as in the suspicions that the Germans were about to perish or the belief that the Jews should. For all its appeal, the union the National Socialists promised rested on violence.

Basic elements of the Nazi worldview, including the moral calculation that to preserve life meant destroying it, circulated widely in the Third Reich, meaning that coercion *always* accompanied consent. Melita Maschmann, watching the parade, glimpsed the blood sacrifice on January 30, 1933. Such violence was never isolated. Germans were perishing, dropping dead, finally awakening so that citizens constantly worked with and debated the evidence as they considered Nazi policies parsing strangers from comrades.

The National Socialists' will to revive Germany depended on a radical reappraisal of the future. History had no predetermined course, and phrases like "old times," "new times," and "good times" calibrated a new epochal way of thinking, one that made the Nazi future seem increasingly compelling and compulsory. When Hitler first addressed the nation over the radio on February 1, 1933, he spoke in terms of a normal legislative period: "Now, Germans," he appealed, "give us the span of four years and then you may pass judgement upon us!" "German *Volk*, give us four years," he repeated ten days later in the Sportpalast. Four years then slipped into forever. "The hour will come at last," he prophesied, to establish "the new German kingdom of greatness and power and glory and justice." Hitler had no intention of giving up power in "four years," of course. "We have power, and we're going to keep it," Hitler told the party's youth leader, Baldur von Schirach, on February 5, a week after he had moved into the Reich Chancellery. "I'm never leaving here."[18] The upcoming election, the new chancellor assured business leaders on February 20, would be the "last election.... There is no going backward." Hermann Göring spoke more precisely: "The election on March 5 would surely be the last for ten years, or even for a hundred years."

After the elections, the "national awakening," celebrated with such fanfare from Könisberg on March 4, hardened into the "national revolution." At a cabinet meeting on March 7, Hitler informed his ministers that he considered "the events of March 5" to be "a revolution." With the National Socialist victories, he explained to crowds in Berlin, "Germany's destiny has not been decided for the next four years; no, it has been decided with finality." The press echoed this idea. "Our state will stand forever," reported a newspaper in July.[19] "We are planning for a long period," Hitler declared at the Nuremberg rally in September, and "just as we shall meet here two years hence, we shall meet here ten years hence and a hundred and even a thousand years hence." Nazi multiplication totaled up a "Thousand Year Reich," which the division of war would destroy in twelve. "When I took power it was a decisive moment for me," Hitler recalled in 1941. "Should we keep the old calendar? Or should we take the new world order to be a sign for a new beginning in time? I told myself: the year 1933 is nothing less than the renewal of a millennial condition."[20]

As soon as Germans accepted the dating of the new calendar, the opponents of the Nazis were doomed, not because they had lost elections or been thrown into concentration camps but because they appeared, even to themselves, obsolescent. In the dramatic debate on the ratification of the Enabling Act on March 23, Social

Democratic leader Otto Wels saluted the final triumph of "justice," "freedom," and "socialism," the shared "principles of humanity." He had faith that the "wheel of history" could never be turned back. But Hitler thought in cosmic dimensions. "You contend," he addressed the Social Democratic legislators, who unanimously and alone voted against the emergency legislation enacting Hitler's dictatorship, "that your star will rise again! Gentlemen, Germany's star will rise and yours will fall. . . . What in the life of a people becomes rotten, old, and infirm will disappear, never to return." The Reichstag minutes recorded "tumultuous cries . . . long-lasting acclamation." The rising star of Germany had broken the "wheel of history." The Nazis believed that their cosmic revolution had deleted the liberal revolution of 1789 from history.[21]

In the debate, Hitler tied the Social Democrats to fourteen years of misrule and to an outdated system. Peace or war? Hitler pointed to the crossroads; the choice was backward or forward, "whiny" or "heroic." The either/or, the unforgiving rhetoric of friend or foe that the Nazis mastered so well, was appropriate to the experience of extreme hardship and the sense of living on the edge of an abyss. It was the basic equation performed by millions of Germans who were hungry and wanted work. "The Weimar Republic is over," concluded the *Vossische Zeitung* the day after the fateful vote. Over the next three days, Wels's honorable speech, which sounded moderate, even apologetic, and Hitler's quick-witted, hot-tempered "impromptu" reply, along with the loud heils and hurrahs and the wicked laughter from the National Socialist benches that interrupted the proceedings, were rebroadcast over the radio ad infinitum. The media gave authority to the "complete dressing down" of the Social Democrats.[22] Wels's humiliation underscored the National Socialists' contention that Germany's socialists were no longer credible. Otto Wels, who died in exile in 1939 at the age of sixty-six, is largely forgotten today.

The "new beginning" resonated with particular force among German Protestants. One historian describes the "Protestant experience" of 1933, when churchgoers and clergy believed that the Nazi seizure of power had brought Germany's Christlike "passion" since 1918 to a redemptive end. In the vein of the disciples' stories in the New Testament, Protestants embroidered the years since the war as a biblical parable of suffering, sacrifice, crucifixion, and resurrection.

During the Weimar Republic, the Protestant churches had felt themselves besieged. In the cities, clergymen melodramatically described irreligion taking root right in front of the church door. In Kreuzberg, one of Berlin's working-class districts, the faithful pointed to "the enemy at the gates who outside on the streets of the big city, in rallies, magazines, and newspapers, uses every opportunity to drag what is holy to us through the mud." Others felt that degeneracy literally surrounded the Kaiser Wilhelm Memorial Church in the center of the city: All around were "beer halls, cafes, showy cinemas, cabarets, bars, sparkling show windows, dazzling advertisements." Saturday night never gave way to Sunday morning. "Life vibrates well past the midnight hour. Bustle, music, noise, pleasure, fancy, eroticism. All around the Memorial Church." The striking spatial images, "at the gates" and "all around" the church, emphasized the physical threat to the very existence of the church.[23] The world of the Protestant Church was in fact quite circumscribed, remembered one theologian; it regarded any willingness to compromise with other parties or tolerate diversity or fancy as a betrayal of well-established tradition: "You cannot put in strong enough terms this opposition between friend and foe, between who belonged and who was alien...between who helped and those who destroyed."[24]

If the cosmopolitan spirit of Weimar appeared life threatening, the church held up an almost biological idea of the German people as the source of vitality and virtue. The ideal of a blessed union between "*Volk* and God" replaced the old alliance of "throne and altar." This direct embrace of the people in a newly renovated *Volkskirche* (people's church) might have led clergymen toward a progressive religious socialism, but instead the "*Volk* and God" doctrine congealed into an exclusive ethnic, even racial, commitment. Like so many other institutions in Germany, the church was profoundly affected by the Great War. Two million German men had died. The "struggle for survival," one of the most emblematic ideas of the early twentieth century, made the church keenly aware of the principle of difference in God's creation of the earth. "God did not create humans as such," argued one theologian, straining to reinterpret Paul's words about the unity of all human beings in Christ in Galatians 3:28; he created "Jews and Greeks, Persians and Indians, Romans and Germans." Since God created separate peoples, it followed that God also commanded his ministry to respect the "law of life" that determined the "internal and external form" of each of these entities.[25] To recognize "each according to his nature" meant that the church's commitment to the German people and to the solidarity and suffering of the German community radically qualified the indivisibility of God's love and introduced ideas of *artfremd* (alien) and *arteigen* (characteristic) into everyday religious practices. The postwar nationalization of the church found concrete form in the pro-Nazi and openly anti-Jewish German Christian movement, which contested church council elections with stunning success in 1932 and 1933.

Prominent theologians such as Karl Barth rejected the Protestant Church's nationalist turn because it introduced "another God" to mediate the relationship between the individual and the divine. Barth would later write that the German Christian heresy was to augment "the holy scripture as the sole revelation of God" with a "second revelation," namely, the "German folk." For years, Barth had objected to hyphenating Christianity into "Christian-social," "evangelical-social," or "religious-social." These combinations drew their legitimacy from historical time and thereby intruded on "God's time." They threatened to secularize and update Christ. This was the strong purist theological position of the "Confessing Church" in the "church struggle" with the German Christians in the years after 1933, but it offered little practical guidance on how to protect civil society. Barth rejected German Christianity in the Third Reich, but he did so in a high-minded way that also undercut any productive reconciliation of Christianity with the Weimar Republic.[26]

For the overwhelming majority of Protestant churchgoers, the Nazi seizure of power was cause for immense joy. It promised to disperse the enemies gathered at the church gates while elevating the German people. Never again during his career, writes one historian, did "Hitler so frequently and so ardently implore God" as he did in the first weeks of his chancellorship. In his first radio address to the German people, the new leader vowed that the new government would "take Christianity under its firm protection." It was "the basis of our entire morality." On the Day of the Awakening Nation, the day before the March 5 elections, Hitler addressed "Lord God" with prayerful hope: "May we never become vacillating and cowardly." The speech concluded with a thanksgiving that recalled the war years: "In battle our God was there standing beside us."[27] But the central motif of Hitler's prayers was not the rightful place of God in the Third Reich but rather God's recognition of the difficult struggle and special place of the German people in history.

The various sermons of German pastors in spring 1933 display a subtle difference in emphasis between those who welcomed wayward Protestants back into the church and those who seized the opportunity to amalgamate the church with the revivified National Socialist people. It was a question of restoration or renewal. A tremendous surge of energy animated the followers of the German Christians who sought renewal by completing the nationalization of the Protestant churches. They believed that God manifested himself in history and in the "great turning point" in Germany's history—"God with us" would be inscribed on the buckles of Wehrmacht soldiers. The church was "alien and indifferent" if it did not embrace the "destiny of the National Socialist movement."[28] A year later, the tide had shifted to favor traditionalists who insisted that "the church remain a church" (and "state remains state") and resisted the establishment of a new "people's church." Both conservative restorers and *völkisch* renewers, however, gave Hitler's national revolution credit for recovering the singularity, unity, and capacity of the German people. The Nazis, they said, had secured Germany's future.

From the perspective of 1945, after years of devastating war and indiscriminate murder, it is hard to fathom the spirit of thanksgiving with which Protestants greeted the new regime in 1933. Hitler appeared to inaugurate a new age, as Luther or Bismarck had; his charismatic appeal rested on the role salvation stories assign to the messiah who emerges in an unexpected way, not from the structure of familiar hierarchies, the "system," but from the people and from the plains—in this case, as a "low-born man" who had fought alongside ordinary Germans in the trenches.[29] Local uniformed SA men and their flags, their *Sieg Heil* salute, and the German greeting *Heil Hitler!* became part of churchgoing rituals in hundreds of Protestant parishes. German Christian sermons resounded with the fighting spirit of National Socialism: struggle, sacrifice, and victory. And services often concluded with the congregation singing the "Horst Wessel Song" accompanied by the triumphant chords of the organ. Archives in the Church of the Good Shepherd in the Berlin neighborhood of Friedenau note the acquisition of Hitler's *Mein Kampf* for the young people's library in August 1933, Hitler portraits in October 1933, and a Hitler oil painting in April 1934. (Indeed, *Mein Kampf* became a standard gift on the occasion of a wedding or a

confirmation.) In the common rooms of the parish hall, churchgoers browsed the pages of the party newspaper, *Völkischer Beobachter*, and the anti-Semitic weekly *Der Stürmer*. Some pastors used
only German wine to celebrate the Eucharist.[30] National Socialist
symbols and practices were not always integrated into old church
rituals, but in the first few months of the Third Reich, the German
Christians set the tone.

Identifying themselves as Jesus Christ's storm troopers, German Christians overreached in their attempt to fully coordinate the
Protestant Church along National Socialist lines. On the one hand,
Nazi leaders were not interested in making even a racialized Protestant Church central to National Socialism (and in 1937 and 1938,
they launched a campaign to pressure party members to leave the
church). On the other, conservatives objected to the whole German
Christian notion that a "second German reformation" was at hand.
The turning point came when, to frantic applause at a November
13, 1933, assembly in the Sportpalast, one leading German Christian
pastor urged Protestants to liberate themselves from the Old Testament's "usurious Jewish morality" with its tales about "cattle trad-
ers and pimps." It was necessary to purge the New Testament of its
theology of "meekness and sin" to remake the "crucified one" into
a completely "heroic figure." German Christians even proposed
replacing the Old Testament with "100% German mythology—
Wotan for Moses, Siegfried for Saul." Saints of the new religion
would include war heroes such as Germany's greatest ace, Manfred von Richthofen. These attacks on sacred texts strengthened
the resolve of the dissenting faction of the Confessing Church to
maintain "the church as church." Their objections constituted one
of the few deliberate attempts by institutions to restrict the influence of the Nazis, though they never coalesced into a wider front,
not even on the issue of Jews. The Confessing Church's references
to "baptized Jews" and "converted Jews" seemed to uphold the idea

that "Jewishness" constituted an almost biologically immutable quality.[31] Neither the Protestant nor the Catholic Church, which also guarded its autonomy on doctrinal issues, stood in the way of the "national community" and the racial and military obligations it required.

Pastors and priests might stand their ground on Sundays, but they could also see how dramatically Nazism had shifted the ground they stood on. The arguments about flags, Hitler portraits, and swastikas and the appeals to nation, race, and the Führer, as well as to God, Christ, and the Holy Word, all indicated the extraordinary force the National Socialist revolution accumulated as it usurped everyday life. More and more Germans accepted the Nazis because they found the promise of national unity and national renewal compelling. They saw themselves in an unexpectedly bright light when they learned new lessons in geography (the unity of all Germans), history (Germany's suffering and salvation), and biology (the "community of blood") during all the other days of the week. As National Socialist ideas about social solidarity and racial uplift gained legitimacy, skeptics found it harder to resist the regime's gravitational pull. From January to May 1933—a span of just one hundred days—the fragmented religious and party-political landscape appeared to have fused into a genuine people's community. This transformation justified violence against unreconciled remnants who appeared traitorous. With each new show of unity, opponents of the Nazis found themselves pushed further to the margins.

A FEW WEEKS after the March elections, forty-four-year-old Luise Solmitz walked along "dangerous streets" where, to her surprise, "the men of the working classes [and] little boys, who all wore badges" greeted her with a *Heil Hitler!*: "That generated a friendly forth-and-back, such a sense of community with these strangers—Hitler's *Volksgemeinschaft.*" She went so far as to explore Hamburg's Gängeviertel, a back-street district near the harbor long regarded as a "breeding ground" for delinquency, prostitution, and communism. In 1933, she suddenly discovered "unimaginably lovely nooks and crannies." With crooked, narrow streets and timbered wooden houses, the district became a favorite weekend destination for "painters and artists."[32] Solmitz recovered an uncomplicated sense of belonging to her city and her country, which in her eyes had finally healed itself after the wounds of 1918. Germany had found the way back to its true self. "From the most simple and remote farmstead, on to the village and small town, and all the way to the big city, there is a completely transformed character to life," wrote one journalist who undertook a "journey through an awakened country" the week after the election, writing, "The great miracle of rediscovering ideals has become reality."[33] People wanted to find images of unity, and because of that desire, its illusion manifested its reality.

The National Socialists manufactured the pastoral of the Third Reich, just as Solmitz had in her own mind. The fashioning of such myths relied on four big celebrations in three months: the torchlight parade on January 30, the Day of the Awakening Nation on March 4, the Day of Potsdam on March 21, and the Day of National Labor on May 1. With each event, the Nazis attracted more participants and staged a more complex choreography. They successfully mobilized local places into the national program and exploited the power of radio to persuasively represent themselves and the "ordinary" representatives they selected as speakers for the nation. Together, these four mass festivals created an unprecedented calendar of national movement in which the German people experienced the new "day" as a turning point in history. New modes of social interaction, the supplanting of the individual, in the streets made legible Nazi ideas about the unity and singularity of the German nation, the people, and the race. These "geography lessons" consolidating national space were augmented by "history lessons," which honored sentimental attachments to the imperial past, underscored the illegitimacy of the Weimar present, and made urgent the need to embrace the militarized National Socialist future. The festivities invited Germans who had until recently so bitterly opposed each other in partisan conflict to reimagine their shared attachment to the nation. While some observers emphasized the falseness of this projection of national unity, most felt the eruption of a new patriotic feeling, even if they didn't know how far it had spread or how true it was. Throughout the Third Reich, Germans debated exactly how the collective nouns "Germans" and "Nazis" overlapped.

The Day of Potsdam, on March 21, was the first day of spring. As the official celebration opening the newly elected Reichstag, it also gave the Nazis the first opportunity to organize a state ceremony in full National Socialist style. For Joseph Goebbels this meant that "the nation" would not simply listen to a daylong broadcast of the events but also decorate houses and balconies with the new national flags, join in torchlight processions through the streets, and light bonfires in hills. The ceremony was held in Potsdam's Garnisonkirche, where Frederick the Great lay buried. The Day of Potsdam connected Hitler with revered Prussian traditions, the Hohenzollern dynasty, and the founding of the German Reich some sixty years earlier. It saluted the heroic sacrifices of the Great War, represented by the "hero of Tannenberg," President Paul von Hindenburg, the man Hitler had so vigorously opposed in presidential elections just one year earlier. Thousands of *akpool* postcards depicted a deferential Hitler shaking Hindenburg's hand with a slight bow to seal the union of new and old Germany. The fanfare of military music and church bells and the intimate scene in the Garnisonkirche made for a great radio broadcast. "With tears, we found our way to each other," reported Luise Solmitz. "The grocer, the shoemaker, the delicatessen owner—in short, everyone we spoke to."[34]

But Hitler's gesture of deference hardly meant that he accepted the authority of tradition. It was really the other way around. Hitler had skipped the morning church services in Potsdam to accompany Goebbels to the graves of fallen SA men in Berlin, signaling the priority of the movement over the ceremony. Moreover, the Day of Potsdam served to cement Hitler's power, since all the parties represented in the new Reichstag (with the exception of the principled Social Democrats), voted to suspend the constitution two days later. The powers of the executive then passed to the chancellor.

The crowds mobilizing in the streets, voting with their bodies, constituted the real Reichstag. It was a Tuesday, and the Day of Potsdam interrupted normal workday routines. Businesses were encouraged to close from ten o'clock to two o'clock so that employees could listen to the broadcast. Authorities canceled classes to emphasize to schoolchildren gathered around the radio that they were experiencing "a new epoch in German history." The special programming extended through the entire day so that broadcasters became the "voice of the nation" as they reported on the crowds streaming into Potsdam, described the events unfolding in the Garnisonkirche, and then transmitted a short address delivered by a blind veteran of the Great War. On this Day of Potsdam, the veteran pronounced that "it was once again spring in Germany"; after "eighteen years of darkness," it was "once again light and beautiful."[35] Across the country, the radio was in the middle of the events, bringing together neighbors gathered in kitchens and taverns to listen to the broadcast. People purchased hundreds of thousands of flags—and when these sold out, sewed together the black-white-red colors—and joined in the street processions in the evening. The Day of Potsdam mobilized millions of Germans in a way that allowed participants to see—to feel—themselves making history as a newly awakened *Volk*.

All accounts stressed the unifying strokes of the Day of Potsdam. "Never before have we had representation," commented the *Kölnische Zeitung*, "in which pure national idealism was so plainly evident." Matthias Mehs saw that almost every householder in Wittlich had put out a black-white-red flag. Thousands of people gathered around loudspeakers to hear the noontime broadcast and enthusiastically join in the singing of the national anthem. Crowds stood "shoulder to shoulder" in Berlin's Lustgarten. Spectators clambered up on statues, window ledges, and street signs. "The really smart ones had taken step ladders from home," placing family members on the rungs from top to bottom. In Braunschweig, the SA brought up the rear of the parade and received the greatest applause: "hats flew off heads, arms rose in salute."[36]

Observers continued to scrutinize the signs of unanimity, noting, for example, that there were more black-white-red imperial flags in the old Prussian city of Potsdam and more swastika flags in Berlin. But most participants considered which flag they flew less important than their involvement in the daylong drama—their experience of what they felt was history in the making. The active roles Germans played throughout the Day of Potsdam generated new affinities with the National Socialist regime and the new age it inaugurated.

As a screenwriter, Erich Ebermayer understood how stage management deceived, but on the Day of Potsdam, he nevertheless acted in the national drama, commenting, "Not even we could exclude ourselves." This was the secret to National Socialist success; Hitler's party represented itself as the legitimate, inevitable steward of the nation while not claiming to be its equivalent. As soon as Ebermayer hauled "the old black-white-red flag from the world war" up from the basement and stored away "the good, disgraced, betrayed, never sufficiently appreciated" black-red-gold flag of the republic, he conceded that a new era had begun. Upstairs, he listened to the ceremonies with his father, who was "deeply moved," and his mother, who had "tears in her eyes." Just the day before, he had reported on "big camps" in Dachau and Oranienburg.[37] Yet the desire to be part of national unity was so strong that it pulled even an anti-Nazi such as him into the new political community.

Ebermayer's contradictory position shows that it was possible to hate the Nazis but still love the Third Reich. It also reveals how the public was rapidly reassembling, perhaps with some reserve, often with a few conditions, around the new Germany. This centripetal force, pulling in people who did not stand with the Nazis, meant there was no more ground on which to oppose the revolution. Ceremony completely overrode the political division that had been so strong just a few weeks earlier. No one wanted to be a Communist anymore.

The Day of National Labor, on May 1, 1933, performed the same sorts of rearrangements, claiming and codifying a date—that is, time—that had long been associated with the Nazis' political enemies. A few days after the Potsdam ceremonies, Hitler agreed to Goebbels's suggestion that the regime declare the first of May, which that year fell on a Monday, as a paid holiday and organize an elaborate commemoration to honor German workers. Socialists around the world had celebrated May Day as a festival of labor since the 1880s, but in Germany they had failed to get official recognition. The Nazis now offered to legitimize the workers' day in a deliberate bid to win over the working class.

The Day of National Labor crafted a spectacle of national unity that was difficult to deny or resist. Visitors to even the smallest towns in Germany could see how local citizens followed Goebbels's cue to "decorate your houses and the streets of your cities and villages with fresh greenery and the flags of the Reich! The pennant of national revival should flutter from every automobile and every truck! There should not be a train or streetcar in Germany without flowers and greenery! The flags of the Reich will fly over factory towers and office buildings! No child without a little [flag]."[38] For one traveler, the new picture of the Reich hardly differed from the moment he crossed the Swiss border in Singen, with a "forest of swastika flags," until he arrived in Berlin, where he got off the train and found his taxi decorated with paper flowers more colorful than a Bavarian "church processional." The man could hardly make out his driver behind the "tangle of green branches."[39]

The Nazis excelled at building elaborate stage sets that were dismantled the next day. Indeed, the spectacle of May 1 was followed on May 2 with storm troopers' sealing off and taking over the operations of the socialist Free Trade Unions and incorporating them into what became the German Labor Front, an integral part of the National Socialist apparatus. This dramatic sequence of events appeared to be a typical Nazi combination of flattery and oppression. But the Day of National Labor was more than an evanescent virtual reality conjuring something that was not really there. When the party's propagandists congratulated the "German people" for having "staged the greatest play imaginable," they put the emphasis on the fact that the people had played an active part in putting on the show.[40] Thousands of Germans had built the proscenium and stepped onstage, a threshold experience in which they reimagined themselves as recognizable, honored parts of the nation. The Day of National Labor did not turn Germans into Nazis, but it did invite them to reflect on their place in the Fatherland and its history.

As was the case on the Day of Potsdam, the emphasis was on movement—walking to and walking with National Socialism. Accompanied by a national radio broadcast, people were on the move all day long on May 1, heading from the band concerts in the market square in the morning to the gigantic assembly to hear Hitler's speech in the evening. National Socialism aimed to break down the insulated milieus—the boxes that kept Catholics, workers, and middle-class professionals apart. When Germans from all walks of life left their neighborhoods to march together in the afternoon, displaying in traditional costumes the part they played in national life and meticulously decorating floats and wagons, they demonstrated their willingness to walk into the Third Reich. Hand-drawn posters heralded the "new age," celebrated the German pastoral, and embraced Hitler as one of their own; in Bochum, carpenters marched under a sign that expressed their own personal pride in the new Germany: "With a plane firm and fine, Hitler smooths Germany back in line."[41] Even a disbeliever like Matthias Mehs heard the people's voice. After seeing a contingent of barbers marching by and admonishing men who owned their own razors, "Do You Want to Doom Our Craft?" Mehs went into town to get a shave. The new Reich persuaded him to put community over self.[42]

All the busy activity came to a halt in the evening with Hitler's nationally broadcast speech, preceded by two minutes of silence. The hush created a sense of anticipation that punctuated the "powerful moment of community" connecting "all classes and estates."[43] Throughout the following years, the silence that only radio could compellingly create was the means to express the fate of the nation; customers in cafes and restaurants were expected to remain silent and even to stand up when radios broadcast the evening news, and during the war "total air silence" preceded special bulletins.[44] Despite ninety powerful loudspeakers set up at Tempelhof Field in Berlin, not everyone could make out Hitler's words. But even on the periphery of the scene, everyone heard the radio silence that pulled together a single listening community. Silence was an unexpected means by which the regime co-opted the body and arrayed it in the formations of the Third Reich.

The sheer movement of people through the streets over the course of the day signaled the reoccupation of German space by the *Volk*. Whereas May Day celebrations during the Weimar Republic had set workers apart along the divide of class, the Day of National Labor was designed to overcome political fragmentation. Radio embellished the "geography lesson" to introduce a shared German homeland. By repeatedly cutting from events in Tempelhof to reportage from onboard the zeppelin to folksy interviews that widened the perspective to far-flung outposts of the Reich and back again, the radio created a single audio space across Germany.[45] Gathered together in the streets or at home to listen to Hitler's speech, millions of Germans incorporated the message of the Day of National Labor even before they had heard it articulated. In the end, Nazi spectacle sought to re-create for every person the experience of Adolf Hitler when he stepped into the patriotic crowd on Munich's Odeonsplatz on August 2, 1914, and recognized how his personhood corresponded with Germany's national and racial identity.

The Day of National Labor was an unabashed celebration of the newly awaked German people. It was also May Day and aimed to demonstrate that "Germany honors labor." When Germany's new ocean-crossing zeppelin circled over the city as part of its twenty-six-hour tour of the nation, it displayed the mechanical skills of German laborers as part of a wider spectacle of national power. In the nationally broadcast events from Berlin, German workers played the major roles. All day long, as Berliners tramped to the parade grounds at Tempelhof, the radio played the songs of "miners, farmers, and soldiers," broadcast a "symphony of work," and featured interviews with (specially selected) ordinary fellows: a dockworker from Hamburg, an agricultural laborer from East Prussia, a metal worker from the (French-occupied) Saar, a miner from the Ruhr, and a vintner from the Mosel Valley. They were the links that composed the great chain of German being, in which a roster of hometowns defined the professions of a people who had recently been sorted by social class.[46]

Most participants did not pay close attention to what Hitler was saying, but the text revealed how he sought to occupy the position of Social Democrats. Hitler, who wore a gray suit with a white carnation rather than a brown SA uniform and swastika pin, spoke to workers as patriots who had served honorably in the war and built Germany's industrial strength—and also as victims oppressed by liberalistic economic orthodoxies. He employed the rhetoric of compassion to recognize the perspective of the working class. Acknowledging social divisions in the past, he attempted to dissolve them for the future. In this way, Social Democracy figured not so much as an opponent of National Socialism as a relic of an older time that had outlasted its usefulness.[47]

With his references to World War I, Hitler sought out the historical ground where the Nazis might have something in common with workers who had been "good comrades" in the trenches. This was the "history lesson." It sought to integrate workers into Germany's past, to reimagine shared collective experience, and thereby to reestablish the national whole. About one-third of all male voters in 1933 had served in the war, and in the last years of the Weimar Republic, they had become receptive to messages honoring the warrior if not the war. Every Sunday, beginning in 1932, crowds inspected the newly installed honor guard, led by a military band, as it marched under the Brandenburg Gate and up the grand boulevard Unter den Linden.[48] Erich Maria Remarque's antiwar novel *All Quiet on the Western Front* was a runaway success in 1929, but in subsequent years audiences also thrilled to films such as Gustav Ucicky's submarine thriller *Morgenrot* (1933), which combined heroic sacrifice with a love story and played as a standard feature in suburban movie houses. Adolescents avidly collected picture cards of the war that could be fished out of cigarette packages. Thus, the memory of the war allowed Social Democrats and other non-Nazis to slip into the Third Reich not by repudiating their autobiographies but by reconfiguring them. In Hämelerwald, Karl Dürkefälden wrote about his brother who took "more interest in tradition" after the "changeover." Willi kept pestering his mother about the whereabouts of his wartime letters and diaries.[49] When two-thirds of all veterans, an astonishing 7.3 million, took the opportunity in summer 1934 to make the effort to fill out an application to receive the "Honor Cross of the World War," they acknowledged the importance of war service to German identity as well as the legitimacy of the Nazi state to act as the executor of the wartime past.[50] German men, including working-class men, saw themselves as the Nazis said they should, as "good comrades."

On May 2, the press reported on the previous day's display. The *Berliner Morgenpost*, its masthead wrapped in fir sprigs, raved about "the largest demonstration of all times." Louis Lochner of the Associated Press agreed: "It was the biggest thing of its kind ever staged anywhere in the world."[51] The numbers bear this out. The Berlin Transport Company (BVG) reported a total of 2.1 million riders on buses, subways, and streetcars, a record number, while the German railways transported another 1.5 million around the city of 4 million inhabitants (on a busy Sunday before Christmas, total ridership was about 2.9 million). In the closely watched "red" region of the Ruhr, 200,000 participants assembled in Dortmund, 100,000 in Bochum, and, in a frenzy of "enthusiasm without end," 120,000 in Gelsenkirchen, "the city of a thousand fires," half of whose 200,000 inhabitants were Catholic and most of whom were ordinary miners. Twenty-five thousand spectators accompanied the parade with 130 decorated floats in sleepy Detmold, a town of 17,000 inhabitants. In precincts across Germany, the Day of National Labor was in fact "the largest demonstration of all times."[52] Was this a case when quantity was transformed into quality, when the millions on the streets manifested a new spirit animating the Third Reich, when the BVG indicated something profound about the NSDAP?

The editors of the *Berliner Morgenpost* imagined the write-up in a "history book in the year 2000": "In spring 1933, the German people, divided and at odds, discovered its community of destiny. After the initial hesitation of many parties, which the Day of Potsdam did not completely overcome, the will to unity blazed a path with such elementary force that in the course of a few weeks, even days, the work of reconciliation culminated in the greatest demonstration of all times on Monday, the first of May." What did history books from the year 2000 really write about the Day of National Labor? In his 1998 biography of Hitler, Ian Kershaw concludes that "many who were far from sympathetic to National Socialism were moved by the occasion." For him, the Day of National Labor represented a successful attempt to win over the "48 percent" who had not voted for Hitler's government on March 5. Richard Evans, who analyzed "the coming of the Third Reich" in 2003, is more skeptical. While "the media blared forth their celebration" that workers had been won over to the new regime, attendance was not entirely voluntary, since workers only got paid if they participated in the march, and "the atmosphere was less than wholly enthusiastic."[53]

It is fun to cite on Evans's behalf the accounts of participants who cut the line. "As the parade passed a pissoir, I said to myself, 'In you go,'" remembered one worker on the way to Tempelhof. Communists from the Wallstrasse in Charlottenburg also needed to "buy cigarettes" or suffered from a "weak bladder."[54] Yet when two workers who ducked out of line to take a pee returned to their flats in Friedrichshain, one of Berlin's proletarian districts, they found that neighbors had draped the tenement facades with Nazi bunting. The two men circumvented party officials at work, yet "nearly fell over" at the sight of so many Hitlerites at home.

The Nazis felt confident enough about the spirit of the ceremonies to arrange a special tour of the festivities in Bremen for select groups of concentration camp inmates. According to an eyewitness, "One group was forced to take a city tour in order to look at the working-class tenements 'decorated' with swastika flags," while another watched the May parade from a nearby police station. When the inmates returned in the evening, the guards compelled Social Democrats and Communists to report on what they had seen. Prisoners could not disguise the genuine "disappointment, fury, and dismay" they felt. In this instance, at least, political opponents accepted Nazi show as political reality.[55]

The speed and scale with which Germans accommodated themselves to the National Socialist regime in the six weeks between the Day of Potsdam and the Day of National Labor are remarkable. Looking back on the Day of National Labor ten years later, Goebbels apprized what it had achieved. "Only at that point was the National Socialist state on stable foundations,"[56] he concluded. It was no coincidence that a few days after the Day of National Labor, Annie Wächter wrote to her sister to guess which of their relatives were "now Nazis too." Her own "decidedly left-wing" neighbors in the Silesian town of Saarau had "all at once taken up patriotism."[57] In Hämelerwald, Karl Dürkefälden expressed dismay at how quickly his father, mother, and sister Emma had turned into enthusiastic supporters of the Nazis. As far as his father was concerned, "the Nazis could do no wrong." "Ordnung mot sein," his father said about the violence. "You have to have order." On the Day of National Labor, almost everyone in the village seemed caught up in the excitement. The streets were full. However, Karl and his wife, Gerda, "stayed at the kitchen window because we didn't want to join in shouting hail to Adolf Hitler. And I didn't want to take off my hat during the 'Horst Wessel Song.'" Karl may have been inside his house looking out, but he was on the outside looking in on a reconstituted Nazi community.[58]

The national "days" of celebrations calibrated Germans to the Third Reich. Calibration: this is an important concept in understanding the times. Already on January 30, 1933, diarists celebrated the "beginning of a new era" and a "new page in the book of history." "At last, at last," wrote Elisabeth Gebensleben, "the goal has been reached; now a beginning." With the frequent use of the word "finally," diarists expressed the enormous hopes and expectations invested in the new regime. They wrote in all capitals or underlined the name Adolf Hitler and doodled swastikas or sketched black-white-red flags on the margins of their chronicles to reinforce the significance of the red-letter date. In many cases, the first day of the Third Reich was a catalyst for young Germans to take up diary writing; national "awakening" prompted personal reflection. Nazi events generated personal entries: "Hitler Reich Chancellor" (January 30), "In the evening listened to Hitler's speech on the radio" (February 2); "Reichstag Elections" (March 5); "No school in observance of the election victory" (March 9); "Listened to the opening of the Reichstag—Hindenburg and Hitler—on the radio" (March 21).[59] Hitler and such seminal dates even intruded into barebones diaries recording expenditures, visits, weather, and baby nap times.

Diarists such as Karl Dürkefälden wrote about the difficulty of grappling with the new times and their estrangement from friends and family who lined up with the National Socialists. The diary became a space for private consolation and personal testimony. "It will soon come to the point that one can only speak with oneself, and then the diary thereby becomes very valuable," wrote one German Jew; "otherwise one forgets what one asked oneself and how one answered and what were the questions the era posed." Diaries would leave a "clear picture" of the "crock of nonsense" that "we have lived through." (Walter Tausk "lived through" some but not all of the Third Reich. The fifty-one-year-old veteran of the war was deported to Kovno on November 25, 1941, and four days later, on arrival, after stripping naked, he was machine-gunned to death. In his Breslau apartment, he left nine suits, two winter coats as well as a summer one, three hats, two sweaters, twenty shirts, ten pairs of underwear, twenty ties and thirty-six collars, five pairs of shoes, and twenty-four pairs of socks, as well as a violin, a suitcase filled with books, and the diary.[60])

Just as many pages were filled by writers who used detail and reiteration to record the ways they felt reconnected to the destiny of the German people and regained energy in their own lives. To understand the momentousness of the German revolution, argued one observer, "future historians" would require the testimony of "genuine" experience that only contemporary diarists could provide. "The coming centuries" have assigned a "huge task" to "those alive today." "A new page in the book of history has turned, for the history of Germany as well as for my own history," reflected one university student upon his conversion to National Socialism in May 1933.[61] Despite her daughter's exasperation, Elisabeth Gebensleben's letters went on and on about Hitler, about the Nazis, about the new Germany. Explaining her obsessiveness but also her righteousness, Elisabeth quoted the Gospel according to Matthew: "For out of the abundance of the heart, the mouth speaks." With the birth of a new era, words tumbled out. In a reflection titled "Christmas 1933," one middle-aged man, a post office employee, stepped back to take stock of the events of the year. "For out of the abundance of the heart, the mouth speaks," he opened his avowal of thanksgiving to the Nazis for granting him a new sense of purpose as a volunteer for the Hitler Youth. "I have once again found a connection," he explained, "a connection to my paddling hobby" and, at the same time, "a connection to the great cause of Hitler! That is what is really most exhilarating." He continued, "I am walking on air. . . . I have never been so happy to be alive. I've got plans, and a passion for work."[62] The daily pages of the diary turned the pages of world history. These are the voices of the Third Reich; they are not silent but energized.

The diary of Wilhelm Scheidler, a local distributor of the detergent Weisse Blüte in the Odenwald, near Aschaffenburg, tracks the experience of calibration and conversion. It comes in two parts. The first remains hidden because Wilhelm and his father packed the diary along with socialist literature and Remarque's *All Quiet on the Western Front* into a wooden box, which they stowed in a safe place on March 10, 1933, right after the election. The second, consisting of the entries Wilhelm wrote up in subsequent weeks, was confiscated upon his arrest for sedition in July 1933 and survived as part of the records of the special court that convicted him. Paradoxically, the second part sketches out Wilhelm's adjustment to the new times. It details his experience between the Day of Potsdam and the Day of National Labor: the sounds on the radio, patriotic flags flying in the small village of Neustadt, the neighbors who were arrested and those who put on brown uniforms to march in the big parades.[63] At first, Wilhelm declared his undiminished faith in freedom and Social Democracy, which he believed would emerge as the "ultimate victor." On the radio, he listened, with contemptuous remarks, to "Chief Murderer Göring," to "Big Mouth Goebbels," and to the "'great' Adolf." He regarded their words as nothing more than "yak-yaking."

Even so, he felt the force of the national tide over the course of the big days. On the Day of Potsdam, when the houses of his Communist town were decked out in black, white, and red, he admitted that "the general enthusiasm was such that it almost swept me in, but I stood my ground"; "even the torchlight parade and bonfires could not sway me." He held firm, ideology against nation, and he greeted the fact that the "proletarians" have "once and for all" united since Communists, whose sports clubs the Nazis promptly prohibited, joined Social Democratic ones. His defiance also registered his growing isolation when he saw more friends in the ranks of the Nazis. "Despite everything," Wilhelm wrote, he stayed true and walked alone; "you can lick my ass." Nonetheless, he found it increasingly difficult to live in a small town where everyone knew his political affiliation. "I am held in such contempt here because everyone despises me," he commented in April. He expressed the desire to withdraw from politics and eventually left his football club because members started to wear swastika badges.

However, Wilhelm did not so much disengage as reengage; nation ultimately trumped ideology. Rattled by the Nazis' insinuation that Social Democrats were not proper Germans, he took the spirit of national awakening seriously. "I am a German," he asserted in March, "but I also love peace and the citizens of other nationalities." Then the emphasis shifted from citizens to Germans. He came to realize that it was a "patriotic duty" to join a nationalist association—"otherwise one is a 5th wheel on the wagon"—and in society you had to be a useful part of a wagon, a member of a team.

Just before the Day of National Labor, Wilhelm abandoned the Social Democratic Party to become a member of the Young German Order to show his political enemies "that I am a German and always have been." The group was middle-aged, both in the age of its members and in the history it revered. He stayed clear of the ceremonies on May 1 but acknowledged that "never before had Neustadt been decorated so festively." Over the next few weeks, he sang and marched and drilled with the Young Germans, who he believed reflected his humanistic values. To make clear that they were not National Socialists, the German "brothers" wore puttees, not boots. Nonetheless, Wilhelm and his new friends honored German martyrs like Albert Leo Schlageter, whom French occupation forces had executed in 1923, prized the well-cut uniforms they received in the mail—"field grey with a hint of green"—and cherished the "true" people's community, which they upheld with the informal *du* greeting.

The Young Germans were the uniformed patriots who allowed Wilhelm to move from the Social Democrats to the National Socialists, from class to nation. He became especially close to Willy Eisele, a blinded veteran of the war. Wilhelm no longer made fun of the "'great' Adolf"; he dropped the irony and congratulated "our Reich chancellor" for his "very restrained" yet "very open" foreign policy speech on May 17, 1933. He came to take the special case of Germany after 1918 seriously. He also cherished the new spirit in his village: the tourists who filled the youth hostels over Easter and wandered up to the Breuberg mountain, the young men who hiked on early mornings in swimming trunks, and the labor brigades who worked to make improvements in town. "There is life here that one has rarely experienced," he observed. The Third Reich had created new life. Social Democrats who underwrote Hitler's patriotic resolve won Wilhelm's praise just as local Nazis who continued to arrest Communists earned his condemnation. The goal was to secure the "greatest and most beautiful happiness": the unity of the German people. For Wilhelm, German unity came to express the old proletarian solidarity, and Germany's freedom, the venerable liberty of workers.

This revaluation of freedom, solidarity, and peace, which took place in countless conversations among Germans, is the astonishing production of the first hundred days. In the Third Reich citizens rediscovered freedom by asserting ethnic sovereignty, and 1933 foreclosed on the liberal ideas that had forged the republic and the constitution in 1919. By the end of May, Wilhelm welcomed National Socialist electoral victories in the city of Danzig, a League of Nations mandate, and a few weeks later regretted that National Socialists had compromised on the supposedly "irrevocable" issue of forbidding Jews to practice law—this from a twenty-one-year-old man who over the Easter holidays still fondly remembered eating the matzos Jewish friends had given him to celebrate Passover.

Wilhelm Scheidler did not believe he was untrue to himself. Through his association with the Young German Order, which was banned as an uncoordinated association in July, the same month Wilhelm was arrested, he entered the Third Reich. And once he did so, he accepted the "people's community," its geography of local color and common unity and its history of passion and martyrdom, and did not question its implied enemies, his own Jewish neighbors.

The images of community exerted real force, diffusing Wilhelm's earlier words of irony. Neighbors who had at first resisted joining in became increasingly estranged from their own insistence on standing firm. "All this being on the sidelines, keeping one's guard—I don't want it anymore," wrote a new Nazi at the end of October 1933. "If you are not organized nowadays, you end up an outsider, and that's not what I want." One playwright imagined the man on the sidelines. "Everybody, even the policemen, sang. Everyone except me," reported one character who felt like "an outsider," completely "alone, like a Jew."[64] And nobody wanted to be a Jew in the Third Reich.

One feature of the Third Reich was that the National Socialists possessed a virtual monopoly on the images that circulated to represent the new spirit of the times. Photographs of the flag-waving crowds and uniformed, brown-shirted marchers can be hard not to take at face value. Produced by small armies of directors, cameramen, and sound engineers, these images made believable the existence of the national community so that bystanders at the window, such as Karl Dürkefälden or the concentration camp inmates on tour in Bremen, felt marginalized. And yet it would be a mistake to think of Hitler simply as a painter, an *Anstreicher*, in this case a painter of the set pieces displaying the new Germany; millions of Germans were first enticed by, intermittently resisted, and then eagerly consumed images of national unity—the bonfires, the bare chests, the spades—which enhanced their credibility.

Today we often forget that contemporaries in 1933 worked to become Nazis and embellish the scene, sewing the brown uniforms at home out of discounted cloth, stitching together colored bands to make a swastika banner, saving tickets to party rallies as souvenirs, cutting their hair in military style, and incorporating the Hitler greeting into rituals at the dinner table. The paradox in trying to understand the rapid emergence of a phenomenon such as National Socialism in the spring and summer of 1933 is that the props of the regime, celebrations such as the Day of National Labor, distort insight even as they provide crucial evidence. In other words, there is no getting around the necessary (but insufficient) task of explaining Nazism with elements of the Nazi world because ideas about the nation, the people's community, and race came to matter to Germans. "There is life here," reported Wilhelm Scheidler. Over the course of 1933, citizens grappled with the new parts of the Third Reich and, in their own individual ways, repositioned and reconfigured themselves, as did Wilhelm. As Germans found that the National Socialist identity fit them well, effort from below matched the pressure from above.

This meant that individuals debated for themselves the whole question of *becoming*: becoming a National Socialist, a comrade, a race-minded German. In the transfer station of the Third Reich, they considered the costs and opportunities of changing trains. They asked themselves about the importance of fitting in, the convenience of going along, and the individual's responsibility to the collective—be it simply going to the barber to get a shave. Thus the careful differentiations that scholars have made as to motivation were themselves objects of scrutiny in Nazi Germany. There was also considerable discussion about the injuries exacted by the

1918 revolution, the expediency of Nazi violence, the assault on the churches, and the morality of anti-Jewish policies. The outcomes of these examinations varied from person to person, but the questions were considered legitimate so that the *process* of examination created ideological congruence. This struggle was the dominant feature of the new time, the main evidence that a new era had dawned. It was what Germans came to share in the Third Reich.

W HEN KARL DÜRKEFÄLDEN stood at the window watching his neighbors assemble under Nazi banners on the Day of National Labor, he was witnessing the final act of a drama in which millions of Germans had taken part over the course of one hundred days. He described this drama as an *Umstellung*, a reorientation or adjustment that he attributed first to sheer opportunism, then also to heartfelt belief. It was one that people examined in diaries and debated around the kitchen table, that they experienced on the streets when Nazis forced mayors to capitulate and pastors to ring church bells in the party's honor. They could hear it on the radio that broadcast the cheering crowds at Hitler's rallies, and they could see it in the movies that replayed the struggles and rallies— the experiences—of becoming a German in the Third Reich. Let's go to the movies.

The 1933 film *Hitlerjunge Quex* retold the events leading up to the "martyrdom" of a young Nazi, modeled on fifteen-year-old Herbert Norkus, who had been stabbed to death by the "Commune" on a Sunday morning on Zwinglistrasse in Berlin's proletarian Moabit district in January 1932. It featured the famous, rough-and-ready actor Heinrich George, who had long been regarded as a leftist. George the actor and Papa Völker—the character he played—both represent telling cases of conversion to Nazism.

Heinrich George. "I ended up getting this mammoth thing of a man," recalled the actress Berta Drews, who married George in 1931.

One scholar took the measure of George with flurries of words. As an actor, George appeared as "a big-shouldered, earth-bound guy; a powerful block-like gnome; a rough, fatty enormous fellow; a brutal man-beast; a gorilla with long clasping arms; a colossus; a giant, broad as a rook; a spooky fiend; a gloomy hulk of meat; a golem with gigantic shoulders; a bearish Titan; a primal force, thick, bloated, stocky, short-necked, massive and broad, and still a sensitive nature." On stage, "he moves to the uttermost, limping, scuffing, hobbling, pacing, stomping, prancing, careening, fluttering through the room, running, swinging his weight, hopping, marching, lurching, parading, strutting, scurrying, crawling, tottering." Born in the Baltic seaport of Stettin, he spoke in a familiar Prussian dialect that appealed to his Berlin audiences. His speech could be "snarling, deep, earthy, terse, tyrannical, razor-sharp, blustery, soldierly, harsh, intemperate, imperious, commanding, broken-up, frightened, vulnerable, brusque, sorrowful, and tender" and also "cold, biting, brutal and raw, panting, flirtatious, boastful, twangy, joking," as well as "affectionate, childish, simple-hearted, compassionate, wonderfully lyrical, and gentle."[65]

Heinrich George played Butch, the jailhouse ringleader, in the German version of the 1930 Hollywood movie *The Big House*, which had made a star of Wallace Beery. A tower of strength, he was cast as the indomitable Émile Zola in *Dreyfus*, Richard Oswald's 1931 film in which the republican hero appealed to "students, artists, workers"—young people—to rekindle the love of freedom and to purge themselves of the childish superstitions of anti-Semitism and the seductions of tyranny, a message from Paris in the late 1890s very much relevant to Berlin in the early 1930s.[66] Even after the Nazis came to power, George was known to play a record of his Zola speech for friends over drinks.

Heinrich George became one of Germany's most recognizable actors after he played the role of Franz Biberkopf in Phil Jutzi's 1931 adaption of Alfred Döblin's big-city novel *Berlin Alexanderplatz*.

A poster for the movie shows the one-armed Biberkopf towering over the busy traffic on Alexanderplatz. Critics remarked that the movie really should have been retitled "Heinrich George as Franz Biberkopf" as it had turned Döblin's novel inside out to feature the unlucky, naive, good-hearted Biberkopf instead of the clash and clang of the city itself. Jutzi straightened out the complexity of the original text with a realist plot line, strong character development, and a happy ending. Like many other Weimar-era directors, Jutzi staged the story amid the gritty proletarian districts of Berlin, giving the film an authentic feel and allowing George's Biberkopf to emerge as an everyman who, down on his luck after his release from prison, pledged to become a "decent man." In the most famous scene, Biberkopf, who lost an arm in an escapade with local gangsters, returned to Alexanderplatz to sell roly-poly dolls or wobbly men, toys with such a low center of gravity that they righted themselves after being pushed. Like Biberkopf himself, the wobbly men overcame adversity without falling down. Heinrich George carried along his Biberkopf characterization for the rest of his life, letting Franz speak for him when he was imprisoned by the Soviets in 1945 as a fascist accomplice: "He always ends up on his feet. Yep, he has metal in the right parts. He can tip over, but always ends up on his feet. And it is on his feet that a person stands, as long as he has two feet."[67] George died in Sachsenhausen in September 1946.

By playing the proletarian figure of Biberkopf in a film directed by a well-known leftist, George burnished the reputation he already had after working for many years with Erwin Piscator in Berlin's Volksbühne. After George became one of the first big stars to join the Nazis, friends asked what had become of the "outstanding battle-ax and ardent militant in the struggle for Germany's free republic" they had once known. However, a wobbly man is a survivor searching for gravity, not a political militant marching forward. Like Franz Biberkopf, George was temperamental and susceptible to the changing situation on the street. In some ways, *Hitlerjunge Quex* carried itself off as a sequel to *Berlin Alexanderplatz* and portrayed the Communist father, Völker, as a plausible version of Biberkopf. The film depicted George playing both himself and the proletarian character, the everyman who over the course of events stepped from the Weimar Republic into the Third Reich.[68]

Ufa, Germany's biggest film company, probably decided to produce a film based on Karl Aloys Schenzinger's novel *Der Hitlerjunge Quex*, which was serialized in the *Völkischer Beobachter* in March and April 1933, so as to take up Goebbels's challenge to awaken to the fact that "the German people has experienced the greatest drama of will power that history has ever known." Film could not merely "follow the times"; its "responsibility was to serve as the flag bearer" for the new age.[69] Directed by Hans Steinhoff, *Hitlerjunge Quex* opens on ground laid out by realist films of the Weimar era such as *Berlin Alexanderplatz*. In the first scene, a boy, who could be the child hero Heini Völker but is not, steals an apple from a cart set up in front of a small shop on a working-class street. "Money?" he asks. "No money, hunger, that's what I have." The shopkeeper catches the boy only to incite a riot in which, true to events throughout Berlin during the depression years, impoverished neighbors plunder his shop. In the second scene, the sense of despair and impending violence is relocated to the cramped apartment in which Völker threatens his harried wife after she refuses to turn over a few nickels so that he can go out for a drink. In the third scene, after Heini returns home from work, the boy drifts over to a nearby carnival where barkers and balladeers confirm the crooked way of life—a familiar setting in the metropolis and in Weimar film.

However, *Hitlerjunge Quex* moves beyond Weimar's chaos and crime to reach the order and collective discipline of the Third Reich. In a series of didactic confrontations between Communists and Nazis, Steinhoff's screenplay restores politics to the story that Jutzi's film had removed from Döblin's novel. Heini is escorted out of the carnival by Stoppel, a local activist who invites him to a Communist outing in the countryside. But the frightening atmosphere of the urban carnival prevails in the rural camp as the young Communists drink, flirt, and play the "spanking game" to verses of "The Internationale." Along the way, Heini bumps into uniformed Hitler Youths, who, in separate groups for boys and girls, have camped nearby. Instead of seeing Nazis as the untouchable class enemy, the "scum of the earth," Heini cherishes the discipline they maintain and the comradeship they express. Back home the next day, he sings the lines of the Hitler Youth song he has learned— "Our flag waves us forward"—infuriating his father, who beats him in rhythm with the lyrics of "The Internationale," which he forces his son to recite. "'So comrades, come rally,' and each time a slap" to the face: thus the war between the Nazis and Communists is enacted on the youthful hero's own body.[70]

Heini has taken sides, which makes tensions in the family unbearable enough that the mother, played by Berta Drews, turns on the gas in the apartment to kill herself and her son while they sleep. The film requires the destruction of the family to fully integrate Heini, who survives the gas—gas is everywhere in 1933—into the collective of the Third Reich. Recovering in the hospital, Heini is visited by both his father and Kass, the Hitler Youth *Bannführer*, who conduct a remarkable conversation about his place in society. Featuring the now familiar new geography and history lessons, the hospital scene narrates in a highly idealized way the conversions to National Socialism that Germans witnessed for themselves in spring 1933. "Where does the boy belong today," Kass asks; "that's precisely the question" that the National Socialist movement posed. Kass hopes to enroll Heini in the struggle for Germany and appeals to the father's service as a soldier in the world war, a time when millions of men left their mothers and fathers to volunteer in the field. Uninterested in the ideals of the "movement," the father recounts that he only experienced movement during the war as a conscript. "On your Feet. Quick. March—that's the movement I understood and then the movement stopped" once he was wounded. "From then on," he added about the bitter years after the war, "I had to limp to the labor exchange. Week in, week out, year after year." At this point, portrayed sympathetically, the Communist father knows where he belongs: "with my friends, from my own class," and "my son belongs too." But Völker also expresses a sense of personal betrayal when he confesses to Kass, "Do you think I got fat through eating too much?" "Of course not," Völker adds. "It was because I was out of a job. Sitting around made me fat." Kass recognizes that Völker, a name that echoes the German word for "people," is ready to consider more movement and works a different angle. He pauses and asks, "Where were you born?" "On the Spree," the father answers, a bit perplexed. "But in what country?" Kass follows up. "In Germany, of course." "Yes," Kass concludes, "in our Germany. Now I want you to think about that."

Kass attempts to get the father out of 1918 and its betrayal and back to 1914 with its ideal of patriotic service. It is a lesson Völker has learned by the time he meets Stoppel and his Communist friends in a tavern. If Communists pick a fight with Franz Biberkopf when he defends Nazi views in the pages of Döblin's novel, they give Völker a respectful hearing in Steinhoff's film.[71] They drink beer, and Völker asks Stoppel where he thinks it was brewed. "In Berlin." "But where is Berlin?" continues Völker, playing the role of Kass. "On the Spree River." "But where is the Spree?" he asks again. Stoppel gives the obvious answer: "The Spree is in Germany." The lesson is almost complete. "Yes," concludes Völker, "in our Germany. You think about that." With these scenes, *Hitlerjunge*

Quex prompted proletarians to "think about that," to reconsider where they belonged in time and place, and to reimagine the streets in which they lived and the beer they drank as a part of "our Germany."

The struggle is not at an end. Local Communists (significantly, Stoppel is not involved) ambush Heini and murder him on the abandoned carnival grounds. Hundreds of boys holding the Hitler flag and singing its anthem take his place, marching offscreen in uniformed columns directly toward the audience. The Nazis would not have altogether disagreed with the conclusion of one historian who argues that *Hitlerjunge Quex* provides a "master narrative" in which "human subjects become state objects . . . political property." The final scenes compose "a dream machine and a death factory . . . a remarkable preview of coming attractions."[72]

Hitler and other Nazi grandees traveled to Munich where *Hitlerjunge Quex* premiered on September 11, 1933. "It is hard to imagine that a film in Germany ever had a premier on such a festive and grand scale," commented *Der Kinematograph* the next day. "Hours before the opening a huge mass of people surrounded the movie house festively furbished with flood lights, fir sprigs, and posters; the Hitler Youth formed a guard of honor straight to the entrance of the auditorium." At the end of the film, the audience in the Phöbus-Palast broke out in chants of "Heil Hitler!" that "rose up through the streets in the dark blue autumn night." The film was "a scene of struggle and victory, a scene of current history." With *Hitlerjunge Quex*, Ufa had its greatest success since the 1931 musical comedy *The Congress Dances*. It sold twice as many tickets as the other leader for 1933, the submarine film *Morgenrot*. In the first three weeks, as many as 2.5 million moviegoers saw *Hitlerjunge Quex*, many of them schoolchildren who attended as part of official school field trips.[73] But thereafter interest in films about the Nazi struggle for the Communist streets dropped off. The "SA films" reviewed—perhaps too attentively—the unsettling conflicts that the National Socialist people's community promised to overcome. *Hans Westmar*, a biopic of Horst Wessel's life and death, featured such dramatic battle scenes between the SA and the Communists that residents in the streets where the movie was shot in July 1933 thought that the "Marxists" had finally launched their long-awaited counteroffensive. (The banners of the movie Nazis read, "Let the Jews Moan and Bloat, the Nazi List Is What We Vote" and "Go and Drain the Scandal Sump, Hitler Is Our Trump."[74])

Before long, Goebbels, the propaganda minister, promoted films that would provide "a showplace for strong feelings and cheerful diversions" rather than "realistic tableaux or topical thematics." He wanted to nestle the Third Reich in a comforting normality, which meant abandoning the political agenda of the years of struggle.[75] Even so, *Hitlerjunge Quex*, "a film by Germany's youth for Germany's youth," remained the standard film to depict the ideals of National Socialism. The pedagogue Hartmut von Hentig remembered his own childhood: "Like other boys, I both loved and envied Quex. I too would have liked to fight and die for a great cause; I also wanted to prove myself and longed to be among the strong who would build the community."[76]

Given Heinrich George's stature, *Hitlerjunge Quex* was as much about the famous actor as about Heini or Völker. In the months that followed the film's opening, George provided proofs of his "Aryan" ancestry, the birth certificates of his parents, which noted the religion of his four grandparents. These sorts of declarations were necessary as the Nazis purged German film and theater of Jews and politically unreliable professionals, hundreds of whom ended up emigrating abroad. One in every three of Germany's leading directors and actors left the country, including Billy Wilder, Fritz Lang, and Peter Lorre (who reassembled in Hollywood, so that Germany's loss was the United States' gain). Goebbels saw them off with a contemptuous snarl: "Let them flail about a while longer in the waters, the fine people in the émigré cafes of Vienna and Paris; their lifelines have been cut; they are corpses on holiday!"[77]

It was, in fact, European exiles, actors as well as characters, who convened in Rick's Café Américain in *Casablanca*, the greatest World War II film—one that told the Allied story, not the German one. The movie premiered in New York City just two weeks after the liberation of Casablanca in Operation Torch in early November 1942. Consider the cast. Conrad Veit, the somnambulist in the classic 1920 expressionist film *The Cabinet of Dr. Caligari*, had left Germany with his Jewish wife in 1933; the highest-paid member of the cast, he starred as Major Heinrich Strasser. Peter Lorre, the child murderer in Fritz Lang's 1931 film *M*, was a Jew who emigrated in 1933—he played Signor Ugarte, who procured visas. Paul Henreid, who emigrated from Vienna in 1935, was cast as Victor Laszlo, the resistance figure. And Curt Bois, also a Jewish émigré from Germany, picked the pockets at Rick's.

George joined in the public "Declarations of German Artists for Adolf Hitler," which Goebbels instigated in November 1933, writing (rather obscurely), "I breathed a sigh of relief, as if waking up from a nightmare, when our Führer, our wonderful people's chancellor and his government, once again gave the world a direct, divinely clear answer to what had apparently been irresolvable and thereby broke the first ground in the hearts of millions of slumbering German comrades on this and the other side of the ocean."[78] George had had a hard time finding well-paying work at the beginning of 1933 due to his reputation as a Communist, but by August he and his wife had lined up lucrative contracts with the Prussian State Theater in Berlin. In 1937 Hitler personally engaged him as the director of the newly renovated Schiller Theater. He established himself as one of Germany's most prominent and wealthy artists, thanks to the state patronage he enjoyed.

Goebbels and Hitler deliberately cultivated a star system to il-luminate the Third Reich. They captured Babelsberg, Germany's Hollywood, and the stars whom Hitler gathered around him were the same ones featured on the postcards that German fans tacked up on the wall, as one English traveler noticed when he bunked down in a bargeman's lodging house in Cologne at the end of 1933: Anny Ondra, Lilian Harvey, Brigitte Helm.[79] The Führer's choice was the people's choice. Göring even married the actress Emmy Sonnemann in a pompous wedding ceremony in April 1935. Her colleague, the exiled Klaus Mann, tried to imagine what this union between the gangster and the celebrity meant. He wrote Sonnemann a public letter:

> Aren't you ever nauseated? And if you are not nauseated, aren't you scared? There must be hours when you are alone—the wedding hoopla can't last forever, and there isn't a dinner party every night. Your fat honorable spouse is out on business—perhaps he is sitting in his office, signing death sentences or planning bombing sorties. It is now dark, and you are alone in your villa. Do ghosts visit you? Behind the luxurious curtains, do you ever see those beaten up in the concentration camps, the mangled bodies of the dead, the prisoners shot while trying to escape, the suicides? Hasn't a bloody corpse already appeared. Perhaps Erich Mühsam—a poet—and wasn't it your profession to quote the lines of poets before you became the first lady of a damned country that clubs to death or banishes the bravest of its poets?[80]

The careers of many stars took off in 1933 thanks to the patron-age of Goebbels's Ministry of Propaganda. With generous fees, fre-quent invitations to meet Goebbels or Hitler, and unprecedented awards and honors, something Weimar governments had never thought of doing—in 1937 Heinrich George was named "state actor"—actors acquired riches and rank as no other artists or intellectuals did. They composed "high society" in the Third Reich and were required to play their parts in making and performing the nation's history.

It fell to stars such as George to participate in winter charity events and travel as VIPs to the Nuremberg rallies. In public events, George was delighted to appear as his favorite character, the free-spirited sixteenth-century imperial knight Götz von Berlichingen, whom Goethe popularized in his eponymous 1773 drama. Standing in a suit of armor and holding his sword, Heinrich George bellowed out Götz's most famous words: "You can lick my ass." These performances typified George's attitude in the Third Reich: loyal but a little bit naughty. The naughtiness represented the zone of artistic freedom he managed to establish for himself; the "little no" validated the declarations of loyalty, the "big yes" that he signed off on.

It took pressure to get Heinrich George to take on the role of the unscrupulous Duke of Württemberg in the 1940 anti-Semitic feature film *Jud Süss*; George, Werner Krauss, and the other actors were not so much concerned about their involvement in Nazi racial propaganda as about the Jewishness that might rub off onto their reputations because of the parts they played. George himself proved unscrupulous when, at the very end of the war, he insisted on a fee of 150,000 marks, rather than the 120,000 at first offered, to play the patriotic mayor in a 1944 *Durchhaltefilm* (or last-ditch defense film) depicting the 1806–1807 French siege of the Pomeranian fortress of Kolberg.[81] *Kolberg* was an extravaganza: it featured a cast of extras numbering nearly 200,000, a total second only to Richard Attenborough's 1982 film *Gandhi*. The patriotic feature had its premiere in Berlin, as well as in the besieged French naval port of La Rochelle, on the twelfth anniversary of the Third Reich, January 30, 1945. Despite its incendiary lines—"the people rise up; the storm breaks out"—more people probably acted in the movie than watched it. By 1945 audiences saw through the false sentimentality of "everything great is born in pain."

George himself was what the Germans call *unübersehbar*: someone you can't overlook. George, a critic remarked, was "the German as such; you couldn't invent him."[82] He was not a romantic figure like the actor Heinz Rühmann, whose photograph Anne Frank kept pasted to the wall of her room in the Secret Annex in Amsterdam. Given his imposing presence, George could speak with collective passion. During the war, it was George, as an emblematic spokesman for the nation, who concluded New Years' Eve programming on the German radio with an address "To the Soldiers," upholding the moral value of resistance at any price. He cited Carl von Clausewitz's 1812 "Profession of Faith," which Hitler himself revered. "I believe and declare," George's low voice rasped the radio waves, "that people have nothing to honor more than the dignity and liberty of their existence, that they must defend these to the last drop of blood." "I believe and declare," he continued, "that I would be only too happy to find a glorious death in the magnificent fight for the freedom and dignity of the fatherland." The pealing of the bells in Potsdam's Garnisonkirche punctuated the end of George's words, which must have struck home in a particularly poignant way at the end of 1944. For his part, Goebbels recognized that "George is still the old valiant warrior for our cause, who will go along with us for good or ill."[83]

George could not have been surprised on the occasion of a hastily organized propaganda rally held in the Sportpalast—it was early in the afternoon on Thursday, February 18, 1943, the day Goebbels delivered his "total war" address to the nation in response to Germany's defeat at Stalingrad three weeks earlier—that black limousines chauffeured by SS drivers parked outside his house on the Wannsee to pick him up or that uniformed personnel met him in the arena to escort him and his wife to seats at the front of the hall along the aisle so that the cameras could film his display of loyalty for the newsreels. George was repeatedly reassigned the role he had played years earlier when Heini Völker's father discovered "our Germany" in *Hitlerjunge Quex*.

The Sportpalast rally marked a pivotal moment in the making and unmaking of George's reputation. One biographer insists that photographs of him applauding Goebbels were fabricated and subsequently spliced in; other witnesses reported seeing a clapping George half rise out of his seat in a burst of enthusiasm. This last scenario seems unlikely since George was more the type to forget to give the Hitler greeting or to do so perfunctorily. But what really got George in trouble was his appeal to the German people to resist the "enemy's barbaric mania of destruction," which was published in the *Völkischer Beobachter* on April 7, 1945. He opened with a Zola-like indictment—"We accuse!"—and concluded by exhorting, "We are stuck in the boots of our hard duty.... Great pathetic words no longer resonate. Actions decide!" To the Soviet "barbarians" who occupied Berlin a few weeks later, George stood out as a "typical representative of fascist art."[84]

These three characters played by Heinrich George tell us a great deal about Heinrich George's motivations in 1933, and film audiences understood the significance because George was so closely identified with the characters he played. As Franz Biberkopf, George certainly understood that he was escorting Döblin's hero into the Third Reich when he agreed to star in *Hitlerjunge Quex*. George knew the public regarded him as a leftist, even if he had come to reject Communist agitprop for diminishing artistic standards. His past became a burden once the Nazis came to power. George also had financial problems. He had a young family to support and a newly acquired villa on the Wannsee, an automobile, and servants to pay for. From this perspective, it made sense to "run with the wolves." *Hitlerjunge Quex* was the perfect opportunity for George to rewrite his autobiography by demonstratively playing himself, the Communist who discovers the truth in the National Socialist cause. Generous fees and state patronage subsequently eased whatever compromises George felt he had to make.

George's identification with Götz von Berlichingen suggests that through the force of his personality and the power of his reputation, he had created liberties for himself that others could not afford in the Third Reich. But George-as-Götz may also have thought that the Third Reich was in fact the realm in which the free nobility could prosper. Like so many other Germans, George certainly did not endorse everything the Nazis did, but that did not keep him from cherishing life in the Third Reich.

Since George made out so well as a "state actor," focusing on his opportunism is easy. According to a fellow prisoner held by the Soviets in 1945, George himself admitted, "Back then, I simply could not see the suffering of the persecuted because personally I was doing so well. And, if I have to be honest," he added, "maybe I also did not want to see. A man in splendor easily becomes near-sighted."[85] Nor did he fully realize what an effective figurehead he was for the Nazis.

Yet George had also learned the same geography and history lessons that Germans like Völker had in 1933. He had been raised in a conservative middle-class family in Stettin; his father, a retired naval officer, used to spruce up the picture of Wilhelm II hanging on the wall with flowers on the occasion of the kaiser's birthday.[86] Although already an aspiring actor, George was encouraged by his father to enlist in 1914 and served honorably, completing an officer reserve training course in Spandau and earning the Iron Cross, before being discharged after a nervous breakdown in March 1917. The three weeks he spent in a sanatorium allowed George to represent himself as someone who embraced the Weimar Republic's "new humanity." But three years a soldier also provided him the credentials to work in the Third Reich.

Long before the Nazis came to power, George had renewed his emotional connections to "our Germany." Like many other successful actors, he was lured to Hollywood, where in spring 1931 he filmed the German production of *The Big House*. But George did not feel at home in California, and he would not or could not learn English. "In my bungalow," he wrote to Drews, "I am not happy in this world so bright and sunny; even though I get all the money, the ocean is still and I have a chill." After he returned home, he explained, "I can only work here; this country is the source of my art, its blood; for better or worse I am with Germany."[87] Germany became the Third Reich in 1933, but that did not fundamentally change George's Germany. For Heinrich George, Germany always remained the same place with its olden imperial past (his father), its struggles in the war (his difficult youth), and its present-day potential (his successful career). Adolf Hitler was Germany, but Germany was also Germany with or without Hitler, a conclusion that explained collaboration in the dark years and the sense of innocence after 1945. Heinrich George, along with his characters, followed the millions of Germans who accepted the Nazis as legitimate stewards of Germany's tradition and Germany's future.

CHAPTER SIX

"Your Jewish Grandmother"

FRANZ GÖLL, a thirty-three-year-old Berliner, worked in the print shop at Julius Springer Publishers. He first took note of the "Hitler movement" in September 1932. Considering the "movement for the renewal of the German people," he predicted that a "radical confrontation" with Jews, the declared enemy of the Nazis, would take place.[1] Göll was right. Just eight weeks after Adolf Hitler assumed power, the Nazi Party organized a headline-grabbing nationwide boycott of Jewish businesses under the slogan "Germans, Defend Yourselves!"

It was an astonishing moment in German history. One citizen was designated for persecution to protect another. Six days after the April 1 boycott, the government itself issued the Law for the Restoration of the Professional Civil Service. The "restoration" was a purge of politically unreliable people as well as Jews, who, with the stroke of a pen, lost their equal rights as citizens. For German Jews,

the terrifying events of April 1933, which, days before the celebration of Passover on April 11, mocked the Lord's "passing over" of
Moses's Jews in his punishment of the Pharaoh's Egyptians, came
as sudden shocks that completely changed the course of their lives.
Over a few weeks, German Jews became one thing only: Jews.

The cumulative effect of the boycott and the civil service law
closed off Germans (or "Aryans") from Jews, who were designated as both alien and dangerous. All the lively, inconclusive discussions present since 1918 about the characteristics of Jews, their
place in German society and the economy, and their parts in war
and revolution calcified into inalterable front lines along which
most Germans came to believe they were defending their lives.
As Germans converted to National Socialism so they could participate in the new community, the community itself was defined
in exclusive racial terms. In other words, consent was generated
through coercion, inclusion and uplift through exclusion. The
"Jewish question" was posed not only forcefully in 1933 but as a
matter of life and death. Consider the chants of the previous years:
"Jews, Drop Dead!" and "Germany, Wake Up!" Call and response,
cause and effect. The boycott on April 1 put forward the conceptual
outline of the Holocaust for the first time. It was Day 61 of the
Third Reich.

As revealed by the thoughts of an ordinary man like Franz Göll,
Germans associated National Socialism with anti-Semitism. Nazis
and other right-wing nationalists obviously relied on ethnic and
racial categories, and as the Nazis got bigger and bigger, Germans
thought more and more carefully about how the collective nouns
"Germans" and "Jews" functioned. In 1932, German Jews suddenly
became the attentively inspected "object of political theories" about
the future and fate of the nation. This scrutiny prepared the selections of the "Final Solution."[2] Intellectuals debated the "Jewish question" in books and on radio programs—but not the "anti-Semitism"

question. Citizens like Franz Göll scrutinized shared, supposedly defining traits with complete confidence in the legitimacy of their inquiry. Not everyone was an anti-Semite, but thinking about Jews provided powerful lessons in civics: What was Germany? How were countrymen bound together? In what ways was the community imperiled?

After the Nazi seizure of power in January 1933, Germans across the political spectrum quickly spoke up as newly recruited experts on the "Jewish question." The issue wasn't whether someone such as Göll did or did not like Jews—Göll, for example, did not know a single Jew; rather the "Jewish question" concerned the validity of the racialized vocabulary of collective nouns and the adjectives attached to them. The rapid authorization of citizens, neighbors, and strangers to reevaluate themselves and others according to two categories—as Germans and Jews, one or the other—was the major historical outcome of the boycott on April 1, 1933. The national revolution suddenly clarified and prioritized things that had been undefined, unsettled, and even unimportant (including anti-Semitism itself). *Guten Tag* became *Heil Hitler!*

Such anti-Jewish rumblings were audible early on. This kind of uninhibited speech grew out of the freedom people felt at Hitler's appointment as chancellor. They felt emboldened: "Now everything will be different." Just three days into the Third Reich, Hertha Nathorff noted in her diary that for the "first time" she heard her patients making "disparaging remarks" about Jews in the waiting room. Startled and a little frightened, Nathorff responded by saying, "Let he who is without guilt cast the first stone." In another instance shortly after Hitler became chancellor, a Jewish schoolteacher in Breslau, Willy Cohn, found the "brown hordes" that he kept bumping into on his way home from work downright menacing. "One is now reluctant to go onto the streets," he wrote on February 8. These "abhorrent brown civil warriors" were loud—marching, stamping, and singing—and the radio amplified their "screams." If you listened, you could hear the brutal slogans of the Nazi marchers—"The Republic is Shit," "Jews, Drop Dead!"—and the song about "Jewish blood spurting from the knife." But as one observer remembered many years later, "Who took that seriously back then?"[3]

Marchers' slogans soon became curbside demonstrations in which SA men wrecked property and assaulted people who looked Jewish. National protests against Jews prompted international protests against Nazis, reconfiguring the battleground of the Great War so that Jewish politics were seen to jeopardize German interests, aided by foreign forces. The defense of German life pointed the way to Jewish death—metaphorically at first (social and economic death by boycott) but then sliding into literal reality.

All these linkages became clear in the run-up to Boycott Saturday. After the March 5 elections, everything changed for Germany's half million Jews, who made up about 1 percent of the total population. Democracy and civil rights died the week after the election. After the Sunday balloting, the SA instigated a reign of terror against political enemies, wrecking trade union and Social Democratic offices and occupying city halls across Germany. And the brownshirts viciously attacked Jews. On Tuesday, March 7, SA men ran amok on Berlin's fancy Kurfürstendamm, beating Jews until, as the correspondent for the *Manchester Guardian* reported, "their heads and faces flowed with blood." The next day, Nazis, who had won an absolute majority in Königsberg, firebombed the city's old synagogue and attacked Jewish shops. Locally prominent Jews were deliberately targeted across Germany: Paul Barnay, the theater director in Breslau, was carted away from his house in the morning and molested outside town on Friday, March 10; Max Naumann, the manager of a Königsberg movie theater, was beaten to death on Monday, March 13; Otto Selz, a businessman in Sträubing, a small town in Bavaria, was abducted from his house and shot and killed in his pajamas by SA men on Wednesday, March 15.[4]

At the same time, SA units infiltrated business districts to force department and discount stores and Jewish businesses to close: Tietz, Wertheim, Karstadt, and even Woolworths, which was neither Jewish nor German. What the liberal *Vossische Zeitung* referred to as a "tumult"—this sort of critical editorial license would last for only a few more days—began on March 8 in Essen, where "unusually large crowds" gathered despite "pouring rain" and spread quickly to Hamborn, Bottrop, and Mühlheim. The next day, "tumultuous performances" shut down department stores in Berlin, Magdeburg, and Kassel, where a civilian with a Leica camera stood by to photograph shoppers who continued to patronize the Tietz department store. Police intervened occasionally, "sometimes with, sometimes without success." Many shopkeepers responded to the Nazi call, "Germans, Shop in German Stores!" They posted signs identifying their premises as "German," "Christian," and even "old Christian."[5]

In an aggressive, unrepentant speech held in Essen on March 10, Hermann Göring, Prussia's police commissar, mocked liberals critical of Nazi violence. "Isn't it normal for us Germans to finally just say, Don't patronize Jews, patronize Germans!" The police should not serve as "a defense force for Jewish department stores!" The implication: The police should only safeguard German lives, and non-German lives threatened German ones. German bodies could thus only be secured by attacking non-German bodies.[6]

That same day, as if on cue, unwittingly playing his part in the drama Göring was constructing, a Jewish lawyer named Michael Siegel reported to the police to protest the arrest of his client, Max Uhlfelder, who had been taken into custody after storm troopers smashed the windows of his department store. At the police station, SA auxiliaries took matters into their own hands. They beat Siegel up, snatched his socks and shoes, and cut his trousers off at the knee. Hanging a sign around his neck that read, "I will never again complain to the police," the "security forces" marched him through city streets. Siegel managed to escape by hailing a taxi.

These sorts of incidents were probably more ordinary than we think, but an enterprising photographer managed to take two snapshots of Siegel's ordeal. He sold them to an American news outfit in Berlin, International News Reel. Two weeks later, newspapers around the world published the photographs, and they immediately became iconic images of Nazi cruelty.[7] (Siegel managed to escape Germany in 1940 with a visa for Peru, where he died in 1979 at the age of ninety-six; Uhlfelder fled Munich in 1938 with a visa for India, although he returned to the city in 1954 to successfully claim compensation. The city museum of Munich stands on and acknowledges the site of the former Uhlfelder department store.)

Göring's widely reported Essen speech (March 10), together with the photograph of miserable Siegel (first published in newspapers on March 22 or 23), set the stage for the first big American rallies protesting Nazi atrocities. Moreover, the foreign press featured the "cleaning out" of Jewish lawyers, doctors, and directors in the second week of March. German diplomats began to feel the mood shift dramatically against Hitler's Germany then. On the Day of Potsdam (March 21), the German Jewish novelist Lion Feuchtwanger published an article on page 11 of the *New York Times* titled "Terror in Germany," featuring stories he had gathered from fellow German refugees in Paris: "people pulled from motor cars and beaten," people almost thrown out of "underground trains in motion because they looked like Jews." "Day after day," Feuchtwanger disclosed, "bodies are discovered mutilated beyond identification. Every Jew in Germany," the refugees reported, "must expect to be assaulted in the street or to be dragged out of bed and arrested, to have his goods and property destroyed, while complaints are met with a shrug from Minister Göring and the remark: 'Where timber is planed, shavings must drop off.'"[8] A few days later, *Newsweek*'s "A Week's Vignettes of Nazi-Land" referred to a "reign of terror" illustrated by a photograph of arrested men with hands above their heads lined up against a wall at night."[9]

Atrocity stories such as the *New York Times* report and the *Newsweek* vignettes turned Hitler's Third Reich into a global event. Since the end of the Great War, the Western world had attempted to stitch together an international order of peace and goodwill supported by the League of Nations. Ties between nations were woven densely enough for global public opinion to matter, especially on issues such as international debt, tariffs, and revision of the terms of the Treaty of Versailles.

Against this background a raucous rally took place in Madison Square Garden on March 27. (Throughout the 1930s, New York City's Madison Square Garden and Berlin's Sportpalast were almost fun house mirror versions of one another, both featuring advertisements for Coca-Cola and playing host to invectives hurled back and forth across the Atlantic. "Smash Hitler" cried New York; "Heil Hitler!" roared Berlin.) Thousands of New Yorkers protested Hitler's "attacks on Jews" and his "reversion to medievalism in the very center of civilization." Every seat in the arena was taken, and those who could not get in milled about the surrounding streets. Demonstrators "jammed into the single block on the south side of the building, in Forty-ninth Street between Eighth and Ninth Avenue. They were huddled shoulder to shoulder, they were packed on the stoops of the tenements." They stood together on rooftops. Uniformed veterans from Brooklyn "marched to Fiftieth Street with bugles blaring and drums thundering." (All this protest had its limits; as late as 1938 more than half of all Americans believed German Jews were partially or entirely responsible for their persecution.[10])

Unsurprisingly, the rally riled up the German public. The American consul described the response in Berlin as "almost hysteria." Such a gut response made it difficult for Germans to objectively see what was going on: that the manager of the movie house had been beaten to death, the lawyer had been paraded through the streets, the businessman had been shot in his pajamas. Otto Dibelius, the influential Protestant bishop in Berlin-Brandenburg, demanded to know how Americans could possibly know what was going on in Germany.[11] He and other Germans considered the reports in the foreign press to be more anti-German propaganda, like when, twenty years prior, the Allies had accused Germans of chopping off the hands of Belgian civilians and murdering women and children, which most had come to believe were wild lies. The atrocity propaganda was "like in the [Great] war, an angry Joseph Goebbels concluded. Newspapers protested "German baiting" and "rabble-rousing according to notorious wartime models." "All the fairy tales that we already know from the war," noted the *Berliner Morgenpost*, "have been reposted."[12] This was not an issue on which Germans disagreed.

The scandal was a Nazi victory because the antiatrocity campaign made the *Volk* feel embattled. Germans read about the April 1 boycott of Jewish businesses as a "declaration of war" against the "crusade of lies" launched abroad. "Jews around the world want to destroy Germany," the poster script read. All the excitement about the "wicked lies" about German atrocities against Jews "will hit the Jews themselves a thousand times harder," the boycott organizers promised. The Nazi Party's proclamation was set to confirm the "truth" of the "stab-in-the-back legend": Jews, acting in the interests of New York, London, and Paris, had subverted the German war effort in 1918, and they were doing the same thing in 1933.[13]

Boycotters detailed the threatened violence of the pulled punch: "not a hair on the head of a Jew has of yet been touched," a gesture of "hospitality" granted to guests who lived among the German people. Casting Jews as guests in Germany further separated Jewish people from Germanness, and the threat of violence was easy to read. A popular joke went like this: A Jewish woman goes to the hairdresser's "to have her hair crimped. 'I regret madam that I am not allowed to.'" "You are not allowed to?" the woman asks. The hairdresser explains, "Impossible! The Führer solemnly promised on the occasion of the boycott of the Jews—and, despite all horror stories to the contrary, it remains true right up to the present day—that no one is to harm a hair on a Jew's head." Audiences laughed and clapped.[14] The joke was silly because the bumpkin had taken literally the Führer's proclamation on Boycott Saturday, but it was frightening because the people clapped their hands and took such obvious delight in the misunderstanding. The denial of atrocity exposed the atrocity.

The newspapers increasingly self-censored themselves at the end of April, but editors nonetheless felt genuine consternation that Germany was once again the target of atrocity propaganda—"like in the war." The *Vossische Zeitung* urged readers to tell the truth about conditions in Germany to anyone abroad who might listen, pleading, "Anyone who has relatives or friends abroad should enlighten them by sending them a letter or newspapers or other propaganda declaring that Germany is unjustly accused, that the German people are completely opposed to the atrocities for which irresponsible agents have blamed them, and that we want to reorder our state by ourselves in peace and quiet."[15] With this appeal, liberal newspapers were also trying to help Germany's Jews by making the boycott unnecessary once the "facts" could be set straight. Even so, Germans' shame about the atrocity propaganda deepened complicity in the persecution of Jews, an indication of how inflexible the categories "German" and "Jew" had already become. The boycott ended up substantiating the accusations it was designed to protest and thereby intensified Germans' sense of aggrievement—a *mise en abyme*. For their part, the Nazis regarded the boycott as a great success because it pushed Germans to see themselves as the Nazis saw Germans—as fundamentally different from and even at war with "the Jews."

Newspaper stories and radio announcements had prepared the German people the week before the boycott. Then, April 1: "Boycott today," announced the headline in the city's biggest newspaper, the *Berliner Morgenpost*. At noon on that Saturday, the streets had become unusually crowded. Uniformed storm troopers were everywhere, but not necessarily to prevent shoppers from entering Jewish stores. The swarms of people who gathered in the centers of towns and cities across Germany were there to watch the spectacle of the Nazi blockade and to learn for themselves which local businesses were, in fact, owned by Jews. The boycott did not deter local folks from shopping by stopping routines. It lured them to town to do something else that was new: to watch and ultimately to participate in the grand spectacle of delivering a message to Germany's Jews. It was street theater, not a blockade. Shop windows were pasted over with preprinted red signs with black letters reading, "Germans, Defend Yourselves! Do Not Buy from Jews!" Never before had undistinguished storefronts received such attention as when the sharp ideas of the Nazis cut through Germany's familiar streets. Over the course of the day, local party members painted their own aggressive addendums: "Beware. Risk of Death. Jews Out" or "Attention, Itzig, Off to Palestine You Go." In other cases, German merrymakers suggested that wealthy Jews were on holiday, putting up signs to indicate that proprietors were "On route to Galicia" or "Traveling in Palestine"—in other words, the Jews had abandoned the Germans.[16]

Trucks with loudspeakers plied streets; choruses of SA men shouted slogans; fresh-faced Hitler Youth handed out leaflets. German shopkeepers posted their own signs, declaring, "German

Business" or "No Jewish Capital" or "No Jewish Employees." Even commodities became "Aryan," as advertisements promoted "German textiles" and "German clothing." On Saturday, brown eggs were indisputably "German." As the number of curious onlookers grew larger, storm troopers fanned out to occupy farther outlying districts. Pedestrians loitered around the posted guards, chatting with the SA and other passersby. The day felt like a "holiday." Swastikas and black-white-red flags affixed to buses, streetcars, and the subways commemorated this day of collective national self-defense.[17] Germans' curiosity was not innocent since the Nazi "action" controlled how people interacted with one another in public that Saturday—to be an onlooker, one had to be "German" rather than a so-called non-German Jew.

Even where it rained, as in Kiel, people showed up to watch the display in large enough numbers to require the police to intervene to unsnarl traffic. ("Holtenauer Strasse had rarely been so busy.") In Berlin, it began to drizzle in the afternoon, but the capital's streets remained packed into the evening as "large numbers of pedestrians crowded the streets and backed up traffic in front of the boycotted businesses." In the Lustgarten, it was already dark at eight o'clock at night when Goebbels assembled the faithful for a big rally, threatening "the Jewish race in Germany" with further boycotts that would end with "annihilation" if foreigners did not put an end to the atrocity propaganda ("dann werde der Boykott der nationalen Erhebung die jüdische Rasse in Deutschland bis zur Vernichtung treffen").[18] On this spring evening, you could hear the deeds of 1941 in the words of 1933.

Hitler received regular updates about the boycott. But he had more glamorous items on his agenda that day. He had lunch with Winifred Wagner, the English-born daughter-in-law of the composer, and her own fifteen-year-old daughter, Friedelind, in the Reich Chancellery. In the afternoon, he attended a tea hosted by

Goebbels honoring the film industry's "The Night of the Stars," a grand fete that took place at the Ufa Palast am Zoo at midnight. "All the stars came," wrote Goebbels, "Brigitte Helm, Asta Nielsen, Renate Müller, Magdo Schneider, Käthe Dorsch, Maria Paudler." The bright constellation made "a thoroughly good impression" on Hitler; the celebrities "feel very much at ease with us." Throughout the city, kiosks featured posters for Greta Garbo's new movie, *Grand Hotel*, playing after noon at the Europa-Palast at 2:30, 4:30, 6:45, and 9:15, alongside announcements reading, "Saturday morning, 10 o'clock. Germans, Defend Yourselves!"[19] At the convention center on the Kaiserdamm, in the city's Westend, Berlin's "water sports and weekend exhibition" was open for business.

(In the *Grand Hotel*, "the revolving door turns and turns—and swings...and swings." "People come, people go. Nothing ever happens." The lobby is "always the same."[20] But Boycott Saturday jammed the revolving doors. Some of the *Menschen im Hotel*, the original title of Vicki Baum's 1929 novel on which the 1932 movie was based, were no longer invited to come and go.)

What did German pedestrians and Nazi storm troopers chat about on the streets that Saturday? They had all been talking for some time, but the boycott gave people a new kind of permission. It seemed as though "everyone suddenly felt himself obligated and entitled to have his own opinion about the Jews and to express it."[21] Perhaps passersby first introduced themselves self-importantly, as members of ethnic clans that had always lived in Germany. My "ancestors on my mother's side were farmers from Schleswig-Holstein," novelist Ernst Johannsen took care to note when responding to the "Jewish question," or my forefathers were "Silesian farmers, who probably came from Franconia in the thirteenth century," surmised Friedrich Hielscher. It was a parody of roots. Richard Euringer also emphasized his "middle-class peasant background," while Friedrich Wilhelm Heinz cherished his "family born in the old free imperial cities." These writers considered their identity and voice through blood and history. (When Jews talked about their origins, they made no mention of parentage; they felt part of a different lineage—that of a civil society composed of citizens with equal rights: "b. 1891 in Prag" [Robert Weltsch] or "born in the year 1899 in Berlin" [Alfred Kantorowicz]).[22]

Plenty of people on the streets were not sure about the overriding importance of race or "Aryan ancestry." Adolf Hitler himself hardly looked like a blue-eyed Nordic man, and many blond-haired Jews were indistinguishable from the "Aryan" prototype. The terms "Nordic" and "Aryan" were used more or less interchangeably but created confusion too: the musty scholarship of the time indicated that "Nordic" or "Germanic" referred to European transplants in the last 2,000 years as opposed to much more ancient Indo-Germanic groups whom philologists collectively denoted with the Sanskrit word for nobleman, *arya*.[23] It was not surprising that people thought of themselves as individuals and not as *arya* since it was as individuals that they made their way in society, found a job, and fell in love. Everybody was different, which made everyone—German or Jew—similarly different.

As a student at the university in Göttingen, Klaus Mühlmann carried on many conversations about racial identity with local Nazis. "The Jewish question," he observed, "is one of the most pressing problems of our times"—pressing or popular? And "not just among National Socialists," he added. Mühlmann himself believed that "it is the spirit that builds the body." He could not accept the premise that "race always generates itself uniformly" and that "outside influences have no role." "Nature is so infinitely varied" that it was not possible to base a worldview on the "shape of a person's nose." Jews had lived in Germany for centuries. He did not understand why the children of a "high-standing" Nordic man and a "high-standing" Jewish woman could be classified as inferior to the children the same man might have with a simple-minded Nordic woman.

In more practical terms, Mühlmann warned against excluding Jews from society since they exercised "enormous" economic influence. Sharper measures against Jews would compel "large numbers of influential Jews in the world" to resort to "countermeasures." In the end, Mühlmann disputed the category of race so inconsistently that he left it intact. The reasons for his anti-anti-Semitism rested in part on anti-Semitic clichés. He was not a Nazi, and his wife underscored the fact in an addendum to the diaries, but he argued in a way that justified the premises of National Socialist racial policies. This sort of forth and back between points about universal principles and concessions on particulars undoubtedly characterized many conversations in front of Jewish stores on Boycott Saturday.[24]

What about the "mean," "horrible" "campaign against the Jews"? Immo asked her mother, Elisabeth Gebensleben. Since her daughter lived in Holland, where Jewish refugees had begun to arrive from Germany, Elisabeth's reply required some thought. She began with a concession, admitting her "sympathy" for "the fate of the individual," but also appealed to the general "happiness" of Germans under Hitler. Thereafter, Elisabeth worked to justify the boycott: "Germany is using the weapon it has" to respond to "the smear campaign" from abroad; Germans were the actual victims. The letter's next word is predictable since discussions about Jewish suffering frequently reshaped themselves into the subject of German suffering: "Versailles" had taken the "opportunities for life" away from Germans, who were now "completely understandably" fighting back on behalf of their "own sons." She argued that German Jews would have to make up for what the Allies had taken from all Germans by restricting their representation in the professions to their proportion in the population: "that is one percent." Elisabeth's reasoning was faulty, but she knew the numbers.[25]

Elisabeth also spoke up as a mother when she made spurious connections between Jewish power and Germany's "own sons." In fact, her own son, Eberhard, a law student in Berlin, was in great difficulty; six weeks earlier, he had recklessly thrown the draft of his dissertation in the fire. (His topic was challenging, but no longer timely: the constitutional issues raised by Franz von Papen's July 20, 1932, coup against the Prussian government.) The humiliating sense of wrongful injury was seemingly so deeply felt that it provoked aggression against an alien malevolent force. In these circumstances of personal endangerment, the National Socialists restored order. Germans defended their streets with the boycott in April, and Eberhard seized the opportunity to toughen himself up in an SA military training camp between semesters in September.[26]

In front of the boycotted stores, many were reluctant to make blanket assertions about Jews, although the fine distinctions they drew did not change the fact that Jews were the particular object of inspection. Sebastian Haffner was astonished at how expert Germans had become when talking about Jews on April 1. There were "'decent' Jews and others," and when some people intervened in a generous spirit to make "mention of their scientific, artistic, medical contributions" to German culture, "as if to exonerate the Jews," others "would reproach them for precisely the same reasons": Jews had "'foreignized' science, art, medicine." The fact that the Jews "comprised such and such a percentage of doctors, lawyers, reporters, etc. would be held against the defenders of the Jews. Indeed, one quite enjoyed deciding the 'Jewish question' by calculating percentages."[27] You could hear bystanders tally them up, as Elisabeth had: 1 percent, 45 percent, and so on. People might concede a great deal to the SA guards by agreeing on the bad influence of Yiddish-speaking "eastern Jews" who had emigrated since the war—these were "kikes" who did not belong in

Germany. But then there were Jewish war veterans: Many shop-keepers stood at the doorways of their boycotted enterprises wear-ing uniforms and medals; 18,000 German Jews had been awarded the Iron Cross (and 12,000 had died) in the Great War. Didn't they belong in Germany?

Liberal Germans who opposed the boycott used the occasion to make their own distinctions. Matthias Mehs had this to say about the boycott in his small town of Wittlich: "it is completely disgust-ing, it is inhumane, it is unchristian, it is a scandal." But he had a "but." "The Jew," he explained, "especially the destructive Jewish spirit, has become too powerful, and that was the case even before the war." For Mehs, it was necessary to "establish limits." Phrasing like "even before" and "the Jew" gave Nazi actions the stamp of long-standing German legitimacy, of historical necessity and prec-edent. Novelist Thomas Mann, an outspoken defender of Weimar democracy, shared prejudices against Jewish intellectuals; he could not believe that not just acerbic critics such as "Tucholski"—a de-liberately alien spelling of the well-known critic Kurt Tucholsky—"but also men and intellectuals such as myself" had been forced into exile. By making distinctions on Boycott Saturday, Mehs and Mann did more than fashion "bad" Jews by speaking up for "good" ones; they created the category of "Jews"—as opposed to "men such as myself."[28]

Sebastian Haffner, the young lawyer, stood out because he knew he had failed his "very first test" when it came to anti-Semitism. In the middle of March 1933, he was sitting in Berlin's superior court library when SA men invaded the building to clear out Jewish law-yers and judges. Suddenly, "the intruders had arrived at the library. The door was thrust open and a flood of brown uniforms surged in." "A brown shirt approached me," Haffner remembered, "and took up position in front of my worktable. 'Are you Aryan?' Before I had a chance to think, I said, 'Yes.'" "A moment too late I felt the shame"—Haffner had "not lied," but he had "allowed something much worse to happen" by answering "the unjustified question as to whether I was 'Aryan' so easily."[29]

H AFFNER HORRIFIED HIMSELF when he answered the brown-shirt's question, but millions of Germans were asked to do exactly this when the Law for the Restoration of the Professional Civil Service went into effect on April 7, 1933. While the party's boy-cott ostensibly punished German Jews for the atrocity propaganda from abroad, the state's legislation sought to exclude Jews from the German national community altogether by denying them public-sector employment. Thousands of civil servants who worked for the post office or the German railways or taught in schools and universities or staffed the courts or practiced medicine in public clinics were retired without pensions.

There was considerable confusion about who was a Jew and whether exceptions could be made for particular classes of Jews (civil servants appointed before the war, or who were frontline vet-erans, or who had lost fathers or sons in combat were exempted at first), but this confusion only multiplied discussions about who was German and who was Jewish, which in turn added to the stig-matization of Jews and then further confirmed that they were not German. Addendums to the law defined a Jew as anyone with one Jewish grandparent—as Jewishness was considered such a strong genetic trait. Grandparents were identified as Jewish based on how they had recorded religious affiliation when they had filled out birth and marriage certificates in the nineteenth century. Religion—rather than race—made grandparents Jewish, and race rather than religion made parents and grandchildren Jewish; conversions to Protestantism or Catholicism or to a nonreligious outlook did not erase Jewishness. It was technically possible for an individual to have eight pious Jewish great-grandparents (who then converted before bearing children) and still be classified as German, while a

Catholic with one nonpracticing Jewish grandparent was classified as a Jew. Racial ancestry mattered above all else, and it structured the lives of millions of people in the Third Reich.

The impact of the law was extraordinary. Thousands of Jews instantly lost their livelihoods. Others lost government contracts. Jews were moved out of municipal nursing homes. The law also targeted politically unreliable elements. In the town of Northeim, for example, about one-quarter of the forty-three people employed in the municipal administration lost their jobs on account of politics, including the manager of the swimming pool, fifteen workers in the construction office, and seven in the town brewery.[30] The purges were more extensive in big cities, and everywhere local Nazis who were unemployed but not necessarily suitable came on as replacements.

Soon almost everyone confronted the question SA toughs had posed to Haffner in the library: "Are you Aryan?" Hundreds of thousands of Germans—civil servants, schoolchildren and their parents, and, by summer 1933, ordinary members of clubs—had to fill out forms to certify under oath that they were in fact German, that they belonged or deserved to belong to the newly reconstituted people's community. This meant that individuals had to figure out the nominal religious affiliation of each of their grandparents for explicitly racial reasons, which swept everybody up in the intellectual confusion of the Third Reich. It brought "the Jew" and the "Jewish question" into every household. The number of professional genealogists soared, and the German radio sponsored a popular weekly program called *Let's Explore Family Ancestry*.[31] In May 1933, Matthias Mehs was busy procuring birth certificates for his uncle Claus and his parents, who no longer lived in Wittlich. The actor Heinrich George signed his declaration in September 1933, finalizing his annual contract for 25,000 marks at the Prussian State Theater. The Breslau schoolteacher Willy Cohn dutifully filled out the required forms. He stated that his grandparents were Jewish and also listed the battles he had taken part in during the war; he declared his membership in the Social Democratic Party, although he wondered to himself whether he should resign since the party was at the point of dissolving itself. Cohn believed his case to be at the discretion of the authorities. In June, he lay in bed bathed in sweat, waiting for a decision, when the custodian from his school came over and handed him the notice that he had been retired, effective immediately.[32]

Everybody learned the lesson of race when they tracked down their grandparents. What was the new curse? "I hope you have a Jewish grandmother!"[33] This curse fell upon Luise Solmitz, a schoolteacher in Hamburg, who in the early 1920s had married Fredy—Friedrich Wilhelm—a converted Jew and disabled war veteran. (In the 1920s Jews often sported the most patriotic German names: Friedrich, Wilhelm, Siegfried, testimony to the promise of acceptance and assimilation.) Both Luise and Fredy identified closely with the National Socialists, and their daughter, Gisela, was completely enthralled with the Nazis. For her thirteenth birthday, on March 4, the day before the big election, she asked her parents to give her the gift of voting for Hitler instead of Alfred Hugenberg: "Tsk, tsk, if you don't do it! I will be very mad." A few days later she came home from school, swearing that she could never fall in love with a Jew. Evidently the elections had loosened German talk about Jews. Her mother said nothing, only remarking that no one obliged her to love a Jew; the Solmitzes had never discussed Fredy's Jewish heritage. Luise confided to her diary, "I did not know if he knew that I knew everything." Before 1933, it did not really matter—Luise and Fredy could express opinions for or against Jews, however defined; celebrate Hitler's triumphs; and choose their own friends. They could fashion their own identities in the "shit" republic. But with the April 7 law, Fredy and his daughter, Gisela, legally became

Jews, and as Jews they had a statutory identity based on race that came with diminished rights.[34]

This is the strange case of Hitler supporters with Jewish grandparents. When the Solmitzes adopted the uniform of National Socialist law, they suffered dire consequences. Who was "us" and who was "them" was a matter not of sympathy or disposition but of decree. The requirement to provide a written declaration attesting to what sort of German one was (or was not) ended any sort of ambivalence or freedom. "Now we have it"—Fredy realized the moment had come that would dictate the course of the family's life in the Third Reich. On May 20, a Saturday, Gisela brought home the form from school and asked her parents, "Am I an Aryan?" As her father began to fill it out, she realized that he was crossing out the wrong words. With the stroke of a pen, Fredy was making her into one of the Jews she knew she could never love. Gisela stormed into her bedroom, while her mother took a bath and Fredy retired to his study. "Time pressed," and Fredy finally went over to Luise, asking her whether she "now" understood why he had not wanted to marry in the first place. "Always, always I dragged this burden around with me," he admitted to his wife about his Jewishness. "I have no right to exist; I shouldn't be here." Fredy anticipated the genocide with thoughts of his own suicide. More curses: "I curse my parents that I am who I am, just as Gisela will eventually curse me." Luise continued to believe that the Nazis' racial legislation was fully justified. Yet she really loved Fredy: "I wanted you; I want you and only you."

The star-crossed couple looked into the abyss: the status of Fredy's pension, the expropriation of savings, Gisela, suicide. Luise was bitter. She had raised Gisela to be "so German," teaching her never to use "foreign words," and now the legal forms turned even a "street urchin" from Hamburg's proletarian districts into a "premium Aryan."[35] It was indeed a matter of "body" over "spirit."

What was Fredy going to say to his daughter, who had turned "pale as a ghost"? When he entered her room, he told her to hold her head up high as she always had and asked for a kiss. But Fredy also organized his own anti-Jewish book burning, just as Nazi students had on May 10, 1933. He asked Luise to throw his grandmother's prayer book, inscribed with the words "Th. Kugelmann 1831," into the stove. But fire was not enough. The Solmitzes knew that neighbors were gossiping about the certificates and about teachers like Cohn who would have to quit their classrooms. Fredy concluded that the family was "now homeless on this earth."[36]

There were no longer any compromises, which is what the end of a free civil society meant. Although her parents managed to enroll Gisela in the girl's section of the German "Colonial Society," a poor substitute for the Hitler Youth, which all her friends had joined, Gisela was turned out of the children's club associated with the Humane Society, and Fredy, after filling out the required forms—one form after the other—was forced to resign from the "Academic Society," the Humane Society, and the Association of Wounded War Veterans, which the Nazis had taken over. Before Gisela had brought the papers from school, Luise herself had noted the names of prominent Jews who had been excluded from German sports organizations. Daniel Prenn had been prohibited from competing in the Davis Cup in April 1933; Nelly Neppach, another Jewish tennis player, was dropped from the German Tennis Association and committed suicide on May 7, 1933. Now the Solmitzes experienced the "cold pogrom" of social exclusion they themselves had previously enforced in their thoughts from the security of the "Aryan" side. Once Nazi legislation had "coordinated" them, friends and neighbors kept their distance. After the spring, there were no more radio evenings with a bottle of wine in the "Mich.'s" garage.

The circumstances did not soften Luise's convictions. She considered "Hitler's racial principles" to be "correct" and unhappily observed that her husband seemed to become more and more a "friend of the Semites." Fredy had asked that she "also recognize 'injustices' etc. Can't do it, I just can't. I will try to keep silent, nothing more. It is curious how strong blood is, both of ours." The "etc." hid everything happening that Luise did not want to see. (The Solmitz family survived the war in difficult circumstances. Fredy died in 1961, Luise in 1973. At the end of the war, Gisela fell in love with a Belgian Jew, married, and moved to France.[37])

Face-to-face relations between Germans and Jews lost all their uninhibitedness as the two groups adjusted their behavior in acknowledgment of the "Jewish question." Following the boycott, *Stammtische*, the regulars' table at the tavern, rearranged their seats after excluding the card player who was Jewish; elsewhere, two gardeners, one Jewish, the other not, who for years had chatted as they weeded, no longer spoke to one another; German children confided to Jewish friends that they could not come over to play anymore.[38] "Former friends provided the most painful evidence of a 'new era,'" writes one historian; Jews remarked on the "disappearance of friendly eyes" and adjusted to a painful "life without neighbors."[39] Averted glances, hostile stares, hushed conversations met Germany's Jews wherever they went. It was as if Jews had interrupted something to which they did not belong. "Suddenly we discovered that we were different," remembered one German Jew.[40] Thousands of Jews abandoned the country in April and May: Otto Frank, Anne's father, left Frankfurt and established a new business in Amsterdam in August. Other families also prepared for the eventuality of emigration. In July 1933, fifteen-year-old Sybille Ortmann, a gifted high school student in Berlin, took up strikingly practical courses in typing and stenography, in French as well as German.[41] The suitcase was already being packed for the journey.

New in all this was not anti-Semitism per se but the termination of ambiguous or indeterminate social relations among neighbors. For many non-Jewish Germans, this required an extraordinarily conscientious public bearing, and for Jewish Germans, it meant "social death." Even when individuals mustered the "civic courage" to shop *beim Juden*, that is, to patronize Jewish businesses, they did so with the same sort of categories in their heads (good prices, high quality) as those who boycotted them. Custom and habit gave way to self-conscious interactions structured by the unambiguous knowledge of race. At this point, Jews tumbled into a "cold pogrom" that frosted over the entire German nation.[42] Some Jews continued to identify with Germany, rooted by their lived experience of its history and culture, but more felt stranded in an alien land. On the day of the boycott, Edwin Landau, who owned a plumbing business in East Prussia, pinned his war medals on his coat and walked around town, proud to visit the stores of fellow Jews. As he passed an SA guard post, he hissed to the brown-shirted men, "I was already out there fighting for this country when you were still in diapers." But after a few hours, he realized, "This country, and this people, whom I had loved and treasured, had suddenly become my enemy. I was no longer a German or wasn't supposed to be one." Landau's surroundings shifted: "the street felt unfamiliar; in fact the whole city had become completely unfamiliar." Like most German Jews, Landau left Germany—the trains out of the country were "long and full" on Boycott Saturday with as many as 3,000 Germans crossing over to Switzerland at Basel that weekend. Landau moved to Palestine in 1934 to establish a plumbing business in Ramat Gan, where he died in 1975.[43]

If the emergency legislation enacted immediately after the Reichstag fire on February 28, 1933, served as "the constitutional charter of the Third Reich," the certificates constituted the administrative charter for social relations in the new Germany. Germans from all walks of life repeatedly established their "Aryan" identity by filling out the preprinted forms. Only once they had signed off were they entitled to employment and government services and to continue to participate in the welter of clubs and associations that made up German social life.

After April 1933, local authorities administrated everyday life. Although officially called off, the boycott remained in effect in precincts across Germany. Signs advertising stores as "German businesses" became part of the street landscape, even after Reich authorities made the postings illegal. Local officials used more menacing methods to get Germans to boycott Jewish businesses. In Kassel, on Boycott Saturday, a public installation on Friedrichplatz featured a donkey in a barbed-wire enclosure adorned with signs that threatened "recalcitrant" shoppers who continued to patronize Jewish businesses with time in a concentration camp. A few days later in Emden, a local Nazi gave a speech in the Neuer Markt, warning that any citizen who continued "to buy from Jews" risked "the same experience as . . . many of town's Communists," who ended up in camps. At the same time, in Krefeld, an SA *Sturmbahnführer* promised to treat trespassing German shoppers in the same manner as "dishonorable broads" who had consorted with Belgian soldiers during the post-1918 Allied occupation. He put residents on notice: "We will keep our eyes peeled."[44] The state of affairs radicalized in just a few days as the announcement of concentration camps on March 21 merged with the boycott on April 1, so that Jews and their friends were just like "Marxists" and other terrorists.

The anonymity of big cities made it difficult to monitor shopping. Even so, a Jewish-looking man was spotted in the textile department in Karstadt, the big department store chain that had fired all Jewish employees in the days leading up the boycott. A prepped employee explained to the sharp-eyed customer, who under no circumstances would allow himself to be served (any longer) by a Jew, "we do have a few Jewish-looking employees in the house, but they are not Jews." Elsewhere, a patron walked up to a Karstadt saleslady, contending, "Actually, Miss, you do still have Jews in the house." " 'That is not true,' [the saleslady] replied, 'this gentleman is not a Jew; he looks very Jewish but is Catholic.'" The customer "thereupon took another very skeptical look" at the man in question.[45] The skepticism was in order: a Catholic could be a Catholic by religion but a Jew by "race," a fact that looking "Jewish" might (or might not) reveal.

In smaller towns, the question of who patronized what business was much easier to answer. A permanent boycott was imposed against Jewish businesses in Quedlinburg, a town of 30,000 mostly Protestant inhabitants, including some one hundred Jews; the local newspaper threatened to expose "noncompliant shoppers" in a column titled *In the Stocks*. In Bavarian Rosstal, the vast majority of citizens signed a document vowing not to patronize Jewish stores. Boycotts could be all-encompassing. The war against the Jews was fought on numerous fronts: the "customer front," in which townsfolk no longer shopped at Jewish stores or paid back their bills; the "supplier front," in which supply contracts were canceled; the "bank front," in which Jews were denied credit; the "press front," in which newspapers refused to publish advertisements for Jewish businesses; and even the "employee front," in which Jewish employers found themselves harassed by their own employees. The marketplace was emptied of Jews, remarked Karl Dürkefälden, but "the churches are now full."[46]

The boycotts relied on entrenched resentments against allegedly wealthy, rapacious, or tricky Jews. But it was not always simply a matter of protecting German or Christian businesses. In a number of cases, National Socialists expanded the boycotts to include Jewish customers who no longer received deliveries of milk or were unable to buy a loaf of bread at the bakery or were refused haircuts. The goal was to force Jews to leave, to make the community "Jew free." "What am I going to do?" wondered Richard Tesch, owner of a bakery in Ballenstedt's marketplace. "Israel has been buying goods from me for a long time. Am I supposed to no longer sell to him?

And if I do it anyway, then I've lost the other customers." However heavy the hand of mean-spirited Nazi politicians, the much larger number of ordinary citizens, the milkman, the baker, and the barber, went along. "What am I going to do?" they asked. "I am not Jewish," they assured themselves. As a result, Jewish families faced outright starvation.[47] The expectations of the new folk community quickly shredded long-established relations among neighbors.

The Law for the Restoration of the Professional Civil Service served as a license to ban Jews from all sorts of spaces and places. During the boycott, Jews had been prohibited from entering the library and the university grounds in Berlin for the day, and in the weeks that followed, bans were extended to recreational spaces, especially swimming pools. In the summer of 1933, the swimming pool became the site of frenzied Nazi activity against Jews. National Socialists insisted on permanently clearing pools of Jews because they believed that physical contact with them was contaminating. The bans on bodies were a prelude to the dehumanization of Jews as pests or rats to be gotten rid of by pogroms. ("Pogrom" was even the name of a rat poison advertised as early as the 1920s by exterminator Albert Feldmann's Pogrom Factory in Hagen in Westphalia.[48]) Germans authorized themselves to scrutinize the Jewish body for supposedly Jewish characteristics to increase the *Volk*'s vigilance and to better keep the Jew out.

The *Hakenkreuzbanner*, a National Socialist newspaper in Mannheim, spoke on behalf of an allegedly scandalized public. "Complaints are piling in," editors wrote on August 1; patrons no longer tolerated encountering "flatfooted and frizzy-haired Lebanese" in the local swimming pool. "Slant-eyed" Jews wearing "the intellectual's horn-rimmed glasses" had turned the place into a "Jews' aquarium." As of August 13, the prohibition against Jewish bathers "freed the pool for Mannheim's inhabitants to use." Over the course of the pleasant summer months, municipal authorities in

Plauen, Sträubing, Nuremberg, and Munich banned Jews. "Well it appears that all they have left is the River Jordan!" joked the *Fränkische Tageszeitung* after the town of Fürth closed its pools to Jews. For good measure, the director of one pool in Baden also turned away girls who smoked or applied makeup.[49]

The Jewish body was scrutinized and mistreated and incarcerated when it came to local policing of "mixed-race" (and until 1935 quite legal) flirtations and affairs between "Germans" and "Jews." In *Mein Kampf*, Hitler had set a lurid scene in which he portrayed Jews as ineradicable pollutants, the premise for keeping Jews out of pools in the summer of 1933. "The black-haired Jew-boy," he fantasized, "lurks for hours, his face set in a satanic leer, waiting for the blissfully ignorant girl whom he defiles with his blood and then steals from her people." (In the end, Hitler rejected the blood-contagion theory of race defilement that Artur Dinter had popularized in his 1917 bestseller *The Sin Against the Blood*, since Nazi legislation based on "genetics" in 1935 only followed Jewishness as far back as the grandparents and later recognized separate categories for individuals with one or two Jewish grandparents.[50]) For Hitler, as for most rabid anti-Semites, the problem was the "Jewish" penis and the vulnerable "Aryan" vagina, all of which was consistent with the imagery of invasion. As a result, mostly Jewish men were persecuted in the vigilante justice directed against the newly classified "mixed-race" couples in summer 1933. Just a few days after the boycott, Walter Tausk, a Jewish businessman, reported that SA troopers were patrolling the "best cafes and pastry shops" in Breslau, throwing out "Jewish-looking people" and hauling those caught sitting with "Christian girls" to the "Brown House" for "interrogation" and "a bit of a beating."[51]

On the summer's weekends, when Germans sat outside in cafes and loitered in restaurants and hotels in the countryside, the campaign against German-Jewish love really took off. It was an extraordinary summer, blessed by gorgeous weather, its recreational pleasures punctuated by Hitler Youth outings, SA rallies, Hitler speeches, and the ruckus over Jews in swimming pools, as well as the excitement of glider competitions and the fright of blaring sirens accompanying the new air-defense exercises. The season was capped by the massive party rally held in Nuremberg at the beginning of September. Nazi authorities repeatedly warned that playtime in summer should not include playing with Jews.

If you "walk around with Jews," warned the *Hessische Volkswacht* in July, "then you will be concentrated!" The weekly newspaper *Der Stürmer*, published in Nuremberg by the city's notorious anti-Semitic Gauleiter, the "Frankenführer" Julius Streicher, policed the relationships between Germans and Jews most energetically. Editors relied mainly on private denunciations to expose Jewish "race defilers" and dishonorable German women and to rouse the righteous anger of the public—Nazi wordsmiths called the collective wrath of the newly awakened people's community *Volkszorn. Der Stürmer* explained the purpose of its muckraking coverage: "If the blood of these 'skirts' doesn't turn them against the Jews, then the fear of public scandal will." The column *In the Stocks* provided the names and addresses of individuals who had transgressed the racial boundaries the Nazis expected Germans to respect. "The Jew E.A., owner of Wellhöfer and Co. in Zirndorf, keeps a palatial bachelor apartment in Adlerstrasse 31/II in Nuremberg....[O]ne often sees the Jew at the side of German girls," for example, "I. M., who lives in Regensburger Strasse 144/II, Nuremberg. She is brazen enough to appear arm-in-arm with the Jew in public premises."[52] Reports such as these exploded the magazine's circulation from an already robust 50,000 in early 1934 (comparable proportionally to that of *People* or *Sports Illustrated* today) to more than ten times that number at the end of 1935. It flooded the editorial offices with anonymous letters. "Keep Your Eyes

Peeled!" the newspaper urged its sun-tanned readers when they visited "outdoor cafes, excursion spots, and public pools" and wandered along "country lanes and hiking paths." Germans needed to learn to look carefully into the faces of people they passed and to provide the *Stürmer* with detail whenever "you encounter a Jewish race defiler with a German girl."[53]

In many grisly examples Jewish men and their German girlfriends were publicly humiliated, beaten up, and even thrown into concentration camps in summer 1933. Incidents in Nuremberg stand out. In what was regarded as the "Nuremberg model," Nazi bosses repeatedly directed the people's wrath against transgressors of community norms. The pillorying also aimed to shut down the potential for empathy. "Well, well, ladies and gentlemen of the moderate bourgeois middle class!" Nuremberg's Nazis scolded citizens who expressed "regrets" when an upstanding businessman had been driven through the streets for his alleged transgressions: "nothing at all happened to you; it was 'just' a housemaid who was defiled. The times of bourgeois sentimentalism are over—take care to remember this from now on." The lesson was that solidarity with the *Volk* trumped sympathy for the individual or a sense of civic decorum.[54]

The public spectacle of *Volkszorn* attracted the notice of passersby who stopped and watched, either in stunned horror or with voyeuristic pleasure. But once in the crowd, they experienced collective indignation. The public, uninhibited nature of the violence sanctioned it and generated more violence.

Almost every week that summer, both Jewish and non-Jewish transgressors were paraded through the streets of Nuremberg. The SA hauled out a former comrade who had stolen a motorcycle, marching him around with placards hung around his neck, front and back. Spectators gathered round to read about his crimes against the *Volksgemeinschaft*: "I stole a motorcycle from my comrade" and "I am a scoundrel!" Photographs appeared in the local newspaper on August 2. Nuremberg's Nazis seized a *Raben-mutter* who had been convicted of neglecting her child and put the woman on display on August 16. Streicher's *Fränkische Tageszeitung* published photographs of the humiliation of "Babette Weschen-felder, residing at Felsenkeller 28." Photographs in the paper on August 18 also showed two other women "running the gauntlet." On August 28, the SA called the employees of the local health insurance office to let a former administrator introduce himself as the embezzler of more than 1,000 marks. This was "Georg Hörmann, Nuremberg, Tannhäuserstrasse 37." Two soldiers accompanied the man through the streets; he wore placards around his neck, detailing his crimes.[55]

The most spectacular incidents, however, involved Nuremberg's Jews. The report of the US consul in Stuttgart on the events of Thursday, July 20, speaks for itself: "It appears that about 5 o'clock in the morning of that day the homes of the members of a Jewish Benevolent Association in Nuremberg were searched by sections of storm troops." When householders called the police, "they received the reply that the police could not assist them." "Following this raid," the report continued, "four hundred Jews ranging in age from twelve to eighty years, women included, were assembled and subjected to degrading indignities." They were "marched through the streets of Nuremberg to be jeered at, spit upon and in some cases severely mishandled by the onlookers at the instigation of the National Socialists." The Jews were assembled on an athletic field on the south side of town and "forced to perform useless hard labor during the day; some were compelled to work in the streets, others to break stone, while still others were made to pull up grass with their hands" and teeth.[56] These horrifying events were designed to show Nuremberg's Jews and the rest of the city's inhabitants that Jews were completely without rights. To Jews who heard about the incident, through either the informal but highly functional "Jewish telegraph" or the foreign press, it became clear that they were *Freiwild*, fair game. The Frankenführer's operation was also the logical consequence of the boycott, which had authorized the SA to organize collective punishment, and of the laws that followed, which underscored that Jews were unwelcome. Streicher made street theater out of the degraded civil and legal circumstances in which the Third Reich had placed German Jews in April 1933.

Throughout Germany, the SA organized public demonstrations against Jewish men who had been caught in the company of "German" women. Nothing compared to what took place in Nuremberg on Sunday, August 6. Postwar trials in 1949 provided details that corroborated eyewitness accounts by shocked British tourists who complained to local authorities and tipped off the *The Times*.[57] On Sunday, Siegfried Reiter was accompanying his fiancé, Emma Baer, on a walk to Brünn outside the city when they decided to swim in a nearby lake. After the couple had put on swimsuits, two forest rangers approached to say that swimming was prohibited because the lake was reserved for trout fishing. They checked the couple's papers. One of the rangers, himself a National Socialist, asked Siegfried if he was a Jew; he answered that he was. The man immediately began screaming, accusing Siegfried and Emma of "race defilement." The ranger telephoned police headquarters in Nuremberg and was told by SA leader Hans-Günther von Obernitz to punish the "forbidden couple" by pillorying the two in public. SA men arrived on the scene and hung a placard with the words "I shall not let myself be defiled again by a Jew" around Emma's neck. Siegfried was forced to wear a placard on the front reading, "I am a Jew, and I have defiled a German girl," and another on the back reading, "I have defiled the German forest." (One really wants to double-click on these pathological details.) The SA set off for little Brünn, where the display did not get the reception the brownshirts wanted, so they moved on to nearby Nuremberg.

"We were jostled, spat on, slapped, and berated by the whipped-up crowd," remembered Emma. *The Times* provided further details:

The parade of the girl was carried out in such a manner that few people in the centre of the town could have failed to see it. The girl, who is described by one of them as being small, fragile, and, in spite of her shaven head and condition, obviously pretty, was marched in and out of the ring of international hotels by the station, through the main streets, where the traffic was blocked by the crowds, and from cabaret to cabaret. Her escort was formed of storm troopers, and a crowd estimated by a trustworthy observer at some 2,000 people followed her about. She occasionally stumbled and was replaced on her feet by the stalwart brownshirts, who sometimes held her aloft in order that more distant onlookers might see her, and on these occasions she was hooted and derided by the crowd and jocularly invited to make a speech.

Once the party was over, the SA brought the victims to headquarters, the Röhm House, where they stripped Emma and Siegfried—the SA men were eager to see a "Jew pecker"—and beat them before leading them through the streets one more time. Siegfried recalled feeling himself to be in the "throes of death." The terrifying procession through the streets felt like a "death march." The next day Streicher's newspaper wrote up the basic outline of the public "stigmatization" of "Siegfried Reiter," who owned a dress shop in town, and the "German girl," this time without a photograph. The "ride" of the "Reiter" ("rider" in German) also served as a warning a few days later to another "Jew bastard," "Helmreich in Lindennaststrasse 10," who had been denounced for going out with "German" girls. (Siegfried Reiter spent two years in Dachau without charges brought against him before he was released and emigrated to South Africa; Emma Baer stayed in Germany and eventually married.[58])

"Keep Your Eyes Peeled!" Germans had long watched one another, but after 1933 it was no longer a game. The imperative strove to get Germans to see through the eyes of a race-conscious people, to police the border between themselves and Jews. Both the boycott and the Law for the Restoration of the Professional Civil Service set in motion a process of supervision, scrutiny, denunciation, and public spectacle to exclude "Jews" from the people's community. "Keep Your Eyes Peeled!" emphasized the "the" in "the Jews," who had become the treacherous object of surveillance by a conscientious folk community. Germans were to keep watch in places where people mixed, in cafes, hotels, and resorts, but also in apartment courtyards, hallways, and stairwells.

In one notorious case, next-door neighbors peering from windows and peeking behind doorways in a tenement building on Nuremberg's Splittertorgraben provided the evidence that convicted Leo Katzenberger, a Jewish businessman, of race defilement due to his (probably innocent) friendship with pretty, well-dressed Irene Seiler, a photographer, who had come to be known locally as the "Jew's floozy." They were searching not for a child murderer, as in the 1931 movie *M*, but for the predatory Jew in the 1933 Nazi production *J*. (Sixty-eight-year-old Katzenberger was arrested in 1941 and guillotined the following year; his trial formed part of the courtroom drama in Stanley Kramer's 1961 movie *Judgement at Nuremberg*; Judy Garland played Irene.[59])

Nearly all cases of "race defilement" rested on individual denunciations by neighbors, and although most Germans did not denounce individuals, plenty showed up for the public pillorying when Jews were paraded around town. The processions of humiliation fortified the idea of the *Volk* by virtue of the extraordinary display of the Jewish body. "The Jew" could only be boycotted in commercial life, banned from swimming pools, and paraded in the street for transgressions if the German people shared the belief that they were part of a collective body under siege. In these conditions, the subject scrutinizing (us) never was or could be the object under scrutiny (them)—this was the premise of vigilante racial justice. Us and them.

According to Franz Göll, Germany's recovery depended on a government that would apply "the motto 'Everything for the whole,'" which he associated with the Nazis. The fate of the individual depended on the security of the collective. "Germany must live, so that we don't go under," he concluded. Given that the Nazis pursued "radical confrontation" with the Jews, the sought-after union of "the whole" and the recovery of Germany's future rested on the exclusion of the Jews.[60] This logic was already at work in the first days of February 1933, when Hitler's new regime permitted patients in Hertha Nathorff's waiting room to slander Jews. The lesson of spring and summer 1933, from the boycott to the ritual humiliation, was a simple one: the remaking of Germany required the unmaking of Jews. German life meant Jewish death.

CHAPTER SEVEN

The Administration of Life

THE DECREE of the Reich President for the Protection of People and State, known colloquially as the "Reichstag Fire Decree," made emergency the foundation of dictatorial rule—the state had to intervene in everyday life to protect the German people, to overcome the "crisis" of the republic. Extended for four years by the Enabling Act on March 23, 1933, the decree served as the "constitutional charter" of the Third Reich. The Law for the Restoration of the Professional Civil Service on April 7, 1933, and the coordinated public booting of Jews associated with it, offered a more precise indication of how the National Socialists intended to manage emergency conditions. The April 7 law established selection as the principle of social regulation, introducing a new vision of society based on discernment and differentiation. The Enabling Act and the civil service law paved the road into the Third Reich.

The administration of everyday life rested on the idea that only a series of state-sponsored measures that grouped people as insiders or outsiders could realize the people's community. The basic distinction in the Third Reich was between "Aryans" and "Jews"; yet safeguarding Germany also meant excluding "Aryans" deemed racially unfit, socially unproductive, or temperamentally unsuited. Concentration camps filled up with "asocials" as political prisoners were released. The differences between "Aryan" Catholics and Protestants were minimized, further unifying an "Aryan people." Breaking down exclusive social milieus, celebrating the military unit, and designing state services to generate racial health—these were all ways that the National Socialists created a single German people.

The sheer number of regulations designed to administer life convinced Germans that "normality" and economic stability depended on administrative innovation. The forms that Germans filled out to attest to "Aryan" ancestry in spring and summer 1933 were just the first installment of a great deal of paperwork in the Third Reich. When in the little town of Hämelerwald, Karl Dürkefälden's father asserted that "Ordnung mot sein," he was speaking in the first place about the necessity of arresting Communists and incarcerating them in concentration camps. Germans learned to live with the camps, and, significantly, they first heard about the opening of Dachau and Oranienburg on March 21, the Day of Potsdam. "Ordnung mot sein" also entailed stepping into line—participating in the celebrations of the folk, greeting neighbors with *Heil Hitler!*, and singing the "Horst Wessel Song." Father admonished son for standing alone at the kitchen window. "Ordnung mot sein" meant accepting the exclusion of Jews from society. And it expected Germans to demonstrate a willingness to learn these new norms of community building by enrolling children in the Hitler Youth, giving to party charities, and heeding guidelines to improve racial health. (All foreignness was suspect, and the organization of civilian air defense showed Germans how the administration of life depended on an authoritarian state able to manage threats posed by foreign powers.) To achieve the order on which Germany's future prosperity depended, Germans had to understand the state's right to sterilize racially undesirable men and women. These clear lines of authority would straighten out the pandemonium of democracy and individual liberty.

Germans themselves did not necessarily learn hatred of Jews. Some became anti-Semites when Adolf Hitler assumed power because they were interested in the Nazis; others did not. Yet the flurry of legislation in 1933 made the imperative of managing danger in any and all of its manifestations impossible to ignore; the new regime presented it as essential to any German recovery. The simultaneity of the Nazis' administrative innovations—the priority of federal power, the one-party state, the leadership principle in civic affairs, community service, sterilization, the exclusion of Jews—added to the legitimacy of each. That was how Germans read things like the (happenstance) juxtaposition on an advertising pillar of a poster advertising Greta Garbo in *Grand Hotel* with the Saturday boycott proclamations ("Germans, Defend Yourselves! Do Not Buy from Jews"); prosperity depended on security and vigilance. Boycott at 10 a.m.; showtime at 6:45. Reconciling these two messages could be exhausting. All around him, noted novelist Hans Carossa, a right-wing fellow himself, Germans "are being cleansed, purged, screened, disinfected, segregated, toughened up, rearranged," and ultimately, he thought, "alienated" from themselves. Carossa really just wanted to go back to the "beautiful old streets" of Vienna where things were as they once had been.[1]

Coercion in the Third Reich was unmistakable, while approval grew deeper and more extensive as Germans created the new community through their own participation in its construction. One way to get around arguments about whether Germans adjusted to or desired the Third Reich is to recognize the broad agreement—one that went well beyond the 52 percent that had voted for the national government in March 1933—that the good life depended absolutely on the administration of life, even if specific requirements appeared onerous or unnecessary. A consensus was emerging around the necessity of compliance, which was considered, justified, and applied by individuals at the grassroots level. (Indeed, the persistence of many features of the administrative state in Germany today confirms the consensus around what constitutes effective government.)

There would have been neither consensus nor compliance if the National Socialists had not been able to improve the economy, or at least not been credited with doing so. It is difficult to believe that many people in Germany truly recognized signs of recovery in winter 1933, before Hitler came to power. The newspaper articles about higher business turnover at Christmastime or the lively drinking crowds at the Bockbierfest at the Neue Welt or the magical interiors of the department stores during the white sales in the new year all expressed the depth of yearning for "normality" and the end of "crisis." Historians have often used the light that journalists believed they could make out at the end of the tunnel in December 1932 as evidence to argue that, had Paul von Hindenburg waited rather than appointing Hitler chancellor when he did, the Weimar Republic could have stabilized itself in the economic fair weather that was coming. All the hopeful sightings of that light, however, more plausibly meant that people were willing to accept "normality" even on terms set by Nazis. In this sense, the credit the liberal press gave to then chancellor Kurt von Schleicher in December actually worked to Hitler's benefit after March 1933 because Hitler imposed the "peace of the fortress" that Schleicher had wanted yet failed to build. The new chancellor brought back 1914's unity of purpose, but at the price of slaying the demons of 1918 that his Nazis had conjured up.

A lot of the stories about the Nazis' "battle for work" in 1933 really concern what people wanted to see. Matthias Mehs recycled the joke about Tünnes and Schäl, favorite characters in Cologne's Hänneschen Puppet Theater, standing on the Rhine Bridge. Good-natured Tünnes says to Schäl, "Don't you see the enormous traffic on the Rhine, the steamers and tugboats, and all the railroad trains and automobiles on either side? The Third Reich has come with such an economic boost." Clever Schäl replies, "I am looking, but with the best of will I can't see anything!" "Oh, jeez," Tünnes asks, "don't you read the papers?"[2]

But new jobs did in fact punctuate the autobiographies of ordinary Germans. As early as spring 1933, a teacher in Berlin remembered children who came to school, beaming to report the news that "Papa found work." The turnaround took some time. In November 1936, a young man ran through crowds on Dresden's Prager Strasse shouting with joy, "I've got work—the first time in three years—and good work—at Renner's—they pay well!"[3] Between these three years, Germany returned to full employment for the first time in a decade (although pay lagged while the number of work hours rose, and, of course, labor unions had been crushed). Germany's recovery also outpaced the economic growth of all other advanced capitalist nations. The pages of graphs and tables in a compilation of labor statistics all paint the same picture: like a roller coaster, unemployment goes up in the winter months and down in the summer, but the ride from 1933 to 1936 drops, plummeting with the improvement of the economy. In summer 1933 there was a dramatic difference in the amount of economic activity, compared with the same period in 1932. And by 1934, unemployment had been cut in half. This holds true for all sectors of the labor market, for all demographic categories, and for all regions of Germany.

In the small town of Fürstenfeldbruck, outside Munich, the numbers of unemployed had reached a high of 2,634 in December

1932, more than 2.5 times the number at the beginning of 1929 and an astonishing figure for a population of 6,000. By April 1933, the number had fallen by half to 1,333 and by October by half again to 722. In winter 1934 and again 1935, the town counted between 1,200 and 1,300 idled workers—for many families, there was no quick resolution to the crisis—but by spring 1934, fewer than 500 people remained unemployed. Over the years, progress was visible as Fürstenfeldbruck's authorities built a new town hall, an athletic facility, and housing developments.[4]

The statistics registered real successes as a result of ambitious state-sponsored work-creation projects in spring and summer 1933 and then a massive rearmament drive after 1935; in fact, rearmament engendered "the largest transfer of resources ever undertaken by a capitalist state in peacetime."[5] Early on, work projects, such as autobahn construction, paid workers low wages, and many were recruited against their will to live in substandard camps in the countryside, where conditions were so terrible that the autobahn was known colloquially as the "hunger and misery bahn." But as the new Reich's labor service expanded, Nazi economic policy also enjoyed the approval of volunteers, whose appearance at the Nuremberg party rally in September 1934 turned out to be a great win for the National Socialists. Thanks to Leni Riefenstahl's 1935 propaganda film *Triumph of the Will*, which featured the stirring roll call "*Heil*, men of labor," the "earth-brown columns" totaling 52,000 men with "shining, shouldered spades marched onto the parade grounds" and into German hearts. The "soldiers of labor" had "captured a place in the sun," remarked the party newspaper, *Völkischer Beobachter*.[6] The retrospective—and in many respects, tendentious—memory of the years before the war as "good times" or a period of "normalcy" rested on the easy credit the Nazis received for winning the "battle for work" and restoring to ordinary people a measure of dignity after years of unemployment.

As men and women found work, the resumption of "normal" life came with important conditions. Germans had to accept the fact that "normal" conditions were now (and presumably forever) premised on the extensive and even violent administration of life. The crisis that was so obvious in the economic downturns, political strife, and bloody confrontations of the post-1918 years largely legitimated the claims of the modern authoritarian state on the German body. Simply having to fill out the form certifying "Aryan" ancestry in order to get a government job after April 1933 tightened the knot tying state supervision and individual well-being together. It was a matter of signing up.

T HE FIRST one hundred days saw the completion of the Nazis' political revolution. Their coalition won 52 percent of the vote in 1933; they assumed total power through the Enabling Act. Yet the Nazi ambition to construct new sorts of human beings made the revolution in 1933 truly revolutionary. In April, anti-Jewish legislation had already clarified the ways in which ideas about race and biology would guide the National Socialists' transformation of German life. In this way, the one hundred days provided the first sketchy blueprints for the design of a new millennium. A clearer outline emerged over the summer, over the course of the second hundred days, which revealed much more definitively how the boycott and the civil service legislation fit into the larger context of social and biological engineering. Boycott Saturday on Day 61 of the Third Reich served as a crucial step toward the sterilization laws promulgated on July 14, Day 166. The public vilification of the Jewish body and the stewardship of the German body it implied became more radical during this period. Citizens learned their biology lessons, in addition to new ones in geography and history.

In early July 1933, Hitler gave a speech to his Reich governors in which he appeared to put brakes on the frenetic, brutal activity of party members. The revolutionary "current," he argued, had to be "redirected into the secure riverbed of evolution." Revolution could not become a "permanent state of affairs." The words unmistakably signaled to the SA to abandon the reign of terror they had imposed on working-class neighborhoods—a week of bloodshed during which the SA tortured and murdered twenty-three "Marxists" in the Berlin suburb of Köpenick had come to an end only on June 26. Hitler went on to offer the Nazi governors, who had taken control of the states in March 1933 under the terms of emergency legislation, a model of good government. He assured governors that the party would not interfere with the "functions of government." Nothing about National Socialism "obliges us to act like fools and upset everything. . . . We must therefore not dismiss a businessman," he explained, "if he is a good businessman," though "not yet" a National Socialist.

The moderate course correction was deceptive, however. Hitler went on to talk about the importance of education, of inculcating in "the people" "the National Socialist conception of the state." A few days earlier, he had developed this pedagogical theme in more detail, declaring that "the new state" would just be "make-believe" (*ein Phantasieprodukt*) "if it did not create a new person."[7]

These addresses in June 1933 confirmed the extreme and radicalizing dynamic of National Socialism. They pointed the way for the transformation of the national revolution and the authoritarian state into something quite different: an innovative and aggressive racial regime that pursued fundamental moral revaluation and extensive social and biological reconstruction. Hitler pulled fascism out of the box.

With the idea of a "new person," Hitler announced a new revolution, far more extensive than the "national revolution" in which the National Socialists had seized "absolute power" and "finally eliminated the political parties." Germany's greatness depended on transforming the national community into a community of blood. Hitler's goal, and the administrative aim of the Third Reich, was to get Germans to heed the principles of race thinking that already underpinned the anti-Jewish objectives of the Law for the Restoration of the Professional Civil Service. The imperative was "thinking with the blood." At the annual party congress in Nuremberg in September 1933, Hitler hammered away at the importance of race: "National Socialism affirms the heroic doctrine of the value of blood, race, and character as well as the eternal laws of selection." This "new orientation" stood in "irreconcilable opposition" to "pacifistic-internationalist democracy," yet remained a work in progress: "The scale of the impact of this great spiritual revolution can hardly be recognized today." To forge the "new person," Germans needed to accept a new social ethic that held individuals accountable to the collective. Nazi propaganda repeatedly urged citizens to abandon Christian caritas and what it mocked as sentimental liberal *Humanitätsduselei*. In the new National Socialist order, "biology became destiny."[8]

The construction of the "community of blood" was an audacious project. "It is not a party badge or a brown shirt that makes you a National Socialist, but rather your character and the conduct of your life," asserted editors of a eugenics journal in July 1933. A "spiritual revolution" had to follow the accomplishments of the political revolution, insisted Walter Gross, director of the Office for Racial Politics in the Nazi Party: It will "fundamentally remodel and reform." The biological revolution will overturn "even those things that seem today completely solid," the young thirty-year-old added ominously.[9] What National Socialist leaders, from Hitler to the local SA *Sturmmann*, announced in summer 1933 was nothing less than a biological engineering project that would affect the lives of millions of Germans and pave the way to global war and genocide.

In no other period in modern history did citizens identify their own personal happiness with the fate of the nation as much as Germans did in the 1930s. War and defeat, then revolution in 1918, the hyperinflation in 1922–1923, and the Great Depression in the early 1930s convinced millions of Germans that they were the victims of history. "Germany must live, so that we don't go under," wrote Berlin diarist Franz Göll in November 1932; the fate of the first person depended on the superordinate collective "we." Once they assumed power, the National Socialists appealed to Germans to fight back against an array of enemies domestic and foreign. The people's community rested on the premise that only collective security made possible individual happiness. Germans had to act for themselves. Organized just sixty days after the seizure of power, the Saturday Boycott was already a giant step forward in race thinking in the name of the community of blood.

National Socialists endeavored to mobilize Germans so that each individual would be capable of defending and strengthening the collective. This was the purpose of the uniforms, the marches, the rallies mobbing the streets in spring and summer 1933. As Karl Dürkefälden's father reminded his son after the May Day celebrations, the first responsibility of the citizen was to stand and march with the new community. Countless campaigns commanded Germans to donate money to charity, to participate in civil defense exercises, to boycott Jewish businesses, and to otherwise enforce the "race" line in daily life. Public life was designed so that it never stood still. Transporting her spunky characters from the Weimar Republic, where the novelist had set her first "modern-life" stories, to the Third Reich, Irmgard Keun caught the spirit of what it was like to be a woman "these days." Well, Keun's narrator notes with exasperation, "she has to read the papers and think about politics. She has to vote and listen to speeches on the radio. She has to go to poison gas drill, and prepare for war."[10] Readers might have wondered about the requirement to vote since there were no more parliamentary elections or competing political parties. But in summer 1933, Nazi leaders anticipated the usefulness of national plebiscites to affirm the popular legitimacy of the regime and to mobilize the population to take part in the national cause.

The outcome of the two referendums held on Sunday, November 12, 1933, to approve the single unity list for the new Reichstag and Germany's withdrawal from the League of Nations was never in doubt. And an astonishing 96 percent of voters turned out to overwhelmingly approve these referendums, by 92 and 95 percent majorities, respectively; about one in seven eligible Germans voted for the first time. The purpose of the election was to build a kind of perpetual-motion machine, churning Germans out to campaign for each other and to recognize and affirm the paramount national interest. In a few weeks, the Nazis transformed the streets into German theater: "innumerable posters on buildings, banners hanging over streets and tied from tree to tree: 'With Hitler for Honor, Equality, and Peace'—'Against the Lunacy of Rearmament.' And just now," the diarist reported on the scene outside, "lights in every window. I've never seen so many flags." Underneath this proscenium, German things were set in motion: "Automobiles drive around with replicas of anti-aircraft batteries, accompanied by the fire department and motorized advertisements with blaring sirens to create propaganda for air defense." With the props of militant Weimar-era politics, the Nazis propelled their own idea of Germany forward.

The crescendo hit when all Germans returned to the stage on the occasion of Hitler's final campaign speech. He stood atop a cable drum on the factory floor of the Siemens Works in Berlin in front of 9,000 workers just after noon on Friday, November 10, demonstratively delivering an impassioned oration. Everything about the show was written in advance: "for one hour work stops, for one minute traffic comes to a standstill—a remarkable picture like a scene in film that is suddenly frozen." With the wail of sirens, "vehicles and pedestrians come to a complete stop, and then the streets empty out as everyone flocks to the radio" to hear Hitler's speech. Scripted silence once again created a national hush. After the collective singing of the "Horst-Wessel Song," the siren sounded one more time, calling people to resume their everyday routines.

The day before the election, huge marches assembled local clubs and organizations and party formations: "the appearance of each man is an unqualified duty." On election day itself, get-out-the-vote teams worked the streets to push Germans along to their polling stations. After depositing the two paper ballots, nearly everyone felt compelled to purchase a little pin, "Ja, 1933," a personal souvenir of national acclamation (hollow but with a gold finish), to show fellow citizens that they had voted and voted with Hitler.[11]

When Germans took their assigned places in the huge marches that crossed towns and cities throughout the country the night before the election, they did so as old members of the traditional clubs into which German social life was woven but also as new members of the Nazi service organizations. These organizations were groups that the party had created as part of its commitment to remake Germany and improve life. With "muscular, problem-solving rhetoric," the new regime set out to clean up factories, carry out charity work, and promote civil defense. "People looked to Nazism as a great and radical surgery" and therefore saw "the movement as a source of rejuvenation" in public life. A heady sense of the possible made this new National Socialist era an appealing agent for the future.[12] The medicalization of politics under the Nazis pulled thousands of biomedical professionals into state service as nurses, teachers, and health-care administrators. Millions of volunteers aided racially desirable but impoverished Germans through the National Socialist People's Welfare Service, which, overseeing charitable activity, was the largest civic organization in the Third Reich.

In Braunschweig, the members of one pro-Nazi family threw themselves into volunteer work. Elisabeth Gebensleben (and her maid Frieda) signed up for Red Cross first aid courses and joined the National Socialist women's organization, while Elisabeth's son, Eberhard, the law student, enlisted in the SA. The whole family pitched in when he prepared to leave for training at a "military sport camp" in Zossen, near Berlin, in September 1933. "You can imagine," his mother wrote, "the bustle of activity at our house until late at night. Packing up all his things ... telephoning with the doctor who was able to give him a checkup at 8 o'clock"; "the last things packed, Eberhard left the station with his heavy bags at 7:15 this morning."[13] Millions of excited leave-takings such as this one took place in the Third Reich. Leadership courses, training camps, paramilitary service—this was the new rhythm of life for ambitious professionals in Nazi Germany.

These auxiliary organizations gave Germans semiofficial responsibilities. Nazi-era volunteering placed thousands of Germans in minor leadership posts where they watched over their small patch of the people's community. The SA, Hitler Youth, and Reich Labor Front all worked the same way, striving to identify a new generation of leaders drawn from all social classes. Leaders honed their skills through special workshops, night courses, and training camps. Even a naysayer such as Karl Dürkefälden served as a deputy air-defense warden for his machine-tool factory in Celle. As Germans enlisted in Nazi service organizations, the old hobby clubs, sport teams, and singing associations lost importance in social life. The Nazis disbanded many working-class groups, especially the athletic clubs, and they coordinated the rest by installing party members on executive boards or merging them with National Socialist organizations. When gatherings began with members greeting one another with *Heil Hitler!* and concluded with everybody singing the "Horst Wessel Song," clubs lost their charming intimacy. Members stopped coming. Townspeople still gathered with friends to take walks in the countryside and relax over coffee and cake or to play cards at the local tavern, but associational life withered, and the collective campaigns organized by uniformed National Socialists never made up the loss. People spoke to each other more often as duty-bound comrades than old friends.[14]

All the busy activity on behalf of the community of blood had the air of fighting a war in a time of peace. According to one Nazi leader, Rudolf Hess, civic work reflected "the true spirit of the wartime front lines." Germans who enthusiastically enrolled themselves in the efforts to strengthen the nation and to attain leadership positions created a huge amount of energy. And this vitality, this sense of national renewal, drew thousands of curious tourists to the Third Reich in the mid-1930s. Nonetheless, citizens unsurprisingly found it onerous to constantly give up time and money. Nazi officials quickly complained that their organizations were filled with masses of "coordinated, but indifferently coordinated" members.[15] However, public commitments became part of everyday life. Ordinary Germans gradually accepted the new practices, and the bundle of regulations, advisories, and prohibitions associated with them, as the best way to manage collective life. And neighbors watched themselves with the expectation that others would fall into line. Artifacts such as gas masks, racial certificates, and badges registered the acceptance of the norms of social compliance that came with membership in the people's community. Slackers brought trouble, while conformists made everything easier.

A glimpse into the front hall of a working-class tenement in Berlin in the summer of 1939 indicates the techniques that German citizens mastered in order to manage their lives in the years after 1933. Journalist Heinrich Hauser led the way inside:

Your eye will first be caught by a series of colorful posters next to the entrance. There is an appeal for contributions to the "Mother and Child" fund, another appeal for the *Winterhilfswerk*. A third is a Party exhortation to visit either an anti-semitic lecture or an anti-semitic film.... A fourth poster, in screaming red, bears the urgent question: "Fellow-countryman, have you bought your gas mask?" A fifth warns you not to throw away such garbage as tinfoil, empty tooth-paste tubes and other metals, even old razor blades, and to collect them in special containers.[16]

Posters, labels, and badges tacked onto the doorways of apartments attested to the fact that nearly all residents belonged to the People's Welfare Service or contributed to the Winter Relief Fund.

The most visible manifestation of the new racial community was the *Winterhilfswerk*, huge winter-relief campaigns overseen by the People's Welfare Service. In accordance with plans drawn up in July 1933, over 1 million party members, Hitler Youth, and other volunteers marched into neighborhoods with their distinctive red boxes to collect the marks that would realize the Nazi maxim that "A People Helps Itself." From October to March, these boys and boxes were among the most familiar sights of the Third Reich. Of course, all this collecting activity, *Duddelkram*, as one housewife put it after the war, was annoying and intrusive. Beginning on October 1, 1933, one-pot meals on the first Sunday of every month—"Aryan stew" the jokester said—invariably concluded with the appearance of party representatives who went door to door in the evening to collect the pennies that had been "saved" and to snoop. In general, however, the regime's "socialism of the deed" enjoyed legitimacy. Nazi leaders regarded every year's record-breaking receipts as an index of political satisfaction and social commitment. In the last year before the war, the revenues collected just on "one-pot Sundays," which were observed in restaurants and hotels as well as at home, totaled 50 million marks, just shy of one mark for each German, one-third of an average daily wage.[17]

The Day of National Solidarity elevated the pitch of the winter-relief campaign to a high point. On the first Saturday in December, beginning with the holiday shopping season in 1934, prominent Nazis, as well as military heroes and celebrities such as Heinrich George, appeared in public to collect money on the streets of Berlin. Newspapers announced their locations the day before so that Berliners knew that Joseph Goebbels would be in front of the Adlon, Joachim von Ribbentrop in front of the Bristol, and Hermann Göring in working-class Wedding, where, reports indicated, he enjoyed outsized popularity.[18] "Crowds became so large that in places progress was impossible and women fainted while trying to reach the collectors," reported *The Times*. Goebbels considered the "celebration and hullabaloo" on the streets of Berlin "unbelievable." "I was almost crushed to death," he wrote, and "twice I had to flee inside the hotel." He saw assembled around him "the marvelous people of Berlin. They gave and gave. The poor most generously." He "reported to the Führer that evening," bragging that he had "filled up 42 collection boxes." Combining celebrity and charity, the 1938 action netted 1 million marks in a city of 4 million people in 2.5 hours.[19]

Winter relief was mostly about ordinary behavior. Germans wore special badges to show that they had donated their marks; the badges functioned to make citizens accountable to each other. On Sundays, when Hitler Youth hit the streets to collect for the Winter Relief Fund, "no one would dare walk outside without a badge pinned conspicuously to his coat."[20] Like *Heil Hitler!*, badges displayed and enforced collective participation. Yet it was just these badges of compliant "good behavior" that became hugely popular collectibles in the Third Reich. Manufactured as novelty items for sale at twenty pfennigs, "the winter-relief badges always offered surprises: sometimes there were brightly painted little porcelain figures in traditional costumes, or the crests of German regions embroidered on silk, or portraits of German poets, philosophers, and musicians made out of plexiglass or synthetic resin." During the 1938–1939 campaign alone, 170 million badges were produced; this was sufficient to give every person in Germany two, if not three.[21] In this way, Germans repossessed for themselves in a homespun way the sacrifices the Nazis demanded. People always felt "forcibly volunteered" in the Third Reich, but the accent should fall on the implications of both words; consent, the spirit of volunteering, as well as the force of compliance structured the practices of everyday life in Nazi Germany.

The directives in the tenement hallway urged Berliners to buy gas masks. The Nazis effectively introduced themselves as the most capable wardens of Germany's national security by dramatizing the nation's vulnerability to air attack. Beginning in summer 1933, propaganda displays of bombs and bombers, and the destruction they could wreak, revealed the exposed, trembling body of the nation, which the Nazis claimed to protect through a nationwide program of air defense. Within a few years, 4 million Germans received special training through the Air Defense League, including 400,000 certified air-raid wardens. Not only did citizens learn how to organize bucket brigades, extinguish fires, and work while wearing gas masks, but many accepted positions of responsibility, as did Karl Dürkefälden for his factory and Franz Göll for his apartment building; however, Fredy Solmitz, a former pilot, lost his position as an air-raid warden as soon as the obligatory forms revealed that he was Jewish. All three of them—Dürkefälden, the skeptic; Göll, the believer who eventually became a nonbeliever; and Solmitz, a believer denied a place in the new world order—readily served the newly activated folk community; 11 million people in total enrolled in the Reich Air Defense League. Not surprisingly, the socialist underground press warned that "in practical terms," air-raid wardens enabled "the fascists" to "occupy every building" in the country.[22]

Again and again, the Nazis used the state of emergency to legitimize the dictatorship and create the conditions of the siege they claimed to protect the people from. In 1933, people kept stumbling onto oblong-shaped bombs, parked tip to tail on city squares, and they shuddered when wails of sirens interrupted the workday for minutes at a time as authorities tested the instruments for loudness and tone. Air-defense exercises scattered traffic as authorities sounded sirens, exploded fireworks in the streets to test the response time of fire brigades, and demonstrated to neighbors the most effective ways to pump water and fight fires. In Breslau, at the end of June 1933, the drills lasted from Monday to Thursday and stretched well into the evening hours. "Theater, nothing else," wrote one incredulous observer. True: the point of the exercises was not so much to train citizens as to dramatize the dangers Germany faced. Civil defense not only legitimated the overreaching authority of the authoritarian state but conscripted the civilian as a soldier and reviewed every building lot as a battlefield. "Military preparedness...pervades every aspect of life in modern Germany," confirmed one American observer. "Every house bears the placards of an organization for defense against air attack. The language of the street, the press, the radio, the newsstand and even the library and classroom smacks of war."[23] Nothing expressed the need for the authoritarian state's administration of life better than the air-defense exercises.

In her novel, Irmgard Keun cast "Aunt Adelheid" as the air-raid warden for her building. When, during a drill, she chased Old Pütz, who was wearing "his one good, dark blue Sunday suit," "up the staircase" of the apartment building with a gas mask strapped to his face, she was the tip of a long spear of conscription and militarization. Out of breath, the pensioner finally collapsed: "a thousand enemy aircraft wouldn't frighten me as much as Aunt Adelheid with a gun and the power to give orders," remarked Keun's narrator. "There will be no need for any enemy airman to drop a bomb on Aunt Adelheid's in order to kill the people inside, because Aunt Adelheid will do the job for him in advance."[24] The authoritarian state manifested itself in many guises.

The Nazis underlined both the danger facing Germany and their unique capacity to contain it, thereby making necessary city-wide air-raid exercises that reproduced almost exactly the boycott against the Jews and the winter-relief campaigns: screaming propaganda, street-corner fanfare, door-to-door bustle, symbolic days of national action. The public enrolled itself in the management of modern life, demonstrating the reach of the militarized new time into the every day. The specter of air war and the strenuous campaigns to fight it were crucial parts of Nazi strategy: the more serious the emergency, the more legitimate social mobilization appeared to be.

More important than protecting Germans was bracing and re-building them. All the practices designed to improve and defend the German body rested on the postulates of race, which held that "Aryans" composed a superior race that could be animated in the "struggle for existence" to conquer new territory and dominate weaker beings. Racial thinking adopted the actual differences among species in the animal kingdom and applied them to visually verifiable, allegedly fundamental, but basically superficial distinctions among people. According to Nazi science, there were only races; there was no such thing as the collective "human" or the singular "man"—the one was dissolved into immutable races, the other sucked up into an embracive racial collective. The universally valid laws of nature demonstrated the "purity" and immutability of the races, "not only the sharp outward delimitation of the various races, but their uniform character in themselves." As Hitler explained in the "Nation and Race" chapter of *Mein Kampf*, "The fox is always a fox, the goose a goose, the tiger a tiger." (All this was weird enough in its speciation of the human species, but Hitler got weirder when he used the field mouse, the common mouse, *and* the titmouse as pseudoscientific examples to illustrate his racist postulates.[25])

Of course, this sort of popular "science" was all nonsense; it made mishmash of the sound science of zoological taxonomy. And the Nazis based their distinctions between "Aryans" and "Jews" not on observed biological characteristics but on religious affiliations reported in the previous century. Nonetheless, a very consequential social Darwinist ethology, or set of practices, was imposed on newly validated biological classifications of race. Hitler and other Nazis were never sure whether they were more comfortable talking about blood or genes, but the quality of the race largely determined the worth of an individual and of a people. The true subjects in history were races, which, following the "law" of the "struggle for existence," had always been locked in ceaseless combat with one another.

The process of imposing the definitive category of race began with the boycott against Jews and the Law for the Restoration of the Professional Civil Service in April 1933 and advanced itself in campaigns to incarcerate and sterilize racially unworthy Germans and protect healthy genetic stock; the struggle finally reached its logical conclusion in Auschwitz. The social policies that applied this "law" to modern German life came in two parts: improvements to the race through fortification and improvements to the race through exclusion and elimination.

Fortification encompassed the winter-relief campaigns and the civil defense exercises as well as the construction of athletic fields and swimming pools, the transformation of sports into paramilitary sport, the expansion of public health care to provide prenatal and neonatal care, and the propaganda in favor of love marriages to promote a rising birth rate. In the years before World War II, public spending for health care increased by some 250 percent, although investments in armaments grew far more rapidly. The number of maternity clinics doubled to almost 15,000 so that medical professionals monitored the vast majority of births in Nazi Germany, which partially explains the decrease in infant mortality. But other indices of health deteriorated: mortality rates for children and adults nudged higher after substantial declines in the 1920s, the postwar increases in the height of children also stalled, and diphtheria became more common. All of this was probably due to the well-known "fat shortage" in the Third Reich; the relatively poor nutrition resulted from a decline in the consumption of animal fats and butter and milk and increasingly autarchic trade policies. After a course correction following the Great Depression, when the birthrate soared from 1.58 per woman in 1933 to 1.93 in 1934, the number of live births more or less returned to the trend line observable in all affluent societies (2.03 in 1935, 2.07 in 1936, and 2.09 in 1937—just below the "replacement level"), despite the enormous propaganda and financial incentives (such as marriage loans that could be paid off in quarter shares with each child) directed at families. More people married but fewer had children. Nazi elites themselves did not produce large families, and even Magda Goebbels, who gave birth to six children between 1932 and 1940, "strenuously objected" when her husband defended the official line that "all women must bear children" as a matter of principle. Nazi Germany's energetic pro-life racial policies were a mixed bag.[26]

With exclusion and elimination, the Nazis were much more successful, limited only by the time and energy it took to realize their extraordinary measures. These encompassed the violent seizure of

Germans to incarcerate them in work details and concentration camps for "asocial" behavior and to sterilize them for alleged mental and physical defects. Unlike the rehabilitative work carried out by millions of activists in the Hitler Youth, the Reich Labor Service, and the People's Welfare Service, smaller but powerful groups of biomedical professionals oversaw the disciplinary part, the identification and segregation of "asocials," and the sterilization of genetically "unfit" Germans. The German medical establishment regarded the national revolution in 1933 as the opportunity finally to abandon liberalism's misguided effort to uphold the sovereignty of the individual; it worked closely with the Nazis to promote therapies to strengthen the collective body of the German people. This meant making judgments about the value of individuals and their ability to lead productive lives.

The Nazis responded to an intense desire for order in Germany in 1933, and this made the public receptive to efforts to sort out the healthy from the unhealthy, the good from the bad. Since millions of Germans remained unemployed, it was difficult to distinguish the dangerous core of criminals and the larger group of what experts identified as "asocials," an underclass of delinquents, prostitutes, beggars, and the work shy, from the much greater numbers of impoverished but virtuous citizens. During the Great Depression, begging was common, but who exactly was at the door? The "truly needy" or "vagrants"? Germans would credit the Third Reich with getting rid of "the mischief of begging."[27] The Nazi years were often remembered as a time when people could once again walk the streets unmolested or leave their bicycles unlocked. In large part, citizens accepted the coercive aspects of the management of modern life. But attentive observers also noticed that life's texture changed. Itinerant musicians, typical big-city characters who, with old-fashioned wooden organs, strolled from one tenement courtyard to another, were fewer. And the ragpicker's familiar cry, "Iron, castoffs, paper," was not heard so much anymore.[28]

The numbers of Communists and Social Democrats held in Germany's concentration camps dropped dramatically after 1934, but the numbers of German citizens caught up in large-scale police sweeps sharply increased; beginning in the summer of 1933, the police arrested thousands of vagrants and "asocials." When police shifted their attention from political Communists to social delinquents, they followed the Nazis' growing preoccupation with genetic and racial dangers rather than political ones. As the head of the police apparatus, Heinrich Himmler explained, "The police has the responsibility to secure the organic unity of the German people, its vital energies, and its facilities from destruction and disintegration."[29] This definition gave the police extremely wide latitude. Anyone who did not fit the normative standards of the people's community or could be construed as an agent of social dissolution theoretically fell under the purview of the police. After the war Germans remembered the Gestapo, the political police, whose numbers they vastly exaggerated, but not the people the police arrested, a silent endorsement of operations against thousands of "asocials."

If "asocials" could be relatively easily identified along the borders of respectability, the so-called genetically unfit, many of whom had children and spouses, were much harder to find. Nazi authorities were not even sure how many German citizens fit their shifting definitions of biological degeneracy. The National Socialist minister of the interior, Wilhelm Frick, usually referred to a figure of about 1 million physically or mentally enfeebled Germans, which corresponded with the estimate of the renowned eugenicist Friedrich Lenz, although he noted that other experts put the number as high as 13 million out of a population of 65 million, a ratio of one in five. Over the radio, Frick hectored Germans to abandon the "'outmoded' command to 'love thy neighbor.'"[30] Public discussions also considered the sterilization of Jews.[31] As it was, the Nazis sterilized over 400,000 Germans, mostly in the prewar years from 1934 to 1939, usually following a diagnosis of congenital "feeblemindedness" or schizophrenia. At least as many citizens faced the threat of sterilization, so that more than 1 million people and their families became entangled in this strand of the state's racial policies. These are extraordinarily high numbers, particularly when compared to the 45,000 individuals sterilized in the United States between 1907 and 1945. (Legal commentators reassured the German public by citing US programs as precedents and quoting Supreme Court Justice Oliver Wendell Holmes's 1927 opinion that "three generations of imbeciles are enough.")

Given the wide social net cast by this racial reclamation project, which included among its victims the niece of Catholic theologian Joseph Sauer, the last Weimar-era rector of the University of Freiburg, there was remarkably little opposition beyond the legal resistance of the defendants themselves. Most candidates for sterilization came from lower-class backgrounds, and since educated middle-class men were making normative judgments about decent behavior, they were both more vulnerable to state action and less likely to arouse sympathy. German Jews, who were very alert to racism in the Third Reich and also disproportionately middle-class, did not refer to racial legislation against non-Jewish Germans; the same goes for German resistance circles.[32] The victims themselves and their families undoubtedly felt ashamed to be officially regarded as "unworthy." All of this indicates the extent to which Germans absorbed Nazis ideas about physical and mental normalcy. (Sterilization forms the unusual basis of the postwar indictments of German judges in the 1961 film *Judgement at Nuremberg*, in which a victim, the "baker's helper," played by Montgomery Clift, does speak out, probably for the first time.)

The Nazis considered biological degeneration to be an immediate and lethal threat to the German people; they moved ahead with great energy. Given that "innumerable inferior and genetically deficient people" produced children without restraint, Frick thought it would take only three generations for "the valuable social groups to be completely overrun by the inferior ones." Hitler himself intervened in cabinet discussions on July 14, 1933, to overrule Franz von Papen's objections, which referred to Catholic teachings on the inviolability of God's creation. Hitler argued that "all measures are justified if they serve the preservation of the nation." He continued to pay close attention to the legislation, insisting that a 1937 documentary film on sterilization, *Victims of the Past*, be "shown in all German cinemas." Perhaps because Goebbels himself described the material as "horrifying," Hitler helpfully suggested that a "nice final image" be included, and the film closed with shots of three healthy children playing together: Helga, Hilde, and Helmut Goebbels. "All three are so sweet," commented their father. (Joseph and Magda Goebbels would poison themselves and all six of their children at the very end of the war, on May 1, 1945.[33])

The rationale for the laws also highlighted the practical administrative aspect. Discussions about the "burden of genes" (*Erblast*) inevitably led to concerns about the "burden of taxes" (*Steuerlast*), which the unhealthy imposed on the healthy. Frick scrupulously outlined the costs: 4 marks a day for a feebleminded person, 3.50 marks for a criminal, and 5 or 6 marks for someone with a disability. By contrast, a skilled worker earned 2.50 marks a day, a civil servant "around 4 marks." Arithmetic problems in schoolbooks added and multiplied the number of "idiots" in Germany. Giving the daily costs of the physically and mentally defective that the state bore, exercises asked students to calculate the total costs "of one cripple and one feebleminded person...if one takes a life span of 45 years for each" or to "calculate the expenditure of the state for one pupil in a special school, and one pupil in an ordinary school over eight years, and state the amount of higher cost engendered by the special school pupil." It was all very self-evident: administrative costs justified the lethal administration of life.[34]

As early as March 1933, Göring explained that the government was exploring the application of "eugenic lessons" in an effort "to reduce expenses for the care of mental and physical inferiors."[35] The Nazis advanced on an astonishing number of fronts in March in order to destroy Communists, attack Jews, occupy city halls, dismantle the parties, expand their support beyond the "52 percent" in a frenzy of national festivity, and identify biologically unworthy Germans. The cabinet promulgated the Law for the Prevention of Genetically Damaged Offspring (along with laws on unemployment insurance, the prohibition of political parties, sabotage, the "German greeting," and plebiscites) on July 14, 1933, a very busy day and, tellingly, Bastille Day—the anniversary of the French Revolution. Racial experts took to radio to alert Germans both to the dangerous creatures they had identified and to the "new human beings" that National Socialism was determined to create.

Sterilization proceedings began immediately after the law went into effect in January 1934. Attending physicians in asylums and hospitals referred most candidates for sterilization to one of Germany's seven hundred public health offices. Health officials also maintained systematic files on welfare recipients, schoolchildren, and convicted felons, and they used these records to identify potential candidates.[36] If local registrars became suspicious, simply the attempt to get married set sterilization proceedings in motion. In Berlin's Charlottenburg neighborhood, for example, officials required one in every nine prospective newlyweds to procure a certificate of genetic health; 5 percent of these were barred from marrying.[37] There were hard lessons to learn, as one young man, a farm worker from Karlsruhe, disclosed, when questioned by the Americans just after the war about his 1935 sterilization: "(he cried bitterly here): 'I never filled out any applications or questionnaires or anything that had to do with the party since then.'"[38]

Once public health offices received a referral, they assigned the case to a physician certified in racial biology. One young woman, accompanied by her fiancé, entered the doctor's office:

> The doctor read from my files and held it against me that my sisters had been in reform school and my mother had had a prior conviction, which I didn't know. I was very embarrassed.... The doctor went from one room to another before he suddenly stopped in front of me and said something like, if 1 pound costs 7 pfennig, how much do 7 pounds cost? Very timidly I said 1.05 Mark. What! screamed the doctor; if ½ pound costs 15 pfennig, how much do seven cost. 70 pfennig I said quietly.

Nothing better represented the revaluation of morality and health in the Third Reich than the Law for the Prevention of Genetically Damaged Offspring. Hitler himself imagined the sacrifice of his mother for the collective racial good. "At least three-quarters" of the questions, he noted, "would have defeated my own good mother. One I recall was: 'Why does a ship made of steel float in the water?' If this system had been introduced before my birth, I am pretty sure I would never have been born at all."[39]

If the consulting physician recommended sterilization, a three-person "sterilization court" issued a final, almost always concurring decision. Appeals could be made within a restricted period but were not usually granted. Almost one in ten candidates for sterilization had to be escorted to the clinics where the operation took place by police force. Faced with her own sterilization, the "schizophrenic" Emma P. objected, "Every person is also different like any other, and every case too."[40] There is no better antifascist statement.

In rare cases, determined individuals obtained court orders that postponed the operation for years. The file of Flora S., a twenty-year-old shop girl who had been a patient in a state asylum in 1933, found its way to the district physician in the public health office of the Berlin district of Tempelhof, who diagnosed "manic depression" and recommended sterilization, particularly in light of the fact that Flora wanted to get married and her grandfather had committed suicide. Flora and her family responded with a long series of appeals, winning several deferrals of the operation, which was initially scheduled for August 1939, rescheduled for May 1944, and finally set for June 1945, by which time the Nazis had been defeated; "for Flora S. the thousand-year Reich was a twelve-year effort to avoid sterilization."[41] Flora was lucky, since most appeals were not granted and most operations not postponed. The thinking was, better one too many sterilizations than one too few.

The idea that race was a fundamental way of being in history worked itself into daily life. The novelist Christa Wolf remembered the new "glitter words," such as "normal," "gene," or "alien," that lit up everyday vocabularies in the years after 1933.[42] When the young high school student Lore Walb met her cousin Günther, they talked about "race," which led to the topics of "blood" and "inheritance." She admired his idealism and considered him a genuine comrade. In other situations, young people did not agree at all. Eberhard Gebensleben and his best friend, Carl-Heinz Zeitler, a medical student, went to the movies one Sunday morning. The feature was paired with "that ridiculous nationalist propaganda film that dealt with population issues." Maybe it was the documentary featuring Goebbels's children at the end or else any one of the other shorts advocating sterilization. On the way home, Eberhard and Carl-Heinz got into a "fierce argument" about race that destroyed their friendship. As adolescents in the 1920s, they had partnered up while handing out campaign literature for the German Nationalists, but the Third Reich divided them. By his own reckoning, Carl-Heinz remained true to ideas of "freedom" and "life," and he could not bear to see Eberhard's party pin or to think about "the German character" it stood for. Only much later would Eberhard reconsider race thinking after he fell in love with a Jewish *Mischling* during the war. "If only the 25% didn't exist (the non-Aryan grandmother)," he sighed, for 25 percent was enough to put his entire career at risk. This was another sign of how central race was to daily life. (He was killed in action in Belgium in 1944; Zeitler emigrated to Switzerland, where he committed suicide after an unhappy homosexual love affair in 1956.[43])

In an age of genes, certificates of racial ancestry, and sterilization, Germans saw themselves in a new light. People made a hobby of tracking blood relatives all the way to 1800, as many as sixty-two lineal family members in all, just as prospective officers in the SS were required to do. They proudly unveiled their *Sippe*, or kin, for show and tell. Victor Klemperer tells the story of a friend, a schoolmaster who decided to retire early rather than join the Nazi Party. While boasting about the "youthful heroic feats" of his grandson, he mentioned the curious name Isbrand Wilderich, which Klemperer inquired about. "The answer was as follows, word for word: 'In the seventeenth century it was the name of one of our kin [*Sippe*], who originally came from Holland.'" For Klemperer the "simple use of the word *Sippe*" indicated how National Socialism had infected even a pious, basically anti-Nazi Catholic. Enthusiasts went so far as to cultivate the genealogies of German dogs and to impose extra taxes on owners of mixed breeds.[44]

Genealogy obsessed Franz Göll, the Berlin diarist. He had always been interested in degeneracy, which he saw in terms of his own darkened circumstances after his father's death in 1915. He was familiar with the eugenic literature that sprouted around themes of love and sex after the turn of the century; he read naturalist novels about the material and biological influences of milieu such as Zola's *The Belly of Paris* and *Nana*; and, after 1933, he expanded his reading list to include Göring, Hitler, and Karl Birnbaum's 1935 study *The World of the Mentally Ill.* But the Law for the Prevention of Genetically Damaged Offspring, which was published on July 25, 1933, and headlined in the newspapers the next day, catapulted him into the busy work of genealogy. Just a few days later, Göll closely studied the "enfeebled mental constitution" of his mother's family, the Liskows:

> Mother's father was a mental weakling, someone who was not able to get what he wanted. As long as life flows uninterruptedly, there are no problems for such mental asthenics. But as soon as someone with asthenic mental constitution butts in, the trouble starts. My grandfather's undoing came in the form of his son-in-law, the husband of his younger daughter, my uncle Carl Amboss. This person knew how to run around my grandfather, to string him along in order to achieve what was to his advantage. Too lazy to support himself and his family, my uncle let my grandfather support him. After failing, despite support, in all manner of professions (cook, dentist, barber, meat inspector), he threw in his lot and was able to get my grandfather to sign over his business to him. In this way, without putting in a penny, my uncle received a house with a grocery store and garden.... Thereafter, my grandfather, who was already a widower, lived in his own house as a barely tolerated tenant.... My grandfather let himself be robbed of his rights instead of taking his son-in-law and his family on as tenants in order to keep some sort of leverage. This shortsighted course of action, combined with his asthenic paralysis of will, this giving in to the encroachments of the outside world without any struggle, is typical of my grandfather's family.[45]

In July 1934, Franz prepared an even more detailed "hereditary biological study" of his uncle's family, the Ambosses:

> The family produced 7 children, of whom one, a girl, died in infancy. In their physical and mental constitution, three of the

remaining children (Martin, Gertrud, Kurt) show the influence of the Amboss, two (Helmut and Margarete †) have a streak of Liskow in them, and one child (Rudolf) is a mixed type (physically = Liskow, mentally = Amboss).

The asthenic effect of the Ambosses is evident in the fact that Martin and Rudolf have made themselves economically independent (each renting or owning a tavern); Gertrud has made a magnificent match considering (Mrs. Captain Matthes), and Kurt is trying hard to make something of himself professionally. The other two children clearly show that they have inherited the weak mental streak of the Liskows. Helmut, who as a child suffered in silence, trained as a baker but is still only an assistant, that is, a wage earner without the prospects to make himself independent anytime soon. Mentally too weak to effectively resist the reality of the ongoing demands of life, Margarete committed suicide. Her motive: a broken heart.[46]

Göll focused on weakness rather than strength; he did not see himself as a mighty Nazi. But by tracking down the particular pathologies of his own family, he worked with the same genetic propositions that enforced the National Socialist laws mandating sterilization. Indeed, he wondered whether he and his elderly mother were "unworthy."

With his reading program and copious scientific notes, Göll illustrated the sheer amount of paperwork that came with thinking about social life in biological terms. Officials published pages and pages comparing, contrasting, measuring, and calculating aspects of racial worthiness—the only thing they could not do was administer a test verifying who was "Aryan" and who was not, as the category had no scientific basis. People believed in or acted on something that did not exist. Germans filled out forms certifying "Aryan" ancestry as the price of employment, to maintain good standing in clubs and associations, to procure a marriage loan, to join the Hitler Youth or other party organizations, to enlist as a "soldier of labor" in the Reich Labor Service, and to serve in the Wehrmacht. (The racial vetting to secure a marriage loan, along with the prohibitions on redeeming the vouchers that came with the loan in department stores or Jewish shops, is a good example of how collective aims regarding race regulated new opportunities for personal prosperity.) The pieces of paper tacked up in the apartment building hallway in Berlin attested to the new ways they had to conduct their lives in accordance with the needs of the *Volk*. The paper trail made the material connection that Franz Göll had: "Germany must live, so that we don't go under." Paper created the case for blood and, with it, an understanding of the dangers the community faced and what was necessary to protect it.

T HE DEFENSE of the nation and the security of the *Volk* were increasingly regarded as the necessary means to achieve individual happiness—that the restoration of "normality" came with the racialized administration of life seemed to make sense to more and more Germans. Gradually, the unemployed returned to work. Business turnover increased; more beers were consumed. But, in many ways, Nazi Germany remained an impoverished country. The idea that German teenagers in the 1930s could afford a used car, be it for $50 or $100, as did Mickey Rooney in the 1940 film *Andy Hardy's Dilemma*, was outlandish—only about 350,000 Germans took a driving test in each of the years of the mid-1930s; most people settled for a bicycle (there were 20 million bicycles in Germany in 1933, one for every three inhabitants).[47] Germans earned about half of what their counterparts did in the United States. They spread more margarine on bread than butter. Today, the Third Reich, with a per capita income of around $4,500, would rank alongside Tunisia or Iran in economic development.[48] But most Germans did not feel that they were confined to that reality; the year 1933 finally pointed the way forward. They cherished the promise of consumption, and the production and purchase of what were standard consumer items in the United States, such as cameras, vacuum cleaners, radios, telephones, and refrigerators, increased in the late 1930s. Nazi Germany was a society of "One Pot Sundays *and* perms," concludes one historian; there was "coffee substitute *and* cinema."[49] The Third Reich advertised itself as the place where Germans could fulfill their personal dreams; the radio noise became less shrill and more fun, the collective marching died down, and May Day ceremonies soon revolved around the theme "Let yourselves enjoy life!"[50]

In keeping with the idea of insiders and outsiders, there was the promise but also the prohibition. Not everyone in Germany was permitted to "enjoy life," and small luxuries became big indicators of who was worthy in the Third Reich and who was not. The prerogatives of consumption were made completely clear in the expropriation of the things Jews in Germany owned in the years before they were deported. "With every car, every radio, every typewriter, every telephone, every camera, every iron" that Jews were required to hand over, the Nazis indicated what they believed "Germans" deserved and Jews did not.[51] Such expropriation was also essential to other forms of exclusion. At the beginning of the war, decrees ordered Jews to turn over their radios to local authorities by September 23, 1939, so that the sets could be "secured" in a safe place (*sicherstellen*), and "excluded" Jews from listening to the radio altogether (*Empfang*, as in the prohibited *Rundfunkempfang*, means "reception" as well as "welcome," and Jews were not welcomed).

One of the most beloved consumer items was the radio—by transmitting public sounds into private spaces, radio gave people the feeling that they were participating in life. "Radioing," you could switch stations, listen to music, hear foreign broadcasts, and follow live events. Although manufacturers sold battery-powered devices, electrification brought radios into German homes. Only 24 percent of Berlin households had been electrified in 1925; seven years later, in 1932, it was 72 percent.[52]

Nazis and radios, which provided much of the noise accompanying the national revolution, came of age together. The notorious French fascist Robert Brasillach explained the ways in which radio collaborated with Hitler in 1933. The radio, the young writer observed, "had virtually waited for this year in order to spread itself everywhere." In the preceding years, he recalled, "it was squeaky and temperamental." With their unreliable sets, only the most patient listeners found themselves "engrossed in searching for a concert amid frightening gurgling noises." But after 1933, "all was ready for us to tune into German stations in the evenings to hear that extraordinary National-Socialist election campaign, with its torrent of bells, drums and violins." The elections set "the demons of music" loose.[53]

The Nazis moved radio to the very center of the election campaign. The airwaves were completely dominated by speeches by Hitler, Göring, and other leading Nazis. The gigantic festivals that the National Socialists organized—the Day of the Awakening Nation on March 4, the Day of Potsdam on March 21, and the Day of National Labor on May 1—hit a dramatic high note with live radio broadcasts of big speeches. Through the radio, people came to feel that they were participating in events. The techniques Nazi broadcasters perfected enhanced the eventfulness of the broadcasts: introductions set the scene, as had those by Goebbels during Hitler's election campaign in February and March 1933 (in the people's vernacular, the radio was known as "Goebbels's snout"), but otherwise the thinking was that "the sounds and speeches of the event should speak for themselves." Microphones picked up the background noise of rallies, the singing and chanting in order to build up the sense of restless expectation, and the cheers that interrupted Hitler's speeches to convey the mood of national acclamation. Reporters bent down low so that the radio broadcast only the rhythmic scuff of boots marching in the streets.[54] Live broadcasts had a much greater impact on listeners than newspaper reports published the next day, and people tended to believe the radio more than the newspaper because it seemed more immediate and unedited—the "real thing." Since events seemed to "speak for themselves," broadcasts gained in authority. Radio broadcasts in a room also invited listening in a way that newspapers on a table did not invite reading. Goebbels himself credited the "much more intensive public management," or *Volksführung*, that radio had made possible with the "vehemence and speed" with which the National Socialist revolution had established itself.[55]

Even those who hated the Nazis often gained their strongest impressions from broadcasts. Listening to Hitler on the radio, writer René Schickele felt "the same fear I had as a child when I would encounter the big dog." "Anschluss! Heil Hitler. Anschluss"—thirteen-year-old Jacques Lusseyran turned the dial and stumbled upon Radio Vienna in March 1938: he heard the "music and voices aimed at you point-bank like loaded pistols." Although blind, Lusseyran believed he could make out "the face of the murderers."[56]

To facilitate participation in the people's community, the Nazis put extraordinary effort into making affordable radios available to the public. In what it touted as the triumph of "socialism of the deed" over "private capitalism" and "economic liberalism," Goebbels's newly established Propaganda Ministry—there were people who simply called it the "Advertising" Ministry—pressured a consortium of radio manufacturers to design and produce a "people's radio," or *Volksempfänger*, for the mass market. Launched in September 1933, the VE 301—the 301 stood for the red-letter date

January 30—was an instant success at seventy-six marks; 1.5 million sets were sold, many of them on installment plans, in the first two years, 1933 and 1934. This was the case because a radio was an entertaining thing to have, but also because many Germans wanted to hear Hitler and the sounds of the Third Reich. Statistics indicate that one-half of the new radio subscribers in 1933 and fully two-thirds in 1934 could be attributed to the availability of the inexpensive people's radio. If one in four households owned radios in 1933, more than one in two did in 1939. Radios moved into living rooms and kitchens, sometimes paired with a framed photograph of Hitler, as depicted in Paul Mathias Padua's iconic 1940 painting, *The Führer Speaks*, in which three generations of a family assemble around a plain wooden table under a radio and Hitler's portrait. Both the price of the sets and the monthly fee kept poorer Germans, especially in rural areas, from making the big-ticket purchase, but in cities almost everyone had a radio.[57]

Nazis condemned radio programming during the Weimar Republic for being too intellectual. It was unfaithful to the "true spirit" of the medium, which was to let the community speak up. "From the people, to the people" was the new watchword. After 1933, the coordinated radio stations endeavored to put in place programs that would put as many ordinary Germans in front of the microphone as possible: Nationwide contests recruited thousands of cub reporters to audition their broadcasting skills. Audience-request shows, especially the popular music show *Wunschkonzert*, let members of the "radioland" audience speak up—these were not on par with the call-in shows featuring Wolfman Jack in 1950s California, but they nonetheless broke new ground to create an appealing cultural vernacular in the Third Reich. *Wunschkonzert*, with its moderator Heinz Goedecke as Germany's "radio uncle," created a national repertoire of "pop" music that broke down distinctions between high and low culture, and "hits" from the Third

Reich remained beloved "evergreens" after 1945. Programming aimed at getting listeners to recognize what they were hearing on the radio as the authentic sounds of the people's community. This way, Goebbels believed, radio would bring into line the 48 percent who had not voted for the Nazis in March 1933.

During the Third Reich, the radio worked itself into the folds of everyday life. The Nazis quickly learned that the value of radio did not lie in the transmission of explicitly political events, and a year into the revolution, they redirected radio programming to light entertainment and variety shows, cheerful slices of German life. Yet when Hitler did speak, almost all radio subscribers listened—and neighbors listened to make sure that neighbors were listening. Subscribers often turned the radio on when they woke up to catch a tune or work out while listening to gymnastic programs; during prime-time listening hours, between seven and ten o'clock in the evening, about 80 percent of radio subscribers tuned in, and they did so with family members; the people listened and responded together as a group. Although the emphasis was on easy listening, Germans made sure to tune into the eight o'clock news broadcast, a (television) habit that remains in place today. Many listeners believed it was their duty to do so. Thus the evening news provided a degree of ideological orientation about the fate of the nation.[58] Grand events of the Third Reich, such as the Anschluss with Austria in March 1938, or the offensive against Poland in September 1939, or even the terrible end of the German army in Stalingrad in January 1943, were experienced primarily as radio events with broadcasts framed by the acoustics of church bells and solemn music. Listeners sat together at home waiting for updates all day long. When Germans tuned in, they tuned into the new times, the gay and happy musical score of the good life, swing to "Ordnung mot sein."

The administration of life promised the good life. National Socialists created a sensible image of the *Volk* mostly by conjuring up the dangers that imperiled the "people's community." But more important than the actual realization of the "people's community," or even the credibility of its promise in the future, was the regime's ability to create a way of life, to put in place, in a seemingly commonsense way, a new mix of social obligations and individual opportunities, and to establish a rhythm of sights and sounds across the weeks and months of the year that added up to the lived experience of the Third Reich. What was the exemplary artifact of the Third Reich? The gas mask? The people's radio receiver? The declaration of "Aryan" ancestry? The newly ironed brown uniform children put on Saturday mornings to get out of the house and skip school? Each item registered the consensus among Germans about compliance and about the returns that compliance dispensed.

CHAPTER EIGHT

"This Enormous Planet"

A FTER 1933, the new Germany rose as an "enormous planet" over the skies of the twentieth century. The world watched in fascination as the country changed. It had once been known for its "poets and philosophers," from whom the great powers had "nothing to fear," according to Madame de Stäel, the nineteenth-century French writer. More recently, it had been reviled during the Great War because of its militaristic, mustachioed kaiser and then later became known as a place notorious for battles among Social Democrats, Communists, and all sorts of other loud, rebellious partisans. Now it had turned into a nation of Aryans, Jews, and "asocials." A romantic fairytale realm, in which the Brothers Grimm served as reliable guides, had become the national community of the Third Reich that indexed passages of Adolf Hitler's *Mein Kampf.* The Sportpalast overawed castles on the Rhine. In one hundred days, the ascent of National Socialism forever scrambled the associations people around the world made with Germany. Just consider the new answers to the old question, Germany, what comes to mind?

Early on, the Third Reich's biggest showman bought a car and took in a movie. But it was Joseph Goebbels's show on the radio and in film that intrigued prospective buyers and terrified captive audiences. One hundred days had made *das Dritte Reich*, the Third Reich, *le Troisième Reich*, and observers in the United States, Britain, France, and elsewhere closely watched the production, its cast of soldiers, and its rapid advance.

The Nazi campaign for the March 5, 1933, Reichstag elections was expensive. As the lead organizer of the last big push, Goebbels had his hands full. His wife had just returned home after spending Christmas and the entire month of January bedridden in a clinic following a miscarriage on December 23, 1932, less than four months after the birth of her first child, Helga Susanne. She remained "sad," Goebbels reported. At the same time, he felt "squeezed" into a corner since the election postponed the creation of the new propaganda ministry he had been promised and a rival had already been appointed as the Prussian minister for cultural affairs. "Not my third Reich," he fumed. And there were huge cash-flow problems. Goebbels spent his days in conference with Nazi leaders who had lots to say but little to offer. Nonetheless, on February 14, even before Hermann Göring invited leading industrialists to meet with Hitler on February 20 in order to extract millions of marks in campaign donations, which broke the logjam ("money's there," Goebbels rejoiced, "here we go"), Goebbels took a break to stroll among the fancy cars on display at Berlin's newly opened International Automobile Exhibition. "What wonderful vehicles! A new Mercedes... that's what I want some day." Two days later, he had worked something out with Jakob Werlin, Hitler's personal automobile salesman. "My Mercedes is a dream," he later swooned. The same day Goebbels visited the automobile show, he also found time to go to the movies to see Greta Garbo in *Grand Hotel*. "I was spellbound," he noted in his diary.[1]

Goebbels coveted a Mercedes and admired Garbo; yet the biggest release in early 1933 was not *Grand Hotel* but Goebbels's production of "The Third Reich." Even before Hitler came to power, Harry Graf Kessler watched the French take in the formidable phenomenon of *le nazisme*. "Today, as during the war, Germany is (alas!) once more the great international star who appears in every newspaper, in every cinema, fascinating the masses with a mixture of fear, incomprehension, and reluctant admiration laced with malicious joy at the trouble we are in. Germany is the great tragic, sinister, and dangerous action figure."[2]

The biggest French daily, *Paris-soir*, which sold more than 1.5 million copies every day, stationed three regular correspondents in Berlin, a team of brothers Jérôme and Jean Tharaud and Jules Sauerwein. They all reported on the first one hundred days. On big occasions like Boycott Saturday, Robert Lorette joined in to report from Berlin, Roger Vailland from Frankfurt, and Jean Marèze from Enschede on the Dutch border, over which hundreds of German Jewish refugees had fled. On the days after the March 5 elections, the Day of Potsdam, Boycott Saturday, and the Day of National Labor, *Paris-soir* splashed photographs of the momentous events, sent the same day by wire (or "Bélinogramme"), on the front pages. Although *Paris-soir*, a center-left paper, had the biggest news operation in Germany, Camille Loutre reported from Berlin for the center-right *Le petit Parisien*, which had a circulation of 1 million, and Philippe Barrès, son of novelist Maurice Barrès, who back in the 1890s had called for a fusion of "socialist nationalism," did so for the rightist daily *Le matin*, with a circulation of about 300,000. In Paris, public lectures also promoted the "Hitler show," covering topics such as the persecution of the Jews by Jérôme and Jean Tharaud, who were themselves admirers of Maurice Barrès, the "great master," and whose fascination with the "chosen people" had turned into aversion, leading them to conclude that Jewry "will never get along with me." The Ciné Paris-soir on the Avenue de la Republique screened documentaries, *L'Allemagne de Guillaume II* and *L'Allemagne de Hitler*, which highlighted "the war, the Ruhr, the inflation, the reign of Hindenburg" and finally "Hitler and his 3rd Reich," from ten o'clock in the morning until midnight.[3]

The British press was well represented in Germany: Vernon Bartlett (*News Chronicle*), Sefton Delmer (*Daily Express*), Norman Ebbutt (*The Times*), Eric Geyde (*Daily Telegraph*), Hugh Carleton Greene (*Daily Telegraph*), Ralph Izzard (*Daily Mail*), Noel Panter (*Daily Telegraph*), G. Ward Price (*Daily Mail*), Rothay Reynolds (*Daily Mail*), Karl Robson (*Morning Post*), John Segrue (*News Chronicle*), Philip Pembroke Stephens (*Daily Express*), Frederick Voigt (*Manchester Guardian*), and Eustace Wareing (*Daily Telegraph*). At the watering hole Taverne on Kurfürstenstrasse, the British were joined after hours by American correspondents such as Ralph Barnes (*New York Herald Tribune*), Frederick Birchall (*New York Times*), John Elliott (*New York Herald Tribune*), Guido Enderis (*New York Times*), Charles Gratke (*Christian Science Monitor*), H. R. Knickerbocker (*New York Evening Post*), Louis B. Lochner (Associated Press), Edgar Mowrer (*Chicago Daily News*), Sigrid Schulz (*Chicago Tribune*), William Shirer (CBS), and Louis Leo Snyder (*New York Herald*).

The reason so many reporters flocked to the Taverne was Adolf Hitler, whose rise led newspapers and radio corporations to establish or expand bureaus in Berlin. Host to over 150 journalists from twenty-nine countries, the city was the world's busiest foreign press hub—Holland sent thirteen correspondents, Sweden eight, Argentina and the Soviet Union four each, and Japan three. Press coverage ensured that Germany's transformation into the Third Reich would be the biggest news story of the twentieth century. Reports from the Reich earned Mowrer a Pulitzer Prize for journalism in 1933 and Birchall one in 1934. Shirer eventually won a National Book

Award for his 1960 *The Rise and Fall of the Third Reich*, and *New York Times* Berlin correspondent Howard K. Smith, author of *The Last Train from Berlin* (1942), coanchored the ABC news from 1969 to 1975.[4] Nazis made news for the rest of the twentieth century.

Hitler's appointment as chancellor on January 30, 1933, generated global headlines, and from then on, the big newspapers' coverage plotted the rise of the Third Reich: Hitler's Sportpalast speech on February 10, the Reichstag fire on February 27, the elections on March 5, the Day of Potsdam on March 21, Boycott Saturday on April 1, the Day of National Labor on May 1, and the book burnings on May 10—a map that traced a new history. There was so much copy that papers frequently misspelled Adolf as "Adolph," which meant that many readers would never get the joke passed around in Germany about the young man who, responding to the name "Adolf," added the telling emendation "but with 'ph.'"

Photographs also accompanied these regular stories, creating an indelible visual canon: of course, the faces of leading personalities—Hitler, Göring, Franz von Papen—but also the torchlight parades at night, the crowds at Nazi rallies, the SA guards in front of Jewish stores. Even small foreign newspapers ran feature stories and tantalizing photographs. The *Henderson Daily Dispatch* (North Carolina), the *Richmond Daily Independent* (California), and the *Delphos Daily Herald* (Ohio) picked up the forced march of Michael Siegel through the streets of Munich on March 10. NBC radio affiliates broadcast Hitler's address to the German people on February 1 across the United States. *Time* magazine's March 13, 1933, cover featured a print of the new chancellor relaxing outdoors; Hitler would appear four more times on the magazine's cover during the Nazi assault on the twentieth century (on April 13, 1936; on January 2, 1939, as "Man of the Year"; on April 14, 1941; and on May 7, 1945, with a big red X drawn on his face). As *Time* introduced prominent members of Franklin D. Roosevelt's new administration (Henry

Wallace, Cordell Hull, Harold Ickes, Frances Perkins), it also featured leading figures of the Third Reich, such as Joseph Goebbels (July 10, 1933) and Hermann Göring (August 21 of that same year).

In just a few weeks, Adolf Hitler, with his toothbrush moustache and side part, was an instantly recognized figure. In April 1933, Madame Tussaud's Wax Museum in London unveiled its model of Hitler, who rubbed wax elbows with the great cricketer Don Bradman ("The Don"), Greta Garbo, and the king and queen. Hitler's was the only figure to be repeatedly defaced.

"Beautiful Adolf," the Austrian housepainter who had become an "apprentice" statesman, was easily mocked. He did not look like most politicians. Journalists could see that he seemed "ill at ease, awkward, and moody" in society. "His coattails embarrassed him." "He crumpled his handkerchief," he "hugged it," and then he "rolled it." He also lacked the brute physicality of new leaders such as Benito Mussolini, who sometimes appeared before the cameras bare chested. (Hitler's skin was visible only around the knees when he wore Tyrolean lederhosen.) According to Dorothy Parker, the man was "formless, almost faceless," a frame "without bones." He didn't even look like a German—"more like a second-rate French hairdresser."[5] "It is easily said: Hitler is not very intelligent," *Paris-soir* admitted, but its reporters on-site in Berlin reminded readers that his cry, "Germany, Wake Up," had roused millions of followers. He was the sentimental lead in a newly invigorated Germany.[6] It was not simply that "Adolf" tickled fancies in 1933; the new giant of the Third Reich turned the year into a milestone. Nineteen thirty-three was a global event because it was immediately recognized as having worldwide political implications; even newspapers in Damascus and Beirut provided running day-to-day commentary. Its suddenness somehow related to fundamentals; the one hundred days pronounced on 1,000 years of history. The "enormous planet" of Germany, wrote nationalist newspaper editor Robert Brasillach, suddenly "took up a position in the very center of the heavens."[7]

Who would disagree? Nineteen thirty-three marked the year that the world slipped from the postwar epoch into a new, dangerous prewar period of international disorder, rivalry, and expansionism. "There has never been so much talk of war as there is to-day," wrote Dorothy Woodman in *Hitler Rearms*. There "will be another European war," predicted Leland Stowe, whose 1933 book title, *Nazi Germany Means War*, stated the argument; "in about two years' time" and "surely within five years...another catastrophe lies directly ahead." For this reason, on both the left and the right, French political commentators responded to the events of 1933 with renewed calls for detente with Germany.

But at issue were not only the injustices of the Peace of Versailles, imposed on Germany from the outside, but also the internal dynamics of National Socialism. The organizing principle of Germany's new militarized society was destruction and expansion. As one author explained, "Fascist self-sufficiency is a contradiction in terms, since Fascism is based" upon "continuous expansion." It has "no fixed political aims.... [T]here is no degree of saturation," confirmed Hermann Rauschning, who observed Nazism close-up as a party member and president of Danzig's senate before abruptly resigning both positions in 1934; it would be futile to try to identify the "final demands" of Germany's "'dynamic' foreign policy," he wrote in his influential book *Germany's War of Destruction*.[8] Fascism appealed to those who believed that the strong needed to destroy the weak in an existential struggle for survival.

In a Hobbesian war of "all against all," Nazi Germany had rolled up all the modern protocols that separated and balanced power and established both sovereignty and tolerance. Franz Neumann compared the "structure and practice of National Socialism" to "Behemoth," the monster who intimidated Job in the Bible. Observers on the left judged Nazism to be an assault on the very credibility of the ideal of progress precisely because it showed that the monstrous creatures of the premodern era—Behemoth, Leviathan,

Amalek—could be reanimated as in some 1930s version of *Jurassic Park*. The "reversion to medievalism in the very center of civilization," as New York senator Robert Wagner described Nazism in Madison Square Garden on March 27, 1933, was as frightening as it was astonishing. Germany was rewriting "the bloodiest chapters of the Middle Ages," confirmed French republicans. Reflecting on Boycott Saturday, Victor Klemperer in Dresden admitted that he had "always imagined the twentieth century and Mitteleuropa" to be "different from the fourteenth century and Romania." "Mistake," he added. Edgar Ansel Mowrer's best-selling book on the rise of Hitler was simply titled *Germany Puts the Clock Back*.[9]

If leftists thought that Hitler's brownshirts were pushing the twentieth century back into some prehistoric time, rightists regarded Nazism as a vanguard force in the defense of contemporary European civilization. The French Right had always mistrusted German power and watched as Germans flexed their muscles—an unreconstructed figure like Charles Maurras of L'Action française believed that Hitler had pushed German Jewish refugees across French borders as part of a grand design to destabilize the country— but for most rightists the clenched fist of world communism posed the greater threat, and Communists and Jews were soon conjoined in the right-wing imagination as a hyphenated hydra, "Judeo-Bolshevism."[10] Given "the frightful experience of Bolshevism," asserted François Coty, the French perfumer and right-wing newspaper financier, Hitler's Germany deserved the "gratitude of the world" for "extirpating from the planet" the "men of prey." In less than one hundred days, Germany had proved that the "European community" could be completely reimagined, as "if a volcano has opened up." That was the bounty of 1933.[11]

HITLER'S FIRST hundred days were widely perceived as a sudden tectonic shift in European politics that threatened the very idea of liberal progress. The reverberations of 1933, the nationalist insurgency and the socialist collapse, shook the continent for many years to come. Events occurring in Germany prompted Europeans to examine their "symptoms"—of mobility unleashed and energy harnessed and of the failure to achieve the same results at home. A new appreciation of power acknowledged its primitive, irrational, and mystical sources and, most of all, recognized that such power was there to be tapped. New histories emerged in the "eruptive violence of time."[12] Precisely the transnational nature of the fascist phenomenon, something confirmed by global responses to the Nazi seizure of power in 1933, enhanced its legitimacy and sturdiness. Even France, the historic foe of Germany, registered in profound ways the shock waves of Hitler's revolution. The turbulence of 1933 later shaped both France's resistance to and its collaboration with the German Nazis.

The magical pull of National Socialism from across the Rhine was irresistible. There can be no doubt that French fascism was a homegrown phenomenon, prepared intellectually in the ferment of the antirepublican and anti-Dreyfusard activity before the Great War and promoted in a more organized, forceful fashion in the early and middle 1920s. In Germany, there had also been mini "Hitlers" before the "Führer" and paler versions of what became recognized as National Socialism before the party's electoral breakthrough in September 1930. Nonetheless, 1933 represented the possibility of radical, unanticipated change. The year scheduled new arrivals and departures in French (and European) politics.

French reporters approached the first hundred days as if they were explorers of a new wilderness. Although *Paris-soir*'s Jules Sauerwein judged Hitler's "mystical discourse" insufficient to "dispel the anxiety" as Germans watched the encroachments of dictatorial rule, he kept coming back to the "blasts of trumpets," to the "intoxication" and ecstasy of the Nazi men, to the religious aspects of Hitler's "sermons," and to the wide appeal of the "ideals, discipline, and hate" of his "crusade."[13] The crowds he surveyed were "immense," the ceremonies "solemn."[14] Nazism proved that a new church of belief could be built.

It was important to keep in mind the "ministerial cocktail" of the new government and to ask whether Adolf Hitler was really "master of the situation in Germany," cautioned Philippe Barrès in *Le matin*, but the more he watched the new regime, the more unrestrained his language became. Hitler spoke the "poetry" of a "demagogic messiah, at once noble and confused." Barrès spent an evening listening to one of Hitler's speeches with a group of German Catholics and reported on their tears of joy; they were "crying like Madeleines," the sponge cakes popular in northern France and immortalized by Marcel Proust. Hitler rallies had the jolly atmosphere of a "county fair." On the Day of National Labor, "everybody was happy."[15]

In his 1939 novel, *Gilles*, Pierre Drieu la Rochelle traced his own autobiographical journey through the wilderness of the 1930s. Attending a Radical Socialist congress in Chateau-le-Roi, the character Gilles found himself among left-leaning centrists who provided the point of gravity to French politics that in Germany had disappeared (he still considered himself to be a republican who believed in the old resonant words "democracy, freedom, equality"). He observed the meeting's proceedings in the shadow of the volcano: "the monstrous conspiracies of the Soviets," "the new Slavic states in which barbarism has hardly been restrained, Italian fascism, the grumbling case of Germany." It suddenly occurred to Gilles that the Radical Socialists on the dais felt completely "exonerated" by their liberal dogmas. They were "untouched" by evidence of other, blazing new life forms. Their "arrogance" veiled a "fainthearted mediocrity." They were "beneficiaries," "successors," "substitutes" who had dug the graves of aristocrats without completing a genuine revolution, leaving France without a path to a vibrant future.[16] Gilles began work at an alternative magazine with the spiteful name *Apocalypse*, though he drifted without being able to make connections and ended the novel by following fellow Catholics to Spain to fight for Francisco Franco on behalf of Europe.

Nineteen thirty-three provided Gilles's creator, Drieu la Rochelle, roiled waters on which to imagine a new society. A year after Hitler came to power, he wrote *Socialisme fasciste*, a book praising Germany's youthful revolution and the honor it accorded to primitive, physical virtue, which formed a "new aristocracy" of action. (Drieu's fascism was incomplete, however. It honored the barbarian but not the demonic character of a war that Drieu, wounded three times as a soldier on the western front, found horrifying.) Many others in France felt themselves drawn into fascism's "magnetic field," a zone of energy, action, and renewal—even some who lacked a résumé of extreme right-wing activity. Novelist Jules Romain and philosopher Emmanuel Mounier carefully disentangled the strands of National Socialism, laying aside the impulse toward totalitarianism and the drive to war but picking up the urgent energy, the collective spirit, and the valorization of sacrifice they hoped to graft onto a reassembled generation of young people to create a confident and dynamic new community in France.[17]

Germany was everything that France was not. "Paris-Berlin" provided *Gringoire* with a fundamental contrast: across the Rhine, "order, discipline, power," and "on the same day, at the same hour, what was happening in Paris?" Another in the "endless series of ministerial crises"—on January 30, 1933, the socialists refused to sign onto party leader Edouard Daladier's program even though they had agreed to participate in his centrist, radical-led government.[18] On the right, French observers cherished the enthusiasm and energy of National Socialism and proposed antiliberal and anti-parliamentarian solutions to restore faith and community at home. Creating a vehicle for decisive, collective action was more important than the precise materials used in building it.

In 1933 the fictional Gilles realized he had misjudged the Radical Socialists, and in June 1933 the very real Marcel Déat appealed to the Socialist Party to conquer "the masses" as the Nazis had and to rejuvenate the nation under a parole—"Order, Authority, Nation"—that superseded "Liberty, Equality, and Fraternity." Outraged socialists quickly kicked Déat and the small number of his supporters out of the party. A new fascist league, the blue-shirted Solidarité Française, sprang into action in 1933 as well, outorganizing the Communists by membership but not winning battles on the streets. Solidarité Française portrayed itself as a movement of renewal, offering the French the "open palm" (that is, the fascist salute) rather than the "clenched fist." Like many fascist groups, the league retained the vocabulary of the French Revolution, honoring ancestors who had taken to the "barricades" to make a "revolution" against feudal privileges and "shocking fiscal inequities." "We are of the people. We go to them, and they listen to us," explained the movement's leader, Jean Renaud, a former military officer who had served in Indochina. But the revolutionary justice he proposed was directed squarely at the Third Republic: "If at seven o'clock in the morning the Solidarité Française attacks and takes power," he fantasized, "at eight o'clock *L'Humanité* will be closed, *Le Populaire* banned, Freemasonry expelled, [and] the Popular Front dissolved. And at nine o'clock, Leon Blum will be taken before a council of state or a High Court." "In ten days," *L'Ami du peuple* claimed as Renaud and his solidaritists watched the resolute action led by the brownshirts in spring 1933, "Marxism will no longer exist in Germany."[19] Without saying as much, Solidarité Française took the Third Reich as a model for what would come after the Third Republic.

Far more important than the blue-shirt imitations of Germany's brownshirts was the veterans' group Croix de Feu, which, in the early 1930s, turned decisively to the right, opening up membership rolls to all citizens and taking to the streets to rally the counter-revolution. Its leader, François de la Rocque, an old military man who before the war had been posted to Algeria and Morocco, spoke constantly of the Croix de Feu's preparation for the "J-Day and H-Hour" of the "National Revolution," offering the propertied middle classes a militarily proficient defense against the socialist Left without going on the attack, a hesitation that probably formed part of its appeal. De la Rocque's "bark was bigger than his bite."[20] Even so, by the mid-1930s, the Croix de Feu had more members than the Socialist and Communist parties combined: 1 million members in a nation of 40 million. Under its own tripartite motto, "Work, Family, Fatherland," which Vichy later adopted, the "cross bearers" mobilized proportionally more citizens in France after 1936 than the Nazis had in Germany before 1933.

The Croix de Feu's battlefield was populated by readers rather than soldiers. There were none of the SA's Sunday morning truck trips through the French countryside. Although it could count on a few thousand paramilitary shock troops, called *dispos* (from the French word *disponible*, meaning "available"), hundreds of thousands of sympathizers saw more action in reading the right-wing press. The daily *L'Action française*, a contemporary remembered, brought "an hour of bliss every morning." You could "denounce liberal errors with an air of self-satisfied superiority, scoff at liberty, equality and fraternity, joke about progress, look skeptical when human dignity and the rights of conscience were spoken of." Yet even reading implied discernment and judgment.

"What is a nation?" asked French historian Ernst Renan in an 1882 lecture at the Sorbonne. "The existence of a nation," Renan had argued, was based on a "daily plebiscite." He rejected the essentials of race, ethnicity, or language to emphasize political culture: commonly held ideas, history, and civic ideals. But in the 1930s, the words that made up this discursive plebiscite began to change so that the idea of the nation shifted as well. The year 1933 reposed Renan's question. For the new Right, to restart France was to move it beyond the uncertainties, contradictions, and discontents of the postwar years and to give France a younger, more dynamic, and leaner form.

To cut France into shape required more clearly defined boundaries. France was not Germany, and the newly energized Right was never comfortable with the "paganism" and violence of the Third Reich. But the French had to assemble just as Germans had under the banner of national community. France needed to be protected from the so-called *métèques*, a word derived from the Greek *metic*, a foreign resident of ancient Athens denied the rights of citizenship. This meant jettisoning universal "general ideas" and affirming a sense of historical, religious, and ethnic identity—making a "France for the French."

To supplement the "old demographic deficiency" of French births, immigration had been allowed to increase dramatically since the Great War. By the early 1930s, France had become the nation most hospitable to immigrants, ahead of the United States. One in ten Parisians was foreign-born. But only in 1933 and 1934, with the rise of Hitler and the power and appeal of ethnic nationalism, did the *métèque* burrow into the thinking of French citizens. Suddenly taking notice, newspapers published dozens more articles than in previous years. All at once *macaronis*, *Polaks*, and "sand niggers" sprang into view. These were identified as Other, not French. Although Italian and Polish immigrants made up the majority of foreigners in France, Jews garnered the most attention. The numbers of foreign-born Jews had increased since the end of the war; other "alien" elements, like French Jews, Protestants, Freemasons, and even the American stars in the popular Hollywood movies (like *King Kong*) playing on the boulevards, attracted coverage as well.[21]

The Jews were named first; other *métèques* were afterthoughts. Of course, it did not take Hitler to recall the French to their own anti-Semitism; at seventy-three, Albert Dreyfus was still alive in 1933. In the beginning of 1932, the republican journal *Le droit de vivre* already lamented the resurgence of anti-Semitism: it was not German; "it is French. It circulates in the veins of the countryside. It has already poisoned the cities. It is no longer a topic of conversation only in the clubs but also on the street." Everyday speech effortlessly passed along the expression "dirty Jew" or the hardly more encouraging amendment "Jewish, but he's a pretty good guy." The firm line in Germany—the boycotts, restrictions, and quotas—gave more precision to anti-Jewish attitudes. Ideas about Jews also spread the concept of Jewish practice and Jewish buildings and notions of infiltration and contamination (and eventually, after 1940, expropriation). The sudden presence of many thousands of German refugees—4,000 by the end of May, 25,000 at the end of the year—most of them Jewish and most of them in Paris, made foreigners even more visible.

"By being persecuted," reflected the journalist Alexander Werth, German "Jews were rendering France a service" for it allowed the country to demonstrate its humanistic values. But Germany's Jews also reminded the French of disorder and uncertainty in international affairs. Jews were the first victims of the war the French wanted desperately to avoid. When Parisians watched German-speaking refugees sitting in the cafes, the police admitted, the attitude was "not generally very warmhearted." Refugees filled the air with "quarrels from beyond our borders," noise that "does not interest us," and posed a threat to the security of the streets.[22] The Jews represented a militant antifascism that disputed the broad French desire for peace; they were associated with the anti-German warmongering party and thus were regarded as a threat to the security of house and home. Even the frightful anti-Semitism that had ejected these people from Germany seemed to prove that Jews were powerful and dangerous.[23]

Anti-Semitic tracts and pamphlets sold well on the streets, and their vocabulary crept into the mainstream press. Distinctions were drawn between "us" and "them," the real French, who wore

regional costumes and ate local fare and took weekend hikes between youth hostels, and the imposters. "Oh! races, races. All
these many races," mused Drieu's Gilles, and "I belong to one."
Just "open the telephone book for the Department of the Seine,"
invited another attentive observer. "The proportion of Jewish subscribers is frightening. The list consisting of 'Lévy' is two times as
long as that of 'Durand' or 'Dupont' combined." (One Café Dupont on the Left Bank tried to get even, posting in 1941 the sign
"Jews and Dogs Prohibited.") And there was more to worry about
since the "invasion" or "colonization" occurred under camouflage. "How many Jews or half-Jews hide themselves behind good
French names?" the writer reminded his readers. (Telephones, like
swimming pools, stipulated an intimacy among strangers and challenged them to live according to abstract or universal norms. Who
was at the other end? In April 1933, the German post office, which
ran the telephone exchanges, amended the phonetic alphabet so
that you no longer spelled out by saying "D as in David," "J as in
Jakob," "N as in Nathan," "S as in Samuel," or "Z as in Zacharias,"
but used "Deutschland," "Joachim," "National," "Siegfried," and
"Zeppelin" instead.[24]) People started calculating the proportions of
foreign-born lawyers, doctors, and university students; compliant
legislators passed laws to limit their numbers. Many foreigners disappeared when 1927 legislation untangled the byzantine natural-
ization process, but this made the problem of camouflage and the
idea of the "real" France all the more compelling. In response to
sentiment like this, Renan's "imagined community" was reimagined in more ethnic-based terms after 1933.

Nuanced discussions that distinguished between "good" and
"bad" Jews gave heart to some, who felt safe on one side of the
line—without fully understanding the violence of line drawing
in the first place. French Jews referred to themselves as *Israélites*,
which was something else and better than *Juifs*, but the distinctions

left collective designations and thus collective prejudices intact. Yiddish-speaking newcomers from Poland, Russia, and Ukraine stood in stark contrast with older French-speaking families; unassimilated Jews, the "strangest of the strangers," in the words of some, differed from assimilated ones, although some Jews were seen to be too assimilated, judging by the alacrity with which they sought out French girls.

Of course, some French Jews had fought bravely in the Great War. Yet anti-Semites disputed even this sacrifice. A long debate ensued about how many Jews had died for France in the years 1914 to 1918. The number was 3,500 according to Paul Ganem, 3,305 if one believed *La France enchaînée*. The propaganda sheet *L'Antijuif* asserted that the dead totaled exactly 1,812, while Robert Brasillach put forward the estimate of 1,700. The number "most frequently advanced" was 1,350, which meant that one soldier died for every thirty-five Jews mobilized as opposed to "one in three" French soldiers, that is, the "true" Frenchmen who had not shirked their duty. (All the figures and conclusions were wrong: out of a 1914 population of 190,000, 32,000 French Jews were mobilized and 6,500 killed, or 1 in 5—compared to 1 in 6.5 for all mobilized Frenchmen. Motivated by like-minded anti-Semitism, Prussia's notorious 1916 "Jew count" registered similarly counterintuitive results. How to explain the disparity? Apt to be middle-class, Jews more likely achieved the rank of noncommissioned officer, the leader of first resort on the dangerous front lines.[25])

By the end of the 1930s, French political discourse examined huge numbers of people for their suitability to live in France: thinking about German Jews led commentators to condemn all refugees, then all immigrants—naturalized or not—and finally French Jews. By drawing careful distinctions between *Israélites* and *Juifs*, the French asked who belonged and who did not, justifying indiscriminate prejudice against those who were labeled outsiders. Alarmed observers regarded Paris as "Canaan-on-the-Seine" or "God's own concentration camp."[26]

Renan's question—"What is a nation?"—was posed with more urgency during the 1933–1934 winter holidays. On Christmas Eve, the morning papers reported on a train wreck in Lagny, outside Paris, the night before. On this "glacial night," delays hampered train traffic from the Gare de l'Est, and the locomotive of a speeding express bound for Strasbourg slammed through the last four wooden carriages of a stalled suburban train. *Le Figaro* reported 113 dead, a figure that was revised upward the next day to nearly 200. The trains had been filled with holiday travelers, their bags packed with Christmas gifts, and the reports of witnesses who described bodies strewn about the wreck, including children still clutching toys, were deeply shocking. Many of the bodies, all of them in the suburban train, were unrecognizable. Three parliamentary deputies were among those killed. Declaring a period of mourning, the president ordered that municipal Christmas trees remain unlit for the remainder of the holidays. It was the grimmest holiday since the war.

Over the course of December 24, as bodies were brought to the baggage rooms at the Gare de l'Est for identification, newspapermen began to ask questions. The accident had occurred just before eight o'clock at night, but organized rescue teams took five hours to arrive to transport the injured to nearby hospitals. Many passengers walked on foot to seek refuge in the nearby towns of Lagny, Ponpomme, and Vaires. Journalists reported that some of the living had rifled through the pockets of the dead. Heavy fog may have explained why the engineers on the express train did not see the red signal on the track, but when the train crossed the signal, detonators should have automatically alarmed the engineer. Were the engineers inattentive or drunk; were the "railway capitalists" slow to install proper safety equipment? The chairman of the Association for the Traveling Public put the blame squarely on the railways, "the real culprits," who had neglected to replace wooden carriages with the metal ones that had saved lives on the Strasbourg express. With every revelation the press uncovered, indignation compounded horror. When the repaired express locomotive was put back in service, trainmen referred to it as "the pork butcher."[27]

On the night of the accident, December 23, inclement weather forced Alexandre Stavisky to abandon the car he was driving and board a train to seek shelter in Chamonix, France's new ski resort in the Alps. A suave former nightclub manager and confidence man, Stavisky had sold fraudulent municipal bonds to insurance companies, which purchased them on the recommendation of Stavisky's confederate, the mayor of Bayonne, and the mayor's contacts in the French cabinet. As the date approached when the worthless bonds would come due, one of Stavisky's agents in Bayonne got cold feet and tipped off the police. Over the Christmas holidays, Stavisky, a *métèque* who had emigrated to France before the war as the child of a Jewish Ukrainian dentist, went deeper into the mountains for cover, followed by Paris police. The chase ended on January 8. The official report stated that Stavisky had committed suicide by a self-inflicted gunshot.

"Le beau Sascha," as Stavisky was called, was one more body in the newspapers. From the very beginning, the story sprang all sorts of leaks. Anyone following leads on Stavisky quickly bumped into the highest levels of French society: Radical Socialists in the Camille Chautemps government who had recommended the bonds; high-level officials in the police and the prosecutor's office who had protected Stavisky, a convicted felon, over the years; newspaper editors who had been bought and sold; and more *métèques*, such as a German émigré novelist and a prominent Russian journalist who had befriended the bon vivant in cafes and casinos. Since the police allowed Stavisky to bleed nearly to death on the floor before calling an ambulance, it was not clear whether the law was on the scene to arrest the man or to murder him. The French political script, quipped one observer, seemed to have been written that winter by the mystery writer Edgar Wallace, the same one who supposedly inspired Göring in Berlin the year before.

Fourteen Parisian newspapers called Stavisky's death a suicide, eight did not, and a few others settled on "suicide by persuasion." The trajectory of the bullet suggested that it had been shot from a distance of three meters, causing some journalists to remark that foreign-born Stavisky must have had a very "long arm." Since Prime Minister Camille Chautemps refused to appoint an investigative commission but accepted the resignation of the implicated cabinet member, the public felt that statesmen at the highest levels had a great deal to hide. Stavisky in a pool of blood at a chalet in Chamonix and the dead arrayed in the baggage rooms at the Gare de l'Est had been the victims of a combination of negligence, embezzlement, and conspiracy. Every revelation the press disclosed about these cases confirmed that "something was rotten in the Republic of France."[28] It was a classic populist scenario: the passengers neglected, the people fleeced, the republic betrayed.

With "another republican scandal," as L'Action française put it, copywriters of the Stavisky affair overwrote it with the story of the Lagny catastrophe. The antirepublican paper had begun to connect these dots even before Stavisky's suicide and, in an appeal "to the People of Paris" on January 7, urged Frenchmen to assemble in large numbers before the Chamber of Deputies to "clamor for honesty and justice." With Stavisky dead, right-wing papers stepped up attacks on the cabinet with headlines like "Down with the Assassins" and "Down with the Thieves." Day after day, they appealed to the public to demonstrate its indignation. Throughout January, protestors organized in the paramilitary leagues, Action français's Camelots du Roi, the Jeunesses Patriotes, the blue-shirted paramilitaries of Solidarité Française, and the Croix de Feu rallied in the Place de la Concorde, provoking the police with "violence rare in recent years" and building improvised barricades out of park benches, metal fencing, and overturned cars before running down side streets.[29]

Readers became demonstrators; the headlines—"À bas les voleurs!" and "À bas les assassins!"—resounded as slogans; songs in the street put into verse the bitter, satirical articles of the right-wing press:

> *Let's string up the deputies*
> *And if we can't string 'em up*
> *Let's beat in their faces*
> *Let's reduce 'em to a pulp!*

Although there was no central organization that could compare with that of Hitler, Goebbels, and the SA, Paris in 1934 began to look like Berlin in 1932.

The public disorder forced Chautemps's resignation at the end of January 1934. The new Daladier government reassigned or fired key figures in the prosecutor's office and the prefect of police, but many observers regarded this as an attempt at damage control. The right-wing press pushed for a confrontation with the republic in front of the Chamber of Deputies in the Palais Bourbon, the "bastion of corruption," on February 6, the day when the Daladier cabinet was to be voted in. "France for the French," the press proclaimed. "Take your brooms and sweep out the rubbish!" There were many newspaper headlines but no itinerary—no exact time or place—whereas the Nazis had been much better organized on January 30, 1933 ("Torchlight Parade, 7 o'clock Grosser Stern"). Ranks of the Croix de Feu lined up in military discipline along the narrow streets abutting the Palais Bourbon on the Left Bank but stayed put. After nightfall, many thousands of demonstrators gathered on the Place de la Concorde on the Right Bank. "Assassins" they shouted in unison. When police stiffened their lines to keep protestors from crossing the Seine, a series of attacks and counterattacks escalated the violence. Protestors defended themselves against the police's horse charges by throwing paving stones and iron railings, setting off firecrackers, and lancing horses with walking canes fitted with razor blades. Over the seven-hour melee, small fires burned, and when the crowds continued to advance, panicked security forces fired their weapons, killing 14 people and injuring 1,300, about half of them police.

February 6 was the most violent night in French history since the Paris Commune in 1871. Talk of a coup was certainly in the air, but the rioters were a mixed lot, more indignant than revolutionary. Outraged by the tragedy at Lagny and the comedy around Stavisky, they rallied against a powerful, self-enriching political establishment. Yet the only song angry taxpayers, the "men in Republican derby hats," the "chaps in Communist caps," and the "middle-aged, medaled war veterans," as well royalist adolescents from the university, had in common was "La Marseillaise," which honored France's republican revolution.[30] A witty comedy two years later staged the dilemma: Martin, the chauffeur, and Claire, the secretary, both employed by a rich industrialist, a Radical Socialist like Gilles, joined together in the streets to protest against the decadent and corrupt republic, only to find that one was a Communist, the other a "cross bearer."[31] Their union dissolved while the industrialist remained upright.

The right-wing demonstrators in 1934 lacked basic organization. There was no plan of attack on the Place de la Concorde that night, no chief of staff to decide what to do the next day, no base of operations in the city or the countryside from which to launch renewed attacks on the republic. After midnight, the rioters dispersed without reaching the Concorde Bridge or the Chamber of Deputies. Sporadic clashes continued over the next days, and young men purposefully dressed their wounds to show off on the boulevards.

Robert Brasillach and his friends organized a pilgrimage to the Place de la Concorde every February to lay violets to honor the demonstrators who had been killed, and Brasillach wrote a final farewell on the eve of his execution for treason by grim coincidence on February 6, 1945: "This evening I am thinking of you, oh dead of February." Yet every year the commemorators "diminished" in number, because, Brasillach lamented, "French patriots are forgetful." In fact, the victims remained anonymous, their lives unexamined, so they never could be claimed as martyrs. There were no grand funerals for activists to turn into angry antirepublican protests. The contrast could not have been greater to the cult of the dead tended by the armies of National Socialists and Communists in Weimar Germany, the legend of Horst Wessel, or the song about the fallen "little trumpeter" or to French republican traditions embellished by the burial of national heroes in the Panthéon or the funerals of writers such as Victor Hugo in 1885. Hostility to the institutions of the Third Republic remained strong, and divisions between socialists and nationalists deepened, but no clear lines of authority translated the large readership of the right-wing newspapers into antirepublican organizations or mass public demonstrations. French fascism was thus more vicarious than real, more theatrical than dangerous. Drieu la Rochelle's Gilles recognized the dream after waking up. "The people are not dead," he enthused about February 6, 1934, but he quickly recognized how short their collective life was: "Yesterday everything was impossible, and tomorrow it will be that way again, but today..."[32]

Gilles did not fill in the ellipsis, and in the end there was no National Socialist French Workers' Party to do so either. Even so, Paris felt different. The crowds who had rallied in January and February brought down two prime ministers: Chautemps and Daladier, who resigned a day after the riots after eights day in power. Gaston Doumerge, who replaced Daladier, relied increasingly on *décret-lois* issued without parliamentary backing. Unappeased militants loitered on the streets. A passerby read a leaflet handed out on the boulevards: it was a call to rally to a national unity front, to shutter Jewish-owned department stores, to bring down the *métèque* André Citroën, the world's fourth-largest automobile manufacturer whose Dutch Jewish grandfather had been a green-grocer and taken the name "Limeonman" (lime man), which the family changed to "Citroen" (lemon) and, after moving to Paris, to Citroën. Lemons and limes incarnated the foreigners' invasion of France. The "contamination of public opinion has set in in France as well," the Parisian pedestrian concluded.[33]

For any number of young French nationalists who gained prominence on the extreme Right in the 1930s, like writers Drieu la Rochelle, Brasillach, Bertrand de Jouvenel, Alfred Fabre-Luce, or Lucien Rébatet, the events of February 6 represented a dramatic turning point. They rejected the crusty, elitist monarchism of Maurras's L'Action française for the streetwise activism of fascist leagues such as the Croix de Feu. Action, violence, and the strikes of decisionism constituted, as a charmed Brasillach summarized, the "extraordinary poetry" of fascism. "I am in seventh heaven," wrote theater critic Paul Léautaud, after seeing all "the warning signs of revolution." With "protestors and police in the street," "my spirits have been revived." In the months after the clash, the 35,000 members of the Croix de Feu had become 150,000, and by 1936, 500,000; when the outlawed league reorganized as a political party, the Parti Social Français, it was France's largest, with as many as 1 million members, more than the socialists and Communists combined. Every week in spring and summer 1934, the league's Paris section recruited several thousand young Parisian men. The novelist Léon Daudet exulted that his city had "never been so reactionary."[34]

The picture postcards that the French sent to each other changed after 1934. They switched out views of the *mécano* and *midinette*, the skilled young worker and the shop girl with an hour of free time at noon, walking in pairs down city streets lined with new shops, snack bars, and movie theaters, for images of militant patriots rallying around national monuments. For Drieu, the mobilization amounted to "national emancipation." "People everywhere have taken to the streets," he observed, and they "have broken the petty chains of the small individual life" to reimmerse "themselves in great communions." "You have lived too long hidden in your houses, cocooned in your little lives," and absorbed in "individual histories," he lectured the French, but after February they had finally rediscovered "the daily rhythm of communal life," "collective fervor," and "unanimous faith." Breathing in "lungfuls of grandeur," they had joined "the great cadenced, reharmonized masses of Fascism, of Hitlerism," and even of Soviet Stalinism. "Revolutionary spectacles" and "mass movement" punctuated the three months since February 6, marveled *L'Action française*.[35]

France learned the same lessons as Germany had, but democratic politics of the street invigorated the Left as well as the Right; citizens assembled on the Place de la Nation in the traditionally poor quarter of eastern Paris, and at the Arc de Triomphe, the symbol of French military glory at the end of the elegant Champs-Élysées on the west side. There was no decisive demonstration of "unanimous faith" as with National Socialism. The "clenched fist" socked it to the "open palm" in the latent civil war among the French that lasted until the end of the collaborationist Vichy regime in 1944. After the riots, on February 9, 1934, Communists rallied against "fascism" in working-class neighborhoods behind the Gare du Nord and the Gare de l'Est and three days later joined a nationwide general strike called by the socialist trade unions. "They will not prevail," the socialists declared, reminting the stirring wartime slogan against the Germans at Verdun in order to resist fascists in postwar Paris: "Ils ne passeront pas!"[36] It was the largest public action in French history, bigger than the strikes on May Day 1920 and a prelude to the great strikes that ushered in the Popular Front in spring 1936. In a counter call to arms, the Croix de Feu's newspaper appealed to the French to mobilize for the "battle of the streets," in which the "national front" faced off against the "Marxist front." For the next two years, this turned all of France into the demonstration ground in a war to claim public space. As many as one hundred demonstrations took place between February 1934 and May 1936 in Paris alone; in what one critic denounced as the "communism of noise," loudspeakers amplified the songs and slogans as street noise echoed across the *quartier* and over the radio.[37]

The Left rallied on May Day 1934, the Right on May 13, the anniversary of the canonization of Joan of Arc in 1920. On Armistice Day, November 11, 1934, traditionally a day of collective mourning, working-class Parisians assembled in their neighborhoods on the east side around the Place de la Republique and the Place de la Nation, while across town the leagues occupied the Place de la Concorde and the Arc de Triomphe. Bastille Day 1935—typically a family holiday—became an "emotionally charged" day of "mass marches and ritual oath-taking."[38] More than 150,000 members of the Croix de Feu and the other right-wing leagues marched up the length of the Champs-Élysées to the Arc de Triomphe, while three or four times as many socialist and Communist partisans marched to the Place de la Nation. Not since the revolutionary years 1793 and 1794 had so many people in France taken to the streets.

The Left rallied more people than the Right, and left-wing militants often made it impossible for the Croix de Feu and other organizations to hold meetings. While 55 percent of the demonstrations in Paris during the "time of troubles" between 1934 and 1936 were held in support of the republic, in the countryside, in the *provence*, the percentage was 83 percent. The contrast with Germany, where the nationalist Right had conquered public places outside the big cities a few years earlier, was stark. Moreover, the French Left mixed politics with fun and added dances to the speeches to provide good-natured celebrations. If the leagues marched their mostly male supporters in military ranks through files of spectators, socialists rallied supporters on the Place de la Republique in the clots of community: a father perched his little girl on his shoulders, and she clenched her fist. Protestors sang "Au-devant de la vie" (Toward life), which was about setting out on the road on weekends, or the more sardonic "Y'a trop de tout" (There's too much of everything) about workers who were expendable and soldiers who were indispensable.[39]

The February riots did not result in a coup; yet no one side won a resounding victory: throughout the 1930s, the Left mobilized against the "fascist" leagues and the "fascist" leagues won support against the specter of "Bolshevism." Unlike in Germany, however, the entire Left rallied to the defense of the republic. Socialists and Communists gained strength as they joined together in an uneasy spirit of working-class cooperation known as the Popular Front. Moreover, the center held, memories of the war united the French more than they divided them, and despite Lagny and Stavisky, there was no melodramatic narrative of national betrayal. There was no November 1918 to corrode August 1914. Although weakened, the "Radicals" joined the Popular Front, which won the 1936 elections and installed Léon Blum as the republic's first socialist prime minister. It was as if Germany's Social Democrats and the Catholic Center Party had forged a political alliance around a Jewish chancellor who was able to count on the toleration of the Communists. But the wave of sit-down strikes in spring 1936 and the Popular Front's pro-labor social legislation unnerved the French Right and definitively lifted the fortunes of antisystem fascist parties such as the Parti Social Français, the successor to the Croix de Feu, and the Parti Populaire Français, founded by Jacques Doriot, the ex-Communist mayor of Saint-Denis. In the venomous conditions of political conflict that resulted, the pissoirs of Paris featured graffiti: "Better Hitler than Blum." "Cross bearers" accused the Comintern of having moved its headquarters from Moscow to Paris.[40] Although the Popular Front succeeded in blocking fascism's drive to power in France, it did not halt its advance.

The basic institutions of the Third Republic remained in place until the fall of France in June 1940, but the price was high. The center-right Daladier government that succeeded the Popular Front—the centrist Radicals ably tacked from left to right—rolled back many of its progressive accomplishments by decree, pursued a vigorous anti-Communist policy, and stiffened antiforeign sentiments in the name of French national virtue and European peace. Daladier had once praised France as "the last trench of freedom," a universal value, but he withdrew republican troops to the rear. Had parliamentary elections been held as scheduled in spring 1940, De la Rocque's right-wing party might have won; its sections had struck deep roots in Catholic associational life, its "comrades" had lifted Joan of Arc up as a symbol of social reconciliation and political crusade, and its leaders had even begun to plan the national *fête*, a French version of the January 30 parades in Germany, to celebrate the triumph of the newly awakened "true" France.[41] The legacy of February 6, 1934, remained unresolved: "If 1936 was the revenge of the Left, 1940 was the revenge of the Right."[42]

Political scientist Karl Loewenstein, a Jewish refugee from Nazi Germany teaching at Yale University, commented at the time that "the unknown x in the political equation of Europe is at the present moment France." Although democratic institutions had survived the challenges of Georges Boulanger in the 1880s and the Dreyfus Affair at the turn of the century, and although the relatively prosperous middle classes remained loyal to the republic in the 1920s, Loewenstein found a "national restlessness" in which fascism had gained credibility as a political alternative. Resentment about decadence and decline washed over crucial sectors of the business and professional elite. Writing in 1935, Loewenstein argued that "two opposing armies of the left and of the right" faced each other, impelling more and more citizens to make a choice in favor of one or the other. Ultimately, Loewenstein expressed confidence in the republican tradition; yet he was not completely sure. Many decades later, scholars continue to examine the x factor, placing France in the "swing zone" to debate whether in the 1930s it illustrated the extent of the postwar fascist "wave" in Europe or the resilience of established liberal institutions.[43]

In 1933, all Europe heard Nazi sounds and saw the Nazi belligerence. Radio broadcast the cries of "Heil, Heil, Heil." Some people were "very impressed"; others found Hitler's "hollering" "horrible." As they watched older "fire-company bands" become loud "Hitler bands," kids on the Swiss side of Lauterbach ran across the old bridge over the Rhine River to see what was going on. "We thought they were a little bit bonkers," but there were energetic, "racy people" among the uniformed groups on the German side.[44] Leni Riefenstahl's acclaimed documentary on the 1934 Nuremberg rally, *Triumph of the Will*, and all the newsreels introduced the future: mass mobilization, collective emotion, preparation for a new era of international warfare. Cinematic images created a new "sensuround," which gave acoustic and visual authority to what had been dispersed symptoms of antidemocratic feeling. Thus, the Third Reich in Germany, the "story of the century," reorganized expectations across Europe and beyond.

I T WOULD BE completely misleading to suggest that Nazi Germany generated by itself a wave of new fascist or authoritarian movements in Europe. In every country, the unfolding of right-wing activity followed older national trajectories. Patriotic and fascist leagues mobilized young people, veterans, and especially university students throughout Europe long before Hitler came to power in 1933. Nonetheless, the example of the Third Reich was compelling. It made credible the idea that the socialist Left could be smashed, and it demonstrated the efficacy of violence. Nazi

Germany created a newly vitalized landscape on which military offensives against political enemies might be conducted. German-speaking Swiss gave a particularly evocative description to the fresh wind blowing in 1933. In the *Frontenfrühling* (front spring), new movements, leagues, and guards shot up like mushrooms. "All at once you could see marching troops with flags and music, and banners and even battle axes marching through the streets or making pilgrimages with song and cheer to 'people's rallies' in the countryside." "The Swiss lands are crisscrossed with fronts; shots fly out in all directions from the trenches."[45] Across Europe, new associations organized while older right-wing groups regained energy. They saw themselves as missionaries of a political offensive that shared antiliberalism, anti-Marxism, anti-Semitism, and usually anticapitalism, plus European-wide experiences of war, revolution, and counterrevolution. The *Frontenfrühling* scored notable successes. It strengthened critiques of democracy and liberalism and of the tendency to identify with a self-serving and self-interested "system" of elites. It also flexed the muscles of anti-Marxism, which identified a "foreign" enemy that Hitler demonstrated could be politically eradicated. Awaiting the "knaves without a fatherland," the "traitors and revolutionaries," was "prison or the gallows" or else the boot "to Palestine or Moscow," promised Emil Sonderegger, the Swiss military officer who had "saved" Zurich from the "red beast" during the general strike in 1918.[46]

Where authoritarian governments had already established themselves—in Austria, Hungary, and Romania—fascism advanced as right-wing statesmen absorbed fascist ideas, even if they repressed specific fascist contenders. Unconditional anti-Marxism was the point of entry, and in the newly established nation-states of central and eastern Europe, a kind of nativist euphoria paved the way for fascists who conceived of the nation as blood and soil, who dramatized its endangerment by meddlesome international powers such as the League of Nations, international capitalism, and

"World Jewry," and who promised an uncompromising, violent struggle to establish a new reign of redeemed national justice. "We are waiting for a nationalist Romania, frenzied and chauvinistic, armed and rigorous, pitiless and vengeful," wrote Mircea Eliade in 1936.[47] To many intellectuals, fascism represented the way forward, sign-posting the open road. In Romania's 1937 elections, the Iron Guard fascists and a right-wing anti-Semitic party won 25 percent of the vote. Two years later, Hungary's Iron Cross movement won 25 percent of the vote, doing especially well in the formerly "red" suburbs around Budapest. In Bucharest, Warsaw, and Vienna, anti-Semitic violence spiked.

The antiliberal, collectivist spirit of fascism resonated in western Europe as well. The National Socialist Movement in the Netherlands won 8 percent of the vote in provincial elections in April 1935. The next year the Rexist party in Belgium won more than 10 percent. France was the x factor in the European political equation because fascist electoral gains there would have likely strengthened right-wing trends in the Low Countries.

But in the absence of a clear French signal, the fascist wave failed to crest. The elections in Holland and Belgium in the mid-1930s represented the high-water mark of fascism's electoral successes. A 1935 frontist referendum in Switzerland proposing a "total revision" of the constitution failed miserably. Also, the arbitrary, state-sponsored violence and anticlerical inclinations of the Third Reich tarnished fascism as a "foreign" product. Ultimately, the democratic parties in western Europe did not succumb to unconditional anti-Marxism. They opposed "totalitarianism" on the fascist Right as well as the Communist Left. Political cabinets moved closer to the center rather than further to the right. Social Democrats, spooked by the destruction of Germany's historic party, also moderated their positions. And effective legislation kept fascists from finding a footing. Already in 1933, Holland, Denmark, Sweden, Norway, and Switzerland enacted "blouse-laws," banning the paramilitary uniforms so central to the public spectacle of fascist mobilization. Western European states also prohibited the formation of private armies and party militias. Legislators toughened laws against the incitement of hate directed at particular groups or religions and the defamation of state authorities. Elsewhere, most notably in Holland, members of extreme parties were purged from the civil service. According to Loewenstein, these were positive signs, indicating that principled "democratic fundamentalism" had stepped over into "militancy," appropriate to "the state of siege" in which democracy found itself in the 1930s, even if this meant sometimes "violating fundamental principles."[48] But for all this to work, it was critical to direct "enabling acts" in defense of democracy at the extreme Right as well as the extreme Left and for the ruling parties to move to the center and not alienate or demonize Social Democrats. If emergency rule suppressed Social Democrats as well as fascists, as was the case in Austria, "authoritarian democracy" collapsed into authoritarianism.

Loewenstein worried that "fundamentalist scruples," especially on the part of center-left parties, would disable the capacity and vigilance of the militant democratic state. But the real problem was the slip to the right. Loewenstein overlooked the revived nationalist spirit by which "militant democracy" countered the extreme or "foreign" fascist threat. In Switzerland, for example, the spirit of "national resistance" celebrated the ancient Swiss history of cantonal representative government but often disparaged the forms democracy took in the twentieth century. It defended the old mountain inhabitants at the expense of the industry and business in the valleys. In an appeal to "roots," an appeal to Swiss or Dutch or French history defended democracy in ways that echoed the fascist parole "Switzerland for the Swiss" or "France for the French" without entirely excising the next thought, which was "Out with the Jews." "Militant democracy" was apt to create in-groups and out-groups. It was suspicious of outsiders, refugees, and Jews, it upheld the notion of an exclusive ethnic or historical polity over pluralist alternatives, and it favored anti-parliamentarian over scrupulously democratic solutions and values over process. It supported historical institutions rather than fundamental principles leading to sustained anticommunism and pacifist appeasement of the Third Reich. In this way, Jews and other opponents of Nazism continued to figure as warmongers, domestic and international partisans of disorder.

One could go to Zurich, Amsterdam, or Paris to tell the story, but the best example is Charles Lindbergh's "America First" speech in Des Moines, Iowa, on September 11, 1941. The famous aviator labeled the British and Jews as "war agitators" whose own interests were understandable yet "not American." Lindbergh counted Jews as victims of Nazi persecution and then went on to recount them as a "dangers to this country" on account of "their large ownership and influence in our motion pictures, our press, our radio and our government." The grammatical effect of the second-person plural in the speech was clear: "them" and "us." Jews needed to take care not to abuse the toleration Americans had afforded them. Lindbergh went on to castigate other usual suspects of instigation, Communists and intellectuals. Much like the Swiss in the mountains, Lindbergh spoke "the cadence of the old West," a virtuous place he believed to be under attack by mass democracy, big-city life, and what his wife, Anne Murrow Lindbergh, considered the utterly false expression of modern times: "high-pressuring newspapers," "flashy and cheap magazines," "racy and material advertising," "sex-appeal movies," and "blustering politicians."[49] The appeal to the "people's community," the "real" America implicit in "America First," always conveyed a fundamental sense of embattlement. The imagined assault on America's character and its interests, the America for Americans, the America misled by Europeans

in the Great War, was another version of the "stab-in-the-back legend," one that held public opinion in sway until the Japanese attack
on Pearl Harbor.

In 1939, before the outbreak of World War II, neither the United
States nor Britain, France, Holland, or Switzerland had succumbed
to fascism; yet the national resistance was expressed in the mistrust-
ful and belligerent language of moral panic. Fascism represented
just one form of the sacralization of politics in which a besieged
in-group reaffirmed forgotten virtue and collective justice against
dangerous outsiders. The effort to resist registered the extent of
fascism's advance. National Socialism was a symptom of a fascist
style in postwar politics that flourished precisely because political
life had become more democratic or populist after the destruction
of the old regimes at the end of World War I. Nazism also strengthened the global appeal of fascism because the first hundred days
demonstrated the extraordinary potential of going to battle to re-
trieve a new idea of the nation; 1933 showed that liberalism and
socialism could be smashed. "Will," "struggle," and violence could
be mobilized to achieve transformative goals, destruction, and creation. What made Germany so interesting to right-wing and fascist
authoritarians was the example of its capacity to disrupt flows of
history and change movements of time.

But the savagery of historical narrative also set Germany apart.
It imposed on generic fascism an extremely personal drama performed by a cast of August patriots and November criminals, sacrificed fathers and avenging sons, wartime victors and betrayed
armies in retreat, as well as corrupt "system" politicians. The script
named names, provided dates, and built landmarks: Hella von
Westarp, November 1918, Versailles, the bleeding border. None of
the events of the twenty years after 1914 left Germans alone: the
war dead, the parades and demonstrations, the strikes, the states
of siege, the currency inflation, the unemployed in the streets,
the beggars at the door. The German crisis arose from not just

numbers but the theater that rendered it an Easter passion. Boycott Saturday is an excellent example of the way "crisis" was translated in Germany. All this was much more difficult to script in France, where mourners gathered on November 11 to honor the war dead in thousands of villages and sang the patriotic "La Marsaillaise." November 1918 meant something very different in Germany: a redemptive story designed to turn back history, to reclaim a moment in August 1914, a fight that would culminate in an extraordinary one hundred days.

CHAPTER NINE

The One Hundred Days

T IME SPED UP in 1933: transformations that would last "one thousand years" occurred in less than "one hundred days." Yesterday the republic, tomorrow the Third Reich. "It was as if I could hear the turning of a page of world history," remembered one eyewitness on the day Adolf Hitler was appointed chancellor, "a page in a book in which the sheets of paper to follow will be inscribed with wild and chaotic, sinister scribblings." Another hand holding the front page of the newspaper "began to tremble."[1]

The "crowding events of the hundred days," as Franklin D. Roosevelt put it in July 1933, certainly seemed to apply to Germany. They also evoked the original template for the one hundred days, Napoleon Bonaparte's return from Elba and the reestablishment of the empire until his abdication in the wake of Waterloo in 1815. Each of the hundred days—Napoleon's, Roosevelt's, and Hitler's— recharged history. The one hundred days consolidating the New

Deal and the Nazi seizure of power gave new shape to the future in the extraordinary year 1933.

I N OCTOBER 1933, Heinrich George detoured to Frankfurt to play the lead in a curious drama, *The Hundred Days*, a piece plotted around Napoleon's return from exile and his renewed drive to remake the world. It was advertised as the collaborative work of Benito Mussolini and the playwright Giovacchino Forzano, although the Italian dictator did little more than add a few lines and ideas. (Forzano presented a copy of the play to Sigmund Freud on behalf of both men in gratitude for the psychoanalyst's willingness to consult with Forzano's daughter. The dedication read, "For Sigmund Freud, who will make the world a better place, with admiration and gratitude.") Mussolini's name made the play remarkably popular in the early 1930s. Malcolm Muggeridge remembered that it was produced at the "Old Vic and kindly received"—although the venue had been the New Theater. The play was performed in cities across Germany in 1933; Hitler himself had seen and admired the premiere in Jena a year before he became chancellor.[2]

Heinrich George would be playing Napoleon. *The Hundred Days* spanned the 112 days in 1815 between March 19, when the newly installed Bourbon king, Louis XVIII, fled Paris before Napoleon and his troops marched into city, and July 8, when the king returned through the gate at Saint-Denis after Napoleon's defeat at Waterloo and his abdication a week later. The interval was hugely dramatic. Napoleon reappeared from his forced exile on Elba and seemed to reverse the tide of history. History had become a category of the sublime, stranger than a Gothic tale. As events turned, the statesmen of France had to decide quickly where they stood: with the restored Bourbons or the renewed dream of Napoleon's empire. "Bonaparte in Paris and Emperor again!" an astounded Englishman wrote in his diary. "These revolutions would be too incredible for romance."³ "No, never shall I forget," recalled Germaine de Stäel, "I thought that the earth was about to open under my feet."⁴ "He's Tyrant again!" wrote Lord Byron, "Thunderer of the scene."⁵ History had taken contemporaries by complete surprise.

Such surprise resonated in the year 1933, when Hitler's sudden rise to power culminated, at a quarter past eleven, with his appointment as chancellor. Europe suddenly slipped from the firm footing of a postwar era into the anxious vertigo of a prewar one. For Hitler, the reversal of fortune had always been a lifeline. Again and again, "a great miracle" had saved him—as after the failed "Beerhall Putsch" in 1923, after the election losses in November 1932, and again, he thought, after Roosevelt's death, on April 12, 1945, less than a month before the German surrender and a little over two weeks before his own suicide.

Mussolini referred to Napoleon more frequently as he consolidated his own power in the late 1920s, modernizing Italy, creating a new fascist order, and reaching a concordat with the Vatican—the "next hundred years belong to us," he boasted. But Forzano's play explored a different theme: How circumstances might fail the dictator. Forzano set the opening of *The Hundred Days* well. Napoleon reappeared after he had already become a figure consigned to history: Soldiers in the armies commented on the weight he had put on, and tourists arrived from England to ogle the emperor, the figure in Madame Tussaud's wax exhibition who had been reanimated. Marshal Ney vowed to capture Napoleon alive and "bring him to Paris in an iron cage," although he defected to Napoleon two days before the emperor made his grand entrance at the Tuileries Palace on March 20, 1815.⁶ (Ney's threat must have made a strong impression on Hitler. At the end of World War II, he expressed his fear that he would be captured and put on public display in a "monkey cage" at the Moscow zoo, a "waxwork figure" exhibited for the amusement of the crowds.⁷)

In the last scenes of the play, however, Napolcon departed with dignity. He abdicated in favor of his son so that the French people would not be forced to dishonorably hand their emperor over to the Allies. Napoleon hoped for exile in the United States or Great Britain, but when on July 15 he surrendered on HMS *Bellerophon*, a ship that had dogged him his entire life (the *Bellerophon* had taken part in the Channel defense in 1794 and seen action in the Battle of the Nile and the Battle of Trafalgar), he was headed to the remote South Atlantic island of St. Helena, where he died in 1821; contemporaries described his fate as "caged." Technically, Napoleon's four-year-old son ruled as Emperor Napoleon II from June 22 to July 7, 1815. And Hitler ordered the remains of the son returned to France in December 1940 (although, because Napoleon II's mother was a Habsburg, the heart and intestines were required to remain in Vienna).

In Forzano's drama, two sources undermined Napoleon's power. The first was the minister of police, Joseph Fouché, whom the emperor cynically reappointed. Fouché played a cunning game, arguing on Napoleon's behalf in the National Assembly but pursuing contacts with the Bourbons, the Orleanists, and France's enemy, Austria. For him, Napoleon had "returned from Elba madder than when he went." The emperor's assumption of the throne was "the last eruption of a volcano which approaches extinction." The second was the National Assembly, elections for which Napoleon magnanimously approved. In the play, the deputies were mostly liberal skeptics of imperial power led by the Marquis de Lafayette, whom Fouché dismissed as "a monument in search of a pedestal." First gathering on the Champ de Mai, where the Eiffel Tower now stands, on June 1, 1815, the assembly turned against Napoleon, convinced that the united powers of Europe had a quarrel with him, not with France. After his defeat at Waterloo, the emperor demanded emergency powers: "Our enemies pretend that I alone am the object of their wrath." They only "wish to destroy me because they know that without me France would be impotent." Napoleon's pleas were in vain. "He alone is the cause of the war," argued one legislator. "Let him perish," declared another. "He must be destroyed.... Long live the Chamber!"

Although Napoleon abdicated so that France would preserve "the sacred right of a land to choose its own sovereign," the victors insisted on the restoration of the unlucky Bourbon king, Louis XVIII. The National Assembly, robust in its democratic opposition to Napoleon and to the Bourbons, miscalculated the intentions of the Allies, who summarily dismissed the representatives. In the end, as German reviews of *The Hundred Days* clarified, "in times of emergency, parliaments can only fail." "Five-hundred happenstance opinions of the fluffed-up representatives of the people," their mouths stuffed with words about "freedom and humanity," thwarted the "ingenuous fellow" who stood ready to accomplish "great things." The "hundred days" represented the apocalyptic moment, testing the mettle of the nation that either remained faithful to the leader or abandoned him and itself.[8]

The true representatives of the people were not the chatty lawyers in the assembly, who, assessing risk like Fouché, deserted the vanquished leader after Waterloo, but the 700,000 soldiers who had fought with Napoleon and rallied once more, willing to die. They and their followers included "the gunsmith of Marseille, who contributes a gift of a hundred muskets; the poor saddler of Boulogne-sur-Mer, who delivered eighty saddles for the cavalry; the workers of Vesoul"—a procession of genuine patriots and heroes who resembled those gathered up on the streets on the Day of Potsdam and the Day of National Labor in 1933—followed by "the peasants of Argonne who threw up trenches and would take no payment" and, behind them, "the soldiers of the seventy-ninth regiment, who are refusing bribes, because they are determined to follow me," and finally "every woman from whom I expected a begging letter and received instead an offer of her savings." "That is the country," Napoleon insisted. And that was exactly as Hitler saw it: Germany was embodied in the brownshirts and not in the Reichstag, in national duty and not democratic representation. Without a people willing to make the sacrifices to defend it, there could be no nation.[9]

German theaters produced *The Hundred Days* in 1933 as a song of triumph, an honor to the dictator who understood the quality of his people and to the people who stood by their leader. The people of France failed Napoleon, but the play appealed to citizens of the new Germany, beneficiaries of a new "hundred days." Heinrich George must have played a magnificent Napoleon Bonaparte.

The "hundred days" was a perennial theme in nineteenth- and twentieth-century literature; Balzac, Stendhal, Dumas, and Hugo all took up this "most romantic enterprise." From the other end of the political world, Joseph Roth, a Jewish journalist who left his position as a feature writer at the *Frankfurter Zeitung* and emigrated to Paris on the very day Hitler came to power, also read or saw Forzano's play. Taking account of the losses of the world, he wrote up his own rendition of "the hundred days" in 1935. Roth's novel is about not an emperor in search of a people but one who came to recognize the fallibility of his own myth. While Forzano made the case for the Hitlers and Mussolinis of the twentieth century, Roth turned the dictators into Job-like figures who learned to face the afflictions of their hubris and the passage of their times. Napoleon's somebody became a nobody and ultimately accepted the end of his own myth by identifying with Job, trading the "scepter" for the "cross." In this novel, Roth performed his own exit from history—his loneliness in postwar Austria, a shrunken state that was no longer an empire; his exile from Germany in 1933; the Paris cafes that emptied at night, leaving alone the man. Was it Roth, a Habsburg or Napoleon, who asked, "Where can I go now?" "I am not a child of my times," Roth admitted. Roth's ballad was a "song of grief" that at once mourned the prewar world of custom and belief in which he had grown up and indicted the brutal postwar usurpers for destroying it. Roth crumbled the history Forzano attempted to brace.[10]

R EADERS WERE FAMILIAR with the tumultuous interval between the emperor's exile on Elba and his exile on St. Helena; according to one estimate, three books have been written about Napoleon for each of the many thousands of days since his abdication in 1815.[11] History has also come to recognize another "hundred days," the first hundred days of the presidency of Franklin Delano Roosevelt, who was inaugurated on Saturday, March 4, 1933, the very day of Germany's Day of the Awakening Nation, on the eve of the fateful Reichstag elections. Such close proximity went unnoted at the time, but since then, historians have twinned the Third Reich and the New Deal and the hundred days on which each was founded. The new president in the United States, who incidentally celebrated his fifty-first birthday on the day Hitler was appointed chancellor, now sits alongside the new Führer in Germany on the newly built stage of twentieth-century world history.

President Franklin Roosevelt first used the term "hundred days" in his third "fireside chat" on July 24, 1933, to refer to the period between the opening of the special session of the 73rd Congress on March 9 and its closing exactly one hundred days later, on June 17. The fireside chats created a nationwide community of radio listeners. Novelist Saul Bellow remembered the "Chicago Midway on a summer evening." Between Cottage Grove and Stony Island, drivers had pulled over, "parking bumper to bumper, and turned on their radios to hear Roosevelt. They had rolled down their windows and opened the car doors. Everywhere the same voice, its odd Eastern accent." The radio audience was as big as those assembled by the Führer's speeches: "You could follow without missing a single word as you strolled by." But "these unknown drivers, men and women smoking their cigarettes in silence," were citizens, not soldiers. July's fireside chat surveyed the first one hundred days, which, the president explained, "had been devoted to the starting of the wheels of the New Deal."[12]

Roosevelt contended that his cabinet had given a "new administrative organization" to the country that strengthened the resilience of both American democracy and American capitalism. "In a flash," writes one historian, Roosevelt "transformed the presidency and the role of Washington D.C.," not only making the federal government an active player in economic policy—by 1936, it consumed 9 percent of the gross national product, up from 3 percent in 1929, and employed 7 percent of the workforce—but giving it a voice in the American conversation.[13] Humorist Will Rogers quipped, "Congress doesn't pass legislation any more, they just wave at the bills as they go by." Roosevelt, however, insisted that the laws were not "just a collection of haphazard schemes." They constituted "parts of a connected and logical whole." The cornerstones to the "new deal" that Roosevelt had pledged for "the American people" upon his nomination in Chicago in July 1932 were the National Industry Recovery Act, which funded a "great public works program" while boosting wages and outlawing child labor, and the "Farm Act," or the Agricultural Adjustment Administration, which set quotas and provided subsidies to cut production and raise prices. A bank holiday and federal insurance for bank deposits ended the banking crisis. Roosevelt's administration also established the Civilian Conservation Corps, which provided temporary employment to a quarter million young people. Other unemployed Americans received direct aid through the temporary Federal Emergency Relief Act.

When Roosevelt spoke to the American people about the early accomplishments of his administration, he referred to a homespun checklist of "good results" "simple purposes," and "solid foundations" and to the general "spirit of understanding and help-fulness." He used the "grammar of mass culture" to address his audiences in a friendly, conversational way. To connect with the American people, he frequently used the pronouns "I," and "you," and "we." In Roosevelt's country, as in Hitler's, more people be-lieved the radio than newspapers, which were uniformly critical of the New Deal and evidently more beholden to financial interests. Radio was regarded not as a medium but as a direct conversation. In his fireside chats, Roosevelt engaged a "prototypical citizenry" that was "patriotic, heroic, brave, and independent."[14] And as the end of the bank panic indicated, Americans responded in the ways they had been engaged. In his inaugural address on March 4, Roo-sevelt raised the possibility that he would have to rely on "broad ex-ecutive power to wage a war against the emergency," as would be the case if the country had been "invaded by a foreign foe." This, rather than the evocative affirmation about the "only thing we have to fear is fear itself," was his big applause line. But Roosevelt's real authority was in fact psychological. He restored confidence in the capacity of American institutions and in the improvement of business conditions. For all the legislative innovation of the first hundred days, he did not dismantle government, or destroy po-litical enemies, or attack a corrupt "system." The administration propped up rather than tore down, providing a "new deal" rather than a "national revolution."

Roosevelt spoke to friends and neighbors, "you and I," and not to an "us" besieged by "them." At one point in July's evening address, "he stopped and asked for a glass of water. After taking time for a sip—audible coast-to-coast," the president remarked to listeners, "It is very hot here in Washington tonight." We are not in Hitler's Berlin. Workers and farmers found themselves in dire straits during the Great Depression in both Germany and Amer-ica, but in the United States they were despondent and frightened, not radicalized or estranged or divided. People felt "dread." They were afflicted by an "awful doom." As poet James Rorty traveled around, he summed up the hitchhikers he picked up on the road as "bewildered souls." Another traveler saw Americans drifting, as if "lost in a fog." Yet in Texas, Florida, and Minnesota, individuals mostly blamed themselves for their misfortune and still believed in the "Horatio Alger Theory." Less than 2.5 percent of American voters cast ballots for the Communist or Socialist Party in 1932, and overall turnout was just 57 percent. There was no "landslide" against the "system" or toward radical alternatives, as in Germany. Social critics consoled rather than indicted readers in Depression-era America; fascism was not part of the atmosphere they described.[15] Meanwhile, Germany's jobless lived in conditions worse than those prevailing in the United States. And all Germans (not just the unemployed) saw their tribulations much more dramatically, as injuries inflicted by traitors and the "system"—Versailles, revolutionaries, Berlin, the Reichstag. They thought about injustice in more collective terms set on an apocalyptic plain, a life-and-death struggle that was fundamentally political.

When Roosevelt pulled up his chair to have his "fireside chat" in July, he explained that he had "purposely refrained from addressing you" in the five weeks since Congress adjourned. He recommended "the opportunity of a little quiet" so that everyone could "examine and assimilate" the "crowding events of the hundred days."[16] This was the traditional calendar of summer and holiday, of leaving town and coming back, of lemonade, ice tea, and glasses of cold water. It was not a revolutionary road to eliminate parties, establish one-party rule, create "new persons," and found a "community of blood." Like the first hundred days of Roosevelt's presidency, the first hundred of Hitler's chancellorship witnessed a flurry of legislation, but in Germany this constituted repeated acts of usurpation that, accompanied by intimidating rather than intimate radio broadcasts, reached far into the private sphere of German citizens. Like Napoleon, in the "hundred days" Hitler and the brownshirts moved unexpectedly and with great force: "Basta! Everything is going to be different." They did not build on state, local, and civic institutions; they inserted the rule of the party, radically transforming the way citizens related to government and authority and how they experienced the balance and accountability of power.

F ORZANO'S *The Hundred Days* played to enthusiastic audiences in German theaters, but the phrase was not applied to the first weeks of the Third Reich. "One hundred days" did not serve as an explicit prelude to "one thousand years." Even so, Nazi leaders were surprised at how much they accomplished in a very short period. "The nation will fall into our hands without a fight," Joseph Goebbels wrote on February 10, 1933. "There is no resistance to speak of." A few weeks later, he celebrated "an unprecedented triumph": "the red majorities have been broken. . . . It is so unbelievable that you can't really comprehend it right now."[17] "So now we are in charge," he reflected after the passage of the Enabling Act on March 23.[18] By spring 1933, the Nazis had concluded the first of their lightning wars.

Not even one hundred days had passed since Hitler's appointment as chancellor when the ambassadors of the great powers wrote up summary reports of the new situation. On March 15, Britain's ambassador Horace Rumbold wrote to the undersecretary of state for foreign affairs in Whitehall that "the National Socialist revolution is now complete." "No Government in this country during the last sixty years has attained to such a position of unchallenged power as the Hitler Government," he explained. There is "homogeneous authority throughout the Reich" untrammeled by "checks or hindrances." Rumbold added that it was "decidedly instructive" to contemplate "the ease with which one-half of the population of the country were suddenly deprived of the right of speech, the right to read, and one might almost say the right to think." The extraordinary thing was not so much that the National Socialists had won elections or imposed authority but that variety, difference, and contradiction had simply been stamped out.[19]

The complete absence of resistance also stunned the French ambassador, André François-Poncet. "In other countries crises bring forth individuals and allow strong personalities to emerge." Soldiers might demonstrate "military bravery," but Germany's citizens lacked "civic courage"; there were neither "martyrs nor heroes." The seizure of power made neither a good story nor tragic history. After "the violent suppression of all non-Hitler entities," only the "dust of personal displeasure" remained. The exorbitant political creatures who were so alive in January 1933 no longer existed. In the ambassador's view, there was not the "slightest reason" to think that "Hitler and his national revolution" would come to an end soon.[20]

With the emphasis on the smothered, cowering opposition, Horace Rumbold and André François-Poncet were still conceptualizing the German scene in terms of the "German crisis." They wrote with the cries of the big January demonstrations echoing in their ears: "Freedom! Freedom! Freedom!" and "Red Front!" They referred to "one-half of the population," to "non-Hitler entities," to the "48 percent." But in one hundred days, something had happened. Opposition was no longer even a possibility. The Day of the Awakening Nation, Boycott Saturday, and the Day of National Labor revealed unanticipated centralizing movements of reunification, renewal, and self-defense that rendered the boundaries between Hitler and not-Hitler unclear.

What made such a sea change possible? The National Socialists built on the fundamental division between the socialist Left and the nationalist Right. They used the resources and armory of the state to fortify the division and relied on deep fears of Communists as well as Social Democrats, which precluded any robust defense of civic institutions and the rule of law. This left the Nazis' opponents completely isolated. The Nazis also acted with unprecedented ruthlessness, checking any meaningful resistance either from civic-minded citizens or the socialist partisans themselves. And they successfully presented themselves as national guardians of German unity and prosperity, consolidating the enthusiasm of the "52 percent" and winning at least the conditional support of most of the remaining "48 percent" relatively quickly. As the events surrounding Boycott Saturday make clear, terror (or rather, counter-terrorism) was effective because it was widely accepted as national defense, and the idea that prosperity depended entirely upon the innovative and even violent administration of life began to make sense to the German people. The nationalist opposition to the republic had been brewing for a long time, but it triumphed only because the National Socialists emerged, after an inspirited interval of one hundred days, as plausible stewards of a redeemed nation. Germany was deeply splintered in winter 1933, without common lore or understanding; the Third Reich, emerging in spring 1933, trafficked in new forms of civic engagement that reunified the nation by "iron and blood," which explains why most exiles never returned to what had become a new place.

In its very first report on conditions in Germany, the dissident socialist group New Beginning got straight to the point. It dispelled any ideas that an "other Germany" or "good Germany" existed in any substantial form in the Third Reich or that National Socialism could be described in terms of the tyranny it had imposed on the defenseless innocent. This is one of the original documents for the critical study of fascism, as it puts into question the very "how" of observation. At the end of November 1933, the anonymous reporter wrote, "The extraordinarily high number of ballots cast for the regime in the referendum of November 12 has led even critical foreign observers to consider the results to have been falsified or to explain them as the result of force and terror." The reality was

quite different: "This assessment is based on an erroneous understanding of the actual inroads that fascist ideologies have made in
all classes of German society. Of course, the plebiscite is not the
expression of the actual opinion of large parts of the population."
The next word, *jedoch* (nevertheless), introduced the difficulty of
analyzing fascism, which was much more than the sum of its violent parts. "Nevertheless," the report continued, "precise obser-
vations of this election reveal that on balance the election results
reflect the actual mood." It was impossible to deny how *"excep-
tionally rapidly and comprehensively* society has become fascist." "All
the voices of discontent," and observers could hear them, "ultimately focus on particular aspects of the regime that do not disturb
the general acceptance of the new system."[21] ("People bitch like
lunatics but are Nazis nonetheless.") Germans did not so much display a startling lack of "civic courage" as demonstrate a surprising
readiness to accept and to participate in the new civic aims of the
regime. They were stepping up, not cowering down. Perhaps the
sounds on the radio were so remarkable, the images of national
union so irresistible, that dissidents gave up, or else they willingly
enrolled themselves in the postulated commonwealth, having reconciled their own ideas of the common good with National Socialism, in the process giving ever greater credence to the big national
idea the Nazis promoted. Opponents, like the fanatics, disappeared
whenever you tried to find them.

New Beginning put forward the premise that insights into fascism or Nazism had to begin with accepting the difficulty of ascer-
taining the nature and extent of its appeal, that more people were
sympathetic to Nazis than a class or political analysis from 1932,
the so-called decision year, might indicate. The analysis disputed
that observable grumbling and dissatisfaction held the answers. It
dismissed the notion that coercion or fraud could explain the obvious evidence of acclamation. Fascism was an immense intellectual
challenge because conventional sociology and political science did

not seem to apply. Somehow the "48 percent" had become some-thing else and something much smaller. More and more Germans participated in the nation's destiny. "One hundred days" stands for the extraordinary extension and speed of the transformation of Germans into Nazis without denying the ways in which the pro-cess was incomplete.

"Keep Your Eyes Peeled!" The "people's community" demanded that comrades watch themselves and others. "This or that?" and "us versus them"—the binaries of National Socialism did great violence to the mottled, baggy, indeterminate relations of liberal society and also led to a continuous state of violence since the cat-egories rested on mutual exclusions. For political dissidents (race traitors), asocials (racial undesirables), and Jews (racial aliens), the distinctions created a literalness of social life. The public at large backed up these distinctions when they thought about Jewish grandmothers, filled out forms, and passed along jokes. This was the consensus of compliance.

"Keep Your Eyes Peeled!" Who actually felt him- or herself to be a genuine member of the national community, and who a physically and racially conscious comrade? There was still a great deal of interpretive work, reading of signs, motivations, and be-haviors, to gauge real consensus or mere compliance so that "lit-erary" approaches continually undercut "literal" classifications. Where exactly were the remnants of the "48 percent," and how actually committed and loyal was the "52 percent"? To what ex-tent did "German" and "Nazi" overlap? Everyone searched daily life for clues and evidence about national belonging, the appeal of National Socialism, the popularity of its initiatives, and the gravity of a grumble. There were no reliable barometers or elections or public opinion polls.

On the one hand, when the Saar (a formerly German territory that had become a League of Nations mandate on the western border after World War I) was authorized to vote on its future on

January 13, 1935, 90 percent of the predominantly Catholic electorate chose to rejoin Germany—whether people in the Saar were
voting to live in the Third Reich or Germany is not clear, but the
Third Reich did not unsettle their ideas about Germany. This 90
percent was consistent with the degree of support that Nazi security officials believed they could count on and with the outcome of
the November 1933 referendum.

On the other hand, in Danzig, the other League of Nations
mandate that administered a prewar German city, populated overwhelmingly with Protestant Germans on the eastern border, local
elections revealed a robust number of voters who, watching the
same developments, did not identify so much with the National
Socialists. In the interval between two elections, one held on May
28, 1933, the other on April 7, 1935, middle-class and "Marxist"
voters moved decisively to the Nazis, who ended up with nearly
60 percent, an impressive majority in a parliamentary system but
not a supermajority and certainly not 90 percent. The "nazified"
population demonstrated extraordinary enthusiasm; the Nazis
counted 45,000 members in a population of 375,000, an organiza-
tional density three times greater than in the Reich. Beginning in
1933, laws required civil servants to use the "German greeting,"
made the "Horst Wessel Song" obligatory in schools, and removed
Danzig's Jews from public office. Nonetheless, one-third of the
population in this little "Third Reich" on the Vistula, which victorious Allies had "torn" from the homeland after the world war, did
not vote for Nazis.[22]

Had an election been held in Germany in 1935, would it have
looked like the one held in the Saar in January 1935 or the one that
took place in Danzig in April, which revealed basic disagreements?
No historian today would dare to consider the question of support
for National Socialism resolved.

Living in the Third Reich was schizophrenic not because
Germans lived "dissonant lives," showing one face in public and

cultivating another in private, but because Germans never knew where the border between inside and outside was drawn. In one hundred days, interpretation stabilized the categories of friend and foe without giving them precise coordinates. On the one side, there was the foe: the Jew, lethal, unambiguous. On the other side, was the "Aryan," who when she looked about was never sure about who really felt at home. More Nazi badges were in circulation than there were German people, but the distribution of all those signs never sorted itself out in a clear way. The society was no longer liberal, nor was it homogeneous. The Nazis created the clear-cut category of the enemy but left unresolved the friendly relations between themselves and other Germans—neither Nazis nor anyone else ever knew who was true. The one hundred days turned Germans into border guards; people constantly made distinctions and apprized categories in conditions of apparent danger. They discussed who crossed, who was in what category, and also what constituted crossing. It was impossible for a neighbor to be recognized simply as a neighbor or for a guard to know the border.

"Immo," Elisabeth Gebensleben's daughter who had moved to Holland in the mid-1920s, discussed borders and neighbors with her patriotic mother who lived in Braunschweig; mother and daughter crossed the borders of the Reich frequently in the 1930s to allow the grandparents to see the grandchildren. They discussed Hitler, and the Jews, and the directions of German foreign policy, which ultimately would install Immo's brother, Eberhard, as a soldier in German-occupied Holland after 1940. When he visited during the war, Immo forbade him to speak German or wear a German uniform in public. Immo's life reveals that there were choices. She learned generosity from the Bresters, her Dutch husband's family. Her future father-in-law had a magnificent sense of humor. After one of his sons came back from military service in the early 1920s, he recounted the experience: "stupid sergeants taught him all that was good and excellent. For example, how to shoot the person next to you through the eyes." "An army chaplain," he continued, "preached many excellent things, but he choked on the words 'love of humanity,' or maybe they just slipped his mind."[23] Immo Brester wrote her mother about the benefit concerts she participated in to help German Jewish refugees in 1933. For a time during the war, Immo and her family hid "Eddy," a young Jewish child. She recognized herself, originally a German youngster enjoying Dutch hospitality right after the end of the Great War, in others.

Elisabeth lived through the very same years, although without the milk and butter of Holland. She also made choices at the border. As she admitted to her daughter, Elisabeth recognized injuries to individuals in spring 1933. She knew Braunschweig's socialist mayor, Ernst Böhme, and his wife quite well, and she read Immo's letters about Jews who had fled Germany for the Netherlands. Nonetheless, she embraced the National Socialists and the embattled view of the world they presupposed. She believed she was protecting her own son and rebuilding the nation that was his future, an endeavor in which she took an active part after 1933. Elisabeth closely identified her person with the national collective and not with individual civility; her rights were German rights. Her admiration for Hitler revealed a veneration for a community in which even the "low born" could lead the nation as Bismarck had. Like millions of other Germans, she wanted to live in a new country, one without Communists but also without monarchists—in her commentary and activism, she had left behind the kaiser and Hindenburg, old figures who belonged to the generation of her parents and grandparents. Hitler country had the energized collectivity of a nation at war: unified, disciplined, reverential to history without being deferential to caste. Elisabeth was among many millions of Germans who believed that the National Socialists offered hope for a new beginning.

Dreaming of "our Hitler," "our Germany," and a place for Germany's "own sons," Elisabeth and her friends built borders to protect against threats posed by outsiders. Elisabeth opened an account book to tally wrongful injuries to family and country, calculating percentages of Jews and quotas on Jews. She went on to propose the incarceration of Communists and Social Democrats in concentration camps to manage alleged terrorist threats. She stepped up as a suspicious border guard, drawing divisions between patriots and socialists, between Germans and Jews, and between misguided empathy and necessary vigilance because she believed the story of Germany's passion, its victimhood and its redemption. As a National Socialist, she advanced the delirium of national crisis and incorporated in her stories the depredations that jeopardized Germany and its renewal. Elisabeth foot-soldiered in a mighty revolution of life and death. The powerful narrative she wrote was one that her daughter tried to cross out. Elisabeth Gebensleben, a last name that in German suggests giving life, "choked on the words 'love of humanity'"; her daughter, Immo, across the border in Utrecht, Holland, spelled them out.

Not everyone kept account books as carefully as Elisabeth, but the large number of Germans who did give an account of themselves in the first hundred days of the Third Reich, and how quickly they did so, stands out. Elisabeth and other witnesses such as the diarists Karl Dürkefälden, who stayed away, and Wilhelm Scheidler, who joined in, saw throngs of people walking over to the new public square and taking part, day after patriotic day. The extraordinary sight of acclamation made skeptical Germans unsure of themselves or their old politics. Coercion played an undeniable role in inhibiting people from making Immo's choices. Economic crisis also justified drastic action. But hard times alone cannot account for Germany's racial panic and ethnic uplift.

The great achievement of the Third Reich was getting Germans to see themselves as the Nazis did: as an imperiled people who had created for themselves a new lease on collective life. This was the moral of the geography and history lessons of the national days of celebration in spring 1933, the stories about 1914 and 1918, about rise and fall, rot and revival. Not everyone agreed with the Nazis on every point, but most adjusted to National Socialism by interpreting it in their own way, adhering to old ideas by pursuing them in new forms. As a result, more and more Germans had accepted the Third Reich. This reassembly closed off any consideration of returning to the democratic governments of the Weimar Republic; it was neither recognized as a possibility nor desired. History had been split into two parts at the end of spring 1933: One was dead, and that death sustained the life of the other part. The narrative became clear. Most citizens believed they confronted a choice between life and death. To make Germany great was to narrate a great awakening, a story that always made it seem like there were more Nazis and fewer resisters, without ever resolving the matter definitively. The flag, the lapel pin, and the salute carried weight that the handshake and the hello did not. This was the new world after one hundred days. At the heart of the tyranny of Nazism was the tyranny of the story Germans came to tell about themselves.

A Postscript and Acknowledgments

L IKE ANY turning point in modern history, the year 1933 must be understood in terms of continuity and discontinuity. Almost a century earlier, in 1835, Heinrich Heine set the scene for what awaited Germany in his essay titled "The History of Religion and Philosophy in Germany." "It is still pretty quiet," he wrote. "It is only the little dogs who run around the empty arena and bark and bite one another." But he considered "the hour" when the "gladiators appear, to fight for life and death." "German thunder," he explained, "rumbles along somewhat slowly." But when it comes—and it will come—it will "crash as nothing ever crashed in German history." I have written this book with an eye not on the quiet before the storm, the overall pattern, but on the thunder. In the preceding chapters, I have emphasized how in one hundred days everything did change, although I have also asked how much. This book has grappled with a basic incongruity: While Hitler's Germany was not inevitable, it also emerged as the twentieth century's most popular dictatorship. We continue to circle around the events of 1933 because the rise of the Nazis exposed so many conflicting motivations about political and social behavior. And we are astonished to see people like ourselves in the galleries of the Third Reich. In the flash of a moment, Adolf Hitler became, and remains, one of the most recognizable figures of world history.

The year 1933 lives on. The events discussed in this book divided my family. My paternal grandfather, Hellmut Fritzsche, director of the mining academy in Aachen and a pro-capitalist rationalizer known unflatteringly to miners as the *Kohlenpapst*, or "coal pope," wrote a letter in November 1932 to urge the leader of the small "national liberal" party he voted for to support a nationalist unity coalition with Hitler; my maternal grandfather, Herbert Lauffer, a Social Democratic lawyer in Berlin charged with investigating the embezzlement of funds by East Elbian Junkers—friends of President Hindenburg—in the "Eastern Aid" scandal, lost his position in the state finance ministry when Papen putsched against Prussia in July 1932. He later defended dissidents in the Third Reich. My father's parents did not attend the wedding—in 1952!

The past also lives on because what was supposed to be behind us suddenly appears up ahead on the right.

If history is continuity and discontinuity, resolution and catastrophe, it is also surprise and unanimity; a total fascist state that in January 1933 was highly contested and rather improbable was widely accepted and broadly realized one hundred days later. History works that way—overriding regular rhythms and the day's expectations, opinion's sensible explanations, and sometimes even scary forecasts for the future. We must not lose our sense of surprise or shock so as to remain true to our faith, but we must also do so without slipping into the complacent thinking that the other side does not exert appeal. A good friend of mine once told me that I was attracted to the fascist aesthetic because I took it seriously. The second part is true: I do take it seriously. Yet I am not attracted to its aesthetic: Fascism disrespects the individual and violates the body. Was fascism less true than liberalism? Is it? I would say yes, but not for a long time, not for everybody, and not when it counted.

A Postscript and Acknowledgments

This book is dedicated to my parents, Hellmut, born in Berlin in 1927, and Sybille, born in the same city in 1931.

Berlin is also the place where all the members of my supportive and indulgent family were either born or have lived for a long time: my in-laws, Andreas and Irene Bautz; my wife, Franziska; and my children, Lauren, Eric, Elisabeth, Joshua, and Matteo. I want to thank two Berliners for their time during interviews: Heinrich George's son, Jan George, down in Dahlem and Jürgen Hochschild, the informal historian of the old socialist settlement "Freie Scholle," up in Tegel. Unfortunately, the "Freie Scholle" did not make it into this book. *Berlinkenner* David Murphy and Jennifer Evans offered valuable readings and valuable advice. I have to shout out to the marvelous staff of the Interlibrary Loan Department at the library of the University of Illinois. I am grateful for the solidarity of my agent, Andrew Wylie, and the comrades there, Kristina Moore and now Hannah Townsend. Writers may write, but they will not publish or speak or make sense or stop without the experts at the editorial office, in this case at Basic Books. Thank you ever so much to Lara Heimert, Brian Distelberg, and Claire Potter in New York City and to Jennifer Kelland in Greece.

Urbana, September 17, 2019

Notes

Introduction: Quarter Past Eleven, One Hundred Days, a Thousand Years

1. Joachim C. Fest, *Hitler* (New York, 1973), 337.

2. Henry Ashby Turner, *Hitler's Thirty Days to Power: January 1933* (Reading, MA, 1996), 137.

3. Karl Kraus, *Die dritte Walpurgnisnacht* (Munich, 1967), 9; Kurt Tucholsky, quoted in Philipp W. Fabry, *Mutmassungen über Hitler. Urteile von Zeitgenossen* (Düsseldorf, 1969), 63.

4. Dorothy Parker, "I Saw Hitler!," *Hearst's International-Cosmopolitan* 92, no. 3 (March 1932): 160.

5. Joseph Goebbels, "Das grosse Wunder," December 24, 1932, in *Wetterleuchten. Aufsätze aus der Kampfzeit* (Munich, 1939), 357.

6. Heinrich Brüning, *Memoiren 1918–1934* (Stuttgart, 1970), 650.

7. This was the case in Berlinchen, a small town northwest of Berlin. See "Frühere Kommunisten verbrennen ihre Fahne," *Berliner Lokal-Anzeiger*, no. 124, March 14, 1933.

8. *Time*, May 22, 1933, 21; *Newsweek*, May 20, 1933, 14. The *Newsweek* reference appears to be the first use of the term "Holocaust" in the context of the Third Reich.

9. Ernst Robert Curtius, quoted in Detlev Grieswelle, *Propaganda der Friedlosigkeit. Eine Studie zu Hitlers Rhetorik 1920–1933* (Stuttgart, 1972), 68.

10. Benjamin Ziemann, "Weimar Was Weimar: Politics, Culture and the Emplotment of the German Republic," *German History* 28, no. 4 (2010): 542–571, at 556.

11. Quoted in Karl Christian Führer, "High Brow and Low Brow Culture," in *Weimar Germany*, ed. Anthony McElligott (Oxford, UK, 2009), 274.

12. Hans Ostwald, *Sittengeschichte der Inflation: Ein Kulturdokument aus den Jahren der Marktsturzes* (Berlin, 1931), 149; Eugen Diesel, *Das Land der Deutschen* (Leipzig, 1931), 222.

13. Heinrich Zille, "Plakatwand [1919]," akg-images, https://www.akg-images.co.uk/archive/Plakatwand-2UMDHUQAZX13.html.

14. Martin Geyer, *Verkehrte Welt: Revolution, Inflation, und Moderne, München 1914–1924* (Göttingen, 1998), 283; entries for September 16 and 21, 1919, in Victor Klemperer, *Leben sammeln, nicht fragen wozu und warum: Tagebücher 1918–1924* (Berlin, 1996), 179, 183; entry for January 6, 1925, in Victor Klemperer, *Leben sammeln, nicht fragen wozu und warum: Tagebücher 1925–1932* (Berlin, 1996), 7.

15. Henry Ashby Turner, *Hitler's Thirty Days to Power: January 1933* (Reading, MA, 1996), 146–147.

16. Entry for September 2, 1941, in Victor Klemperer, *I Will Bear Witness, 1933–1941: A Diary of the Nazi Years* (New York, 1998), 428.

17. Entries for April 12, 1933, and March 17, 1940, in Victor Klemperer, *I Will Bear Witness, 1933–1941: A Diary of the Nazi Years* (New York, 1998), 14, 329.

18. "April [1935] Bericht über die Lage in Deutschland," in *Berichte über die Lage in Deutschland. Die Meldungen der Gruppe Neu Beginnen aus dem Dritten Reich 1933–1936*, ed. Bernd Stöver (Bonn, 1996), 444.

19. Entry for March 22, 1933, in Victor Klemperer, *I Will Bear Witness, 1933–1941: A Diary of the Nazi Years* (New York, 1998), 8–9.

20. Entry for September 11, 1938, in Victor Klemperer, *I Will Bear Witness, 1933–1941: A Diary of the Nazi Years* (New York, 1998), 267–268.

21. *Völkischer Beobachter*, no. 151, May 31, 1931, quoted in Thomas Balistier, *Gewalt und Ordnung. Kalkul und Faszination der SA* (Muenster, 1989), 92.

Chapter One: "Crisis, if You Please"

1. Egon Jacobsohn, "12 Stunden unerkannt durch Gross-Berlin," *Berliner Morgenpost*, no. 317, November 16, 1919.

2. Alfons Arenhövel, *Arena der Leidenschaften: Der Berliner Sportpalast und seine Veranstaltungen 1910–1973* (Berlin, 1990); Eugen Szatmari, *Das Buch von Berlin* (1927; rpt. Leipzig, 1997), 171–172.

3. "Krise gefällig?," *BZ am Mittag*, no. 109, May 7, 1932.

4. Alexander Graf Stenbock-Fermor, *Deutschland von unten. Reise durch die proletarische Provinz*, eds. Christian Jäger and Erhard Schütz (1931; rpt. Berlin, 2016), 203; Heinz Rein, *Berlin 1932: Ein Roman aus der grossen deutschen Arbeitslosigkeit* (Berlin, 1946), 170. Rein drafted his novel in 1935.

5. Heinz Rein, *Berlin 1932: Ein Roman aus der grossen deutschen Arbeitslosigkeit* (Berlin, 1946), 169.

6. Entry for November 24, 1932, in Abraham Plotkin, *An American in Hitler's Berlin. Abraham Plotkin's Diary, 1932–33*, eds. Catherine Collomp and Bruno Groppo (Urbana, 2009), 14–16.

7. Franz Hessel, *Walking in Berlin: A Flaneur in the Capital* (Cambridge, 2017), 211–212.

8. Walter Schönstedt, *Kämpfende Jugend—Roman der arbeitenden Jugend* (Berlin, 1932), 7, 80; Harry Schreck, "Im Spiegel des Schlagers," *Vossische Zeitung*, no. 83, February 18, 1933.

9. Justus Ehrhardt, *Strassen ohne Ende* (Berlin, 1931), 44; Walter Schönstedt, *Kämpfende Jugend—Roman der arbeitenden Jugend* (Berlin, 1932), 7.

10. Entry for December 10, 1932, in Abraham Plotkin, *An American in Hitler's Berlin. Abraham Plotkin's Diary, 1932–33*, eds. Catherine Collomp and Bruno Groppo (Urbana, 2009), 57; "Berlin zu 72% elektrifiziert," *Deutsche Allgemeine Zeitung*, no. 520, November 4, 1932; on toilets, see Jens Flemming, Klaus Saul, and Peter-Christian Witt, eds., *Familienleben im Schatten der Krise: Dokumente und Analysen zur Sozialgeschichte der Weimarer Republik* (Düsseldorf, 1988), 107.

11. Entry for December 10, 1932, in Abraham Plotkin, *An American in Hitler's Berlin. Abraham Plotkin's Diary, 1932–33*, eds. Catherine Collomp and Bruno Groppo (Urbana, 2009), 57–58.

12. "Unser Täglich Brot . . . ," in Ruth Fischer and Franz Heimann, eds., *Deutsche Kinderfibel* (Berlin, 1933), 95–100.

13. See the comparison between 1907 and 1926 in Jens Flemming, Klaus Saul, and Peter-Christian Witt, eds., *Familienleben im Schatten der Krise: Dokumente und Analysen zur Sozialgeschichte der Weimarer Republik* (Düsseldorf, 1988), 75.

14. "Auf dem Arbeitsnachweis," *Arbeiter Illustrierte Zeitung*, no. 5 (1930).

15. "'Freizeit' ohne Ende. Vier Arbeitslose erzahlen aus ihrem Leben . . . ," *Berliner Tageblatt*, no. 563, November 27, 1932; Bruno Nelissen Haken, *Stempelchronik. 261 Arbeitslosenschicksale* (Hamburg, 1932), 32.

16. Jens Flemming, Klaus Saul, and Peter-Christian Witt, eds., *Familienleben im Schatten der Krise: Dokumente und Analysen zur Sozialgeschichte der Weimarer*

Republik (Düsseldorf, 1988), 176–177; Detlev Peukert, "The Lost Generation: Youth Unemployment at the End of the Weimar Republic," in *The German Unemployed: Experiences and Consequences of Mass Unemployment from the Weimar Republic to the Third Reich*, eds. Richard J. Evans and Dick Geary (New York, 1987), 179; Heinz Rein, *Berlin 1932: Ein Roman aus der grossen deutschen Arbeitslosigkeit* (Berlin, 1946), 18–20, 41, 65.

17. "Auf dem Arbeitsnachweis," *Arbeiter Illustrierte Zeitung*, no. 5 (1930).

18. Walter Schönstedt, *Kämpfende Jugend—Roman der arbeitenden Jugend* (Berlin, 1932), 22–23.

19. Justus Ehrhardt, *Strassen ohne Ende* (Berlin, 1931), 32–33.

20. *Süd-Berlin*, no. 39, February 15, 1933. Advertisements in *Berliner Tageblatt*, no. 516, October 30, 1932; no. 3, January 3, 1933; *Süd-Berlin*, no. 9, January 11, 1933.

21. "Eine Verkäuferin verfolgt eine Plündererbande. Schliemannstrasse im Berliner Norden," *Deutsche Allgemeine Zeitung*, no. 22, January 13, 1933.

22. "'Freizeit' ohne Ende. Vier Arbeitslose erzahlen aus ihrem Leben...," *Berliner Tageblatt*, no. 563, November 27, 1932; "Jedem Bettler 2 Pfennig," *Vossische Zeitung*, no. 593, December 11, 1932; Elisabeth Gebensleben to Irmgard Brester, February 3, 1933, in Hedda Kalkshoven, ed., *Between Two Homelands: Letters Across the Borders of Nazi Germany* (Urbana, 2014), 57.

23. "Täglich 225,000 Fahrgäste weniger," *Vossische Zeitung*, no. 622, December 28, 1932.

24. "Not—wie noch nie—Ansprüche wie noch nie," *Tempo*, no. 258, November 4, 1931; H. R. Knickerbocker, *The German Crisis* (New York, 1932), 29.

25. Jochen Hung, "'Die Zeitung der Zeit.' Die Tageszeitung Tempo und das Ende der Weimarer Republik," in *"Der ganze Verlag ist einfach eine Bonbonniere." Ullstein in der ersten Hälfte des 20 Jahrhunderts*, eds. Davil Oels und Ute Schnieder (Berlin, 2015), 146; entry for August 19, 1933, in Victor Klemperer, *I Will Bear Witness, 1933–1941: A Diary of the Nazi Years* (New York, 1998), 30.

26. "Die Fahrt ins Blaue," *Ulk*, no. 42, October 20, 1932, reprinted in Erich Mühsam, *Berliner Feuilleton. Ein poetischer Kommentar auf die missratene Zähmung des Adolf Hitlers*, ed. Heinz Hug (Grafrath, 1992).

27. See, for example, "Österreicher Alpenwinter," *Vossische Zeitung*, no. 41, January 25, 1933; Oskar Maria Graf, *Der Abgrund* (1936; rpt. Munich, 1994), 77, 80.

28. Elisabeth Gebensleben to Irmgard Brester, July 21 and December 11, 1931, in Hedda Kalshoven, ed., *Between Two Homelands: Letters Across the Borders of Nazi Germany* (Urbana, 2014), 31, 39.

29. Elisabeth Gebensleben to Irmgard Brester, March 4 and June 22, 1932, in Hedda Kalshoven, ed., *Between Two Homelands: Letters Across the Borders of Nazi Germany* (Urbana, 2014), 44, 48.

30. Elisabeth Gebensleben to Irmgard Brester, December 7, 1929, October 18, 1931, and July 20, 1932, in Hedda Kalshoven, ed., *Between Two Homelands: Letters Across the Borders of Nazi Germany* (Urbana, 2014), 18, 36, 52.

31. Elisabeth Gebensleben to Irmgard Brester, March 4 and June 22, 1932, in Hedda Kalshoven, ed., *Between Two Homelands: Letters Across the Borders of Nazi Germany* (Urbana, 2014), 44, 48.

32. Entries for January 4 and 24, 1933, in Abraham Plotkin, *An American in Hitler's Berlin. Abraham Plotkin's Diary, 1932–33,* eds. Catherine Collomp and Bruno Groppo (Urbana, 2009), 94, 98, 101, 127.

33. Entries for January 26–28 and 30, 1933, in Abraham Plotkin, *An American in Hitler's Berlin. Abraham Plotkin's Diary, 1932–33,* eds. Catherine Collomp and Bruno Groppo (Urbana, 2009), 129–130, 133.

34. Elisabeth Gebensleben to Irmgard Brester, November 10, 1931, and December 1, 1932, in Hedda Kalshoven, ed., *Between Two Homelands: Letters Across the Borders of Nazi Germany* (Urbana, 2014), 38, 55.

35. "Conférence zwischen Eisbein und Molle," *8-Uhr Abendblatt,* no. 289, December 9, 1932; Harry Schreck, "Traktat vom Rodeln," *Vossische Zeitung,* no. 95, February 25, 1933.

36. Siegfried Kracauer, "Schreie auf der Strasse," *Frankfurter Zeitung,* July 19, 1930, reprinted in Kracauer, *Strassen in Berlin und anderswo* (Berlin, 1987), 27–29.

37. Karl Aloys Schenzinger, *Der Hitlerjunge Quex* (Berlin, 1932), 109–110.

38. Entries for January 4 and 7, 1933, in Abraham Plotkin, *An American in Hitler's Berlin. Abraham Plotkin's Diary, 1932–33,* eds. Catherine Collomp and Bruno Groppo (Urbana, 2009), 92, 106.

39. Karl Aloys Schenzinger, *Der Hitlerjunge Quex* (Berlin, 1932), 100; Sebastian Haffner, *Defying Hitler: A Memoir* (New York, 2002), 92, 109.

40. "Es kamen fast 10,000," *Tempo,* no. 249, October 22, 1932; J. K. von Engelbrechten and Hans Volz, eds., *Wir wandern durch das nationalsozialistische Berlin: Ein Führer durch die Gedenkstätten des Kampfes um die Reichshauptstadt* (1937; rpt. Dresden, 2007), 201.

41. Eugen Szatmari, *Das Buch von Berlin* (1927; rpt. Leipzig, 1997), 197; Magnus Brechtken, *Albert Speer. Eine deutsche Karriere* (Munich, 2017), 31–36. On the "Neue Welt," see the advertisements in almost any January issue of the *Berliner Morgenpost.*

42. Martin Schuster, "Die SA in der nationalsozialistischen »Machtergrei-fung« in Berlin und Brandenburg 1926–1934" (PhD diss., Technical University, Berlin, 2004), 45, 50–51; Ruth Glatzer, ed., *Berlin zur Weimarer Zeit: Panorama einer Metropole* (Berlin, 2000), 413; J. K. von Engelbrechten and Hans Volz, eds., *Wir wandern durch das nationalsozialistische Berlin: Ein Führer durch die Gedenkstätten des Kampfes um die Reichshauptstadt* (1937; rpt. Berlin, 2007), 36–37.

43. Joseph Goebbels, *Kampf um Berlin. Der Anfang* (Munich, 1932), 60.

Chapter Two: Mystery Tour

1. David Andrew Hackett, "The Nazi Party in the Reichstag Election of 1930" (PhD diss., University of Wisconsin, 1971), 224–225; Detlev Grieswelle, *Propaganda der Friedlosigkeit. Eine Studie zu Hitlers Rhetorik 1920–1933* (Stuttgart, 1972), 31, 33; Thomas Balistier, *Gewalt und Ordnung. Kalkul und Faszination der SA* (Muenster, 1989), 63.

2. Friedrich Kurz, "Meine Erlebnisse in der Kampfzeit," December 25, 1936, Bundesarchiv Berlin, NS26/529.

3. Thomas Balistier, *Gewalt und Ordnung. Kalkul und Faszination der SA* (Muenster, 1989), 63; Sven Reichardt, *Faschistische Kampfbünde. Gewalt und Gemeinschaft im italienischen Squadrismus und in der deutschen SA* (Cologne, 2002), 103.

4. Georg Bernhard, *Die deutsche Tragödie. Der Selbstmord einer Republik* (Prag, 1933), 275; "Das grosse Zirkussterben," *Berliner Tageblatt*, no. 223, May 12, 1932; "Ein Zirkus vor dem Bankrott," *Vossische Zeitung*, no. 625, December 30, 1932; Hans Fallada, *Little Man, What Now?*, trans. Susan Bennett (Brooklyn, 2009), 59.

5. William Sheridan Allen, *The Nazi Seizure of Power: The Experience of a Single German Town, 1922–1945*, rev. ed. (Brattleboro, 2014), 142–143.

6. Thomas Childers, *The Nazi Voter: The Social Foundations of Fascism in Germany, 1919–1933* (Chapel Hill, 1983), 268–269.

7. Jürgen Falter, "The Two Hindenburg Elections of 1925 and 1932: A Total Reversal of Voter Coalitions," *Central European History* 23 (1990): 225–241.

8. Diary entries for June 24 and 26, 1934, in Theodore Abel, *The Columbia Circle of Scholars: Selections from the Journal (1930–1957)*, ed. Elzbieta Halas (Frankfurt, 2001), 178, 181.

9. Theodore Abel, *Why Hitler Came to Power* (New York, 1938).

10. Trude Mauerer, "From Everyday Life to a State of Emergency: Jews in Weimar and Nazi Germany," in *Jewish Daily Life in Germany, 1618–1945*, ed. Marion A. Kaplan (Oxford, 2005), 335.

11. Ian Kershaw, *Hitler, 1889–1936: Hubris* (New York, 1999), 36, 60.

12. Klaus Theweleit quoted in Josef Kopperschmidt, "War Hitler ein grosser Redner? Ein redekritischer Versuch," in *Hitler der Redner*, ed. Josef Kopperschmidt (Munich, 2003), 190.

13. Detlev Grieswelle, *Propaganda der Friedlosigkeit. Eine Studie zu Hitlers Rhetorik 1920–1933* (Stuttgart, 1972), 79, 85; "Hitler Would Scrap Versailles Treaty and Use Guillotine," *New York Times*, September 26, 1930.

14. Gerhard Paul, *Aufstand der Bilder: Die NS-Propaganda vor 1933* (Bonn, 1990); Peter Kurth, *American Cassandra: The Life of Dorothy Thompson* (Boston, 1990), 157.

15. Knickerbocker quoted in Volker Ullrich, *Hitler: Ascent, 1889–1939* (New York, 2016), 385.

16. Werner Goerendt, "Meine Erinnerungen aus der Kampfzeit," n.d. [1937], Bundesarchiv Berlin, NS26/530.

17. Elisabeth Gebensleben to Irmgard Brester, October 18, 1931, in Hedda Kalshoven, ed., *Between Two Homelands: Letters Across the Borders of Nazi Germany* (Urbana, 2014), 34–37.

18. According to Michael Mann, *Fascists* (Cambridge, 2004), 14, "fascism is the pursuit of a transcendent and cleaning nation-statism through paramilitarism."

19. Benjamin Carter Hett, *The Death of Democracy: Hitler's Rise to Power and the Downfall of the Weimar Republic* (New York, 2008), 30.

20. Daniel Siemens, *The Making of a Nazi Hero: The Murder and Myth of Horst Wessel* (London, 2013), 65; Peter H. Merkl, *Political Violence Under the Swastika: 518 Early Nazis* (Princeton, 1975).

21. Gabriel Tergit, "Atmosphäre des Bürgerkriegs," *Berliner Tageblatt*, December 18, 1931, republished in Gabriel Tergit, *Wer schiesst aus Liebe? Gerichtsreportagen* (Berlin, 1999), 166–167; "SA-Männer zur Aufgebung des SA Verbots," *Der Angriff*, no. 126, June 17, 1932.

22. Gabriel Tergit, "Atmosphäre des Bürgerkriegs," *Berliner Tageblatt*, December 18, 1931, republished in Gabriel Tergit, *Wer schiesst aus Liebe? Gerichtsreportagen* (Berlin, 1999), 166–167; Karl Aloys Schenzinger, *Der Hitlerjunge Quex* (Berlin, 1932), 129; Victor Klemperer, *The Language of the Third Reich: LTI—Lingua Tertii Imperii* (London, 2000), 4.

23. Rolf Bjerke quoted in Horst Matzerath and Brigitte Holzhauser, eds., *". . . vergessen kann man die Zeit nicht, das ist unmöglilch . . .": Kölner erinnern sich an die Jahre 1929–1945* (Cologne, 1984), 76–77.

24. Thomas Balistier, *Gewalt und Ordnung. Kalkul und Faszination der SA* (Muenster, 1989), 117.

25. Gottfried Niedhart, "Sangeslust und Singediktatur im Nationalsozialistischen Deutschland," in *Lieder in Politik and Alltag des Nationalsozialismus*, eds. Gottfried Niedhart and George Broderick (Frankfurt, 1999); George Broderick and Andrea Klein, "Das Kampflied der SA," in *Lieder in Politik and Alltag des Nationalsozialismus*, eds. Gottfried Niedhart and George Broderick (Frankfurt, 1999), 81.

26. "Riesenpropaganda der 'meuternden' SA," *Der Angriff*, no. 73, September 11, 1930; J. K. von Engelbrechten, *Ein brauen Armee entsteht. Die Geschichte der Berlin-Brandenburger SA* (Munich, 1937), 107–108, 137, 139. See also the film *Hans Westmar* (1933).

27. Walter Schönstedt, *Kämpfende Jugend—Roman der arbeitenden Jugend* (Berlin, 1932), 19–20.

28. J. K. von Engelbrechten, *Ein brauen Armee entsteht. Die Geschichte der Berlin-Brandenburger SA* (Munich, 1937), 107; Walter Schönstedt, *Kämpfende Jugend—Roman der arbeitenden Jugend* (Berlin, 1932), 122.

29. See the movie *Hans Westmar* (1933) and "Ein kleineres Übel—Riesengross. Bülowplatz und die Folgen," *Vossische Zeitung*, no. 39, January 24, 1933.

30. See, for example, entries for September 5 and 6, 1931, in André Postert, ed., *Hitlerjunge Schall. Die Tagebücher eines jungen Nationalsozialisten* (Munich, 2016), 80.

31. Sven Reichardt, *Faschistische Kampfbünde. Gewalt und Gemeinschaft im italienischen Squadrismus und in der deutschen SA* (Cologne, 2002), 452, 514–515.

32. Wilfrid Bade, *Die SA erobert Berlin* (Berlin, 1937), 176–177.

33. Hitler in an interview with the *Daily Express*, May 4, 1931, quoted in Karen Bayer, *"How Dead Is Hitler?" Der britische Starreporter Sefton Delmer und die Deutschen* (Mainz, 2008), 47; Hanns Heinz Ewers, *Horst Wessel. Ein deutsches Schicksal* (Stuttgart, 1933), 40.

34. Gerhard Paul, *Aufstand der Bilder: Die NS-Propaganda vor 1933* (Bonn, 1990), 207; Heinrich August Winkler quoted in Benjamin Carter Hett, *The Death of Democracy: Hitler's Rise to Power and the Downfall of the Weimar Republic* (New York, 2008), 139.

35. "Fanfaren der Wahl," *Berliner Tageblatt*, no. 122, March 12, 1932; "Berlin vor der Entscheidung," *Berliner Tageblatt*, no. 123, March 13, 1932.

36. Karl Aloys Schenzinger, *Der Hitlerjunge Quex* (Berlin, 1932), 222.

37. *Vossische Zeitung*, no. 173, April 10, 1932.

38. Entries for March 12, 13, and 14, 1933, in Elke Fröhlich, ed., *Die Tagebücher von Joseph Goebbels. Teil I: Aufzeichnungen 1923–1941* (Munich, 1998), part 2, 2:239–242.

39. Heinrich Hoffmann, ed., *Hitler über Deutschland* (Munich, 1932).

40. "Fahnen in allen Strassen," *Vossische Zeitung*, no. 363, July 30, 1932; Siegfried Kracauer in *Frankfurter Zeitung*, April 24, 1932, quoted in Ruth Glatzer, ed., *Berlin zur Weimarer Zeit: Panorama einer Metropole* (Berlin, 2000), 417–418.

41. Christopher Isherwood, *The Berlin Stories* (1935; rpt. New York, 1963), 86.

42. Thomas Balistier, *Gewalt und Ordnung. Kalkul und Faszination der SA* (Muenster, 1989), 159–160; entries for March 28 and July 12 and 14, 1932, in Elke Fröhlich, *Die Tagebücher von Joseph Goebbels: Sämtliche Fragmente* (Munich, 1987), part 1, 2:148, 203–204.

43. Anthony McElligott, *Contested City: Municipal Politics and the Rise of Nazism in Altona, 1917–1937* (Ann Arbor, 1998), 193; Harry Kessler quoted in Volker Ullrich, *Hitler: Ascent, 1889–1939* (New York, 2016), 311.

44. Hans Joachim Hildenbrand, "Der Betrug mit dem Fackelzug," in *Wir erlebten das Ende der Weimarer Republik. Zeitgenossen berichten*, ed. Rolf Italiaander (Dusseldorf, 1982), 165.

45. Oskar Maria Graf, *Der Abgrund* (1936; rpt. Munich, 1994), 64–67, 148–150.

46. Hans Fallada, *Little Man, What Now?*, trans. Susan Bennett (Brooklyn, 2009), 19; Karl Aloys Schenzinger, *Der Hitlerjunge Quex* (Berlin, 1932), 90–91; Heinz Horn, "Abschnitte und Erlebnisse aus meiner Kampfzeit!," December 29, 1936, and Paul Schneider, "Bericht über meine Kampfjahre 1925–1933," Dessau, December 16, 1936, Bundesarchiv Berlin, NS26/528, as well as Karl Mernberger, "Kampferlebnisse vor der Machtübernahme," December 6, 1936, Bundesarchiv Berlin, NS26/530.

47. Albert Speer, *Erinnerungen* (Berlin, 1969), 34.

48. Jürgen Falter, *Hitlers Wähler* (Munich, 1991), 372.

49. Entry for August 1, 1932, in Elke Fröhlich, *Die Tagebücher von Joseph Goebbels: Sämtliche Fragmente* (Munich, 1987), part 1, 2:211.

50. Entry for August 7, 1932, in Victor Klemperer, *Leben sammeln, nicht fragen wozu und warum: Tagebücher 1925–1932* (Berlin, 1996), 758; entry for August 5, 1932, in Elke Fröhlich, ed., *Die Tagebücher von Joseph Goebbels. Teil I: Aufzeichnungen 1923–1941* (Munich, 1998), part 2, 2:333.

51. *Vossische Zeitung*, no. 366, August 1, 1932.

52. Hans V. Kaltenborn, "An Interview with Hitler, August 17, 1932," *Wisconsin Magazine of History* 50, no. 4 (1967): 287; entry for August 8, 1932, in Elke Fröhlich, *Die Tagebücher von Joseph Goebbels: Sämtliche Fragmente* (Munich, 1987), part 1, 2:218; entry for August 11, 1932, in Elke Fröhlich, ed., *Die Tagebücher von Joseph Goebbels. Teil I: Aufzeichnungen 1923–1941* (Munich, 1998), part 2, 2:337.

53. According to Hitler biographer Ian Kershaw, Hindenburg made the often-cited remark in an August 10, 1932, meeting with Chancellor Franz von Papen. See Ian Kershaw, *Hitler, 1889–1936: Hubris* (New York, 1999), 371.

54. Entry for August 12, 1932, in Elke Fröhlich, *Die Tagebücher von Joseph Goebbels: Sämtliche Fragmente* (Munich, 1987), part 1, 2:223.

55. Entry for August 14, 1932, in Elke Fröhlich, *Die Tagebücher von Joseph Goebbels: Sämtliche Fragmente* (Munich, 1987), part 1, 2:226.

56. Harald Sandner, *Hitler: Das Itinerar: Aufenthaltsorte und Reisen von 1889 bis 1945, Band II 1928–1933* (Berlin, 2016), 982.

57. Entries for September 29, November 3 and 11, and December 31, 1932, quoted in Werner Jochmann, ed., *Nationalsozialismus und Revolution. Ursprung und Geschichte der NSDAP in Hamburg 1922–1933* (Frankfurt, 1963), 413, 416–418, 420; Elisabeth Gebensleben to Irmgard Brester, November 23 and December 1, 1932, in Hedda Kalshoven, ed., *Between Two Homelands: Letters Across the Borders of Nazi Germany* (Urbana, 2014), 55.

58. "Der matte Wahlkampf," *Berliner Tageblatt*, no. 526, November 5, 1932. The remark comes from July. See "Vor den Wahlen. Die Propagandatätigkeit in Berlin," *Berliner Tageblatt*, no. 258, July 30, 1932.

59. *Vossische Zeitung*, no. 582, December 5, 1932; Heiden quoted in Volker Ullrich, *Hitler: Ascent, 1889–1939* (New York, 2016), 330.

60. "Schleicher, ein stellenloser General?," *Neue Zürcher Zeitung*, no. 190, January 31, 1933.

61. Theodor Wolff, "Schleicher," *Berliner Tageblatt*, no. 575, December 4, 1932.

62. Johannes W. Harnisch, "Rund um Schleicher," *Berliner Lokal-Anzeiger*, no. 573, December 3, 1932.

63. Entry for December 17, 1932, in Elke Fröhlich, ed., *Die Tagebücher von Joseph Goebbels. Teil I: Aufzeichnungen 1923–1941* (Munich, 1998), part 2, 3:85.

64. Entry for December 8, 1932, in Elke Fröhlich, *Die Tagebücher von Joseph Goebbels: Sämtliche Fragmente* (Munich, 1987), part 1, 2:296.

65. "Die Welle sinkt," *Vossische Zeitung*, no. 606, December 19, 1932; "Wahl in Dorfe Binow," *Vossische Zeitung*, no. 40, January 25, 1933.

66. See Henry Ashby Turner, *Hitler's Thirty Days to Power: January 1933* (Reading, MA, 1996), 1, on press commentary on January 1, 1933.

67. "Hitlers Abstieg begonnen," *8 Uhr-Abendblatt*, no. 262, November 7, 1932; Julius Elbau, "Jahr der Entscheidung," *Vossische Zeitung*, no. 1, January 1, 1933.

68. "Der goldene Strom," *Vossische Zeitung*, no. 606, December 19, 1932; "Goldener Sonntag," *Deutsche Allgemeine Zeitung*, no. 593, December 18, 1932; "Unsere Meinung," *Deutsche Allgemeine Zeitung*, no. 595, December 20, 1932.

69. *Vossische Zeitung*, no. 607, December 20, 1932.

70. Entry for December 8, 1932, in Bella Fromm, *Blood and Banquets: A Berlin Social Diary* (New York, 1942), 60; Kolnai quoted in Dan Stone, *Responses to Nazism in Britain, 1933–1939: Before War and Holocaust* (Basingstoke, 2003), 28.

71. See, for example, "Kommt die Grosse Konzentration?," *Deutsche Allgemeine Zeitung*, no. 524, November 7, 1932; "Zerstörter Nimbus. Hitlers Verluste in Thüringen und die Reichspolitik," *Berliner Tageblatt*, no. 576, December 5, 1932.

72. Peter Longerich, *Die braunen Bataillone. Geschichte der SA* (Munich, 1989), 159; Conan Fischer, *Stormtroopers: A Social, Economic, and Ideological Analysis, 1929–1935* (London, 1983), 210.

73. Max Domarus, *Hitler: Speeches and Proclamations, 1932–1945* (Wauconda, IL, 1990), 1:201.

74. "Sitzung des Parteiausschusses am 10 November 1932," in *Anpassung oder Widerstand? Aus den Akten des Parteivorstands der detuschen Sozialdemokratie 1932/33*, ed. Hagen Schulze (Bonn, 1975), 18–19; "Stiller, zäher Kampf auf dem Lande," *Berliner Tageblatt*, no. 258, July 30, 1932.

75. "Proclamation to the Party," November 25, 1932, in Max Domarus, *Hitler: Speeches and Proclamations, 1932–1945* (Wauconda, IL, 1990), 1:193.

76. John Wheeler-Bennett, *Wooden Titan: Hindenburg in Twenty Years of German History, 1914–1934* (New York, 1936).

77. Julilus Elbau, "Kanzlersturz—und dann?," *Vossische Zeitung*, no. 49, January 29, 1933; "Hitler oder Papen," *Frankfurter Zeitung*, no. 80 (Morgenausgabe), January 30, 1933; "Unsere Meinung," *Deutsche Allgemeine Zeitung*, nos. 51–52, February 1, 1933.

78. Henry Ashby Turner, *Hitler's Thirty Days to Power: January 1933* (Reading, MA, 1996), 77; Max Domarus, *Hitler: Speeches and Proclamations, 1932–1945* (Wauconda, IL, 1990), 1:203; Goebbels, "Das grosse Wunder," December 24, 1932, and "Das grosse Wunder," February 2, 1933, in Joseph Goebbels, *Wetterleuchten. Aufsätze aus der Kampfzeit* (Munich, 1939), 356–357, 365–366.

79. Herbert Wichmann, "Die letzte Chance?," *Süd-Berlin*, no. 13, January 15, 1933; "Lippe, nicht Deutschland," *Tempo*, no. 13, January 16, 1933; "Das Orakel von Lippe," *Vossische Zeitung*, no. 26, January 16, 1933.

80. "Unter Polizei-Schutz," *Berliner Tageblatt*, no. 38, January 23, 1933.

81. Theodor Wolff, "Der gefährliche Bülowplatz," *Berliner Tageblatt*, no. 37, January 22, 1933; Jay W. Baird, *To Die for Germany: Heroes in the Nazi Pantheon* (Bloomington, 1990), 87; "Ein kleineres Übel—reisengross. Bülowplatz und die Folgen," *Vossische Zeitung*, no. 39, January 24, 1933; *Vorwärts*, quoted in Volker Ullrich, *Hitler: Ascent, 1889–1939* (New York, 2016), 360.

82. Entries for January 22 and 23, 1933, in Elke Fröhlich, ed., *Die Tagebücher von Joseph Goebbels. Teil I: Aufzeichnungen 1923–1941* (Munich, 1998), part 2, 3:112–113; *Der Angriff*, January 23, 1933, quoted in Martin Loiperdinger, "'Hans Westmar': Faschistische und kommunistische Oeffentlichkeit kämpfen um den Besitz der Strasse," in *Märtyrerlegenden im NS-Film*, ed. Martin Loiperdinger (Opladen, 1991), 73.

83. Entry for January 23, 1933, in Elke Fröhlich, ed., *Die Tagebücher von Joseph Goebbels. Teil I: Aufzeichnungen 1923–1941* (Munich, 1998), part 2, 3:123; entry for January 20, 1933, in Abraham Plotkin, *An American in Hitler's Berlin. Abraham Plotkin's Diary, 1932–33*, eds. Catherine Collomp and Bruno Groppo (Urbana, 2009), 117.

84. Max Domarus, *Hitler: Speeches and Proclamations, 1932–1945* (Wauconda, IL, 1990), 1:220.

85. Henry Ashby Turner, *Hitler's Thirty Days to Power: January 1933* (Reading, MA, 1996), 112–116.

86. Entry for January 26, 1933, in Abraham Plotkin, *An American in Hitler's Berlin. Abraham Plotkin's Diary, 1932–33*, eds. Catherine Collomp and Bruno Groppo (Urbana, 2009), 129; Friedrich Stampfer, "Wieder Bülowplatz," *Vorwärts*, no. 43, January 26, 1933.

87. Entry for January 29, 1933, in Abraham Plotkin, *An American in Hitler's Berlin. Abraham Plotkin's Diary, 1932–33*, eds. Catherine Collomp and Bruno Groppo (Urbana, 2009), 132–133.

88. "Krisenwende?," *Berliner Tageblatt*, no. 1, January 1, 1933; "Wird es besser werden?," *Kölnische Zeitung*, no. 1, January 1, 1933.

89. Oliver Lubrich, eds., *Travels in the Reich, 1933–1945: Foreign Authors Report from Germany* (Chicago, 2010), 56.

90. "Bockbierzauber," *Süd-Berlin*, no. 4, January 5, 1933; Alfred Döblin, *Berlin Alexanderplatz: The Story of Franz Biberkopf* (New York, 1997), 91–96. See also Jérôme et Jean Tharaud, "En attendant sans fièvre les élections les Berlinois fêtent joyeusement la bière," *Paris-soir*, February 4, 1933.

Chapter Three: Assault

1. Hans Bausch, "Frühe Erfahrungen," in *Wir erlebten das Ende der Weimarer Republik. Zeitgenossen berichten*, ed. Rolf Italiaander (Dusseldorf, 1982), 206.

2. Hans Bausch, "Frühe Erfahrungen," in *Wir erlebten das Ende der Weimarer Republik. Zeitgenossen berichten*, ed. Rolf Italiaander (Dusseldorf, 1982), 206; Elisabeth Gebensleben to Irmgard Brester, February 3, 1933, in Hedda Kalshoven, ed., *Between Two Homelands: Letters Across the Borders of Nazi Germany* (Urbana, 2014), 57; Ursula Sobottka, "Alles wird anders und besser," in *Wir erlebten das Ende der Weimarer Republik. Zeitgenossen berichten*, ed. Rolf Italiaander (Dusseldorf, 1982), 164; entry for January 30, 1933, in Thea Sternheim, *Tagebücher 1903–1971, Band 2, 1925–1936* (Göttingen, 2002), 470; Bernd Küster, *Max Liebermann—ein Malerleben* (Hamburg, 1988), 216.

3. Entry for January 30, 1933, in Erich Ebermaycr, *Denn heute gehört uns Deutschland . . .* (Hamburg, 1959), 11–14.

4. *Der Angriff*, no. 25, January 30, 1933.

5. Melita Maschmann, *Account Rendered: A Dossier on My Former Self*, ed. Geoffrey Strachan (London, 1964), 10–13; Melita Maschmann, *Fazit. Mein Weg in der Hitler-Jugend* (Stuttgart, 1979), 7–13.

6. "Fackelzug für Hindenburg, Hitler und Seldt," *Deutsche Allgemeine Zeitung*, no. 51, January 31, 1933.

7. "Der Aufbruch der Nation," *Der Angriff*, no. 26, January 31, 1933.

8. Entry for July 26, 1933, in Thomas Mann, *Dairies 1918–1939*, ed. Hermann Kesten (New York, 1982), 167; entry for November 27, 1933, in Thomas Mann, *Tagebücher 1933–1934*, ed. Peter de Mendelssohn (Frankfurt, 1977), 259.

9. "Fackelzug für Hindenburg, Hitler und Seldt," *Deutsche Allgemeine Zeitung*, no. 51, January 31, 1933; entry for January 30, 1933, in Elke Fröhlich, *Die Tagebücher von Joseph Goebbels: Sämtliche Fragmente* (Munich, 1987), part 1, 2:360; Andreas Dorpalen, *Hindenburg and the Weimar Republic* (Princeton, 1964), 455. Bella Fromm transcribed a slightly different version of the joke in her diary on January 31, 1933, in *Blood and Banquets: A Berlin Social Diary* (New York, 1942), 74. See also Lilian T. Mowrer, *Journalist's Wife* (New York, 1937), 281.

10. "War das Berlin? Nachwort zu einem 'historischen Tag,'" *Vorwärts*, no. 53, February 1, 1933; Martin Schuster, "Die SA in der nationalsozialistischen 'Machterfreigung' in Berlin und Brandenburg, 1926–1934" (PhD diss, TU Berlin, 2005), 51; the 700,000 figure is quoted in *Süd-Berlin*, no. 27, February 1, 1933.

11. *Berliner Tageblatt*, no. 33, January 20, 1933; *Deutsche Allgemeine Zeitung*, no. 58, February 4, 1933; entry for February 10, 1933, in Elke Fröhlich, ed., *Die*

Tagebücher von Joseph Goebbels. Teil I: Aufzeichnungen 1923–1941 (Munich, 1998), part 2, 3:125 ("Tuesday" was evidently February 7); Heinrich Böll, *What's to Become of the Boy* (New York, 1984), 9–10.

12. *Berliner Morgenpost*, no. 26, January 31, 1933, and no. 27, February 1, 1933.

13. "Anstehen—zum Rodeln" and "Rekordbesuch," *Berliner Tageblatt*, no. 86, February 20, 1933; "Der Kölner Karneval," *Berliner Tageblatt*, no. 99, February 28, 1933.

14. *Berliner Tageblatt*, no. 56, February 2, 1933; Max Osborn, "Jüdisches Museum," *Vossische Zeitung*, no. 41, January 25, 1933.

15. Kurt Schumacher quoted in Josef and Ruth Becker, eds., *Hitlers Machtgreifung 1933. Vom Machtantritt Htilers 30. Januar 1933 bis zur Besiegelung des Einparteienstaates 14 Juli 1933* (Munich, 1983), 45–47.

16. Sebastian Haffner, *Defying Hitler: A Memoir* (New York, 2002), 105; entry for January 30, 1933, in Johann Wilhelm Brügel and Norbert Frei, eds., "Berliner Tagebuch 1932–1934: Aufzeichnungen des tscheschoslowakischen Diplomaten Camill Hoffmann," *Vierteljahrshefte für Zeitgeschichte 36*, no. 1 (1988): 131–183, at 159.

17. Anthony McElligott, *Contested City: Municipal Politics and the Rise of Nazism in Altona, 1917–1937* (Ann Arbor, 1998), 177; entry for February 2, 1933, in Hertha Nathorff, *Das Tagebuch der Hertha Nathorff. Berlin–Newyork: Aufzeichnungen 1933 bis 1945*, ed. Wolfgang Benz (Munich, 1987), 35; Stéphane Roussel, *Die Hügel von Berlin. Erinnerungen an Deutschland* (Hamburg, 1986), 177.

18. William Sheridan Allen, *The Nazi Seizure of Power: The Experience of a Single German Town, 1922–1945*, rev. ed. (Brattleboro, 2014), 154; entry for February 6, 1933, in "Tagebuch Luise Solmitz," in Frank Bajohr, Beate Meyer, and Joachim Szodrzynski, eds., *Bedrohung, Hoffnung, Skepsis. Vier Tagebücher des Jahres 1933* (Göttingen, 2013), 155–156.

19. "Der Reichstag ist aufgelöst," *Vossische Zeitung*, no. 55, February 2, 1933.

20. "Das Kabinett Hitler," *Neue Zürcher Zeitung*, no. 187, January 31, 1933.

21. Horace Rumbold to John Simon, February 23, 1933, in E. L. Woodward and Rohan Butler, eds., *Documents on British Foreign Policy, 1919–1939*, second series (London, 1950), 4:425.

22. "Das Staatsbegräbnis im Dom," *Vossische Zeitung*, no. 60, February 4, 1933; *Berliner Morgenpost*, no. 31, February 5, 1933, and no. 33, February 8, 1933.

23. Entry for February 5, 1933, in Abraham Plotkin, *An American in Hitler's Berlin. Abraham Plotkin's Diary, 1932–33*, eds. Catherine Collomp and Bruno Groppo (Urbana, 2009), 145; "Maikowski Trauerfeier," *Berliner Morgenpost*, no. 32, February 7, 1933.

24. Jay W. Baird, *To Die for Germany: Heroes in the Nazi Pantheon* (Bloomington, 1990), 95.

25. Theodor Heuss, "Begräbnis eines ermorderten SA-Mannes," *Die Hilfe*, February 18, 1933, quoted in Josef and Ruth Becker, eds., *Hitlers Machtgreifung 1933. Vom Machtantritt Hitlers 30. Janaur 1933 bis zur Besiegelung des Einparteienstaates 14 Juli 1933* (Munich, 1983), 80.

26. "Eine Volksrede Hitlers," *Neue Zürcher Zeitung*, no. 259, February 12, 1933.

27. "Kampfruf an die Nation!," *Der Angriff*, no. 36, February 11, 1933; Goebbels's radio text, "Welche eine Wendung durch Gottes Fügung!," February 10, 1933, in Josef and Ruth Becker, eds., *Hitlers Machtgreifung 1933. Vom Machtantritt Htilers 30. Januar 1933 bis zur Besiegelung des Einparteienstaates 14 Juli 1933* (Munich, 1983), 57–59.

28. See *Deutsche Allgemeine Zeitung*, no. 57, February 3, 1933.

29. Joachim C. Fest, *Hitler* (New York, 1973), 323–324.

30. Max Domarus, *Hitler: Speeches and Proclamations, 1932–1945* (Wauconda, IL, 1990), 1:247; Klaus Scholder, *The Churches and the Third Reich*, vol. 1: *Preliminary History and the Time of Illusions, 1918–1934* (Philadelphia, 1988), 223; entries for February 10 and 11, 1933, in Elke Fröhlich, *Die Tagebücher von Joseph Goebbels: Sämtliche Fragmente* (Munich, 1987), part 1, 2:372–373.

31. Ansgar Diller, *Rundfunkpolitik im Dritten Reich* (Munich, 1980), 109.

32. Karen Bayer, *"How Dead Is Hitler?" Der britische Starreporter Sefton Delmer und die Deutschen* (Mainz, 2008), 56.

33. Joseph Goebbels, "Die zukünftige Arbeit und Gestaltung des deutschen Rundfunks," March 25, 1933, in *Goebbels Reden 1932–1945*, ed. Helmut Heiber (Gondrom, 1991), 87.

34. Ansgar Diller, *Rundfunkpolitik im Dritten Reich* (Munich, 1980), 61–69; "Politischer Rundfunk," *Vossische Zeitung*, no. 91, February 23, 1933.

35. Hermann Probst, "Besuch beim Rundfunkwerbewagen," *Die Sendung* 9, no. 12 (March 18, 1932), 247.

36. Entry for May 10, 1933, in Erich Ebermayer, *Denn heute gehört uns Deutschland . . .* (Hamburg, 1959), 78.

37. Elisabeth Gebensleben to Irmgard Brester, March 2, 1933, in Hedda Kalshoven, ed., *Between Two Homelands: Letters Across the Borders of Nazi Germany* (Urbana, 2014), 62; entry for February 21, 1933, in Matthias Joseph Mehs, *Tagebücher. November 1929 bis September 1946. Band I. November 1929 bis Januar 1936* (Trier, 2011), 243.

38. Entries for February 2, 10, 11, 25, and 26 and March 21, 1933, in "Tagebuch Luise Solmitz," in Frank Bajohr, Beate Meyer, and Joachim Szodrzynski, eds., *Bedrohung, Hoffnung, Skepsis. Vier Tagebücher des Jahres 1933* (Göttingen, 2013), 153, 158–159, 162–163, 178.

39. Victor Klemperer, *I Will Bear Witness, 1933–1941: A Diary of the Nazi Years* (New York, 1998), 155; Andrew Stuart Bergerson, "Listening to the Radio in Hildesheim, 1923–1953," *German Studies Review* 24, no. 1 (February 2001), 83–113, at 96.

40. Inge Marssolek and Adelheid von Saldern, "Das Radio als historisches und historiographisches Medium," in *Zuhören und Gehörtwerden I. Radio im Nationalsozialismus*, eds. Marssolek and von Saldern (Tübingen, 1998), 33; Uta C. Schmidt, "Radioaneigung," in *Zuhören und Gehörtwerden I. Radio im Nationalsozialismus*, eds. Marssolek and von Saldern (Tübingen, 1998), 297.

41. Uta C. Schmidt, "Radioaneigung," in *Zuhören und Gehörtwerden I. Radio im Nationalsozialismus*, eds. Inge Marssolek and Adelheid von Saldern (Tübingen, 1998), 332; Jacques Lusseyran, *And There Was Light. Autobiography of Jacques Lusseyran, Blind Hero of the French Resistance* (New York, 1963), 106; Werner Hensel and Erich Keller, *1000 Hörer antworten...* (Berlin, 1935), 16–18, 30; Friedrich Bischoffs, "Hallo! Hier Welle Erdball!," quoted in Irmela Schneider, ed., *Radio-Kultur in der Weimarer Republik* (Tübingen, 1984), 122–124; A. H. Schelle-Noetzel [Arnolt Bronnen], *Kampf im Aether, oder Die Unsichtbaren* (Berlin, 1935), 404.

42. Jason Loviglio, *Radio's Intimate Public: Network Broadcasting and Mass-Mediated Democracy* (Minneapolis, 2005), xiv.

43. Annette Kolb, "Radiofreuden und Radioleiden," in *Beschwerdebuch* (Berlin 1932), 10; Rebecca P. Scales, *Radio and the Politics of Sound in Interwar France, 1921–1939* (Cambridge, 2016), 23, 49–50; Victor Engelhardt, "Die kulturelle Bedeutung," *Die Sendung* 1 (April 1924), quoted in Heinz Pohle, *Der Rundfunk als Instrument der Politik* (Hamburg, 1955), 340.

44. Entries for February 21 and March 4, 1933, in Elke Fröhlich, *Die Tagebücher von Joseph Goebbels: Sämtliche Fragmente* (Munich, 1987), part 1, 2:380, 386; "Der 'Tag der erwachenden Nation,'" *Deutsche Allgemeine Zeitung*, no. 109, March 5, 1933. See also entry for February 11, 1933, in Erich Ebermayer, *Denn heute gehört uns Deutschland...* (Hamburg, 1959), 21–22.

45. Jules Sauerwein, "Le peuple allemand est allé aux urnes avec passivité," *Paris-soir*, March 6, 1933.

46. Entries for February 21 and March 4, 1933, in Elke Fröhlich, *Die Tagebücher von Joseph Goebbels: Sämtliche Fragmente* (Munich, 1987), part 1, 2:380, 386.

47. Theodor Wolff, "Der 5. März," *Berliner Tageblatt*, no. 61, February 5, 1933; entry for March 3, 1933, in Walter Tausk, *Breslauer Tagebuch 1933–1940* (Berlin, 1975), 30.

48. *Berliner Morgenpost*, no. 28, February 2, 1933, and no. 32, February 7, 1933; *Tempo*, no. 27, February 1, 1933.

49. See the headlined articles in the *Deutsche Allgemeine Zeitung*, nos. 55–56, February 2–3, 1933.

50. Friedrich Stampfer, "Für die Wahrheit! Der Blutsonntag in Eisleben," *Vorwärts*, no. 75, February 14, 1933; "Strassenkampf nach KPD-Ueberfall," *Berliner Lokal-Anzeiger*, February 13, 1933.

51. *Berliner Morgenpost*, no. 30, February 4, 1933; no. 40, February 16, 1933; no. 41, February 17, 1933; no. 42, February 18, 1933.

52. Sebastian Haffner, *Geschichte eines Deutschen: Die Erinnerungen 1914–1933* (Stuttgart, 2000), 119.

53. "Unsere Meinung," *Deutsche Allgemeine Zeitung*, nos. 75–76, February 15, 1933.

54. "Wahlfieber," *Deutsche Allgemeine Zeitung*, nos. 89–90, February 23, 1933; "Unsere Meinung," nos. 59–60, February 5, 1933.

55. "Die Hitlerwahl," *Deutsche Allgemeine Zeitung*, nos. 97–98, February 28, 1933.

56. Fritz Klein, "Nun an die Arbeit," *Deutsche Allgemeine Zeitung*, nos. 121–122, March 14, 1933.

57. "Unsere Meinung," *Deutsche Allgemeine Zeitung*, nos. 151–152, March 31, 1933.

58. Karl Dietrich Bracher, "Stufen der Machtergreifung," in *Die nationalsozialistische Machtergreifung. Studien zur Errichtung des totalitären Herrschaftssystems in Deutschland 1933/34*, eds. Karl Dietrich Bracher, Wolfgang Sauer, and Gerhard Schhulz (Cologne, 1960), 67–73; "Ein Erlass Görings an die Polizei," *Berliner Morgenpost*, no. 44, February 21, 1933.

59. Rudolf Diels, *Lucifer ante Portas...es spricht der erste Chef der Gestapo* (Stuttgart, 1950), 182–183.

60. Ernst Fraenkel, *The Dual State: A Contribution to the Theory of Dictatorship* (New York, 1941), 3, 5; On Hussong, "Die Magna Charta des neuen Reichs," *Berliner Lokal-Anzeiger*, no. 141, March 24, 1933.

61. Rudolf Diels, *Lucifer ante Portas...es spricht der erste Chef der Gestapo* (Stuttgart, 1950), 194.

62. Sefton Delmer, *Trail Sinister: An Autobiography* (London, 1961), 1:188.

63. Goebbels quoted in Karl Dietrich Bracher, "Stufen der Machtergreifung," in *Die nationalsozialistische Machtergreifung. Studien zur Errichtung des totalitären Herrschaftssystems in Deutschland 1933/34*, eds. Karl Dietrich Bracher, Wolfgang Sauer, and Gerhard Schhulz (Cologne, 1960), 77.

64. Irene Strenge, *Machtübernahme 1933—Alles auf legalem Weg?* (Berlin, 2002), 165.

65. Benjamin Carter Hett, *Burning the Reichstag: An Investigation into the Third Reich's Enduring Mystery* (New York, 2014).

66. Entry for February 27/28, 1933, in Erich Ebermayer, *Denn heute gehört uns Deutschland . . .* (Hamburg, 1959), n.p.; entry for February 28, 1933, in Matthias Joseph Mehs, *Tagebücher. November 1929 bis September 1946. Band I. November 1929 bis Januar 1936* (Trier, 2011), 245.

67. Sefton Delmer, *Trail Sinister. An Autobiography* (London, 1961), 1:191.

68. "Der Menschenstrom zur Brandstätte," *Vossische Zeitung*, no. 100, February 28, 1933; "An der Brandstätte des Reichstags. Tägliche Fuehrung," *Berliner Morgenpost*, no. 54, March 4, 1933.

69. "Unsere Meinung," *Deutsche Allgemeine Zeitung*, nos. 99–100, March 1, 1933; "Unsere Meinung," nos. 103–104, March 3, 1933.

70. "Rheinische Fahrt," *Neue Zürcher Zeitung*, no. 396, March 5, 1933.

71. Entry for February 28, 1933, in Matthias Joseph Mehs, *Tagebücher. November 1929 bis September 1946. Band I. November 1929 bis Januar 1936* (Trier, 2011), 245.

72. Otto Braun at "Sitzung des Parteivorstands mit Vertretern der Reichstagsfraktion und des ADGB am Vormittag des 30. Januar 1933 im Reichstag," in *Anpassung oder Widerstand? Aus den Akten des Parteivorstands der detuschen Sozialdemokratie 1932/33*, ed. Hagen Schulze (Bonn, 1975), 135.

73. *Vorwärts*, no. 65, February 8, 1933; entry for February 7, 1933, in Abraham Plotkin, *An American in Hitler's Berlin. Abraham Plotkin's Diary, 1932–33*, eds. Catherine Collomp and Bruno Groppo (Urbana, 2009), 150; William Sheridan Allen, *The Nazi Seizure of Power: The Experience of a Single German Town, 1922–1945*, rev. ed. (Brattleboro, 2014), 155.

74. See, for example, "SPD Versammlung in Lindengarten in Hermsdorf," *Nord-Berliner Tagespost*, no. 52, March 2, 1933.

75. Reichsbanner leader Karl Höltermann quoted in "'Freiheit!' Mächtige Kundgebung des Reichsbanners im Lustgarten," *Berliner Tageblatt*, no. 86, February 20, 1933.

76. "KPD-Versammlung aufgelöst," *Vorwärts*, no. 93, February 24, 1933.

77. Entry for February 27, 1933, in Abraham Plotkin, *An American in Hitler's Berlin. Abraham Plotkin's Diary, 1932–33*, eds. Catherine Collomp and Bruno

Groppo (Urbana, 2009), 169–172; "Karl Marx Kundgebung aufgelöst," *Vorwärts*, no. 99, February 28, 1933.

78. Entry for March 5, 1933, in "Tagebuch Luise Solmitz," in Frank Bajohr, Beate Meyer, and Joachim Szodrzynski, eds., *Bedrohung, Hoffnung, Skepsis. Vier Tagebücher des Jahres 1933* (Göttingen, 2013), 167.

79. Horace Rumbold to John Simon, March 7, 1933, in E. L. Woodward and Rohan Butler, eds., *Documents on British Foreign Policy, 1919–1939*, second series (London, 1950), 4:445; "Blick über die Reichshauptstadt" and "In den süddeutschen Ländern," *Kölnische Zeitung*, no. 128, March 6, 1933.

80. "Blick über die Reichshauptstadt," *Kölnische Zeitung*, no. 128, March 6, 1933.

81. Entry for March 6, 1933, in Elke Fröhlich, ed., *Die Tagebücher von Joseph Goebbels. Teil I: Aufzeichnungen 1923–1941* (Munich, 1998), part 2, 3:141; entry for March 12, 1933, in Elke Fröhlich, *Die Tagebücher von Joseph Goebbels: Sämtliche Fragmente* (Munich, 1987), part 1, 2:391–392.

82. "Die Bilanz des 5. März," *Berliner Morgenpost*, no. 56, March 7, 1933.

Chapter Four: The "Communist Beast"

1. Eric Rentschler, *The Ministry of Illusion: Nazi Cinema and Its Afterlife* (Cambridge, 1996).

2. Entry for May 7, 1933, in Karl Dürkefälden, *"Schreiben wie es wirklich war..." Aufzeichungen Karl Dürkefäldens aus den Jahren 1933–1945*, eds. Herbert and Sibylle Obenaus (Hannover, 1985), 48.

3. Hans Speier, "Nazi Propaganda and Its Decline," *Social Research* 10 (1943): 358–377, at 376.

4. Entry for October 17, 1931, in André Postert, ed., *Hitlerjunge Schall. Die Tagebücher eines jungen Nationalsozialisten* (Munich, 2016), 90.

5. Sebastian Haffner, *Defying Hitler: A Memoir* (New York, 2002), 7.

6. See "The History of the Karl Liebknecht House," Die Linke, https://archiv2017.die-linke.de/partei/organe/karl-liebknecht-haus/die-geschichte-des-karl-liebknecht-hauses (accessed on April 20, 2018). "The Left," the successor party to the Communists, today has its headquarters in the building.

7. Rudolf Diels, *Lucifer ante Portas...es spricht der erste Chef der Gestapo* (Stuttgart, 1950), 188–189; "Geheimgewölbe im Liebknecht-Haus," *Vossische Zeitung*, no. 97, February 26, 1933.

8. Horace Rumbold to John Simon, March 7, 1933, in E. L. Woodward and Rohan Butler, eds., *Documents on British Foreign Policy, 1919–1939*, second series

(London, 1950), 4:444; Georg Bernhard, *Die deutsche Tragödie. Der Selbstmord einer Republik* (Prague, 1933), 6.

9. Göring on the "kommunistischen Aufstandsversuch," March 1, 1933, in Axel Friedrichs, ed., *Dokumente der Deutschen Politik*, vol. 1: *Die nationalsozialistische Revolution, 1933* (Berlin, 1939), 19–21; "Göring begründet die Notverordnung. Mitteilungen über die kommunistische Gefahr," *Vossische Zeitung*, no. 103, March 3, 1933.

10. Elisabeth Gebensleben to Irmgard Brester, March 2, 1933, in Hedda Kalshoven, ed., *Between Two Homelands: Letters Across the Borders of Nazi Germany* (Urbana, 2014), 62.

11. Hermann Göring, "Wir tragen die Verantwortung" (Frankfurt, March 3, 1933), in *Reden und Aufsätze* (1938; rpt. Munich, 1943), 22–27.

12. Nikolaus Wachsmann, *KL: A History of the Nazi Concentration Camps* (New York, 2015), 24–25; Kim Wünschmann, *Before Auschwitz: Jewish Prisoners in the Prewar Concentration Camps* (Cambridge, 2015), 66; Peter Fritzsche, *An Iron Wind: Europe Under Hitler* (New York, 2016), 142.

13. Hermann Göring, "Wir tragen die Verantwortung" (Frankfurt, March 3, 1933), in *Reden und Aufsätze* (1938; rpt. Munich, 1943), 22–27.

14. Otto Michael Knab, *Kleinstadt unterm Hakenkreuz. Groteske Erinnerungen aus Bayern* (1934; rpt. Starnberg, 2014), 6–7.

15. Entry for March 6, 1933, in Johann Wilhelm Brügel and Norbert Frei, eds., "Berliner Tagebuch 1932–1934: Aufzeichnungen des tscheschoslowakischen Diplomaten Camill Hoffmann," *Vierteljahrshefte für Zeitgeschichte* 36, no. 1 (1988): 131–183, at 166.

16. *Kölnische Zeitung*, nos. 133–134, March 8–9, 1933.

17. Entries for March 9 and 10, 1933, in Walter Tausk, *Breslauer Tagebuch 1933–1940* (Berlin,1975), 32–35; Peter Longerich, *Die braunen Bataillone. Geschichte der SA* (Munich, 1989), 167; Franz F. Nöhbauer and Ludwig Hüttl, eds., *Die Chronik Bayerns* (Gütersloh, 1994), 482.

18. "Breslauer Intendant misshandelt," *Berliner Morgenpost*, no. 60, March 11, 1933; *Frankfurter Zeitung*, March 12, 1933, quoted in Comité des Délégations Juives, ed., *Das Schwarzbuch: Tatsachen und Dokumente. Die Lage der Juden in Deutschland 1933* (Paris, 1934), 495–496; entry for March 11, 1933, in Jochen Klepper, *Unter dem Schatten Deiner Flügel: Aus den Tagebüchern der Jahre 1932–1942* (Stuttgart, 1972), 38.

19. "Jews from Germany," *The Times*, March 10, 1933.

20. "Eine scharfe Rede Görings. Nationalsozialistische Kundgebung in Essen," *Vossische Zeitung*, no. 119, March 11, 1933. "Old Aunties" is from the *Völkischer Beobachter*; see *Vossische Zeitung*, no. 116, March 9, 1933.

21. Hitler to Papen, March 11, 1933, in Dirk Erb, ed., *Gleichgeschaltet. Der Nazi-Terror gegen Gewerkschaften und Berufsverbände 1930–1933. Eine Dokumentation* (Göttingen, 2001), 141–144.

22. "Ausserordentliche Zurückhaltung der Presse," *Vossische Zeitung*, no. 121, March 12, 1933.

23. On Sollmann, see *Berliner Morgenpost*, no. 59, March 10, 1933. On Ottendorf, see Madeleine Kent, *I Married a German* (London, 1938), 178; "Radeberger Land unter dem Hakenkreuz," Bund der Antifaschisten, Region Dresden e.V., http://aardb.blogsport.de/images/RadebergerLandunterdemHakenkreuz.pdf.

24. Entry for April 4, 1933, in "Tagebuch Cornelius Freiherr v. Berenberg-Gossler," in Frank Bajohr, Beate Meyer, and Joachim Szodrzynski, eds., *Bedrohung, Hoffnung, Skepsis. Vier Tagebücher des Jahres 1933* (Göttingen, 2013), 318.

25. "Terror in Braunschweig, Bericht der Kommission zur Untersuchung der Lage der politischen Gefangenen, Zurich, Oktober 1933," in Dirk Erb, ed., *Gleichgeschaltet. Der Nazi-Terror gegen Gewerkschaften und Berufsverbände 1930–1933. Ein Dokumentation* (Göttingen, 2001), 130–134; Elisabeth Gebensleben to Irmgard Brester, March 10, 1933, in Hedda Kalshoven, ed., *Between Two Homelands: Letters Across the Borders of Nazi Germany* (Urbana, 2014), 64.

26. "Terror in Braunschweig, Bericht der Kommission zur Untersuchung der Lage der politischen Gefangenen, Zurich, Oktober 1933," in Dirk Erb, ed., *Gleichgeschaltet. Der Nazi-Terror gegen Gewerkschaften und Berufsverbände 1930–1933. Eine Dokumentation* (Göttingen, 2001), 130–134; *Wolfenbütteler Zeitung*, March 13, 1933, in Reinhard Bein, *Zeitzeichen. Stadt und Land Braunschweig 1930–1945* (Braunschweig, 2000), 182.

27. Ernst-August Roloff, *Braunschweigs Weg ins Dritte Reich: Bürgertum und Nationalsozialismus 1930–33* (Braunschweig, 1980), 142; Elisabeth Gebensleben to Irmgard Brester, March 14, 1933, in Hedda Kalshoven, ed., *Between Two Homelands: Letters Across the Borders of Nazi Germany* (Urbana, 2014), 68.

28. Robert Gehrke, *Aus Braunschweigs dunkelsten Tagen—Der Rieseberger Massenmord. Über den Widerstand im ehemaligen Freistaat Braunschweig 1933–1945* (Hanover, n.d.), 64; Reinhard Bein, *Zeitzeichen. Stadt und Land Braunschweig 1930–1945* (Braunschweig, 2000), 41, 44.

29. Joachim C. Fest, *Hitler* (New York, 1973), 424.

30. *Chemnitzer Tageblatt und Anzeiger*, March 11, 1933, quoted in Klaus Hesse and Philipp Springer, *Vor aller Augen: Fotodokumente des nationalsozialistischen Terrors in der Provinz* (Essen, 2002), 57.

31. Madeleine Kent, *I Married a German* (London, 1938), 172–173.

32. "Schaufahrt 1933," Karlsruher Stadtwiki, https://ka.stadtwiki.net/Scha ufahrt_1933; "Schaufahrt als öffentliche Demütigung," Karlsruhe, May 10, 2013, http://web1.karlsruhe.de/Aktuell/Stadtzeitung13/sz1913.htm; Martin Schumacher, ed., *M.d.R. Die Reichstagsabegeordneten der Weimarer Republik in der Zeit des Nationalsozialismus. Politische Verfolgung, Emigration und Ausbürgerung 1933–1945* (Düsseldorf, 1994), 309. On trauma, see Marum's letter to his wife, May 21, 1933, quoted in Guido Fackler, *"Des Lagers Stimme"—Musik im KZ. Alltag und Häftlingskultur in den Konzentratonslagern 1933 bis 1936* (Bremen, 2000), 125.

33. "Schaufahrt 1933," Karlsruher Stadtwiki, https://ka.stadtwiki.net/Scha ufahrt_1933.

34. "Eine scharfe Rede Görings. Nationalsozialistische Kundgebung in Essen," *Vossische Zeitung*, no. 119, March 11, 1933.

35. I have drawn heavily from Jan Petersen, *Unsere Strasse* (1935; rpt. Munich, 1978), but the details are corroborated by historical records detailing the terror against "Marxist" neighborhoods.

36. Kim Wünschmann, *Before Auschwitz: Jewish Prisoners in the Prewar Concentration Camps* (Cambridge, 2015), 23; "Keine Sabotage des Volkswillens mehr!," *Völkischer Beobachter*, August 11, 1932, cited in Christian Goeschel and Nikolaus Wachsmann, eds., *The Nazi Concentration Camps, 1933–1939: A Documentary History* (Lincoln, 2012), 9; Nikolaus Wachsmann, *KL: A History of the Nazi Concentration Camps* (New York, 2015), 29; Slavko Goldstein, *1941: The Year That Keeps Returning* (New York, 2013), 310.

37. Detlef Schmiechen-Ackermann, *Nationalsozialismus und Arbeitermilieus: Der nationalsozialistische Angriff auf die proletarischen Wohnquartiere und die Reaktion in den sozialistischen Vereinen* (Bonn, 1998), 403, 411; Detlev Peukert, *Die KPD im Widerstand. Verfolgung und Untergrundarbeit an Rhein und Ruhr 1933 bis 1945* (Wuppertal, 1980), 87.

38. "16 mars 1933, les elections du 12 mars et les developpements de l'action hitlerienne," in Jean-Marc Dreyfus, ed., *Les rapports de Berlin; André François-Poncet et le national-socialisme* (Paris, 2016), 66; "The Terror in Germany," *Manchester Guardian*, March 29, 1933.

39. Irmgard Litten, *A Mother Fights Hitler* (London, 1941), 33.

40. Stephen Greenblatt, *Tyrant: Shakespeare on Politics* (New York, 2018), 73.

41. Charlotte Beradt, *The Third Reich of Dreams* (New York, 1968), 21; Charlotte Beradt, "Dreams Under Dictatorship," *Free World* 6 (October 1943), 333–337, at 333. The storm trooper dream is Beradt's own.

42. Entry for September 17, 1933, in "Tagebuch Kurt Fritz Rosenberg," in Frank Bajohr, Beate Meyer, and Joachim Szodrzynski, eds., *Bedrohung, Hoffnung, Skepsis. Vier Tagebücher des Jahres 1933* (Göttingen, 2013), 114–115.

43. "Keine Sabotage des Volkswillens mehr!," *Völkischer Beobachter*, August 11, 1932, quoted in Christian Goeschel and Nikolaus Wachsmann, eds., *The Nazi Concentration Camps, 1933–1939: A Documentary History* (Lincoln, 2012), 9.

44. Hitler's speech at the Düsseldorf Industry Club on January 26, 1932, quoted in Joachim C. Fest, *Hitler* (New York, 1973), 310.

45. Nikolaus Wachsmann, *KL: A History of the Nazi Concentration Camps* (New York, 2015), 36.

46. Willi Veller to Gregor Strasser, August 16, 1930, quoted in Joachim C. Fest, *Hitler* (New York, 1973), 295; Thomas Balistier, *Gewalt und Ordnung. Kalkul und Faszination der SA* (Muenster, 1989), 158; David Pietrusza, *1932: The Rise of Hitler and FDR—Two Tales of Politics, Betrayal, and Unlikely Destiny* (Guilford, CT 2016), 232.

47. Ludwig August Jacobsen, *So hat es angefangen. Ein Bericht aus den Tagen der "nationalen Erhebung" in Köln* (Cologne, 1987), 36; Eric A. Johnson, *Nazi Terror: The Gestapo, Jews, and Ordinary Germans* (New York, 1999), 182, 191, 193.

48. Stefan Szende, *Zwischen Gewalt und Toleranz: Zeugnisse und Reflexionen eines Sozialisten* (Frankfurt, 1975), 19.

49. Stefan Szende, *Zwischen Gewalt und Toleranz: Zeugnisse und Reflexionen eines Sozialisten* (Frankfurt, 1975), 15, 17–18; J. K. von Engelbrechten and Hans Volz, eds., *Wir wandern durch das nationalsozialistische Berlin: Ein Führer durch die Gedenkstätten des Kampfes um die Reichshauptstadt* (1937; rpt. Dresden, 2007), 59.

50. "Vernehmungsprotokoll der Berliner Kriminalpolizei," May 17, 1933, in Josef and Ruth Becker, eds., *Hitlers Machtgreifung 1933. Vom Machtantritt Htilers 30. Januar 1933 bis zur Besiegelung des Einparteienstaates 14 Juli 1933* (Munich, 1983), 150–153; World Committee for the Victims of German Fascism, *The Brown Book of the Hitler Terror and the Burning of the Reichstag* (New York, 1933), 206–211.

51. Stefan Szende, *Zwischen Gewalt und Toleranz: Zeugnisse und Reflexionen eines Sozialisten* (Frankfurt, 1975), 51; Felix von Papen, *Ein von Papen spricht . . . über seine Erlebnise im Hitler Deutschland* (Amsterdam, 1939), 11.

52. Rudolf Diels, *Lucifer ante Portas . . . es spricht der erste Chef der Gestapo* (Stuttgart, 1950), 251, 255.

53. Ludwig August Jacobsen, *So hat es angefangen. Ein Bericht aus den Tagen der "nationalen Erhebung" in Köln* (Cologne, 1987), 51, 87, 119.

54. Joachim C. Fest, *Hitler* (New York, 1973), 375–376.

55. "Konzentrationslager," *Berliner Morgenpost*, no. 68, March 21, 1933.

56. Elisabeth Gebensleben to Irmgard Brester, March 22, 1933, in Hedda Kalshoven, ed., *Between Two Homelands: Letters Across the Borders of Nazi Germany* (Urbana, 2014), 72.

57. Richard J. Evans, *Rituals of Retribution: Capital Punishment in Germany, 1600–1987* (New York, 1996), 644–659; entry for August 8, 1933, in "Tagebuch Luise Solmitz," in Frank Bajohr, Beate Meyer, and Joachim Szodrzynski, eds., *Bedrohung, Hoffnung, Skepsis. Vier Tagebücher des Jahres 1933* (Göttingen, 2013), 228; "Axe Restored in the Reich," *New York Times*, August 4, 1933.

58. "Das neue Spiel: SA räumt Liebknechthaus," *Illustrierter Beobachter*, no. 15, April 15, 1933.

59. *Coburger Zeitung* quoted in Klaus Drobisch and Günther Wieland, *System der NS-Konzentrationslager 1933–1939* (Berlin, 1993), 90; "Schutzhäftlinge kommen aus Dachau zurück—und ein neuer Transport geht ab," *Fränkische Tageszeitung*, no. 62, August 12, 1933.

60. Werner Schäfer, *Konzentrationslager Oranienburg. Das Anti-Braunbuch über das erste detusche Konzentrationslager* (Berlin, 1934), 23; "Konzentrationslager: Eine notwendige Frage und ihre befriedigende Lösung," *Nachrichten für den Kreis Niederbarnim*, August 19, 1933, quoted in Christian Goeschel and Nikolaus Wachsmann, eds., *The Nazi Concentration Camps, 1933–1939: A Documentary History* (Lincoln, 2012), 58.

61. Entry for July 3, 1933, in Walter Tausk, *Breslauer Tagebuch 1933–1940* (Berlin, 1975), 87; entry for October 11, 1933, in "Tagebuch Luise Solmitz," in Frank Bajohr, Beate Meyer, and Joachim Szodrzynski, eds., *Bedrohung, Hoffnung, Skepsis. Vier Tagebücher des Jahres 1933* (Göttingen, 2013), 246.

62. "Dachau ab: 12.40 Uhr," *Fränkische Tageszeitung*, no. 27, July 3, 1933. See also no. 43, July 21, 1933, and no. 61, August 11, 1933.

63. Max Tabaschnik, "Königstein," in *Konzentrationslager. Ein Appell an das Gewissen der Welt* (Karlsbad, 1934), 107.

64. Klaus Drobisch and Günther Wieland, *System der NS-Konzentrationslager 1933–1939* (Berlin, 1993), 51.

65. Fritz Ecker, "Die Hölle Dachau," in *Konzentrationslager. Ein Appell an das Gewissen der Welt* (Karlsbad, 1934), 40.

66. Günther Kimmel, "Das Konzentrationslager Dachau. Eine Studie zu den nationalsozialistischen Gewaltverbrechen," in *Bayern in der NS-Zeit II: Herrschaft und Gesellschaft im Konflikt*, eds. Martin Broszat and Elke Fröhlich (Munich, 1979), 363–364.

67. Werner Schäfer, *Konzentrationslager Oranienburg. Das Anti-Braunbuch über das erste detusche Konzentrationslager* (Berlin, 1934), 173; *Völkischer Beobachter*, August 11, 1933, quoted in Martin Knop, Hendrik Krause, Roland Schwarz, "Die Häftling des Konzentrationslagers Oranienburg," in *Konzentrationslager Oranienburg*, ed. Günter Morsch (Oranienburg, 1994), 50; Wolfgang Langhoff, *Rubber Truncheon: Being an Account of Thirteen Months Spent in a Concentration Camp* (New York, 1935), 200–204; Klaus Drobisch and Günther Wieland, *System der NS-Konzentrationslager 1933–1939* (Berlin, 1993), 123.

68. Kim Wünschmann, *Before Auschwitz: Jewish Prisoners in the Prewar Concentration Camps* (Cambridge, 2015), 84; Fritz Ecker, "Die Hölle Dachau," in *Konzentrationslager. Ein Appell an das Gewissen der Welt* (Karlsbad, 1934), 29; Guido Fackler, *"Des Lagers Stimme"—Musik im KZ. Alltag und Häftlingskultur in den Konzentratonslagern 1933 bis 1936* (Bremen, 2000), 176.

69. *Fränkische Tageszeitung*, no. 62, August 12, 1933.

70. "Sondergerichte arbeiten," *Berliner Morgenpost*, no. 85, April 9, 1933; "Sondergerichts-Urteile," *Vossische Zeitung*, no. 216, May 6, 1933; "Gefängnis für Greuelmärchen," *Vossische Zeitung*, no. 202, April 28, 1933; Nikolaus Wachsmann, *KL: A History of the Nazi Concentration Camps* (New York, 2015), 76.

71. Von Pfeffer, "Denunziantentum," September 6, 1933, in Thomas Klein, ed., *Die Lageberichte der Geheimen Staatspolizei über die Provinz Hessen-Nassau 1933–1936*, Teilband II (Cologne, 1986), 618; Irmgard Keun, *After Midnight* (New York, 2011), 100.

72. "Aus der Schutzhaft. Zurück in die Volksgemeinschaft," *Berliner Morgenpost*, no. 5, January 6, 1934; Nikolaus Wachsmann, *KL: A History of the Nazi Concentration Camps* (New York, 2015), 76–77. For a different version of the joke, see the entry for August 7, 1933, in "Tagebuchaufzeichnungen von Klaus Mühlmann 1928 bis 1936," Akademie der Künste, Berlin, 1174/1, 259.

73. Nikolaus Wachsmann, *KL: A History of the Nazi Concentration Camps* (New York, 2015), 68; Felix von Papen, *Ein von Papen spricht … über seine Erlebnise im Hitler Deutschland* (Amsterdam, 1939), 12. See also Samantha Seithe, "Die vergessene Geschichte des Felix Maria Michael von Papen," History.Scheidingen.de, http://history.scheidingen.de/Schlagwort/felix-von-papen.

74. Ausländer in Hans-Rainer Sandvoss, *Die "andere" Reichshauptstadt: Widerstand aus der Arbeiterbewegung in Berlin von 1933 bis 1945* (Berlin, 2007), 163.

Chapter Five: The German Spring

1. Sabine Friedrich, *Wer wir sind* (Munich, 2012), 1118.

2. Entries for March 8 and 21, April 30, and May 1, 1933, in Matthias Joseph Mehs, *Tagebücher. November 1929 bis September 1946. Band I. November 1929 bis Januar 1936* (Trier, 2011), 249, 253–254, 270–273.

3. Entry for June 21, 1933, in Matthias Joseph Mehs, *Tagebücher. November 1929 bis September 1946. Band I. November 1929 bis Januar 1936* (Trier, 2011), 297.

4. Madeleine Kent, *I Married a German* (London, 1938), 225.

5. Reinhard Bein, "Die Uniform. Jungvolk-Ausruestung," in *Zeitzeichen. Stadt und Land Braunschweig 1930–1945* (Braunschweig, 2000), 106; Axel Schildt, "Jenseits der Politik? Aspekte des Alltags," in *Hamburg im "Dritten Reich,"* ed. Forschungsstelle für Zeitgeschichte in Hamburg (Göttingen, 2005), 250; entries for April 22 and 23 and May 25, 1933, in "Tagebuch Luise Solmitz," in Frank Bajohr, Beate Meyer, and Joachim Szodrzynski, eds., *Bedrohung, Hoffnung, Skepsis. Vier Tagebücher des Jahres 1933* (Göttingen, 2013), 195, 197, 210.

6. Entry for May 28, 1933, in Willy Cohn, *Kein Recht, nirgends. Tagebuch vom Untergang des Breslauer Judentums* (Cologne, 2006), 1:49; Sebastian Haffner, *Defying Hitler: A Memoir* (New York, 2002), 145–146; entry for August 18, 1933, in Erich Ebermayer, *Denn heute gehört uns Deutschland…* (Hamburg, 1959), 155.

7. Entries for May 12 and 15 and June 21, 1933, in Matthias Joseph Mehs, *Tagebücher. November 1929 bis September 1946. Band I. November 1929 bis Januar 1936* (Trier, 2011), 278–280, 297.

8. Entries for April 20 and 24, 1933, Karl Dürkefälden, *"Schreiben wie es wirklich war…" Aufzeichungen Karl Dürkefäldens aus den Jahren 1933–1945*, eds. Herbert and Sibylle Obenaus (Hannover, 1985), 38, 40–41.

9. Otto Michael Knab, *Kleinstadt unterm Hakenkreuz. Groteske Erinnerungen aus Bayern* (1934; rpt. Starnberg, 2014), 22, 25.

10. Björn Weigel, "'Märzgefallene' und Aufnahmestopp im Frühjahr 1933" in *Wie wurde man Parteigenosse? Die NSDAP und ihre Mitglieder*, ed. Wolfgang Benz (Frankfurt, 2009), 94.

11. "Werner Finck," Wikipedia, https://de.wikipedia.org/wiki/Werner_Finck.

12. Lieselotte G., diary entry for April 22, 1945, in Ingrid Hammer and Susanne zur Nieden, eds., *Sehr selten habe ich geweint: Briefe und Tagebücher aus dem Zweiten Weltkrieg von Menschen in Berlin* (Zurich, 1992), 311.

13. Entry for July 28, 1933, in Victor Klemperer, *I Will Bear Witness, 1933–1941: A Diary of the Nazi Years* (New York, 1998), 27.

14. Tilman Allert, *The Hitler Salute: On the Meaning of a Gesture* (New York, 2008), 38.

15. Martha Dodd, *My Years in Germany* (London, 1939), 28, 100; Virginia Woolf's diary entry for May 9, 1935, quoted in Oliver Lubrich, ed., *Travels in the Reich, 1933–1945: Foreign Authors Report from Germany* (Chicago, 2010), 74; Frederick T. Birchall, "Third Reich Builds on Colossal Scale," *New York Times*, September 15, 1937.

16. Entry for May 1, 1933, in Matthias Joseph Mehs, *Tagebücher. November 1929 bis September 1946. Band I. November 1929 bis Januar 1936* (Trier, 2011), 273.

17. Hans Mommsen quoted by Michael Wildt, "*Volksgemeinschaft*: A Modern Perspective on National Socialist Society," in *Visions of Community in Nazi Germany: Social Engineering and Private Lives*, eds. Martina Steber and Bernhard Gotto (Oxford, 2014), 49.

18. Volker Ullrich, *Hitler: Ascent, 1889–1939* (New York, 2016), 412, 415; Sportpalast speech of February 10, 1933, quoted in Max Domarus, *Hitler: Speeches and Proclamations, 1932–1945* (Wauconda, IL, 1990), 1:250.

19. Hermann Beck, *The Fateful Alliance: German Conservatives and Nazis in 1933. The Machtergreifung in a New Light* (New York, 2008), 114; Hitler quoted in the *Berliner Morgenpost*, no. 61, March 12, 1933; "Unser Staat wird ewig stehen," *Fränkische Tageszeitung*, no. 33, July 10, 1933.

20. Frederick T. Birchall, "Hitler Sees Reich, Nazi for All Times; Aides Assail Jews," *New York Times*, September 3, 1933; Volker Ullrich, *Hitler: Ascent, 1889–1939* (New York, 2016).

21. "Reichstag—2. Sitzung. Donnerstag, des 23 März 1933," *Verhandlungen des Reichstags. VIII. Wahlperiode 1933* (Berlin, 1934), 33, 36.

22. "Das Regierungsprogramm," *Vossische Zeitung*, no. 42, March 24, 1933.

23. Manfred Gailus, *Protestantismus und Nationalsozialismus. Studien zur nationalsozialistische Durchdringung des protestantischen Sozialmilieus in Berlin* (Cologne, 2001), 58, 85–88.

24. Wolf-Dieter Zimmermann, *Gerechtigkeit für die Väter* (Berlin, 1983), 69, 73.

25. Hans-Gerhard Koch, "Evangelium und Rasse," *Evangelium im Dritten Reich. Sonntagsblatt der Deutschen Christen* 1 (December 18, 1932); Wilhelm Stapel cited in Klaus Scholder, *The Churches and the Third Reich*, vol. 1: *Preliminary History and the Time of Illusions, 1918–1934* (Philadelphia, 1988), 421.

26. Klaus Scholder, *The Churches and the Third Reich*, vol. 1: *Preliminary History and the Time of Illusions, 1918–1934* (Philadelphia, 1988), 41, 51.

27. Klaus Scholder, *The Churches and the Third Reich*, vol. 1: *Preliminary History and the Time of Illusions, 1918–1934* (Philadelphia, 1988), 222–224.

28. Emanuel Hirsch quoted in Klaus Scholder, *The Churches and the Third Reich*, vol. 1: *Preliminary History and the Time of Illusions, 1918–1934* (Philadelphia, 1988), 420.

29. Elisabeth Gebensleben to Irmgard Brester February 3, 1933, in Hedda Kalshoven, ed., *Between Two Homelands: Letters Across the Borders of Nazi Germany* (Urbana, 2014), 57.

30. Manfred Gailus, *Protestantismus und Nationalsozialismus. Studien zur nationalsozialistische Durchdringung des protestantischen Sozialmilieus in Berlin* (Cologne, 2001), 171–172; Eberhard Funk, "Die evangelische Kirchengemeinde Berlin-Tempelhof, 1933–1945," in *Kirchengemeinden im Nationalsozialismus: Sieben Beispiele aus Berlin*, ed. Manfred Gailus (Berlin, 1990), 173, 177.

31. Klaus Scholder, *The Churches and the Third Reich*, vol. 1: *Preliminary History and the Time of Illusions, 1918–1934* (Philadelphia, 1988), 552–553; Kurt Meier, *Kreuz und Hakenkreuz. Die evangelische Kirche im Dritten Reich* (Munich, 1992), 49–51. On the new saints, see "Foreign News: Germany," *Time*, April 17, 1933, 18.

32. Entries for March 23 and May 17, 1933, in "Tagebuch Luise Solmitz," in Frank Bajohr, Beate Meyer, and Joachim Szodrzynski, eds., *Bedrohung, Hoffnung, Skepsis. Vier Tagebücher des Jahres 1933* (Göttingen, 2013), 197, 205. See also Michael Grüttner, "Soziale Hygiene und Soziale Kontrolle. Die Sanierung der Hamburger Gängeviertel 1892–1936," in *Arbeiter in Hamburg*, eds. Arno Herzig, Dieter Langewiesche, and Arnold Sywottek (Hamburg, 1983).

33. Frank Arnau, "Fahrt durch erwachtes Land," *Berliner Lokal-Anzeiger*, no. 124, March 14, 1933.

34. Entry for March 21, 1933, in "Tagebuch Luise Solmitz," in Frank Bajohr, Beate Meyer, and Joachim Szodrzynski, eds., *Bedrohung, Hoffnung, Skepsis. Vier Tagebücher des Jahres 1933* (Göttingen, 2013), 178.

35. "Funktag der ganzen Nation," *Die Sendung* 10 (April 1, 1933): 298; Thomas Wernicke, "Der Handschlag am 'Tag von Potsdam,'" in *Der Tag von Potsdam: Der 21. März 1933 und die Errichtung der nationalsozialistischen Diktatur*, eds. Christoph Kopke and Werner Tress (Berlin, 2013), 26.

36. "Erneuerung im Geiste von Potsdam," *Kölnische Zeitung*, no. 158, March 21, 1933; "Hunderttausende in Potsdam. Das Volksfest der Reichstagseröffnung," *Berliner Morgenpost*, no. 69, March 22, 1933; Elisabeth Gebensleben to Irmgard

Brester, March 22, 1933, in Hedda Kalshoven, ed., *Between Two Homelands: Letters Across the Borders of Nazi Germany* (Urbana, 2014), 71.

37. Entries for March 20 and 21, 1933, in Erich Ebermayer, *Denn heute gehört uns Deutschland*... (Hamburg, 1959), 44, 47.

38. Michael Schneider, *Unterm Hakenkreuz: Arbeiter und Arbeiterbewegung 1933 bis 1939* (Bonn, 1999), 92; Hans Wendt, *Der Tag der Nationalen Arbeit. Die Feier des 1. Mai 1933* (Berlin, 1933), 11.

39. "Der Feiertag der deutschen Arbeit," *Neue Zürcher Zeitung*, no. 788, May 2, 1933.

40. "Kommentar zur 1. Mai Feier," May 10, 1933, quoted in Karlheinz Schmeer, *Die Regie des öffentlichen Lebens im Dritten Reich* (Munich, 1956), 157.

41. Werner Freitag, "Der Führermythos im Fest. Festfeuerwerk, NS-Liturgie, Dissens und '100% KdF Stimmung,'" in *Das Dritte Reich im Fest: Führermythos, Feierlaune und Verweigerung in Westfalen 1933–1945*, ed. Werner Freitag (Bielefeld, 1997), 27.

42. Entry for October 22, 1933, in Matthias Joseph Mehs, *Tagebücher. November 1929 bis September 1946. Band I. November 1929 bis Januar 1936* (Trier, 2011), 352.

43. Entry for May 1, 1933, in Elke Fröhlich, *Die Tagebücher von Joseph Goebbels: Sämtliche Fragmente* (Munich, 1987), part 1, 2:414–415.

44. Cathryn Birdsall, *Nazi Soundscapes: Sound, Technology and Urban Space in Germany 1933–1945* (Amsterdam, 2012), 113.

45. Reinhard Döhl, *Das Hörspiel zur NS-Zeit: Geschichte und Typologie des Hörspiels* (Darmstadt, 1992), 132–133.

46. The radio broadcast for the Day of National Labor can be found in Wieland Elfferding, "Von der proletarischen Masse zum Kriegsvolk: Massenaufmarsch und Öffentlichkeit im deutschen Faschismus am Beispiel des 1. Mai 1933," in *Inszenierung der Macht: Ästhetische Faszination im Faschismus* (Berlin, 1987), 26.

47. Eberhard Heuel, *Der umworbene Stand: Die ideologische Integration der Arbeiter im Nationalsozialismus 1933–1935* (Frankfurt, 1989).

48. Wolfgang Seiferth, "Die aussterbenden Kriegsteilnehmer: Kriegserlebnis und politische Willensbildung," *Das Reichsbanner*, no. 47, November 23, 1929; "3 mars 1932, renaissance de l'esprit militaire en Allemagne," in Jean-Marc Dreyfus, ed., *Les rapports de Berlin; André François-Poncet et le national-socialisme* (Paris, 2016), 56.

49. Entries for May 24 and 29, 1933, in Karl Dürkefälden, *"Schreiben wie es wirklich war..." Aufzeichnungen Karl Dürkefäldens aus den Jahren 1933–1945*, eds. Herbert and Sibylle Obenaus (Hannover, 1985), 53.

50. Arndt Weinrich, "Zwischen Kontinuität und Kritik: Die Hitler-Jugend und die Generation der 'Frontkämpfer,'" in *Nationalsozialismus und Erster Weltkrieg*, ed. Gerd Krumeich (Essen, 2010), 282.

51. "Wie Berlin den Ersten Mai feierte. Der groesste Aufmarsch aller Zeiten!," *Berliner Morgenpost*, no. 104, May 2, 1933; Louis P. Lochner to Betty Lochner, May 28, 1933, in "Round Robins from Berlin: Louis P. Lochner's Letters to His Children, 1932–1941," *Wisconsin Magazine of History* 50, no. 4 (1967): 29.

52. "Ausklang der Maifeier," *Berliner Morgenpost*, no. 105, May 5, 1933; Eberhard Heuel, *Der umworbene Stand: Die ideologische Integration der Arbeiter im Nationalsozialismus 1933–1935* (Frankfurt, 1989), 130–131; Werner Freitag, "Der Führermythos im Fest. Festfeuerwerk, NS-Liturgie, Dissens und '100% KdF Stimmung,'" in *Das Dritte Reich im Fest: Führermythos, Feierlaune und Verweigerung in Westfalen 1933–1945*, ed. Freitag (Bielefeld, 1997), 21. See also "Silbersonntag—guter Sonntag," *Vossische Zeitung*, no. 595, December 12, 1932.

53. Ian Kersaw, *Hitler, 1889–1936: Hubris* (New York, 1999), 476; Richard Evans, *The Coming of the Third Reich* (New York, 2003), 357.

54. Cited in Wieland Elfferding, "Von der proletarischen Masse zum Kriegsvolk: Massenaufmarsch und Öffentlichkeit im deutschen Faschismus am Beispiel des 1. Mai 1933," in *Inszenierung der Macht: Ästhetische Faszination im Faschismus* (Berlin, 1987), 24n2; Jan Petersen, *Unsere Strasse* (1933; rpt. Munich, 1978), 115.

55. Klaus Dyck and Jens Joost-Krüger, "Unsere Zukunft eine Gasse! Eine Lokalgeschichte der Bremer Maifeiern," in *100 Jahre Zukunft. Zur Geschichte des 1. Mai*, ed. Inge Marssolek (Frankfurt, 1990), 222.

56. Entry for May 2, 1943, in Joseph Goebbels, *Die Tagebücher von Joseph Goebbels: Sämtliche Fragmente*, ed. Elke Fröhlich (Munich, 1994), part 1, 8:197.

57. "Annie Wächter" quoted in Janosch Steuwer, *"Ein Drittes Reich, wie ich es auffasse." Politik, Gesellschaft und privates Leben in Tagebüchern 1933–1939* (Göttingen, 2017), 142.

58. Entries for March 20, April 24, and May 2, in Karl Dürkefälden, *"Schreiben wie es wirklich war . . ." Aufzeichnungen Karl Dürkefäldens aus den Jahren 1933–1945*, eds. Herbert and Sibylle Obenaus (Hannover, 1985), 37, 42–43, 46–47.

59. Janosch Steuwer, *"Ein Drittes Reich, wie ich es auffasse." Politik, Gesellschaft und privates Leben in Tagebüchern 1933–1939* (Göttingen, 2017), 57–64; Elisabeth Gebensleben to Irmgard Brester, February 3, 1933, in Hedda Kalshoven, ed., *Between Two Homelands: Letters Across the Borders of Nazi Germany* (Urbana, 2014), 57; Hanns Theodor Flemming, "'Intellektueller' wurde zum Schimpfwort," in

Wir erlebten das Ende der Weimarer Republik. Zeitgenossen berichten, ed. Rolf Ital-iaander (Dusseldorf, 1982), 174.

60. Entries for June 25 and August 8, 1933, in Walter Tausk, *Breslauer Tage-buch 1933–1940* (Berlin, 1975), 80, 100, and 16.

61. "Die künftigen Historiker," *Die Tat* 25, no. 3 (1933), quoted in Janosch Steuwer, *"Ein Drittes Reich, wie ich es auffasse." Politik, Gesellschaft und privates Leben in Tagebüchern 1933–1939* (Göttingen, 2017), 231; entry for July 12, 1933, in "Tagebuchaufzeichnungen von Klaus Mühlmann 1928 bis 1936," Kempowski-Archive 1174/1, Akademie der Künste, Berlin.

62. Elisabeth Gebensleben to Irmgard Brester, February 14, 1934, in Hedda Kalshoven, ed., *Between Two Homelands: Letters Across the Borders of Nazi Germany* (Urbana, 2014), 97; Janosch Steuwer, *"Ein Drittes Reich, wie ich es auffasse." Politik, Gesellschaft und privates Leben in Tagebüchern 1933–1939* (Göttingen, 2017), 74–75.

63. What follows is based on the entries for March 10, 11, 17, 21, 23, and 30, April 15, 19, 24, and 25, and May 7, 17, and 24, 1933, in "Tagebuch Wilhelm Scheidler," NS-Dokumentationszentrum Rheinland-Pflaz, Osthofen, 2/27/2.

64. "Inge Thiel," quoted in Janosch Steuwer, *"Ein Drittes Reich, wie ich es auffasse." Politik, Gesellschaft und privates Leben in Tagebüchern 1933–1939* (Göttingen, 2017), 148; Ferdinand Bruckner, *Races* (New York, 1934) [originally *Die Rassen* (Zürich, 1933)], 32.

65. Peter Laregh, *Heinrich George: Komödiant seiner Zeit* (Munich, 1992), 164; Horst Mesalla, "Heinrich George: Versuch der Rekonstrukton der schauspieler-ischen Leistung utner besonderer Berücksichtigung der zeitgenössischen Pub-lizistik" (PhD dissertation, Freie Universität Berlin, 1969), 182, 188–189.

66. Peter Laregh, *Heinrich George: Komödiant seiner Zeit* (Munich, 1992), 146.

67. Joachim A. Lang, *Heinrich George. Eine Spurensuche* (Leipzig, 2013).

68. Peter Jelavich, *Berlin Alexanderplatz: Radio, Film, and the Death of Weimar Culture* (Berkeley, 2006), 245.

69. "Aufgaben des deutschen Films," *Berliner Morgenpost*, no. 29, March 1933.

70. Heinrich George's son, Jan, quoted in Joachim A. Lang, *Heinrich George. Eine Spurensuche* (Leipzig, 2013), 110–111.

71. Peter Jelavich, *Berlin Alexanderplatz: Radio, Film, and the Death of Weimar Culture* (Berkeley, 2006), 245.

72. Eric Rentschler, *The Ministry of Illusion: Nazi Cinema and Its Afterlife* (Cambridge, 1996), 53, 55, 69.

73. "Der Kinematograph," September 12, 1933, quoted in Kurt Fricke, *Spiel am Abgrund: Heinrich George, eine politische Biographie* (Halle, 2000), 95; Horst

Claus, *Filmen für Hitler. Die Karriere des NS-Starregisseurs Hans Steinhoff* (Vienna, 2013), 291; Gerd Albrecht, ed., *Arbeitsmaterialien zum Nationalsozialistischen Propagandafilm Hitlerjunge Quex* (Frankfurt, 2006), 27.

74. Gerhard Stahr, *Volksgemeinschaft vor der Leinwand? Der nationalsozialistische Film und sein Publikum* (Berlin, 2001), 123; "Hereingefallene Hetzer! 'Blutige Unruhen' in der Reichshauptstadt," *Fränkische Tageszeitung*, no. 50, July 29, 1933.

75. Eric Rentschler, *The Ministry of Illusion: Nazi Cinema and Its Afterlife* (Cambridge, 1996), 19.

76. Klamm, "Ein Film der deutschen Jugend für die deutsche Jugend: *Hitlerjunge Quex*," *Der Film*, September 23, 1933, quoted in Kurt Fricke, *Spiel am Abgrund: Heinrich George, eine politische Biographie* (Halle, 2000), 94; Hentig in Horst Claus, *Filmen für Hitler. Die Karriere des NS-Starregisseurs Hans Steinhoff* (Vienna, 2013), 292.

77. Peter Laregh, *Heinrich George: Komödiant seiner Zeit* (Munich, 1992), 186.

78. "Kundgebungen deutscher Künstler für Adolf Hitler," *Völkischer Beobachter*, November 3, 1933, quoted in Kurt Fricke, *Spiel am Abgrund: Heinrich George, eine politische Biographie* (Halle, 2000), 62.

79. Patrick Leigh Fermor, *A Time of Gifts* (New York, 2005), 53.

80. Quoted in Tilman Lahme, *Die Manns. Geschichte einer Familie* (Frankfurt, 2015), 113.

81. Werner Maser, *Heinrich George. Mensch aus Erde gemacht* (Berlin, 1998), 319.

82. *Tempo*'s Lucy von Jacobi quoted in Berta Drews, *Mein Mann Heinrich George* (Munich, 2013), 17.

83. Kurt Fricke, *Spiel am Abgrund: Heinrich George, eine politische Biographie* (Halle, 2000), 168, 259. Goebbels's December 23, 1944, diary entry quoted in Felix Moeller, *The Film Minister: Goebbels and the Cinema in the "Third Reich"* (London, 2000), 183. See also Bernd Wegner, "The Ideology of Self-Destruction: Hitler and the Choreography of Defeat," *German Historical Institute London Bulletin* 26 (November 2004), 30.

84. Kurt Fricke, *Spiel am Abgrund: Heinrich George, eine politische Biographie* (Halle, 2000), 170–171, 260.

85. Werner Maser, *Heinrich George. Mensch aus Erde gemacht* (Berlin, 1998), 174.

86. Peter Laregh, *Heinrich George: Komödiant seiner Zeit* (Munich, 1992), 35.

87. Kurt Fricke, *Spiel am Abgrund: Heinrich George, eine politische Biographie* (Halle, 2000), 46, 74.

Chapter Six: "Your Jewish Grandmother"

1. Entry for September 20, 1932, in "Tagebuch 1. January 1919–31.XII. 1932; 3. Buch," Nachlass Franz von Göll, Landesarchiv Berlin, E Rep. 200-43, Acc. 3221, no. 3.

2. Werner E. Mosse, "Die Niedergang der Weimarer Republik und die Juden," in *Entscheidungsjahr 1932: Zur Judenfrage in der Endphase der Weimarer Republik*, ed. Mosse (Tübingen, 1965), 40.

3. Entries for January 30 and February 2, 1933, in Hertha Nathorff, *Das Tagebuch der Hertha Nathorff. Berlin–Newyork: Aufzeichnungen 1933 bis 1945*, ed. Wolfgang Benz (Munich, 1987), 35; entries for February 8, 12, 24, and 26, 1933, in Willy Cohn, *Kein Recht, nirgends. Tagebuch vom Untergang des Breslauer Judentums* (Cologne, 2006), 1:8, 10, 13; entry for February 6, 1933, in "Tagebuch Luise Solmitz," in Frank Bajohr, Beate Meyer, and Joachim Szodrzynski, ed., *Bedrohung, Hoffnung, Skepsis. Vier Tagebücher des Jahres 1933* (Göttingen, 2013), 155–156.

4. Michael Wildt, *Hitler's* Volksgemeinschaft *and the Dynamics of Racial Exclusion: Violence Against Jews in Provincial Germany, 1919–1939* (New York, 2012), 80; "Aus dem Halbmonatsbericht des Regierungspräsidenten von Niederbayern und der Oberpfalz," March 30, 1933, quoted in Martin Broszat, Elke Fröhlich, and Falk Wieseman, eds., *Bayern in der NS-Zeit: Soziale Lage und politisches Verhalten der Bevölkerung im Spiegel vertraulicher Berichte* (Munich, 1977), 432.

5. "Schliessung jüdische Geschäfte," *Vossische Zeitung*, no. 115, March 9, 1933; "Tumulte vor Geschäften," *Vossische Zeitung*, no. 17, March 10, 1933; on Kassel, see *Frankfurter Zeitung*, March 10, 1933, quoted in Comité des Délégations Juives, ed., *Das Schwarzbuch: Tatsachen und Dokumente. Die Lage der Juden in Deutschland 1933* (Paris, 1934), 285.

6. "Eine scharfe Rede Görings," *Vossische Zeitung*, no. 119, March 11, 1933.

7. Eric Schmalz, "The Story of Dr. Michael Siegel," History Unfolded; US Newspapers and the Holocaust, US Holocaust Museum and Memorial, https://newspapers.ushmm.org/blog/2017/12/19/dr-siegel. See also entry for March 23, 1933, in "Tagebuch Kurt Fritz Rosenberg," in Frank Bajohr, Beate Meyer, and Joachim Szodrzynski, ed., *Bedrohung, Hoffnung, Skepsis. Vier Tagebücher des Jahres 1933* (Göttingen, 2013), 31.

8. Lion Feuchtwanger, "Terror in Germany Amazes Novelist," *New York Times*, March 21, 1933, 11. See also George S. Messersmith to Cordell Hull, Dispatch no. 1196, March 21, 1933, Box 1 F7, and Messersmith to Hull, Dispatch no. 1205, March 25, 1933, Box 1 F8, George S. Messersmith Papers, University of Delaware Library.

9. "A Week's Vignettes of Nazi-Land," *Newsweek*, March 25, 1933.

10. "55,000 Here Stage Protest on Hitler Attacks on Jews; Nazis Order a New Boycott," *New York Times*, March 28, 1933, 1; Michaela Hoenicke Moore, *Know Your Enemy: The American Debate on Nazism, 1933–1945* (Cambridge, 2010), 73.

11. George S. Messersmith to Cordell Hull, Dispatch no. 1210, March 28, 1933, Box 1 F8, George S. Messersmith Papers, University of Delaware Library; Dibelius in Berlin's *Der Tag*, March 26, 1933, quoted in Klaus Scholder, *The Churches and the Third Reich*, vol. 1: *Preliminary History and the Time of Illusions, 1918–1934* (Philadelphia, 1988), 263.

12. Paul Moore, "German Public Opinion on the Nazis' Concentration Camps, 1933–1939" (PhD diss., University of London, 2010), 30; "Gegen die Greuel-Märchen," *Berliner Morgenpost*, no. 73, March 26, 1933.

13. Klaus Scholder, *The Churches and the Third Reich*, vol. 1: *Preliminary History and the Time of Illusions, 1918–1934* (Philadelphia, 1988), 264; "Deutscher Abwehr wirkt," *Berliner Morgenpost*, no. 75, March 29, 1933; "Der Abwehrkampf," *Kölnische Zeitung*, no. 176, March 30, 1933.

14. Entry for August 28, 1933, in Victor Klemperer, *Ich will Zeugnis ablegen: Tagebücher 1933–1945*, 2 vols. (Berlin, 1995), quoted and translated in Victor Klemperer, *The Language of the Third Reich: LTI—Lingua Tertii Imperii*, trans. Martin Brady (New York, 2000), 38.

15. "Helft alle mit! Die Wahrheit ins Ausland," *Vossische Zeitung*, no. 152, March 30, 1933.

16. "Heute Boykott, dann Frist bis Mittwoch," *Berliner Morgenpost*, no. 78, April 1, 1933; entry for April 1, 1933, in "Tagebuch Luise Solmitz," in Frank Bajohr, Beate Meyer, and Joachim Szodrzynski, ed., *Bedrohung, Hoffnung, Skepsis. Vier Tagebücher des Jahres 1933* (Göttingen, 2013), 185; Frank Bajohr, "Von der Ausgrenzung zum Massenmord. Die Verfolgung der Hamburger Juden 1933–1945," in *Hamburg im "Dritten Reich*," ed. Forschungsstelle für Zeitgeschichte in Hamburg (Göttingen, 2005), 482; "La grande journée en Allemagne de boycottage antisémite," *Le petit Parisien*, April 2, 1933.

17. *Frankfurter Zeitung*, April 2, 1933, quoted in Comité des Délégations Juives, ed., *Das Schwarzbuch: Tatsachen und Dokumente. Die Lage der Juden in Deutschland 1933* (Paris, 1934), 307; "La grande journée en Allemagne de boycottage antisémite," *Le petit Parisien*, April 2, 1933.

18. *Kieler Neueste Nachrichten*, no. 79, April 2, 1933, quoted in Erich Hoffmann and Peter Wulf, eds., *"Wir bauen das Reich": Aufsteig und erste Herrschaftsjahre des nationalsozialismus in Schleswig-Holstein* (Neumünster, 1983), 343; "Ruhiger

Verlauf des Boykott-Tages," *Berliner Morgenpost*, no. 79, April 2, 1933; "Berlin nach der Aktion," *Vossische Zeitung*, no. 157, April 2, 1933.

19. See the advertisements in the *Berliner Morgenpost*, nos. 76–77, March 30 and 31, 1933; entry for April 2, 1933, in Elke Fröhlich, ed., *Die Tagebücher von Joseph Goebbels. Teil I: Aufzeichnungen 1923–1941* (Munich, 1998), part 2, 3:160.

20. Vicki Baum, *Grand Hotel* (New York, 1931), 8, 309.

21. Sebastian Haffner, *Defying Hitler: A Memoir* (New York, 2002), 142.

22. *Klärung. 12 Autoren, Politiker über die Judenfrage* (Berlin, 1932), 10, 32, 44, 89, 126.

23. Roman Töppel, " 'Volk und Rasse': In Search of Hitler's Sources," *German Yearbook of Contemporary Research* 3 (2018): 91–92.

24. Entry for January 29, 1931, "Tagebuchaufzeichnungen von Klaus Mühlmann 1928 bis 1936," Kempowski-Archive 1174/1, Akademie der Künste, Berlin.

25. Irmgard Brester to Elisabeth Gebensleben, April 3, 1933, and Elisabeth Gebensleben to Irmgard Brester, April 6, 1933, in Hedda Kalshoven, ed., *Between Two Homelands: Letters Across the Borders of Nazi Germany* (Urbana, 2014), 73–75.

26. Elisabeth Gebensleben to Irmgard Brester, February 16 and April 6, 1933, in Hedda Kalshoven, ed., *Between Two Homelands: Letters Across the Borders of Nazi Germany* (Urbana, 2014), 60, 73–75.

27. Sebastian Haffner, *Defying Hitler: A Memoir* (New York, 2002), 142.

28. Entry for April 1, 1933, in Matthias Joseph Mehs, *Tagebücher. November 1929 bis September 1946. Band I. November 1929 bis Januar 1936* (Trier, 2011), 260; entry for April 2, 1933, in Thomas Mann, *Tagebücher 1933–1934*, ed. Peter de Mendelssohn (Frankfurt, 1977), 32.

29. Sebastian Haffner, *Defying Hitler: A Memoir* (New York, 2002), 151.

30. William Sheridan Allen, *The Nazi Seizure of Power. The Experience of a Single German Town, 1922–1945*, rev. ed. (Brattleboro, 2014), 176.

31. Monika Pater, "Rundfunkangebote," in *Zuhören und Gehörtwerden I. Radio im Nationalsozialismus*, eds. Inge Marssolek and Adelheid von Saldern (Tübingen, 1998), 146.

32. Entry for May 12, 1933, in Matthias Joseph Mehs, *Tagebücher. November 1929 bis September 1946. Band I. November 1929 bis Januar 1936* (Trier, 2011), 278; entries for May 22 and June 18, 1933, in Willy Cohn, *Kein Recht, nirgends. Tagebuch vom Untergang des Breslauer Judentums* (Cologne, 2006), 1:46, 52.

33. Entry for July 2, 1933, in Matthias Joseph Mehs, *Tagebücher. November 1929 bis September 1946. Band I. November 1929 bis Januar 1936* (Trier, 2011), 302.

34. Entries for February 28 and May 20, 1933, in "Tagebuch Luise Solmitz," in Frank Bajohr, Beate Meyer, and Joachim Szodrzynski, eds., *Bedrohung, Hoffnung, Skepsis. Vier Tagebücher des Jahres 1933* (Göttingen, 2013), 163, 206.

35. Entry for May 20, 1933, in "Tagebuch Luise Solmitz," in Frank Bajohr, Beate Meyer, and Joachim Szodrzynski, eds., *Bedrohung, Hoffnung, Skepsis. Vier Tagebücher des Jahres 1933* (Göttingen, 2013), 206–207.

36. Entries for May 21, 23, and 28, 1933, in "Tagebuch Luise Solmitz," in Frank Bajohr, Beate Meyer, and Joachim Szodrzynski, eds., *Bedrohung, Hoffnung, Skepsis. Vier Tagebücher des Jahres 1933* (Göttingen, 2013), 207, 209, 211.

37. Entries for October 18 and November 25, 1933, in "Tagebuch Luise Solmitz," in Frank Bajohr, Beate Meyer, and Joachim Szodrzynski, eds., *Bedrohung, Hoffnung, Skepsis. Vier Tagebücher des Jahres 1933* (Göttingen, 2013), 196n49, 249, 261.

38. Frances Henry, *Victims and Neighbors: A Small Town in Germany Remembered* (South Hadley, MA, 1984), 56; Marion Kaplan, *Between Dignity and Despair: Jewish Life in Nazi Germany* (New York, 1998), 37; Saul Friedlander, *Nazi Germany and the Jews: The Years of Persecution, 1933–1939* (New York, 1997), 38.

39. Marion Kaplan, *Between Dignity and Despair: Jewish Life in Nazi Germany* (New York, 1998), 40; Joachim Prinz, "Das Leben ohne Nachbarn. Versuch einer ersten Analyse," *Jüdische Rundschau* 40, nos. 31/32 (April 17, 1935).

40. Saul Friedlander, *Nazi Germany and the Jews: The Years of Persecution, 1933–1939* (New York, 1997), 38.

41. Peter Crane, *Wir leben nun mal auf einem Vulkan* (Bonn, 2005), 78.

42. The term is from the *The Times*, commenting on the Nuremberg Laws on November 8, 1935, cited in Robert Gellately, *Backing Hitler: Consent and Coercion in Nazi Germany* (New York, 2001), 122. Jochen Klepper described these early weeks as a "silent pogrom." See entry for March 27, 1933, in Jochen Klepper, *Unter dem Schatten Deiner Flügel: Aus den Tagebüchern der Jahre 1932–1942* (Stuttgart, 1955), 45.

43. Entry for April 1, 1933, in Thomas Mann, *Tagebücher 1933–1934*, ed. Peter de Mendelssohn (Frankfurt, 1977), 31; "Zur Einreise deutscher Juden," *Neue Zürcher Zeitung*, no. 645, April 8, 1933; Monika Reicharz, ed., *Jüdisches Leben in Detuschland. Selbstzeugnisse zur Sozialgeschite 1918–1945* (Stuttgart, 1982), 104.

44. Michael Wildt, *Hitler's* Volksgemeinschaft *and the Dynamics of Racial Exclusion: Violence Against Jews in Provincial Germany, 1919–1939* (New York, 2012), 90; *Krefelder Generalanzaiger*, April 11, 1933, quoted in Comité des Délégations Juives, ed., *Das Schwarzbuch: Tatsachen und Dokumente. Die Lage der Juden in Deutschland 1933* (Paris, 1934), 351.

45. Comité des Délégations Juives, ed., *Das Schwarzbuch: Tatsachen und Dokumente. Die Lage der Juden in Deutschland 1933* (Paris, 1934), 389–390.

46. Michael Wildt, *Hitler's* Volksgemeinschaft *and the Dynamics of Racial Exclusion: Violence Against Jews in Provincial Germany, 1919–1939* (New York, 2012), 113; "Es geht auch ohne Juden," *Fränkische Tageszeitung*, no. 56, August 5, 1933; Axel Bruns-Wüstefeld, *Lohnende Geschäfte. Die "Entjudung" der Wirtschaft am Beispiel Göttingens* (Hanover, 1997), 72–73; entry for May 21, 1933, in Karl Dürkefälden, *"Schreiben wie es wirklich war..." Aufzeichnungen Karl Dürkefäldens aus den Jahren 1933–1945*, eds. Herbert and Sibylle Obenaus (Hannover, 1985), 52.

47. Entries for August 12, 19, and 26, 1935, in Karl Windschild, *Mit Finger vor dem Mund: Ballenstedter Tagebuch des Pfarrers Karl Fr. E. Windschild, 1931–1944*, eds. Günther Windschild and Helmut Schmid (Dessau, 1999), 267–273; Hannah Ahlheim, *"Deutsche, kauft nicht bei Juden!" Antisemitismus und politischer Boykott in Deutschland 1924 bis 1935* (Göttingen, 2011), 344–348. See also Wolfgang Mück, *NS-Hochburg in Mittelfranken. Das völkische Erwachen in Neustadt a. d. Aisch 1922–1933* (Neustadt a.d. Aisch, 2016).

48. *Braunschweiger Landeszeitung*, July 7 and October 23, 1920.

49. *Hakenkreuzbanner*, August 1, 11, and 13, 1933, quoted in Comité des Délégations Juives, ed., *Das Schwarzbuch: Tatsachen und Dokumente. Die Lage der Juden in Deutschland 1933* (Paris, 1934), 460; *Fränkische Tageszeitung*, nos. 61–62, August 11 and 12, 1933.

50. Hitler quoted in *The Yellow Spot: The Outlawing of Half a Million Human Beings* (London, 1936), 216. See also Cornelia Essner, *Die "Nürnberger Gesetze" oder die Verwaltung des Rassenwahns 1933–1945* (Paderborn, 2002).

51. Entry for April 3, 1933, in Walter Tausk, *Breslauer Tagebuch 1933–1940* (Berlin, 1975), 59.

52. *Hessische Volkswacht*, July 12, 1933, quoted in Dietfrid Krause-Vilmar, "Das Konzentrationslager Breitenau 1933/34," in *Hessen unterm Hakenkreuz. Studien zur Durchsetzung der NSDAP in Hessen*, ed. Eike Hennig (Frankfurt, 1983), 475; "Am Pranger," *Der Stürmer*, July 11, 1933, quoted in Comité des Délégations Juives, ed., *Das Schwarzbuch: Tatsachen und Dokumente. Die Lage der Juden in Deutschland 1933* (Paris, 1934), 462.

53. "Augen auf!," *Der Stürmer* (1935), quoted in Daniel Roos, *Julius Streicher und "Der Stürmer" 1932–1945* (Paderborn, 2014), 242.

54. "Rothenburg. Unterm Brennglas," *Fränkische Tageszeitung*, no. 59, August 9, 1933.

55. "Ich bin ein Lump," *Fränkische Tageszeitung*, no. 53, August 2, 1933; "Rabenmutter am Pranger," *Fränkische Tageszeitung*, no. 66, August 17, 1933; "Spiessrutenlaufen eines Schmarotzers," *Fränkische Tageszeitung*, no. 76, August 29, 1933.

56. Leon Dominian, US-Generalkonsul, "Continued Persecution of Jews in Germany, Stuttgart, 17 August 1933," in *Fremde Blicke auf das "Dritte Reich." Berichte ausländische Diplomaten über Herrschaft und Gesellschaft in Deutschland 1933–1945*, eds. Frank Bajohr and Christoph Strupp (Göttingen, 2011), 387. See also Jacob Billikopf to Herbert H. Lehmann, "The Terrorism in Germany," September 1, 1933, Box 3 F18, George S. Messersmith Papers, University of Delaware Library; and "Nazis Round Up 300 Jews in Nuremberg; Business Men Are Paraded Through City," *New York Times*, July 21, 1933.

57. "Hitler Salute Incident," *The Times*, August 19, 1933. As many as 2,000 tourists, including about 100 Britons and Americans anxious to see the new Germany, stayed in the medieval city every night during the summer holidays. See Statistisches Amt, *Statistisches Jahrbuch Nürnberg der Stadt der Reichsparteitage* (Nürnberg, 1937), 49–50. In his best seller, *In the Garden of Beasts: Love and Terror in Hitler's Berlin* (New York, 2011), Erik Larson refers to this incident and puts Martha and William Dodd, the grown children of the American ambassador, at the scene (95–96). It is possible that the Dodds, accompanied by Quentin Reynolds, an American newspaperman stationed in Berlin, stumbled onto a public shaming in the streets of Nuremberg, where they had stopped as part of their motorcar tour through Germany. Their reports were published in the British and American press and match the events of August 6 in many striking respects. But the Dodds could not have been eyewitnesses since they arrived in Nuremberg more than a week later—the diary of their father has them in Leipzig on August 14, after which they motored on to the west. Setting the scene, Reynolds also mentions a municipal double-decker bus, which apparently did not exist in any official capacity in Nuremberg at the time. See Martha Dodd, *My Years in Germany* (London, 1939), 29; William E. Dodd Jr. and Martha Dodd, eds., *Ambassador Dodd's Diary, 1933–1938* (New York, 1941), 22; Quentin Reynolds, *By Quentin Reynolds* (New York, 1963), 118–122; "Foreigners in Germany," *The Times*, August 23, 1933.

58. Franco Ruault, *"Neuschöpfer des deutschen Volkes": Julius Streicher im Kampf gegen "Rassenschande"* (Frankfurt, 2006), 348–351; "Eine Warnung fuer deutsche Mädchen und Frauen," *Fränkische Tageszeitung*, no. 57, August 7, 1933. See also *Fränkische Tageszeitung*, no. 62, August 12, 1933.

59. Christiane Kohl, *The Maiden and the Jew: The Story of a Fatal Friendship in Nazi Germany* (Hanover, NH, 2004).

60. Entries for September 20 and October 10, 1932, in "Tagebuch 1. Jan. 1919–31.XII. 1932; 3. Buch," Nachlass Franz von Göll, Landesarchiv Berlin, E Rep. 200-43, Acc. 3221, no. 3.

Chapter Seven: The Administration of Life

1. Hans Carossa to Erika Mitterer, April 28, 1933, quoted in Josef and Ruth Becker, eds., *Hitlers Machtgreifung 1933. Vom Machtantritt Htilers 30. Janaur 1933 bis zur Besiegelung des Einparteienstaates 14 Juli 1933* (Munich, 1983), 272.

2. Entry for February 11, 1934, in Matthias Joseph Mehs, *Tagebücher. November 1929 bis September 1946. Band I. November 1929 bis Januar 1936* (Trier, 2011), 408–409.

3. Nele Prüfer, "Papa hat Arbeit bekommen," in *Wir erlebten das Ende der Weimarer Republik. Zeitgenossen berichten*, ed. Rolf Italiaander (Düsseldorf, 1982), 191; entry for November 24, 1936, in Victor Klemperer, *I Will Bear Witness, 1933–1941: A Diary of the Nazi Years* (New York, 1998), 201.

4. Ulrich Herbert and Lutz Raphael, eds., *Statistiken zu Detlef Humann: "Arbeitsschlacht." Arbeitsbeschaffung und Propaganda in der NS-Zeit 1933–1939* (Göttingen, 2011); Paul Hoser, "Kommunalpolitik in Fürstenfeldbruck 1933–1945," in *Fürstenfeldbruck in der NS-Zeit: Eine Kleinstadt bei München in den Jahren 1933 bis 1945*, eds. Ferdinand Kramer and Ellen Latzin (Regensburg, 2009), 93.

5. Adam Tooze, *The Wages of Destruction: The Making and Breaking of the Nazi Economy* (New York, 2007), xxv.

6. Sabine Neumann, "Wir Schülerinnen politisierten viel," in *Wir erlebten das Ende der Weimarer Republik. Zeitgenossen berichten*, ed. Rolf Italiaander (Düsseldorf, 1982), 132–133; Kiran Klaus Patel, *Soldiers of Labor: Labor Service in Nazi Germany and New Deal American, 1933–1945* (Cambridge, 2005), 92–96.

7. "Erziehung des deutschen Menschen," *Völkischer Beobachter*, July 4, 1933; "Adolf Hitler über Staat und Wirtschaft," *Völkischer Beobachter*, July 8, 1933.

8. "Nationalsozialismus als Weltanschuung," *Völkischer Beobachter*, September 2, 1933; Lawrence Preuss, "Racial Theory and National Socialist Political Thought," *Southwestern Social Science Quarterly* 15 (September 1934): 103–118. See also Julius Streicher, *Reichstagung in Nürnberg 1933* (Berlin, 1933); Renate Bridenthal, Atina Grossman, and Marion Kaplan, eds., *When Biology Became Destiny: Women in Weimar and Nazi Germany* (New York, 1984).

9. *Neues Volk* 1 (July 1933); Walter Gross, "Von der äusseren zur inneren Revolution," *Neues Volk* 2 (August 1934).

10. Irmgard Keun, *After Midnight* (New York, 2011), 93.

11. Entry for November 11, 1933, in "Tagebuch Kurt Fritz Rosenberg," in Frank Bajohr, Beate Meyer, and Joachim Szodrzynski, eds., *Bedrohung, Hoffnung, Skepsis. Vier Tagebücher des Jahres 1933* (Göttingen, 2013), 124. See also Guido Enderis, "Hitler Stops All Industry an Hour for Final Plea for Unanimous Vote," *New York Times*, November 11, 1933, 1.

12. Robert N. Proctor, *The Nazi War on Cancer* (Princeton, 1999), 7–8, 114; Detlef Peukert, *Max Webers Diagnose der Moderne* (Göttingen, 1989), 69, 110–111.

13. Elisabeth Gebensleben to Irmgard Brester, September 15, 1933, in Hedda Kalshoven, ed., *Between Two Homelands: Letters Across the Borders of Nazi Germany* (Urbana, 2014), 85–86.

14. See the local studies of Northeim by William Sheridan Allen, *The Nazi Seizure of Power: The Experience of a Single German Town, 1922–1945,* rev. ed. (Brattleboro, 2014), 223–232, and of Greifswald by Helge Matthiesen, *Greifswald in Vorpommern: Konservatives Milieu im Kaiserreich, in Demokratie und Diktatur 1900–1990* (Düsseldorf, 2000), 385–399, as well as Detlef Schmiechen-Ackermann, *Nationalsozialismus und Arbeitermilieus: Der nationalsozialistische Angriff auf die proletarischen Wohnquartiere und die Reaktion in den sozialistischen Vereinen* (Bonn, 1998), 480–614.

15. Bernhard Gotto, "Die NSDAP in Fürstenfeldbruck," in *Fürstenfeldbruck in der NS-Zeit: Eine Kleinstadt bei München in den Jahren 1933 bis 1945,* eds. Ferdinand Kramer and Ellen Latzin (Regensburg, 2009), 133.

16. Heinrich Hauser, *Battle Against Time: A Survey of Germany of 1919 from the Inside* (New York, 1939), 11–12.

17. No. 61704, June 17, 1945, Schedule B interviews, United States Strategic Bombing Survey, National Archives and Records Administration, RG 243, 64b, f21; Herwart Vorländer, *Die NSV: Darstellung und Dokumentation einer nationalsozialistischen Organisation* (Boppard, 1988), 51.

18. *Deutschland-Berichte der Sozialdemokratischen Partei Deutschlands (Sopade) 1934–1940. Vierter Jahrgang 1937* (Frankfurt, 1980), 483.

19. *The Times*, December 10, 1934, quoted in Thomas E. de Witt, "'The Struggle Against Hunger and Cold': Winter Relief in Nazi Germany, 1933–1939," *Canadian Journal of History* 12 (1978): 369; entry for December 10, 1934, in Elke Fröhlich, ed., *Die Tagebücher von Joseph Goebbels. Teil I: Aufzeichnungen 1923–1941* (Munich, 1998), part 3, 1:151.

20. Heinrich Hauser, *Battle Against Time: A Survey of Germany of 1919 from the Inside* (New York, 1939), 11–12.

21. Eva Sternheim-Peters, *Die Zeit der grossen Täuschungen. Mädchenleben im Faschismus* (Bielefeld, 1987), 86; Herwart Vorländer, *Die NSV: Darstellung*

und Dokumentation einer nationalsozialistischen Organisation (Boppard, 1988), 54; Hans Dieter Schäfer, *Das Gespaltenes Bewusstsein: Über deutsche Kultur und Lebenswirklichkeit 1933–1945* (Munich, 1984), 140–141.

22. Bernd Lemke, *Luftschutz in Grossbritannien und Deutschland 1923 bis 1939: Zivile Kriegsvorbereitungen als Ausdruck der staats- und gesellschaftspolitischen Grundlagen von Demokratie und Diktatur* (Munchen, 2005), 255–256; "Dezember-Bericht über die Lage in Deutschland (Abgeschlossen Ende November 1933)," in Bernd Stöver, ed., *Berichte über die Lage in Deutschland. Die Meldungen der Gruppe Neu Beginnen aus dem Dritten Reich 1933–1936* (Bonn, 1996), 21–22.

23. Entry for June 25, 1933, in Walter Tausk, *Breslauer Tagebuch 1933–1940* (Berlin, 1975), 79; Clifford Kirkpatrick, *Nazi Germany: Its Women and Family Life* (Indianapolis, 1938), 26.

24. Irmgard Keun, *After Midnight* (New York, 2011), 10–11.

25. Adolf Hitler, *Mein Kampf* (New York, 1941), 389–390 (chapter 11, "Nation and Race").

26. Jörg Baten and Andrea Wagner, "Autarchy, Market Disintegration, and Health: The Mortality and Nutritional Crisis in Nazi Germany, 1933–1937," *Economics and Human Biology* 1 (2003): 1–28; entry for May 17, 1935, in Elke Fröhlich, ed., *Die Tagebücher von Joseph Goebbels. Teil I: Aufzeichnungen 1923–1941* (Munich, 1998), part 3, 1:233.

27. Eva Sternheim-Peters, *Die Zeit der grossen Täuschungen. Mädchenleben im Faschismus* (Bielefeld, 1987), 52.

28. Wolfgang Ayass, *"Asoziale" im Nationalsozialismus* (Stuttgart, 1995), 39.

29. Ulrich Herbert, *Best: Biographische Studien über Radikalismus, Weltanschauung und Vernunft 1903–1989* (Bonn, 2001), 167.

30. Michael Burleigh, *The Third Reich: A New History* (New York, 2000), 382; Claudia Koonz, *The Nazi Conscience* (Cambridge, 2003), 104.

31. "Frick Plan Proposes Sterilization of Jews," *Jewish Telegraphic Agency*, June 30, 1933; "Urge Sterilization Law Apply to Intermarriages," *Jewish Telegraphic Agency*, July 30, 1933.

32. Christopher Dipper, "'20 July and the 'Jewish Question,'" in *Probing the Depths of German Antisemitism: German Society and the Persecution of the Jews, 1933–1941*, ed. David Bankier (New York, 2000), 497.

33. Udo Benzenhöfer, *Zur Genese des Gesetzes zur Verhüttung erbkranken Nachwuchses* (Muenster, 2006), 88–89, 124; Bill Niven, *Hitler and Film: The Führer's Hidden Passion* (New Haven, 2018), 39–41.

34. Wilhelm Frick, "Sachverständigenbeirats für Bevölkerungs- und Rassenpolitik über die Rassengesetzgebung," June 28, 1933, Ministry of the Interior, in Axel

Notes to Chapter Seven

Friedrichs, ed., *Dokumente der Deutschen Politik*, vol. 1: *Die nationalsozialistische Revolu-tion, 1933* (Berlin, 1939), 1:172; Lisa Pine, *Education in Nazi Germany* (Oxford, 2010), 52.

35. "Eugenische Sterilisierung?," *Vossische Zeitung*, March 15, 1933.

36. Gisela Bock, *Zwangssterilisation im Nationalsozialismus: Studien zur Rassenpolitik und Frauenpolitik* (Opladen, 1986), 189–190.

37. Johannes Vossen, *Gesundheitsämter in Nationalsozialismus: Rassenhygiene und öffentliche Gesundheitsfürsorge in Westfalen 1900–1950* (Essen, 2001), 423, 448, 334.

38. No. 62203, July 10, 1945, Schedule B interviews, United States Strategic Bombing Survey, National Archives and Records Administration, RG 243, 64b, f9.

39. Thomas Childers, *The Third Reich: A History of Nazi Germany* (New York, 2017), 339.

40. Gisela Bock, *Zwangssterilisation im Nationalsozialismus: Studien zur Rassenpolitik und Frauenpolitik* (Opladen, 1986), 285, 209.

41. Gisela Bock, *Zwangssterilisation im Nationalsozialismus: Studien zur Rassenpolitik und Frauenpolitik* (Opladen, 1986), 216–219.

42. Christa Wolf, *Patterns of Childhood* (New York, 1980), 57–58, 60.

43. Entry for February 6, 1936, in Lore Walb, *Ich die Alte, ich, die junge: Konfrontation mit meinen Tagebüchern 1933–1945* (Berlin, 1997), 58; Carl-Heinz Zeitler to Irmgard Brester, November 28, 1935, and October 6, 1947, and Minna von Alten to Irmgard Brester, August 29, 1940, in Hedda Kalshoven, ed., *Between Two Homelands: Letters Across the Borders of Nazi Germany* (Urbana, 2014), 108, 227–228, 159.

44. Victor Klemperer, *The Language of the Third Reich. LTI—Lingua Tertii Imperii* (London, 2000), 80. On the application of racial principles to dogs, see "Grenzen der Kunst, zu organisieren," *Das Schwarze Korps*, September 28, 1940; "Leipzig Bans Half-Breed Dogs in 'Racial Purity' Campaign," *Jewish Telegraphic Agency*, October 20, 1933.

45. Entry for July 30, 1933, in "Tagebuch 16. Jan. 1933–12. März 1938. 4. Buch," Nachlass Franz von Göll, Landesarchiv Berlin, E Rep. 200-43, Acc. 3221, no. 4. See also "Literatur-Tagebuch," Nachlass Franz von Göll, Landesarchiv Berlin, E Rep. 200-43, Acc. 3221, no. 32.

46. Entry for July 28, 1934, in "Tagebuch 16. Jan. 1933–12. März 1938. 4. Buch," Nachlass Franz von Göll, Landesarchiv Berlin, E Rep. 200-43, Acc. 3221, no. 4.

47. Richard Vahrenkamp, *The German Autobahn, 1920–1945* (Cologne, 2010), 96–97; Curt Risch, "Vorbemerkungen," in *Der öffentliche Personennahverkehr*, eds. Risch and Friedrich Lademann (Berlin, 1957), 6.

48. Adam Tooze, *The Wages of Destruction: The Making and Breaking of the Nazi Economy* (New York, 2007), 138.

49. Birthe Kundrus, "Greasing the Palm of the *Volksgemeinschaft?* Consumption Under National Socialism," in *Visions of Community in Nazi Germany: Social Engineering and Private Lives*, eds. Martina Steber and Bernhard Gotto (Oxford, 2014), 164.

50. Eberhard Heuel, *Der umworbene Stand: Die ideologische Integration der Arbeiter im Nationalsozialismus 1933–1935* (Frankfurt, 1989), 187.

51. Birthe Kundrus, "Greasing the Palm of the *Volksgemeinschaft?* Consumption Under National Socialism," in *Visions of Community in Nazi Germany: Social Engineering and Private Lives*, eds. Martina Steber and Bernhard Gotto (Oxford, 2014), 164–165.

52. "Berlin zu 72% elektrifiziert," *Deutsche Allgemeine Zeitung*, no. 520, November 4, 1932.

53. Robert Brasillach, *A Translation of* Notre avant-guerre/Before the War, trans. Peter Tame (Lewiston, NY, 2002), 143.

54. Kate Lacey, *Listening Publics: The Politics and Experience of Listening in the Media Age* (Oxford, 2013), 108.

55. Alfred Schmidt, *Publizistik im Dorf* (Dresden, 1939); Joseph Goebbels, "Anlässlich der Gründung der Kommission zur Bewahrung von Zeitdokumenten am 29. Juni 1937," Reichsministerium für Volksaufklärung, Bundesarchiv Berlin, R 55/1241/95.

56. Jacques Lusseyran, *And There Was Light. Autobiography of Jacques Lusseyran, Blind Hero of the French Resistance* (New York, 1963), 106.

57. Wolfgang König, *Volkswagen, Volksempfänger, Volksgemeinschaft: "Volksprodukte" im Dritten Reich. Vom Scheitern einer nationalsozialistischen Konsumgesellschaft* (Paderborn, 2004), 83–85; Heinz Pohle, *Der Rundfunk als Instrument der Politik* (Hamburg, 1955), 249; Uta C. Schmidt, "Radioaneigung," in *Zuhören und Gehörtwerden I. Radio im Nationalsozialismus*, eds. Inge Marssolek and Adelheid von Saldern (Tübingen, 1998), 291.

58. A. Wulf, "500 Berliner Volksschulkinder erzählen vom Radio," *Rufer und Hörer* 4 (1934/1935), 115–124, 176–183; Janosch Steuwer, "*Ein Drittes Reich, wie ich es auffasse.*" *Politik, Gesellschaft und privates Leben in Tagebüchern 1933–1939* (Göttingen, 2017), 401.

Chapter Eight: "This Enormous Planet"

1. Entries for February 6, 15–17, and 22, 1933, in Elke Fröhlich, ed., *Die Tagebücher von Joseph Goebbels. Teil I: Aufzeichnungen 1923–1941* (Munich, 1998), part 2,

3:125, 129–131, 133; entry for February 15, 1933, in Elke Fröhlich, *Die Tagebücher von Joseph Goebbels: Sämtliche Fragmente* (Munich, 1987), part 1, 2:375.

2. Entry for August 26, 1932, in Harry Graf Kessler, *Tagebücher 1918–1937* (Frankfurt, 1961), 684.

3. Jérôme and Jean Tharaud, *Quand Israël n'est plus roi* (Paris, 1933), 254; advertisement in *Paris-soir*, March 22, 1933.

4. Carmen Müller, *Weimar im Blick der USA: Amerikanische Auslandskorrespondenten und Öffentliche Meinung zwischen Perzeption und Realität* (Münster, 1997), 75–76; *Verein der Ausländischen Presse zu Berlin* (Berlin, 1933).

5. *Gringoire*, February 10, 1933, quoted in Robert J. Soucy, "French Press Reactions to Hitler's First Two Years in Power," *Contemporary European History* 7 (1998): 24; entry for February 10, 1933, in Bella Fromm, *Blood and Banquets: A Berlin Social Diary* (New York, 1942), 74–75; Dorothy Parker, "I Saw Hitler!," *Hearst's International-Cosmopolitan* 92, no. 3 (March 1932): 160; Alexander Werth, *France in Ferment* (London, 1934), 25.

6. Jérôme and Jean Tharaud, "Le calme règne à Berlin," *Paris-soir*, February 3, 1933; Philippe Barrès, "Hitler est nommé chancelier du Reich," *Le matin*, January 31, 1933.

7. Gotz Nordbruch, "Defining the Nation: Discussing Nazi Ideology in Syria and Lebanon During the 1930s," in *Nazism, the Holocaust, and the Middle East: Arab and Turkish Reponses*, eds. Francis R. Nicosia and Gogaç A. Ergene (New York, 2018), 131; Robert Brasillach, *A Translation of* Notre avant-guerre / Before the War, trans. Peter Tame (Lewiston, NY, 2002), 144.

8. Dan Stone, *Responses to Nazism in Britain, 1933–1939: Before War and Holocaust* (Basingstoke, 2003), 52–57; Hermann Rauschning, *Germany's War of Destruction* (London, 1939).

9. "55,000 Here Stage Protest on Hitler Attacks on Jews; Nazis Order a New Boycott," *New York Times*, March 28, 1933; *L'Oeuvre*, March 15, 1933, quoted in Ralph Schor, *L'Antisemitisme en France pendant les années trente* (Paris, 1992), 294; entry for March 30, 1933, in Victor Klemperer, *I Will Bear Witness, 1933–1941: A Diary of the Nazi Years* (New York, 1998), 9.

10. *L'Ami du peuple*, February 7, 1933, quoted in Robert J. Soucy, "French Press Reactions to Hitler's Frist Two Years in Power," *Contemporary European History* 7 (1998): 25–26.

11. "La fin de la Republique allemande," *L'Action française*, no. 66, March 7, 1933.

12. Michel Foucault, *The Order of Things: An Archeology of the Human Sciences* (New York, 1971), 132.

13. Jules Sauerwein, "Le peuple allemand est allé aux urnes avec passivité," *Paris-soir*, March 6, 1933; Jules Sauerwein, "Une immense vague de fond a passé hier sur l'Allemagne," March 7, 1933.

14. "Une foule innombrable a célébre solennellement à Potsdam l'avène-ment officiel de la nouvelle Allemagne," *Paris-soir*, March 22, 1933.

15. Philippe Barrès, "Adolf Hitler semble vraiment maitre de la situation en Allemagne," *Le matin*, February 1, 1933; Philippe Barrès, "Le président Hinden-burg dissout le Reichstag," *Le matin*, February 2, 1933; Philippe Barrès, "Berlin a célébre la fête nationale-socialiste du travail," *Le matin*, May 2, 1933.

16. Pierre Drieu La Rochelle, *Die Unzulänglichen* (Berlin, 1966), 381–382, 386–390.

17. Philippe Burrin, "La France dans la champ magnétique des fascismes," *Le debat*, no. 32 (November 1984): 52–72.

18. "Paris-Berlin," *Gringoire*, no. 222, February 3, 1933.

19. Robert Soucy, *French Fascism: The Second Wave, 1933–1939* (New Haven, 1995), 55, 83, 86, 89, 96; Simon Arbellot, "La solidarité française," *Le temps*, January 29, 1935.

20. Robert Soucy, *French Fascism: The Second Wave, 1933–1939* (New Haven, 1995), 173.

21. Eugen Weber, *The Hollow Years: France in the 1930s* (New York, 1994), 87; Ralph Schor, *L'Opinion francaise et les etrangers en France 1919–1939* (Paris, 1985), 27, 38–39, 550–551.

22. Ralph Schor, *L'Antisemitisme en France pendant les années trente* (Paris, 1992), 24, 26; Gaëtan Sanvoison, writing in *Le Figaro*, September 25, 1933, quoted in Rita Thalmann, "L'Immigration allemande et l'opinion publique en France de 1933 à 1936," in *La France et l'Allemagne 1932–1936*, ed. Centre National de la Recherche Scientifique (Paris, 1980), 160.

23. Jérôme and Jean Tharaud, *Quand Israël n'est plus roi* (Paris, 1933), 1; Alex-ander Werth, *France in Ferment* (London, 1934), 25; Vicki Caron, *Uneasy Asylum: France and the Jewish Refugee Crisis, 1933–1942* (Stanford, 1998), 67–72.

24. Michel Winock, "Une parabole fasciste: 'Gilles' de Drieu la Rochelle," *Le mouvement social* 80 (July–September 1972), 29–47, at 37; Ralph Schor, *L'An-tisemitisme en France pendant les années trente* (Paris, 1992), 71–72; Jeremy Josephs, *Swastika over Paris: The Fate of the French Jews* (London, 1989), 59. It was true: according to the *Annuaire officiel des abonnés au téléphone (région de Paris)* (Paris, 1936), subscribers included 516 Lévys (not counting 67 Levis) and 135 Duponts and 182 Durands. So what?

25. Ralph Schor, *L'Antisemitisme en France pendant les années trente* (Paris, 1992), 98.

26. Eugen Weber, *The Hollow Years: France in the 1930s* (New York, 1994), 105, quoting novelist Paul Morand.

27. I am following David Clay Large, *Between Two Fires: Europe's Path in the 1930s* (New York, 1990), 25, in putting the train disaster in the context of the February 6, 1934, riots. See also Edgar A. Haine, *Railroad Wrecks* (New York, 1994), 155–156; William Beaumont, "Communists and Cheminots: Industrial Relations and Ideological Conflict in the French Railway Industry, 1919–1939" (PhD diss., University of Exeter, 2011), 198–201; *Le matin*, December 24 and 25, 1933; *Paris-soir*, December 25, 1933.

28. Janet Flanner, "Stavisky," in *Paris Was Yesterday, 1925–1939* (New York, 1972), 111; David Clay Large, *Between Two Fires: Europe's Path in the 1930s* (New York, 1990), 43; Alexander Werth, *France in Ferment* (London, 1934), 77.

29. Sean Kennedy, *Reconciling France Against Democracy: The Croix de Feu and the Parti Social Français, 1927–1945* (Montreal, 2007), 44; Alexander Werth, *France in Ferment* (London, 1934).

30. Janet Flanner, "Bloody Tuesday," in *Paris Was Yesterday, 1925–1939* (New York, 1972), 112.

31. Pierre Chaine, *L'Heure H* (Paris, 1936).

32. Pierre Drieu La Rochelle, *Die Unzulänglichen* (Berlin, 1966), 415, 419.

33. Entry for February 14, 1934, in Thea Sternheim, *Tagebücher 1903–1971, Band 2, 1925–1936* (Göttingen, 2002), 563.

34. Robert Soucy, *French Fascism: The Second Wave, 1933–1939* (New Haven, 1995), 111; entry for February 7, 1934, in Paul Léautaud, *Journal littéraire* (Paris, 1986), 2:1368; Daudet quoted in Danielle Tartakowsky, "Stratégies de la rue: 1934–1936," in *La France en mouvement, 1934–1938*, ed. Jean Bouvier (Paris, 1986), 32.

35. Drieu in *L'Emancipation nationale*, August 1, 1936, quoted in Frederick Brown, *The Embrace of Unreason: France, 1914–1940* (New York, 2014), 237; Danielle Tartakowsky, "Stratégies de la rue: 1934–1936," in *La France en mouvement, 1934–1938*, ed. Jean Bouvier (Paris, 1986), 39.

36. Frederick Brown, *The Embrace of Unreason: France, 1914–1940* (New York, 2014), 208; Dietrich Orlow, *The Lure of Fascism in Western Europe: German Nazis, Dutch and French Fascists, 1933–1939* (New York, 2009), 55; Charles Rearick, *The French in Love and War: Popular Culture in the Era of the World Wars* (New Haven, 1997), 183.

37. *L'Ami du peuple* quoted in Danielle Tartakowsky, "Stratégies de la rue: 1934–1936," in *La France en mouvement, 1934–1938*, ed. Jean Bouvier (Paris, 1986), 32,

39; Rebecca P. Scales, *Radio and the Politics of Sound in Interwar France, 1921–1939* (Cambridge, 2016), 50–51.

38. Charles Rearick, *The French in Love and War: Popular Culture in the Era of the World Wars* (New Haven, 1997), 185.

39. Charles Rearick, *The French in Love and War: Popular Culture in the Era of the World Wars* (New Haven, 1997), 199–200.

40. George Seldes, *Even the Gods Can't Change History: The Facts Speak for Themselves* (Secaucus, NJ, 1976), 90; Sean Kennedy, *Reconciling France Against Democracy: The Croix de Feu and the Parti Social Français, 1927–1945* (Montreal, 2007), 123.

41. Jessica Wardhaugh, "Demokratische Experimente in der politischen Kultur Frankreichs," in *Normalität und Fragilität: Demokratie nach dem Ersten Weltkrieg*, eds. Tim Müller and Adam Tooze (Hamburg, 2015), 239.

42. Alexander Werth, *France in Ferment* (London, 1934), 3; Peter Davies, *The Extreme Right in France, 1789 to the Present: From de Maistre to Le Pen* (London, 2002), 98.

43. Karl Loewenstein, "Autocracy Versus Democracy in Contemporary Europe, II," *American Political Science Review* 29 (October 1935), 769–774; Michael Mann, *Fascists* (Cambridge, 2004), 38.

44. Christof Dejung, Thomas Gull, and Tanja Wirz, eds., *Landigeist und Judenstempel: Erinnerungen einer Generation 1930–1945* (Zurich, 2002), 22, 25.

45. Konrad Zollinger, *Frischer Wind oder faschistische Reaktion? Die Haltung der Schweizer Presse zum Frontismus 1933* (Zürich, 1991), 23; Willy Bretscher, "Eine nationale Gefahr," *Neue Zürcher Zeitung*, July 24, 1933, reprinted in Bretscher, *Im Sturm von Krise und Krieg: Neue Zürcher Zeitung, 1933–1944. Siebzig Leitartikel* (Zürich, 1987), 193.

46. Sonderegger speaking in Basel on June 15, 1933, cited in Erich Holliger, *Frontenfrühling oder Die Ordnung im Staat: Die freie Rekonstruktion einer Grosskundgebung der Nationalen Front im Frühling 1933* (Basel, 1974), 12.

47. Michael Mann, *Fascists* (Cambridge, 2004), 278.

48. Karl Loewenstein, "Militant Democracy and Fundamental Rights, I," *American Political Science Review* 31 (June 1937): 432; Karl Loewenstein, "Militant Democracy and Fundamental Rights, II," *American Political Science Review* 31 (August 1937): 649, 656.

49. Diary entry for April 29, 1939, in Anne Morrow Lindbergh, *War Within and Without: Diaries and Letters of Anne Morrow Lindbergh, 1939–1945* (New York, 1980), xxv, 4.

Chapter Nine: The One Hundred Days

1. Entry for January 30, 1933, in Hertha Nathorff, *Das Tagebuch der Hertha Nathorff. Berlin–Newyork: Aufzeichnungen 1933 bis 1945*, ed. Wolfgang Benz (Munich, 1987), 35; entry for January 30, 1933, in Erich Ebermayer, *Denn heute gehört uns Deutschland . . .* (Hamburg, 1959), 12.

2. Manfred Flügge, *Stadt ohne Seele: Wien 1938* (Berlin, 2018), 375; C. E. J. Griffiths, *The Theatrical Works of Giovacchino Forzano—Drama for Mussolini's Italy* (Lewiston, NY, 2000), 121; Craig Raine, "Mussolini's London Triumph," *Grand Street* 8 (winter 1989): 188–191; John London, "Non-German Drama in the Third Reich," in *Theatre Under the Nazis*, ed. London (Manchester, 2000), 225.

3. Entry for March 18, 1815, quoted in Clive Emsley, *British Society and the French Wars, 1793–1815* (London, 1979), 168.

4. Germaine de Staël, *Considerations on the Principal Events of the French Revolution* (London, 1818), 3:136.

5. Byron quoted in Jeffrey N. Cox, *Romanticism in the Shadow of War: Literary Culture in the Napoleonic War Years* (Cambridge, 2014), 68.

6. Benito Mussolini and Giovacchino Forzano, *Napoleon: The Hundred Days*, trans. John Drinkwater (London, 1932); Beatrice Corrigan, "Scenario by a Dictator," *Queen's Quarterly*, January 1, 1947, 215–216; C. H. Gifford, *History of the Wars Occasioned by the French Revolution from the Commencement of Hostilities in 1792 to the End of the Year 1816* (London, 1817), 2:1248, 1660.

7. Joachim Fest, *Inside Hitler's Bunker: The Last Days of the Third Reich* (New York, 2004), 107.

8. John London, "Non-German Drama in the Third Reich," in *Theatre Under the Nazis*, ed. London (Manchester, 2000), 225; Hans Knudsen, "Berliner Theater," *Preussische Jahrbücher* 253, no. 3 (1934): 273–276.

9. Benito Mussolini and Giovacchino Forzano, *Napoleon: The Hundred Days*, trans. John Drinkwater (London, 1932), 38.

10. Anka Muhlstein, "The Genius in Exile," *New York Review of Books*, November 6, 2014; Bruce M. Broerman, "Joseph Roth's *Die hundert Tage*: A New Perspective," *Modern Austrian Literature* 11, no. 2 (1978): 35–50; Wolfgang Mueller-Funk, *Joseph Roth* (Munich, 1989), 110; Alfred Kazin, "Forlorn Little Man Back from Elba," *New York Herald Tribune*, August 23, 1936. See also Bernard Gendrel and Mireille Labouret, eds., *Les cent-jours vus de la littérature* (Strasbourg, 2017).

11. F. L. Lucas, "Long Lives the Emperor," *Historical Journal* 8, no. 1 (1965): 126–135, at 130.

12. "The President's Speech," *New York Times*, July 25, 1933; Saul Bellow in *It All Adds Up*, quoted in Jason Loviglio, *Radio's Intimate Public: Network Broadcasting and Mass-Mediated Democracy* (Minneapolis, 2005), xiii.

13. Jonathan Alter, *The Defining Moment: FDR's Hundred Days and the Triumph of Hope* (New York, 2006), 306; David M. Kennedy, *Freedom from Fear: The American People in Depression and War, 1929–1945* (New York, 1999), 55, 285.

14. Amos Kiewe, *FDR's First Fireside Chat: Public Confidence and the Banking Crisis* (College Station, TX, 2007), 21; "The President's Speech," *New York Times*, July 25, 1933; William Stout, *Documentary Expression and Thirties America* (Chicago, 1986), 80–81.

15. Erik Barnouw, *A History of Broadcasting in the United States*, vol. 2: *The Golden Web: 1933–1953* (New York, 1968), 8; H. R. Knickerbocker, *The German Crisis* (New York, 1932), 11; David P. Peeler, *Hope Among Us Yet: Social Criticism and Social Solace in Depression America* (Athens, 1987), 19, 27–28, 49.

16. "The President's Speech," *New York Times*, July 25, 1933.

17. Entries for February 10 and March 12, 1933, in Elke Fröhlich, *Die Tagebücher von Joseph Goebbels: Sämtliche Fragmente* (Munich, 1987), part 1, 2:371, 391–392. The only references to an interval of time such as the "hundred days" are Otto Nippold, *180 Tage Revolution* (Diessen, 1934), and the "resistance" pamphlets *Hundert Tage illegaler Kampf* (Moscow, 1933) and *60 Tage Drittes Reich* (Vienna, 1933).

18. Entry for March 24, 1933, in Elke Fröhlich, ed., *Die Tagebücher von Joseph Goebbels. Teil I: Aufzeichnungen 1923–1941* (Munich, 1998), part 2, 3:154.

19. Horace Rumbold to Robert, March 15, 1933, in E. L. Woodward and Rohan Butler, eds., *Documents on British Foreign Policy, 1919–1939*, second series (London, 1950), 4:459–460.

20. André François-Poncet on April 5, 1933, quoted by Max Braubach, "Hitler's Machtergreifung: Die Berichte des französischen Botschafters Francois-Poncet über die Vorgänge in Detuschland von Juli 1932 bis Juli 1933," in *Festschrift fur Leo Brandt zum 60. Geburtstag*, eds. Josef Miexner and Gerhard Kegel (Cologne, 1968), 456–460.

21. "Dezember-Bericht über die Lage in Deutschland (Abgeschlossen Ende November 1933)," in Bernd Stöver, ed., *Berichte über die Lage in Deutschland. Die Meldungen der Gruppe Neu Beginnen aus dem Dritten Reich 1933–1936* (Bonn, 1996), 2.

22. Peter Liver Loew, *Danzig. Biographie einer Stadt* (Munich, 2011), 191, 208.

23. Jan Brester to Irmgard Gebensleben, September 21, 1920, in Hedda Kalshoven, ed., *Between Two Homelands: Letters Across the Borders of Nazi Germany* (Urbana, 2014), 3–4.

Index

Index

Index

Index

Sterilization, 285–290, 292–293

Sternheim, Thea, 92

Storm troopers, 46–47, 49–50, 55–63, 69, 72, 80, 85–86, 93–96, 98, 101–102, 104–106, 116–117, 119–121, 124–125, 141–144, 146–152, 155–160, 179–180, 192, 232–233, 238–239, 244, 257–260, 270, 275

    in concentration camps, 124, 162–165

    and museums, 164

Stowe, Leland, 307

Streicher, Julius, 256

Stützel, Karl, 143

Der Stürmer, 193, 256–257

Switzerland, 329–332

Tausk, Walter, 207–208, 255

Tesch, Richard, 253–254

Thälmann, Ernst, 45, 61

Tharaud, Jérôme and Jean, 303

Thompson, Dorothy, 55

Thousand-Year Reich, 8, 10, 186–187

Time, 13, 186–188, 207

Time (magazine), 9, 305

The Times (London), 260

Trade unions, 200

Treaty of Versailles, 15, 53, 57, 242, 307, 334

Triumph of the Will, 268, 329

Tucholsky, Kurt, 244

Turner, Henry Ashby, 86

Uhlfelder, Max, 233–234

Ulbricht, Walter, 45, 62

Unemployment. See Great Depression

United States, 333–334, 342–346

Vacations, 38–39, 53–54, 211, 315–316

Vailland, Roger, 303

Veit, Konrad, 222

Veterans, 58, 204

Vichy France, 313, 325, 328

Victims of the Past, 287

Volksfreund House (Braunschweig), 148–151

Volksgemeinschaft. See People's community

Vorwärts, 117–118,129

Wächter, Annie, 206

Wagner, Robert, 308

Wagner, Winifred, 239

Wallace, Edgar, 138, 320

Walldorf, Claire, 129–130

Weimar Republic, 1, 3, 11–15, 189–190

    end of, 20, 53–54, 82–83, 121–125, 188

Wels, Otto, 81, 188

Weltsch, Robert, 241

Werlin, Jakob, 302

Werth, Alexander, 315

Weschenfelder, Babette, 258

Wessel, Horst, 60, 85, 221, 323

Westarp, Hella, 140, 334

Wilder, Billy, 221

Wilhelm II (ex-kaiser), 3, 13, 51, 137, 227, 301

Wilhelm, Prince of Prussia, 104

Winter Relief, 224, 277–279, 295

Wolf, Christa, 290

Wolff, Theodor, 77

Wolfman Jack, 298

Woodman, Dorothy, 307

Woolf, Virginia, 183

PETER FRITZSCHE is the W. D. & Sarah
E. Trowbridge Professor of History at
the University of Illinois and author of
ten previous books, including *An Iron
Wind: Europe Under Hitler* and the award-
winning *Life and Death in the Third Reich*.
He lives in Urbana, Illinois.

DATE DUE
